A WEBER-MARX DIALOGUE

Edited by Robert J. Antonio
and Ronald M. Glassman

University Press of Kansas

© 1985 by the University Press of Kansas

Published by the University Press of Kansas
(Lawrence, Kansas 66045), which was organized
by the Kansas Board of Regents and is operated
and funded by Emporia State University, Fort
Hays State University, Kansas State University,
Pittsburg State University, the University of
Kansas, and Wichita State University

Library of Congress Cataloging in Publication
Data
Main entry under title:
A Weber-Marx dialogue.
    Includes bibliographies and index.
    1. Weber, Max, 1864–1920—Addresses,
essays, lectures. 2. Marx, Karl, 1818–1883—
Addresses, essays, lectures. 3. Marxian school of
sociology—Addresses, essays, lectures. I. Antonio,
Robert J. II. Glassman, Ronald M.
HM22.G3W468 1985   301′.01   85-3148
ISBN 0-7006-0265-8   ISBN 0-7006-0312-3 (pbk.)

Printed in the United States of America
10 9 8 7 6 5 4 3

Designed by Steve Skaggs

A Weber-Marx Dialogue

V/////\

CONTENTS

v

vi

PART IV / History

PART V / Politics

ACKNOWLEDGMENTS

The editors wish to express their appreciation of the generous extra help provided by several contributors to this work. Stephen Kalberg and Lawrence Scaff offered excellent critical suggestions and gave valuable assistance at key points throughout the process of developing this collection. Gerd Schroeter's sharp eye for detail helped us avert several problems, and his extensive editorial comments contributed significantly to the two translations. Because the present work was stimulated by dialogue begun at several "Max Weber Colloquia and Symposia," the many scholars who participated in them deserve our thanks. Vatro Murvar, who initiated the Colloquia, has been a significant force in promoting wider communication concerning Weber and Weberian scholarship; our work benefits from his efforts. We appreciate the assistance and advice given by Guenther Roth, who has made a wide-ranging contribution to Weber scholarship. Several others deserve recognition: Sharon Cox typed the manuscript and helped solve numerous editorial problems; Scott McNall promoted a work environment in which the volume could be completed; Norman Yetman provided generous criticism and advice; and David Willer was a seemingly endless source of stimulating ideas about Weber and classical theory. Their friendship and support as well as their more direct assistance facilitated the completion of this volume. Finally, the authors are grateful to the departments of sociology and the administrations at the University of Kansas and at William Paterson College for their continuing support of this project.

I/X/XI

INTRODUCTION

Scholarly interest about the relationship between Karl Marx and Max Weber is hardly new. As Gerd Schroeter demonstrates in this volume, the contours of the Weber-Marx dialogue began to take shape in the 1930s. Interpretations of the relationship between the ideas of these two great thinkers and the philosophical, political, methodological, comparative-historical, and empirical issues raised by them have varied greatly. Yet, and despite an increasing discussion over the last fifty years, the exact boundaries of the dialogue have not been fixed to this day.

In the history of this dialogue the most common reflex is to use Marx as a baseline for interpreting Weber's contributions. The extent to which Weber's work represents a dialogue with "the ghost" of Marx is a central issue in the history of sociological theory. This volume offers a fresh approach: it reverses the typical order by viewing issues in Marxist thought against a Weberian backdrop. This is a timely orientation because "crises" in Marxist theory, due to twentieth-century historical developments, have underscored the significance of several of the primary components of Weber's corpus. For example, Weber's emphases on the state, political forces, bureaucracy, and status groups address major critical points that have been raised about Marxist theory. This volume begins with a close consideration of these Weberian issues and then relates them to Marx and Marxism.

These essays represent the efforts of scholars who are fashioning readings of Weber and Marx appropriate for today's intellectual and historical context. The work originated in discussions at several recent "Weber Colloquia" and professional meetings and has unfolded from rather· frequent critical interchanges among many of its authors. An alternative is presented to neoidealist as well as "decisionist" and "instrumentalist" interpretations of Weber, and a framework is offered that avoids the many Weberian and Marxist orthodoxies, which too often have perpetuated a totally oppositional view of these theorists. Our aim is to stimulate new discussion about the development, nature, and problems of corporate capitalism and state socialism in the late twentieth century.

In the 1950s and early 1960s American sociology remained relatively oblivious to continental perspectives and devoted little attention to detailed consideration of classical theory. Occasionally, major European theorists were invoked, though mainly in order merely to enamor and provide a legitimating luster to empirical studies or to pose as the forerunners of modern theoretical perspectives. Marx was seldom read, and Weber was embraced superficially. For example, although Weber's texts contradicted such interpretations, he was associated with functionalism and neoevolutionism.[1] Moreover, his semiautocratic concept of "mass democracy" and his "realist" approach to capitalilsm (which stressed domination and inequality) were too frequently understated or ignored.[2] Instead, Weber was often portrayed as a precursor of modern theories that heralded the development of substantive democracy. Democratic capitalism "delivered the goods," leveled arbitrary inequalities, and increased political participation. Although these conditions were not presaged directly in Weber's work, they were viewed as consistent with or as logical extensions of his analysis of rationalization. Weber was thought to have inspired a theory of progressive rationalization which held that substantive rationality increased with formal rationality.[3] Yet this interpretation directly opposed Weber's explicit reference to a fundamental contradiction between the two types of rationality, a contradiction that he considered inherent in modern capitalism.[4] For example, he implied that capitalist cost accounting required the systematic subordination and exploitation of workers.[5]

After World War II American sociology linked Weber with an image of capitalism in the process of overcoming its contradictions. This Weber, when pitted directly against Marx, seemed to reveal deep flaws in Marxist thought. Marx's ideas about the ruling class, capitalist collapse, proletarian revolution, and socialist democracy seemed bankrupt in an era of apparent middle-class expansion, vast capitalist economic growth, fullbellied suburbanite workers, and Stalinism. Even the spiritual father of the New Left, Herbert Marcuse, spoke of capitalism's "sweeping rationality" and argued that both "the bourgeoisie and the proletariat" possess "an overriding interest in the preservation and improvement of the institutional status quo."[6] The same historical conditions that stimulated Marcuse's reaction provoked a mood of such virulent anti-Marxism among many sociologists and political theorists that the Weber-Marx confrontation in American thought was reduced to: Weber over Marx; *The Protestant Ethic* . . . over *Capital;* ideas and values over material factors; leadership over domination; and ultimately, rational capitalism over irrational socialism. Above all, the complexity and ambivalence of Weber's stance toward capitalism was obscured totally: *The Protestant Ethic and the Spirit of Capitalism* was read as a refutation of Marxism, and capitalism became the product of religious ideas instead of material development and class struggle. Scholars such as Reinhard Bendix, H. H. Gerth, Guenther Roth, and C. Wright Mills had a much more sophisticated understanding of Weber, but their views did not shape the conventional wisdom. Moreover, Weber's growing popularity was based in part upon the perception that he provided a politically acceptable alternative to Marxism. Within this postwar milieu, little receptivity to a Weber-Marx dialogue could develop among American sociologists.

The "functionalism-conflict" debate of the middle and late 1960s proved to be the first step toward a disintegration of the liberal consensus in sociology. By the early 1970s functionalist theory, positivist legitimations of empirical methods, and post-industrial optimism faced a challenge from a vast array of political and economic events in the broader society and no longer dominated American sociology. The growing awareness that corporate capitalism had not eliminated its contradictions became widespread, as did acknowledgment of the persistent economic, political, and social inequalities earlier emphasized by both Marx and Weber. While the works of both classical theorists were inspected increasingly for guidance throughout the 1970s and into the 1980s, Marx and Weber scholarship experienced a renaissance, one manifested not only by the proliferation of specialized books, journals, and associations but also in an increased interest in these two thinkers among non-Marxist and non-Weberian sociologists. Most importantly this awakening reflects the desire for an analytic framework sufficiently comprehensive to interpret critically the intensifying political and socioeconomic dislocations of the last decade. In an era of intense specialization and proliferation of "middle-range" theories, the approaches of Marx and Weber provide coherent and exhaustive conceptual frameworks for the analysis of a seemingly fractured social world.

Marx and Weber have been most seminal contributors to classical sociological theory and global political thought. Though they differ on the relative merits of capitalism and socialism, numerous aspects of their analyses of the origins of modernity and the rise of modern capitalism are complementary or convergent. For example, both stress the refinement of productive forces, increased rationalism and exact calculation, centralization of political and economic power, the perpetuation of sharp social inequalities, and vast expansion of bureaucratic organizational forms. A century later, because these issues are still crucial, Weber and Marx have remained integral to debates within contemporary sociological and political theory on subjects as diverse as critical theory, neo-Marxism, post-industrial society, democracy, pluralism, modernization and dependency, functionalism, and comparative-historical sociology. Most importantly Weber and Marx continue to be injected into arguments about the nature and desirability of contemporary capitalist and state-socialist regimes. Their ideas are central to debates over contemporary values and political questions as well as social-scientific discourse. Indeed, the present tone of urgency, which surrounds discussions of social conflicts and social problems, leads unavoidably to repeated confrontations with the theories of Marx and Weber. Their works may not offer the most appropriate solutions today, but they provide a basis for rational discourse that broadens our understanding of modern-day social dilemmas through systematic reflection as well as sophisticated theoretical frameworks.

This volume brings together contributions from sociology, history, political theory, and philosophy. Its title, *A Weber-Marx Dialogue,* implies two understandings. First, most of the authors have been active in the recent Weber renaissance and have an enduring interest in Weber scholarship; however, not all of the authors are "Weberians," and several lean more strongly toward Marx. The point is that Weber's name appears first because the majority of papers focus more centrally on his ideas, and this reflects the approach of the collection to analyze Marx against a Weberian backdrop. Second, the Weber-Marx relationship and the debates surrounding it are too broad to be covered comprehensively in a single volume. Moreover, this work constitutes one style of reading Weber and therefore does not intend to cover all points of view. The Parsonsian position and more recent German approaches that stress evolution and "progressive rationalization" (e.g., Tenbruck and Schluchter) are not represented. On the other hand, orthodox Marxist perspectives are also absent. Rather than a polemical rejection of these positions, the present collection is based on our belief that idealist and materialist interpretations pit the two theorists against each other and, in so doing, tend to fail to stimulate the fruitful Weber-Marx dialogue we desire.

Although it would be presumptuous to describe this collection as representing a school of thought, several common elements are integral to most of the contributions. The scholars writing in this volume remain outside the functionalist and neoevolutionist camps. Also, instead of espousing idealist, materialist, or structuralist determinisms, most contributors retain a balanced concern for material and ideal interests, uphold a historical/developmental rather than a teleological understanding of global developments, and are open-minded to the projects of both Marx and Weber.

The collection is arranged in five self-explanatory sections—the limits of the dialogue, theory, method, history, and politics. The headings designate general topics which constitute the range of issues covered by our dialogue. However, there are more finite substantive foci that traverse these general areas. These foci are relevant to many facets of the debate and therefore are mentioned at numerous junctures throughout the volume. These important issues are best introduced through a discussion of the contributions that address each of them most directly.

The nature, development, problems, and possibilities of *capitalism and socialism* constitute a central point of departure and a crucial substantive issue in any discussion of the Weber-Marx relationship. Although this issue is implicit in each contribution, it is the primary focus in three essays. A new and improved English translation of Wolfgang Mommsen's essay covers this topic broadly and perceptively. While he dismisses views that exaggerate the differences between Marx and Weber, he identifies key points of convergence in their articulation and conceptualization of the development and problems of capitalist society. However, Mommsen stresses a crucial point of disagreement: Weber feared the effects of socialist centralization and control more than he feared the effects of capitalist concentration of property. Mommsen comprehensively outlines key similarities and differences between the two theorists in a fashion that demonstrates their continued relevance for comprehending corporate-capitalist and state-socialist development.

Stephen Turner contends that Weber's Protestant-ethic thesis does not constitute a rejection of Marx's vision of capitalist development. Although it could be construed as an attack on crude materialism, the Protestant-ethic thesis incorporates major components of Marx's theory into a contrasting conceptual framework and a different historical mosaic of capitalist development than Marx's overall theory. Turner also demonstrates the manner in which the divergent approaches to capitalism relate to fundamental methodological differences between the two theorists. Finally, Franco Ferrarotti explains how the warm reception of Weber's *The Protestant Ethic and the Spirit of Capitalism* by anti-Marxist thinkers distorted the Weberian position into an idealist rebuttal of Marx. Ferrarotti, like Mommsen and Turner, explicates Weber's approach and demonstrates that there are key points of convergence and divergence in Weber's and Marx's style of analyzing capitalist development.

As Schroeter makes clear, the question of *materialism versus idealism* has long been central in debates over the Weber-Marx relationship. The papers by Mommsen, Turner, Ferrarotti, and Antonio stress the important role that material factors played in Weber's sociology and Weber's explicit denial that his approach was an idealist alternative to Marx.

Johannes Weiss provides the most detailed English-language account of the treatment of Weber in recent Eastern-European literature. Weiss dissects the Eastern Marxist accusation that Weber is guilty of subjectivism and agnosticism. From Lenin's critique to recent Marxist broadsides, Weber's alleged substantive errors are traced to his idealist, neo-Kantian roots. Weiss contends that this is a distorted view because the positions of Weber and Marx agree that material and ideal interests organize reality. The fundamental difference between the theorists is not between idealism and materialism; rather, it involves Weber's rejection of Marx's claims that core-determining features of social life could be elaborated and that value judgments could be determined scientifically. Weber was a nonbeliever in both respects and was adverse to Marx's attempt to develop a philosophy of history.

Mommsen contends that the crucial point of epistemological disagreement between Marx and Weber concerned the issue of ideal interests. Marx tended to treat these as epiphenomena, while Weber stressed that they are frequently significant and sometimes even the most important factors in historical change. Weber did not present a detailed analytic explanation of ideal interests, although they are central to his substantive analyses and represent a major divergence between his thought and that of Marx. Thus, Stephen Kalberg's systematic, theoretic account of Weber's interpretation of ideal interests is an especially important contribution. Kalberg carefully demonstrates how Weber explained the emergence of certain explicit forms of ideal interests from specific types of historical conditions and how these interests orient action in patterned ways. Kalberg presents a complex picture that avoids invoking the tired idealism-materialism polarity, which has often obfuscated the relationship between the theorists. Instead, the role of ideal interests is presented in a manner that delineates the differences with historical materialism and also preserves Weber's appreciation of the import of material interests.

The relation between *Weber and critical Marxism* is an important issue because critical Marxism represents a muted Weber-Marx dialogue, an implicit and incomplete synthesis of their theories. The issue of critical Marxism also revives the debate over the relation between science and politics, a most important disagreement between Weber and Marx. Douglas Kellner presents a detailed explanation of the treatment of Weber by the Frankfurt School and by recent critical theorists. His major point is that critical Marxists have been influenced by Weber and have integrated aspects of Weber's thought into their theories; however, they have tended not to acknowledge Weber's influence nor to engage in overt attempts to reconstruct Weber's perspective. Not until the most recent work of Jürgen Habermas has a critical theorist provided concrete and detailed treatment of Weber. Kellner's essay is the first English-language attempt to trace critically and comprehensively the role of Weber's ideas in the critical Marxist tradition.

Weiss's critical comments about Marcuse's attack on Weber raise points concerning the relations between values and facts and between science and politics, which have been prominent issues in critical Marxist circles. Jürgen Kocka's classic article, appearing for the first time in English, provides a basis for framing analytically the differences between Weberians and critical Marxists. Kocka presents a highly sophisticated analysis of Marx's and Weber's treatment of the subject-object relation and its connection to arguments over Marxian "dogmatism" and Weberian "decisionism." Ultimately, Kocka's paper raises questions about how scientific problems are defined and how the portions of reality under investigation are determined. Marxists who argue that science must be guided by immanent emancipatory ends are often accused of pseudoscientific legitimation of arbitrarily imposed values. On the other hand, Weberians who argue that science should maintain a pluralistic value base are frequently attacked for portraying the choice of objects of inquiry as merely a matter of individual taste; thus, it is claimed that scientific questions are somewhat randomly and arbitrarily selected. Kocka argues that Weber recognized that material culture constrains the randomness of choice and that this "ontic dimension" provides a basis for developing a new position that reconciles some of the major differences between Marx and Weber.

Guenther Roth's paper adds to the discussion of capitalism and socialism, but it also contributes centrally to dialogue about *democracy*. Roth critically analyzes Marx's and Weber's predictions about the United States in light of contemporary history and shows that both were, in important respects, "poor forecasters." He implies that they were overly optimistic about the possibilities of liberation from traditional domination ("personal rulership"), on the one hand, and material progress stimulated by capitalist development on the other. Although Marx was prescient in his prediction about the shifting of the center of the capitalist world market to the Pacific and about the weakening of Europe's economic position, he believed mistakenly that capitalist expansion would occur at a much more rapid rate. Moreover, he was unaware of the possible constraints on the development of productive forces and on material affluence (e.g., resource exhaustion and environmental problems). On the other hand, although Weber was correct in his prediction that the United States would be transformed into a "welfare and garrison state," he was wrong in his prognostications about the development of an "exclusivist" status-group hierarchy and of a bureaucratic party system. Roth's most provocative analysis concerns the nature and consequences of what he refers to as the "universalist personalism" of American politics. He describes a peculiar form of democracy, one in which politicians must continually bend to please their constituents (and the popularity polls) and wherein the President must negotiate constantly with Congress over every law. At the same time, neopatrimonial appointees of each administration work to sabotage laws and policies of their predecessors. Although this system undermines rationalization and efficiency, Roth implies that it has functioned reasonably well and believes that existing reform models do not promise potentially more effective alternatives. Roth's vision of American democracy conflicts with Marxian conceptions of class struggle and with Weberian themes of bureaucratic petrifaction.

Ira Cohen argues that, by devoting their attention almost exclusively to obstacles to democracy, Marx and Weber failed to provide the conceptual basis for adequately recognizing and comprehending the significance of the recent democratic achievements of Western societies. Cohen asserts that their sensitivities to antidemocratic forces remain relevant and should be retained; however, he stresses the need for theoretical innovations, designed to take account of substantive, democratic developments. Modern social theory must amplify the meaning of such institutions as representative political mechanisms and legally protected political rights. These are not ideological chimera nor mere means of bureaucratic manipulation; rather, they are vital foundations for the development of democratic public spheres and progressive social movements. Cohen's point is that the dialogue on the Marx-Weber relationship either must be expanded to confront these issues or must risk being irrelevant to some of the most important contemporary possibilities for political change.

Lawrence Scaff and Thomas Arnold focus on Marx's and Weber's *conceptions of history* by comparing how these two approaches were employed in the two theorists' concrete historical analyses. The authors contend that in Marx's analysis of class conflict and politics in mid-nineteenth-century France, he was forced to abandon historical materialism for the dramatic and ironic interpretations of events. In contrast, Weber successfully retained and employed his developmental approach to history in his study of class and revolution in early twentieth-century Russia. By explaining systematically the type of events that Marx interpreted as irrational and paradoxical, Weber realized more fully than Marx could, Marx's own goal of a scientific understanding of history. This paper not only contributes an innovative interpretation of how Marx and Weber analyzed history, but it also describes Weber's work on events in Russia, which is still only partly available in English.

Robert Antonio criticizes the Marxian theory of history, particularly its teleological elements, which Marx assumed would guarantee proletarian revolution and inevitable socialism. Antonio also points to a strain in Weber's theory between his neo-Kantian emphasis on ethical individualism and the Nietzschean theme of value pluralism. He questions whether Weber's approach is sufficient to promote the autonomy of the social sciences in a bureaucratic age and whether its pessimistic perspective toward domination and inequality can adequately stimulate the needed dialogue about the Enlightenment goals of rationality and freedom. Marx's and Weber's approaches to history circumscribe the vision of potential social transformation. Antonio's paper points to elements from both approaches which, if modified, could contribute to a broader discussion about late-twentieth-century possibilities for progressive change. This paper connects the two theorists' visions of history to issues in critical Marxism, which are elaborated further in the papers by Kellner, Kocka, and Weiss.

The articles by Alan Sica and Stephen Esquith focus on rather subtle topics. Sica examines the previously unexplored issue of the irrational in the theories of Marx and Weber and the influence of Goethe on both thinkers. Such a concern is highly significant because Marx's and Weber's respective concepts of rationality and irrationality are central to their views of history and are therefore intimately related to controversies over teleology in Marx and decisionism in Weber. Esquith analyzes the "historicity" of the value of work in Marx's and Weber's theories and the impact of these respective conceptions on their ideas about historical possibility. For Marx the value of work was central to his vision of the working class transcending fetishism and building a collective political movement. Although Weber did not derive a theory of emancipatory action from his approach to labor, he did relate the concept of scientific vocation to his hopes for national renewal, which he considered an important means to oppose the fragmentation generated by formal rationalization.

Finally, the issue of *epistemology* is a prominent theme in several of the papers. For example, Kalberg elaborates Weber's logic of interpreting ideal interests, Turner demonstrates how Weber's concept of causality affected his interpretation of capitalist development, Scaff explains Marx's and Weber's respective methods of historical explanation and their influence on substantive analyses, and Kocka describes how conflicting epistemological assumptions shape their frameworks and underlie their contrasting views of the relation of science and politics. Finally, Mommsen, Weiss, and Antonio discuss various aspects of the epistemological differences that derive from the contradictions between Marx's Hegelian philosophical base and Weber's neo-Kantian and Nietzschean network of meta-assumptions.

These comments are a brief introduction to some of the issues in the following essays. Gerd Schroeter, in the initial contribution, amplifies this introductory discussion by carefully tracing the past fifty years of scholarly analyses of the Weber-Marx relationship. Schroeter's paper is probably the most thorough and systematic English-language account of this literature.

The aims of this collection are to generate critical rethinking of theoretical matters and, through the lens of the Weber-Marx relationship, to stimulate ideas and questions that will foster social and political dialogue about pressing social issues. Finally, before new attempts are made to overcome the fragmentation of theory that followed the breakdown of the Parsonsian consensus, it would be wise to reassess our stance toward the two most important and systematic "founders" of twentieth-century social thought.

Notes

Stephen Kalberg and Norman Yetman provided extensive substantive and editorial criticism of this introduction. Ira Cohen, Lawrence Scaff, and Gerd Schroeter also provided helpful suggestions.

1. Although Talcott Parsons undoubtedly possessed a sophisticated understanding of Weber's thought, he incorrectly traced his own neoevolutionist and functionalist approach back to Weber. E.g., see Talcott Parsons, *The System of Modern Societies* (Englewood Cliffs, N.J.: Prentice Hall, 1971), 2; Parsons, "Review Article: Max Weber," *American Sociological Review* 25 (1960): 752. Parsons's own statements, as well as distorted elaborations by his epigones, were major factors in bringing Weber into the orbit of post-industrial and "end of ideology" thinking.

2. Of course, this criticism does not apply to the work by competent Weber scholars in this period. E.g., see H. H. Gerth and C. Wright Mills, "Introduction: The Man and His Work," in Max Weber, *From Max Weber: Essays in Sociology,* ed. and trans. H. H. Gerth and C. W. Mills (New York: Oxford University Press, 1946), 3–74; Guenther Roth, "Introduction," in Max Weber, *Economy and Society,* ed. G. Roth and C. Wittich (New York: Bedminster Press, 1968), 1: xxvii–ciii.

3. Again, statements by Parsons and some of his followers contributed to this view. E.g., see Talcott Parsons and Neil J. Smelser, *Economy and Society* (New York: Free Press, 1956), 291–92.

4. Weber, *Economy and Society* 1: 85–86.

5. Ibid., 183, 140.

6. Herbert Marcuse, *One Dimensional Man* (Boston: Beacon Press, 1964), xiii.

PART I / The Limits of the Dialogue

⚡

Gerd Schroeter	**Dialogue, Debate, or Dissent?** **The Difficulties of Assessing Max** **Weber's Relation to Marx**

I

Until twenty years ago, sociological discussions of Weber's relation to Marx were essentially dominated by four sources. The most frequently footnoted was undoubtedly Karl Löwith's essay "Max Weber und Karl Marx," which had been originally published in 1932 and was subsequently included among Löwith's collected writings;[1] it has only recently become available in an English translation.[2] The most influential, however, in Europe as well as in North America, was probably a short section of Gerth and Mills's introduction to their volume *From Max Weber.*[3] The work of Talcott Parsons, beginning with his translation of "The Protestant Ethic and the Spirit of Capitalism" in 1930, contains scattered references to the ways that Marx's writings influenced Weber's thinking, which were clearly important for shaping many people's attitudes and interpretations, again on both sides of the Atlantic. Less significant, but catchy, were some comments by Albert Salomon dating from 1935 and 1945. Löwith's contention was that, although both Marx and Weber were preoccupied with capitalism and goaded by similar impulses, their epistemological assumptions and their views of human beings were so divergent that he had to discuss them in alternating sections of his article. Gerth and Mills, on the other hand, believed that "there is a definite drift of emphasis in [Weber's] intellectual biography towards Marx."[4] Though Salomon felt that "the works of Weber and Marx appear antagonistic to each other,"[5] he also claimed: "Max Weber . . . became a sociologist in a long and intense dialogue with the ghost of Karl Marx."[6] Parsons insisted, however, that Weber engaged in a "direct polemical challenge to the Marxian type of explanation."[7]

This was the level of analysis until the middle of the 1960s, when a number of important articles appeared, revealing for the first time the myriad complexities of establishing even a universe of discourse and reaching some basic consensus on how to assess the Marx-Weber nexus.[8] Thus began a steady trickle of essays and monographs which continues into the present.[9]

II

Those who familiarize themselves with the range of secondary literature on Weber's relation to Marx are bound to become thoroughly confused. On one hand are writers who, if not stressing outright antagonism, view the differences between Marx and Weber as being more significant than the similarities. Thus, Wolfgang Mommsen refers to Weber as "perhaps the most important theoretical opponent of Marx"[10] and also calls him "the great bourgeois antipode of Marx"[11] because, although Weber always took the theoretical work of Marx seriously, "he did not agree with him."[12] Jürgen Kocka goes further, claiming that "even if Weber had construed Marx more adequately, he would still have rejected his premise."[13] On the other hand there are those who see Weber as essentially an epigone of Marx. George Lichtheim, echoing an earlier statement by Schumpeter, observed that "the whole of Weber's sociology of religion fits without difficulty into the Marxian scheme."[14] Others claim that Weber's sociology "builds upon Marxian fundamentals"[15] or reveals "a deep intellectual dependency"[16] on Marx. Tom Bottomore even maintains that "the greater part of Weber's sociology can be read more properly as a prolonged and varied commentary upon the Marxist theory . . . than as an original, systematic theory of society."[17] In the middle are those writers who acknowledge the differences between Marx and Weber but want to emphasize their convergence; Gerth and Mills belong here. More recently, Benjamin Nelson, for example, suggested that "both Weber and Marx are the heirs, executors and gravediggers of the German idealist tradition,"[18] and thirty years after publishing his well-known essay, Löwith was musing that "it is odd how neither Marxist nor bourgeois sociology has noticed that Weber's sociology is *the* twin of Marx's *Capital.*"[19] Johannes Weiss refers specifically to "the convergence between Marx's and Weber's statements."[20]

How can this range of divergent evaluations possibly be explained? Two decades ago Bendix warned that Weber's work "offers points of departure for the most varied interpretations,"[21] and this suggests that a great number of decisions must be made before any interpretation can even be attempted.[22] In addressing the question of Weber's relation to Marx one must make a fundamental decision about whether: (a) to concentrate on Weber's explicit statements about Marx, Marxism, and socialism, as well as to consider the question whether Weber ever went through a "Marxist phase"; (b) to draw comparisons between certain of Marx's and Weber's scholarly publications; or (c) to ascribe similarities and differences in terms of the alleged historical, philosophical, and political milieus in which both of them were active. Let us examine the ramifications of each of these choices.

III

To analyze and evaluate the statements that Weber actually made about Marx, Marxism, historical materialism, and socialism is not as simple an option as it may appear to be at first blush. Explicit references to Marx or to Marx's writings are few in number, and as Guenther Roth has pointed out, it is difficult to tell which of Marx's works Weber read.[23] But there are frequent references to historical materialism and to Marxism in Weber's publications and in his 1918 speech on the topic of socialism. This has led to the widespread assumption that Weber did not realize the difference between Marx's own formulations and their distortion among his followers, with the result that "his argumentation did not rise beyond the vulgar-Marxist interpretations of his time."[24] If this were indeed true, then Weber's criticisms of historical materialism and socialism are inadequate assessments of Marx, and this would result in a rather futile approach to understanding Marx-Weber relations. However, that is not the case.

There is no question at all that misconstructions of his ideas were considerable while Marx was still alive; otherwise, why would he have insisted that he himself was not a "Marxist"? One of the best-known contemporary interpreters of Marx, whom Weber esteemed highly as a scholar, was Werner Sombart. Sombart's popularizations had received Engels's approval in volume 3 of *Capital,* where he stated that "Werner Sombart gives an outline of the Marxian system which, taken all in all, is excellent."[25] Yet, when we look at what Sombart actually wrote in such books as *Socialism and the Social Movement,* we find that he played down all dialectical elements of Marx's thinking and even insisted that "when the socialist theorists cut themselves loose from the Marxian system their minds were at ease at once."[26] If Weber was indeed unaware of these distortions, unaware that Engels had often complained towards the end of his life that his and Marx's theories were being widely misinterpreted,[27] then Weber would not have felt obliged to investigate the distinctions between the original writings and popular Marxism or to study these *Urtexte* himself. However, there is enough scattered evidence to throw serious doubt on such a conclusion.[28]

First, there are some general statements. In the essay on " 'Objectivity' in Social Science" Marx is called "the great thinker,"[29] and during his address to Austrian army officers on the subject of socialism, Weber referred to the *Communist Manifesto* as a "scientific achievement of the first order."[30] In addition, there is the comment attributed to him shortly before he died: "The world in which we ourselves exist intellectually is a world that has been extensively shaped by Marx and Nietzsche."[31] By examining Weber's own publications, we find that the *Communist Manifesto* is referred to in three other essays[32] and *Capital* is also mentioned three times;[33] there is one reference to *The Poverty of Philosophy,*[34] and if *General Economic History* is included (not strictly a "publication" by Weber), there are a number of references to Marx and one to the *Manifesto.*[35]

In the same paragraph of the "Objectivity" essay in which Marx is identified as a *great thinker,* Weber also wrote the following: "We have intentionally avoided a demonstration with respect to that instance of ideal-typical constructs which is the most important one to us: namely Marx. This was done in order not to complicate the exposition any further by introducing interpretations of Marx [*Marx-Interpretationen*]."[36] It appears that it was Weber's intention here to distinguish clearly between the original Marx and current "interpretations." In the Stammler essay he made this statement: "We are not concerned with the question whether Stammler's representation of the 'materialist conception of history' is *sound.* From the *Communist Manifesto* to the work of the contemporary epigones of Marx, this theory has passed through very different forms."[37] In a footnote, Weber then added that "on the meaning of 'materialist' in the works of Marx, see Max Adler, . . . (a sound criticism of Stammler)."[38] Not only can this be seen as an attempt to identify the vulgar Marxist interpretations and to differentiate between the materialist conceptions of history and "the works of Marx" but even as an effort to *defend* Marx against Stammler.[39]

By far the most interesting comments, though, that Weber made about Marx were recorded at conferences in which Weber participated. These comments strongly suggest that he was well able to distinguish between Marx's own theories and their distortion by "Marxists." In addition, they throw doubt on the validity of Mommsen's assertion that "at least to 1906 Max Weber referred to Marxism in the vulgar versions of the day rather than to the original writings of Marx and Engels themselves."[40] At the founding meeting of the *National-Soziale Verein* in 1896, Weber spoke of the need for the psychological emancipation of the workers because "the Social Democratic Party does not tolerate freedom of thought, since it presses Marx's fragmented system into the heads of the masses as dogma."[41] This implies that Weber was well aware of the extent to which Marx's fusion of theory and practice had been thoroughly fragmented by his epigones. A more explicit statement occurred at the first meeting of the German Sociological Society in 1910. Commenting on a paper by Sombart, Weber charged that "so-called historical materialism is being represented today by totally obscuring its actual meaning. . . . Naturally, the materialist conception of history, as Marx intended it, has completely lost its cutting edge."[42]

Although it would be desirable to have a greater number of detailed statements, the above suggest strongly, on the basis of his own pronouncements, that a full decade before 1906 Weber was quite capable of distinguishing vulgar-Marxist interpretations, along with the slogans of the Social Democrats, from the teachings of Marx. Whether he always did so in practice is, of course, another matter. Yet, this differentiation has rarely been made in the literature on Weber, and thus it remains a major stumbling block in deciding how often he was, in fact, confusing Marx's shadow (or ghost) with Marx himself.[43] One of the few authors to draw such a distinction has been Anthony Giddens,[44] who was subsequently commended by Paul Walton for introducing a much-needed "breath of reason" into discussions of this topic.[45] The sharpest criticism (directed in particular at Löwith) of the prevailing tendency to gloss over the differences between Marxism and Marx can be found in Zander's book.[46]

An alternate path to analyzing Weber's relation to Marx is to see a "Marxist phase" reflected in some of his early research.[47] The most comprehensive statement of this position was made by Fleischmann, who argued that Weber conceptualized much of his substantive research under the influence of Marxian ideas, but that he gradually moved closer to Nietzsche as he replaced a focus on economic factors by a stress on volition and values. Thus, for Fleischmann, Weber's criticism in 1918 of socialism was in effect "the public confession of a 'disenchanted' ex-believer, who had at one time hoped for much more from Marxism [*sic*] than it could possibly deliver."[48] Most writers on this aspect have concentrated on the period before Weber's nervous breakdown in 1898. An analysis by Vernon Dibble of the study that Weber carried out in 1892 for the *Verein für Sozialpolitik* of agricultural workers in the East Elbian provinces of Prussia led him to conclude that "Weber took Marx seriously and learned from Marx."[49] Kozyr-Kowalski made a similar point: "His theory shows that up to 1896 Max Weber was under the overwhelming influence of historical materialism."[50] The support for such a claim was widely assumed to be found in Weber's use of the concepts "superstructure" and "infrastructure" during his explanation of the collapse of ancient Roman civilization, which he delivered that year as a public lecture and subsequently published.[51] Two years earlier, in 1894, Weber had advanced the idea at a meeting of the *Evangelisch-Soziale Kongress* that "class conflict" should be considered as an integrative element of modern industrial society.[52] After Weber resumed writing in 1902, he never used such explicit Marxian language again, and Kozyr-Kowalski suggested that the frequent criticism of historical materialism during the last two decades of his life may have been partly an expression of self-criticism.

The only one to challenge directly this question of a Marxist interlude is Guenther Roth. His point is simply that among Weber's teachers and colleagues economic determinism was fashionable for a while, and anticapitalist sentiments were common. If today's students knew more about the literature of the period and about the intellectual setting in which Weber matured, they would be less prone to assume such direct influences.[53] Roth concludes, therefore, that "Weber never had a Marxist phase."[54]

An oblique attempt to revive this question is Jonathan Wiener's recent review essay of *The Agrarian Sociology of Ancient Civilizations,* which contains Weber's 1896 essay on "The Social Causes of the Decline of Ancient Civilization" and the first translation of his long 1909 encyclopedia article literally entitled "The Agrarian Conditions of Antiquity."[55] Wiener's essay includes phrases such as: "Weber thus adopts the essence of Marx's position," "Weber's analysis . . . is compatible with Marxist theory," and "[his] method is precisely the Marxist one."[56] Yet, despite an arresting title, Wiener claims that he is merely trying to trace the parallels and similarities between Marx's and Weber's approaches and to argue that Weber's account is "the other side of the causal chain" referred to in the 1920 introduction to "The Protestant Ethic."[57] Wiener concludes that he does not in any way "wish to imply that Weber studied Marx, or that he considered himself a 'Marxist,'"[58] but the reader must pay close attention to the final paragraph in order to realize this.

It should be obvious that this first approach to our question of Weber's relationship to Marx contains a variety of pitfalls. Weber did not make many explicit references to Marx, and he never engaged in any type of critique. In addition, the ascription of "similarity" or "influence" is much more complex than merely counting footnotes.[59] Finally, as Giddens points out: "While one must, of course, respect Weber's own statements on the subject of his relationship to Marx, these cannot be used as a sufficient index of the true nature of the substantive connections between the writings of the two authors."[60] Thus, we must consider alternative procedures.

IV

Drawing comparisons between selected publications, the second mode of approach, also presents a number of thorny problems. One must choose between focusing on the epistemological (i.e., defining concepts or justifying "methodology") level or the more substantive (i.e., empirical) level[61] and between the youthful work or the mature work of each author. The debate within Marxian scholarship about the merit of the early writings versus the later writings is well known. Among Weberians the disagreement about what is his most important work has only come to the fore recently; it is still quite muted. For a long time *Economy and Society* stood as Weber's magnum opus; Marianne Weber labeled it as such in her introduction to the first edition and made a similar statement in her biography.[62] The fact that the English translation of these volumes is the most painstakingly done of all his books strengthens this assumption. Some doubts were raised by Bendix as long ago as 1960,[63] but they have been most strongly expressed recently by Tenbruck.[64] Both agreed that during the last seven years of his life Weber was preoccupied with the link between religion and rationalization; thus, the collected essays on the sociology of religion, along with the "Author's Introduction" and the 1920 revisions to "The Protestant Ethic and the Spirit of Capitalism" essay, must actually be seen as his major achievement.[65] Several years ago Bendix restated his own position as follows: "The differences between Weber's studies of the sociology of religion and the universal-historical intention of his theoretical categories in *Wirtschaft und Gesellschaft* have been pointed out. . . . In my opinion both studies should be considered of equal importance."[66]

Guenther Roth, however, has rejected this interpretation. On the basis of letters which Weber wrote to his publisher Roth claims categorically that Weber looked upon the old manuscript of *Economy and Society* (i.e., Part Two) as the major accomplishment of his life, and he regarded it as both more difficult and more significant than his essays on world religions.[67] (He agrees that Weber preferred to work on the religion essays during the war, rather than *Economy and Society*, but insists this was simply because they required less effort and concentration.) Thus, Roth concludes that *Economy and Society* must continue to be treated as his magnum opus.

Several scholars have argued that it is Weber's strictly methodological writings which deserve priority, and for Dennis Wrong they represent "probably his greatest achievement";[68] certainly, as Roth made clear, these essays have figured prominently in many attempts to interpret the Marx-Weber nexus over the past fifty years. However, when making this choice, it is important to keep in mind that

the word *'Wissenschaftslehre'* does not appear in any of the essays contained in the *Wissenschafts-lehre.* Nor is there any reason to believe that Weber himself would have collected these various essays and monographs—published over a period of more than fifteen years, composed under very different circumstances, and written for a variety of purposes—into a single volume. We owe both the volume and the word to Marianne.[69]

Randall Collins proposes still another candidate; he maintains that the volume on *General Economic History,* the first to be translated into English but long ignored, ought to receive more attention because *it* is the one that best reflects Weber's mature thinking.[70] Roth and others scoff at such a claim for the transcript of a series of lectures which was never even seen by Weber himself.[71]

One further aspect of this issue of identifying the most representative of both Marx's and Weber's publications is the question of how isomorphic Weber's own substantive studies actually are with his "methodological" writings. His investigations of contemporary agricultural and industrial workers, as well as the various historical analyses that he conducted (apart from "The Protestant Ethic"), have received relatively little attention until now, even though there is a general awareness among those interested in Weber that in practice he did not adhere closely to his own guidelines for doing "sociology."[72] Furthermore, as Anthony Giddens emphasizes: "There are many sorts of processes and influences which have causal relevance for social life which are not 'understandable,' but the importance of which Weber by no means discounts."[73]

Marx's and Weber's writings on "capitalism" offer popular grounds for comparison on the above questions of Marx's influence on Weber and Weber's own consistency. Often distinctions are drawn in the literature between: (a) explanations of the genesis of capitalism; (b) descriptions of the characteristics of mature capitalism; and (c) evaluations of capitalism. Both Marx and Weber wrote on each of these dimensions, and they appear to have disagreed strongly only when assessing capitalism and predicting its evolvement. The best recent discussions on the question of *origins* are Giddens's 1970 essay and the one by Randall Collins published ten years later.[74] Giddens concludes that there is a "general theoretical congruity [between] much of what Marx and Weber wrote on the history and origins of capitalism."[75]

The most detailed comparison of perspectives on life within a capitalist economic system was carried out by Löwith, who saw both Marx and Weber concerned with the "mode of being human" under capitalism. The former focused on self-alienation (due to private property and money as the intermediary between people), while the latter emphasized the possible implications of a thoroughly rationalized way of life. Löwith's novel approach suggested that although rationalization for Weber clearly implied specialization, bureaucratic organization, and general disenchantment (literally "de-magicization"), it also meant that some human beings could have an opportunity for a new type of freedom. Thus, he believed that "Weber fundamentally *affirms* what Marx describes as a self-alienated humanity because, for him, precisely this form of existence did not merely permit the maximum 'freedom of movement' but enforced it."[76] Others who compare Marx's and Weber's analyses of capitalist society include Giddens,[77] Mommsen,[78] and Mueller.[79]

While there was general consensus on the characteristics of mature capitalism, when it came to *evaluating* it or discussing how it would (or could) be transcended, Marx and Weber disagreed sharply. Weber stated his position most clearly in his 1918 address on socialism, which challenged Marxists with the statement: "It is the dictatorship of the official, not that of the worker, which, for the present at any rate, is on the advance."[80] Mommsen sums it up by concluding that "Weber, indeed, did not try to cover up the shortcomings of capitalism although he could not see any viable alternative to it."[81] While Marx never went into much detail, he retained his faith in such a viable alternative until he died.[82]

One of the fundamental difficulties involved in carrying out such a series of comparisons is that although Marx and Weber often *described* "capitalism" in much the same manner: as a historical phenomenon of world-wide significance, the concept nevertheless had very different connotations for each of them.[83] For Marx it involved distinctive social relations of production and was inextricably linked with social inequality and exploitation (e.g., the production of surplus value), which were a necessary stage on the road to the perfect social order. For Weber capitalism was but one dimension of "occidental rationalism," which had gradually led to the specialization and bureaucratic mechanization of every dimension of social life, so that eventually competitive capitalism itself became stifled by rampant rationalization. The end of this development was a world populated by "specialists without spirit, sensualists without heart,"[84] which Weber abhorred, but from which he saw no possible escape. This distinction implies that whereas Marx assumed he was describing the dynamics of capitalism as experienced during the eighteenth and nineteenth centuries, Weber looked upon the rationalism and asceticism at the heart of his ideal type of "capitalism" as the preferred norms for the German population of his day. Therefore, what he described as the characteristics of capitalism were, to a large extent, "Max Weber's personal ideals, which had only a limited (historical) value for explaining reality, but to which, as a politician, Weber tried to make reality correspond more closely. . . . Max Weber did everything he could as a writer and a propagandist in order to advance on the political front those very factors which he regarded as vital to [classical] capitalism."[85] We are obviously only at the periphery of a highly complicated question which has, as yet, been very inadequately researched, but it must be clear that any textual comparison will be fraught with difficulties as long as the political and normative motivations which guided both Marx and Weber are ignored. (According to Mommsen, divorcing Weber the scholar from Weber the politician can only result in a "sterile interpretation" of his sociology.[86] Is this any less true for Marx?)

V

The third general type of approach is to de-emphasize (or even ignore) publications as such and to concentrate on the milieus and the alleged philosophical traditions into which both men were locked. Most simply this means to categorize Max Weber as a Kantian or a neo-Kantian (i.e., a nominalist and methodological individualist) and to see Karl Marx as shaped by early Hegelian influences (i.e., holism and dialectics). The clearest example of this appears in a talk delivered by Carl Mayer in 1974, which ends with the statement: "The fundamental problem . . . , which is posed with the confrontation of Marx and Weber, is the problem of Hegel vs. Kant, or of Kant vs. Hegel,"[87] but there are many others as well.[88] I find it difficult to understand what is accomplished by assigning either of them to such rubrics; it seems quite similar to criticizing a film which one has not seen simply on the basis of its country of origin and the name of the director.[89] Guy Oakes also refers to the "scholastic sterility" of the debate whether "Weber [was] a neo-Kantian, an idealist, a bourgeois Marx, an Aristotelian, a Hegelian, or perhaps even an existentialist."[90]

In order to promote some rapprochement between the analyses of Weber and Marx, Jürgen Kocka argues that there is, in fact, an "ontic" dimension to Weber's substantive work which has been largely ignored because it seems to be at odds with the methodological writings.[91] Lately this interpretation has been elaborated by Bryan Turner, who contends that "Weber's analyses of 'social formations' adhere far more closely to a

Marxist structuralism than they do to *verstehen* principles" and that "the key to Weber's sociology is not his epistemological distinctions" but rather "the analysis of the ineluctable processes of rationalization, routinization and secularization."[92] Let us quickly look at several examples. When Vernon Dibble examined Weber's 1892 study of agricultural workers in East Elbia, he concluded: "Weber's colleagues saw individual people interacting with one another, while Weber saw, first of all, the system that constrained them."[93] In a letter which he wrote to Tönnies in 1908 Weber himself referred to a "super-individual structural system."[94] Another example can be found towards the end of *Economy and Society*, where Weber wrote that "in principle, the behavior of any individual cannot be so questioned, since it is prescribed in all relevant respects by objective situations."[95] An illustration of Weber's use of the concept totality occurred when he explained the permanence of Indian village life and insisted that "the caste order as a whole must be regarded as the bearer of stability."[96] These examples should make it clear how facile it is to label Weber as a Kantian; examples of Marx's writings which demonstrate that he was not locked into strictly Hegelian modes of thinking are more widely known and therefore will not be discussed here.[97]

VI

Our brief survey, concentrating on the literature which has gradually accumulated over the past twenty years, leads to a number of conclusions:
1. Whether Weber's unbridled criticism of Marxism, the materialist conception of history, socialism, and the German Social Democrats may be interpreted as a criticism of Marx as well is a subject of controversy which has its roots in Löwith's 1932 essay.[98]
2. Agreement on what is each man's major, or representative, body of work is still lacking.
3. There is no consensus on whether an understanding of Weber's relation to Marx is best achieved by comparing their epistemological positions or their substantive analyses.
4. The significance of relying on discrete philosophical categories (e.g., Kantian vs. Hegelian; idealist vs. materialist; nominalist vs. realist; decisionist vs. determinist; etc.) is unclear but contentious.
5. As a result, it is easy to marshal support for a wide range of mutually exclusive interpretations and points of view to address Max Weber's relation to Karl Marx.

I hope that I have succeeded in pointing out some of the decisions which cannot be evaded when formulating comparisons between two such complex and prolific writers as Weber and Marx, both of whom were involved in politics and journalism besides their more "scholarly" work. In addition, each had a magnetic personality, so we also have a body of reminiscences (by both adherents and opponents) which needs to be taken into account and weighed against the primary publications.[99] Other comparisons and contrasts between Marx and Weber are, of course, also vital. For example, such topics as (a) the dialectical elements in their thinking, (b) their emphases on "conflict," or (c) the tension between agnosticism and "praxis," should be carefully assessed. I have stressed what I consider to be the most basic questions which must be confronted before attempting detailed comparisons.

Notes

1. *Archiv für Sozialwissenschaft und Sozialpolitik* 67 (1932): 53–99, 175–214; Karl Löwith, *Gesammelte Abhandlungen* (Stuttgart: Kohlhammer, 1960), 1–67. Note this telling comment: "Löwith's books are often discussed, and I list them primarily for that reason." Harold Alderman, *Nietzsche's Gift* (Athens, Ohio: Ohio University Press, 1977), 183.

2. Karl Löwith, *Max Weber and Karl Marx* (London: Allen & Unwin, 1982).

3. H. H. Gerth and C. Wright Mills, eds., *From Max Weber: Essays in Sociology* (New York: Oxford University Press, 1946), 46–50.

4. Ibid., 63. For a discussion in 1960 of Weber's relation to Marx, Bendix suggested only the Löwith piece and the section in *From Max Weber*. Reinhard Bendix, *Max Weber: An Intellectual Portrait* (Garden City, N.Y.: Doubleday, 1960), 66n.

5. Albert Salomon, "Max Weber's Political Ideas," *Social Research* 2 (1935): 369.

6. Albert Salomon, "German Sociology," in *Twentieth Century Sociology*, ed. Georges Gurvitch and Wilbert Moore (New York: Humanities Press, 1945), 596. This statement became the organizing principle for Irving Zeitlin, *Ideology and the Development of Sociological Theory* (Englewood Cliffs, N.J.: Prentice-Hall, 1968); it is repeated by Ian Robertson in his introductory text, *Sociology* (New York: Worth, 1981), 14. See also Franco Ferrarotti, *Max Weber and the Destiny of Reason* (Armonk, N.Y.: Sharpe, 1982), who insists that "throughout his life [Weber] was obsessed by a question which recurs in all his work, explicitly or implicitly: What if Marx was right?" (p. 89).

7. Talcott Parsons, *The Structure of Social Action* (1937; Glencoe, Ill.: Free Press, 1949), 510. On Parsons's significance as an interpreter of Weber, from a German perspective, see Dirk Käsler, *Einführung in das Studium Max Webers* (Munich: Beck, 1979), 203.

8. For example, Eugène Fleischmann, "De Weber à Nietzsche," *European Journal of Sociology* 5 (1964): 190–238; Jürgen Kocka, "Karl Marx und Max Weber. Ein methodologischer Vergleich," *Zeitschrift für die gesamte Staatswissenschaft* 122 (1966): 328–57 (reprinted twice with minor revisions and in English translation in this volume); Guenther Roth, "Das historische Verhältnis der weberschen Soziologie zum Marxismus," *Kölner Zeitschrift für Soziologie und Sozialpsychologie* 20 (1968): 429–47 (see also a translation with some omissions in *Scholarship and Partisanship*, ed. Reinhard Bendix and Guenther Roth [Berkeley: University of California Press, 1971], 227–46); Stanislaw Kozyr-Kowalski, "Weber and Marx," *The Polish Sociological Bulletin*, 1968, no. 1: 5–17.

9. For example, Anthony Giddens, "Marx, Weber and the Development of Capitalism," *Sociology* 4 (1970): 289–310; Paul Walton, "Ideology and the Middle Class in Marx and Weber," *Sociology* 5 (1971): 389–94, and Giddens's "Reply," pp. 395–97; Wolfgang J.

Mommsen, "Max Weber als Kritiker des Marxismus," *Zeitschrift für Soziologie* 3 (1974) (reprinted in Mommsen, *Max Weber: Gesellschaft, Politik und Geschichte* [Frankfurt: Suhrkamp, 1974], translated in *Canadian Journal of Sociology* 2 [1977], and newly translated in this volume); Carl Mayer, "Max Weber's Interpretation of Karl Marx," *Social Research* 42 (1975): 701-19; Helmut R. Wagner, "Marx and Weber as Seen by Carl Mayer," *Social Research* 42 (1975): 720-28; Veit Michael Bader et al., *Einführung in die Gesellschaftstheorie: Gesellschaft, Wirtschaft und Staat bei Marx und Weber* (Frankfurt, New York: Campus, 1976); Jürgen Zander, *Das Problem der Beziehung Max Webers zu Karl Marx* (Frankfurt: Haag & Herchen, 1978); Randall Collins, "Weber's Last Theory of Capitalism: A Systematization," *American Sociological Review* 45 (1980): 925-42; Johannes Weiss, *Das Werk Max Webers in der marxistischen Rezeption und Kritik* (Opladen: Westdeutscher Verlag, 1981); Gert H. Mueller, "Socialism and Capitalism in the Work of Max Weber," *British Journal of Sociology* 33 (1982): 151-71; Jonathan M. Wiener, "Max Weber's Marxism," *Theory and Society* 11 (1982): 389-401.

10. Wolfgang J. Mommsen, "Max Weber as a Critic of Marxism," *Canadian Journal of Sociology* 2 (1977): 374.

11. Wolfgang J. Mommsen, *The Age of Bureaucracy* (New York: Harper & Row, 1974), 43.

12. Mommsen, "Max Weber as a Critic of Marxism," 375.

13. Kocka, "Karl Marx und Max Weber," 335.

14. George Lichtheim, *Marxism: A Historical and Critical Study* (London: Routledge & Kegan Paul, 1964), 385.

15. Randall Collins, "The Empirical Validity of the Conflict Tradition," in *Sociology Since Midcentury* (New York: Academic Press, 1981), 38.

16. Gertraud Korf, "Die Marxismus-Kritik in der Methodologie Max Webers," in *Die philosophische Lehre von Karl Marx und ihre aktuelle Bedeutung,* ed. Dieter Bergner et al. (Berlin: Deutscher Verlag der Wissenschaft, 1968), 253. According to Fleischmann, "it was probably Marx who exerted the strongest and most lasting influence on Weber." "De Weber à Nietzsche," 194.

17. Tom Bottomore, "Marxism and Sociology," in *A History of Sociological Analysis,* ed. T. Bottomore and R. Nisbet (New York: Basic, 1978), 129-30.

18. Benjamin Nelson, "Dialogs across the Centuries: Weber, Marx, Hegel, Luther," in *The Origins of Modern Consciousness,* ed. John Weiss (Detroit, Mich.: Wayne State University Press, 1965), 153.

19. Karl Löwith, "Die Entzauberung der Welt durch Wissenschaft," *Merkur* 28 (1964): 504.

20. Weiss, *Das Werk Max Webers,* 103. For Ernst Nolte, also, "Marx is always conceived [by Weber] as a kindred thinker, never as an enemy." "Max Weber vor dem Faschismus," *Der Staat* 2 (1963): 6.

21. Reinhard Bendix, "Max Weber's Sociology Today," *International Social Science Journal* 17 (1965): 9. However, he went on to add: "It is unprofitable to uphold this or that interpretation as being the only possible one" (p.10).

22. By stating the problem in this way, I am aligning myself with the Weberian position that "research, and the conceptual system in which it is expressed, seems to be dominated by the initial, and at the same time basic, dimension of *choice."* Ferrarotti, *Max Weber and the Destiny of Reason,* 37.

23. Roth, "Das historische Verhältnis der weberschen Soziologie," 433; Roth, "The Historical Relationship to Marxism," in *Scholarship and Partisanship,* 228.

24. Mommsen, "Max Weber as a Critic of Marxism," 380. See also Löwith, *Max Weber and Karl Marx,* 68, 100; Kocka, "Karl Marx und Max Weber," 329.

25. Friedrich Engels, "Supplement," to Karl Marx, *Capital* (New York: International Publishers, 1967), 3: 893.

26. Werner Sombart, *Socialism and the Social Movement* (London: Dent, 1908), 90.

27. See, for example, Engels to Conrad Schmidt, 5 August 1890 and 27 October 1890, and Engels to J. Bloch, 21 September 1890. All letters reprinted in Lewis S. Feuer, ed., *Marx and Engels: Basic Writings on Politics and Philosophy* (Garden City, N.Y.: Doubleday, 1959).

28. According to Honigsheim, Weber was sensitive to falsification occurring in the transmission of religious ideas, since "he distinguished carefully between German Lutheranism conceived as an historically explainable aberration from the basic attitude of the founder, and the young monk from Wittenberg." Paul Honigsheim, "Max Weber: His Religious and Ethical Background and Development," *Church History* 19 (1950): 239. Would he not have applied the same caution to Marxism and Marx?

29. Max Weber, *The Methodology of the Social Sciences* (Glencoe, Ill.: Free Press, 1949), 103.

30. J. E. T. Eldridge, ed., *Max Weber: The Interpretation of Social Reality* (London: Michael Joseph, 1970), 205. The *Communist Manifesto* is mentioned in this speech thirteen times!

31. Eduard Baumgarten, *Max Weber: Werk und Person* (Tübingen: Mohr, 1964), 555.

32. Weber, *Methodology,* 68; Weber, *Critique of Stammler* (New York: Free Press, 1977), 69; Weber, "Deutschlands künftige Staatsform," in *Gesammelte Politische Schriften* (Tübingen: Mohr, 1971), 460.

33. Max Weber, *Roscher and Knies: The Logical Problems of Historical Economics* (New York: Free Press, 1975), 220n.37; Weber, *Methodology,* 149; Weber, *Economy and Society* (Berkeley: University of California Press, 1978), 305.

34. Weber, *Economy and Society,* 112.

35. Max Weber, *General Economic History* (London: Allen & Unwin, [1927]), 162, 290, 352.

36. Max Weber, *Wissenschaftslehre* (Tübingen: Mohr, 1968), 204. (My translation differs slightly from the one found in *Methodology,* 103.)

37. Weber, *Critique of Stammler,* 69.

38. Ibid., 174n.4.

39. This is the position taken by Zander, *Das Problem der Beziehung,* 80.

40. Mommsen, *The Age of Bureaucracy,* 49.

41. Weber, *Gesammelte Politische Schriften,* 26.

42. Max Weber, *Gesammelte Aufsätze zur Soziologie und Sozialpolitik* (Tübingen: Mohr, 1924), 450.

43. While the English version of Salomon's essay on "German Sociology" (see note 6) pointed to a dialogue with Marx's "ghost," in the French edition (1947) this was changed to his "shadow." Ferrarotti, *Max Weber and the Destiny of Reason,* also sees him obsessed by "the imposing shadow of Marx" (p. 8). Is it farfetched to suggest that Marx's *ghost* was historical materialism while his *shadow* was the German Social Democratic Party?

44. Giddens, "Marx, Weber and the Development of Capitalism," 296.

45. Walton, "Ideology and the Middle Class."

46. Zander, *Das Problem der Beziehung,* 78–80, 148.

47. Again, the important conceptual distinctions between "Marxian," "Marxist," and "historical materialist" are often blurred, as in the following statement: "It is impossible to fully grasp Weber's work, unless it is seen in the context of how Marx's thinking was understood within bourgeois circles." Maurice Weyembergh, *Le voluntarisme rationnel de Max Weber* (Brussels: Palais des Académies, 1972), xxv.

48. Fleischmann, "De Weber à Nietzsche," 218.

49. Vernon K. Dibble, "Social Science and Political Commitments in the Young Max Weber," *European Journal of Sociology* 9 (1968): 99.

50. Kozyr-Kowalski, "Weber and Marx," 7.

51. See Max Weber, "The Social Causes of the Decay of Ancient Civilization," *The Journal of General Education* 5 (1950): 75–88, esp. 78. Reprinted in Eldridge, *Max Weber,* and in Max

Weber, *The Agrarian Sociology of Ancient Civilizations* (London: New Left Books, 1976). Weyembergh insists that "especially in his study of 1896, [Weber] applies a strictly Marxist approach" as he then understood it. *Le voluntarisme rationnel,* 30. See also Fleischmann, "De Weber à Nietzsche," 194.

52. *Verhandlungen des Evangelisch-Sozialen Kongresses,* 1894, 73. See also Wolfgang J. Mommsen, *Max Weber und die deutsche Politik, 1890–1920* (Tübingen: Mohr, 1974), 109.

53. Cf. Maximilien Rubel, "Premiers contacts des sociologues du XIXe siècle avec la pensée de Marx," *Cahiers internationaux de sociologie* 31 (1960): 175–84; Dieter Lindenlaub, *Richtungskämpfe im Verein für Sozialpolitik* (Wiesbaden: Steiner, 1967), chap. 4.

54. Roth, "The Historical Relationship to Marxism," 240.

55. Wiener, "Max Weber's Marxism," 389–401.

56. Ibid., 390, 393, 394.

57. Ibid., 390. Cf. Max Weber, *The Protestant Ethic and the Spirit of Capitalism* (New York: Scribner's, 1958), 27.

58. Ibid., 398.

59. Jones refers to this as "Q-similarity," usually the least interesting or significant type. W. T. Jones, "On the Meaning of the Term 'Influence' in Historical Studies," *Ethics* 53 (1943): 198.

60. Giddens, "Marx, Weber and the Development of Capitalism," 290.

61. "Almost always comparisons between Marx and Weber have been made on the level of the philosophy of history or of the methodology of social science, from Karl Löwith's well-known essay of 1932 up to the recent investigations by Kocka." Roth, "The Historical Relationship to Marxism," 228. For Johannes Winckelmann, though, "the key to understanding the scholarly [*wissenschaftlich*] work of Max Weber lies unequivocally in his *substantive* research." "Die Herkunft von Max Webers 'Entzauberungs'-Konzeption," *Kölner Zeitschrift* 32 (1980): 43.

62. Marianne Weber, *Max Weber: A Biography* (New York, London: Wiley, 1975), 420.

63. Bendix, *Max Weber: An Intellectual Portrait,* 20.

64. Friedrich H. Tenbruck, "Das Werk Max Webers," *Kölner Zeitschrift* 27 (1975): 663–702, esp. 669 (a slightly condensed version appeared as "The Problem of Thematic Unity in the Works of Max Weber," *British Journal of Sociology* 31 [1980]: 316–51). See also Tenbruck, "Abschied von *Wirtschaft und Gesellschaft,*" *Zeitschrift für die gesamte Staatswissenschaft* 133 (1977): 703–36. Salomon had already made the same point in the 1920s: Albert Salomon, "Max Weber," *Die Gesellschaft* 3 (1926): 131.

65. Tenbruck, "Das Werk Max Webers," 693; Tenbruck, "Wie gut kennen wir Max Weber?," *Zeitschrift für die gesamte Staatswissenschaft* 131 (1975): 726. In addition, see Benjamin Nelson, "Max Weber's 'Author's Introduction' (1920): A Master Clue to his Main Aims," *Sociological Inquiry* 44 (1974): 269–78. Nelson stressed the point, similar to Bendix and Tenbruck, that until the *Collected Essays on the Sociology of Religion* and *Economy and Society* along with their related papers are assembled and analyzed in proper sequence, "anyone who wishes will only have to fix upon one or another passage or essay in Weber's massive corpus to find grounds for his preferred image of Weber and Weber's sociology" (p. 274).

66. Reinhard Bendix, "Western Europe as the Object and Source of Social Science Research," *Social Research* 46 (1979): 796n.7.

67. Guenther Roth, "Abschied oder Wiedersehen?," *Kölner Zeitschrift* 31 (1979): 324. See also Wolfgang Schluchter, "Max Webers Gesellschaftsgeschichte: Versuch einer Explikation," *Kölner Zeitschrift* 30 (1978): 440f.; Martin Riesebrodt, "Ideen, Interessen, Rationalisierung: Kritische Anmerkungen zu F. H. Tenbrucks Interpretation des Werkes Max Webers," *Kölner Zeitschrift* 32 (1980): 109–29; and, for references to additional literature,

Stephen Kalberg, "The Search for Thematic Orientations in a Fragmented Oeuvre: The Discussion of Max Weber in Recent German Sociological Literature," *Sociology* 13 (1979): 127–39.

68. Dennis Wrong, *Max Weber* (Englewood Cliffs, N.J.: Prentice-Hall, 1970), 8.

69. Guy Oakes, "Introductory Essay," in Weber, *Critique of Stammler*, 41n.4.

70. Collins, "Weber's Last Theory of Capitalism."

71. The following admonition is also applicable here: "We need to distinguish between what Marx published, what he left unfinished, and what he wrote at one time for his own use, which was then published long after his death as the result of a kind and indiscrete adulation." Louis Dumont, *From Mandeville to Marx* (Chicago: University of Chicago Press, 1977), 113. Surely students' lecture notes need to be treated with particular caution.

72. For example, while Rehberg claims that Weber "did not become a prisoner to his methodological stipulations" (Karl-Siegbert Rehberg, "Rationales Handeln als gross-bürgerliches Aktionsmodell," *Kölner Zeitschrift* 31 [1979]: 216), Merleau-Ponty emphasizes that "[Max Weber's] methodological writings postdate his scientific applications" (Maurice Merleau-Ponty, *Adventures of the Dialectic* [Evanston, Ill.: Northwestern University Press, 1973], 11).

73. Anthony Giddens, *Capitalism and Modern Social Theory* (Cambridge: Cambridge University Press, 1971), 150.

74. Giddens, "Marx, Weber and the Development of Capitalism"; Collins, "Weber's Last Theory of Capitalism."

75. Giddens, "Marx, Weber and the Development of Capitalism," 302. Cf. Wiener, "Max Weber's Marxism." The trailblazing essay by Norman Birnbaum, "Conflicting Interpretations of the Rise of Capitalism: Marx and Weber," *British Journal of Sociology* 4 (1953): 125–41, contains several conceptual confusions, which led to the unfortunate choice of title.

76. Löwith, *Max Weber and Karl Marx*, 58 (emphasis added). I do not have the space here to discuss the numerous flaws in Löwith's reading of Weber, but I have done so in a review essay, "Exploring the Marx-Weber Nexus," in the *Canadian Journal of Sociology* 10 (1985): 69–87. Completely at variance with his interpretation is a forceful statement which Weber made during the 1905 revolution in Russia: "It is highly ridiculous to attribute to contemporary mature capitalism (this 'inevitability' of our economic development), . . . , an elective affinity with 'democracy' or 'freedom' in any literal sense." Max Weber, "Zur Lage der bürgerlichen Demokratie in Russland," in *Gesammelte Politische Schriften*, 63–64.

77. Giddens, "Marx and Weber: A Reply to Mr. Walton," *Sociology* 5 (1971): 395–97.

78. Mommsen, "Max Weber as a Critic of Marxism"; Mommsen, *The Age of Bureaucracy*, chap. 3.

79. Mueller, "Socialism and Capitalism," esp. 160–62.

80. Eldridge, *Max Weber,* 209.

81. Mommsen, "Max Weber as a Critic of Marxism," 394. There is also a short, lucid discussion in Mueller, "Socialism and Capitalism," 164–65.

82. See the section "Future Society" in *Karl Marx: Selected Writings in Sociology and Social Philosophy*, ed. T. B. Bottomore and M. Rubel (Harmondsworth: Penguin, 1961), 249–63.

83. Cf. Andrew Arato and Eike Gebhardt, *The Essential Frankfurt School Reader* (New York: Urizen Books, 1978), 191, 348; and Richard Münch, "Max Webers 'Anatomie des okzidentalen Rationalismus': Eine systemtheoretische Lektüre," *Soziale Welt* 29 (1978): 225.

84. Weber, *The Protestant Ethic,* 182.

85. Lindenlaub, *Richtungskämpfe im Verein für Sozialpolitik*, 296–97. In the same vein, Mommsen contends that "Weber's well-known investigation of 'The Protestant Ethic and the

Spirit of Capitalism' was *also* an attempt to help revitalize this bourgeois-puritan (class) consciousness.'' *Max Weber und die deutsche Politik,* 417. See also 65–66, 100.

86. *Max Weber und die deutsche Politik,* 447.

87. Mayer, ''Max Weber's Interpretation of Karl Marx,'' 719.

88. ''Both conventional sociology and Marxism concur that Weberian sociology *is* neo-Kantian.'' Bryan S. Turner, *For Weber: Essays on the Sociology of Fate* (London, Boston: Routledge & Kegan Paul, 1981), 4. Examples of such labeling are: Korf, ''Die Marxismuskritik,'' 255; Julien Freund, *The Sociology of Max Weber* (New York: Pantheon Books, 1968), 39; David Goddard, ''Max Weber and the Objectivity of Social Science,'' *History and Theory* 12 (1973): 3, 12, 18; Jürgen Kocka, ''Kontroversen über Max Weber,'' *Neue Politische Literatur* 21 (1976): 288; Zander, *Das Problem der Beziehung,* 104. Those who reject this interpretation include, besides Turner, Heinrich Rickert, *Die Grenzen der naturwissenschaftlichen Begriffsbildung* (Tübingen: Mohr, 1921), xx; Fleischmann, ''De Weber à Nietzsche,'' 197; Martin Barker, ''Kant as a Problem for Weber,'' *British Journal of Sociology* 31 (1980): 242; Weiss, *Das Werk Max Webers,* 39; Ferrarotti, *Max Weber and the Destiny of Reason,* 10. Despite his complex relationship to Hegel, Marx held him in the highest esteem, and he is commonly seen as more of a disciple than a dissenter. See Lloyd Easton, ''Alienation and History in the Early Marx,'' *Philosophy and Phenomenological Research* 22 (1961): 193–205. Among those who question this inference are Martin Nicolaus, ''Proletariat and Middle Class in Marx: Hegelian Choreography and the Capitalist Dialectic,'' *Studies on the Left* 7 (1967): esp. 33; Dumont, *From Mandeville to Marx,* 113, 166; Henry Veltmeyer, ''Marx's Two Methods of Sociological Analysis,'' *Sociological Inquiry* 48 (1978): 101–12; Mueller, ''Socialism and Capitalism,'' 168n.20.

89. As we are told at the beginning of a recent study of Nietzsche: ''We can understand his work without knowing who his friends were.'' Alderman, *Nietzsche's Gift,* 3.

90. Guy Oakes, ''Introductory Essay,'' to Weber, *Roscher and Knies,* 43–44.

91. Kocka, ''Karl Marx und Max Weber,'' 355. Cf. note 71.

92. Turner, *For Weber,* 9, 101–2.

93. Dibble, ''Social Science and Political Commitments,'' 96.

94. Quoted in Baumgarten, *Max Weber,* 399.

95. Weber, *Economy and Society,* 1186.

96. Max Weber, *The Religion of India: The Sociology of Hinduism and Buddhism* (Glencoe, Ill.: Free Press, 1958), 111.

97. Examples of sensitivity to a ''social interactionist'' approach are expressed by Marx and Engels most clearly in *The Holy Family* (1845) and *German Ideology* (1845–46), but also in Marx's letter to Annenkov (28 December 1846) and in Engel's book *Ludwig Feuerbach und der Ausgang der Klassischen deutschen Philosophie* (1888).

98. We should note that both Roth and Mommsen speak of the ''relationship to Marxism'' or the ''criticism of Marxism,'' but in fact they discuss mainly the relationship to, and criticism of, Marx.

99. This is a very significant issue in evaluating Weber, for as Tenbruck points out: ''In the case of no other sociologist has the biography assumed such broad and significant influence for [subsequent] interpretation. All those who knew him report how they were overwhelmed by his personality rather than his work.'' Tenbruck, ''Das Werk Max Webers,'' 666.

//////

| Robert J. Antonio | Values, History, and Science: The Metatheoretic Foundations of the Weber-Marx Dialogue |

Talcott Parsons's interpretation of Max Weber emphasized the contribution of religious ideas to progressive, societal rationalization and implied that the thrust of Weber's work was a desirable alternative to Marx's materialism. Parsons portrayed both his own early action theory and his later evolutionary functionalism as "in the spirit of Weber's work."[1] Parsons's theories as well as his widely read translations and interpretations of Weber have had immense influence on conventional understanding of the Weber-Marx relation. However, subtleties in Parsons's analyses are frequently overlooked, resulting in the conflation of his position with that of Weber.[2]

In the 1970s the so-called "Parsonized" Weber came under attack,[3] but at the same time new German interpretations revived the Parsonsian emphases on religious ideas and progressive rationalization.[4] However, the tendency of American sociologists to see Weber's work as a rebuttal of materialism is not a direct product of these sophisticated idealist readings; the tendency results from the impact of such interpretations on an audience more receptive to ideas than to material factors and who, until recent years, summarily rejected Marx's thought. In short, conventional sociologists, rather than Weber, have been preoccupied with refuting Marxism.

Certain scholars have demonstrated that Weberian theory is not antithetical to Marxism, although they sometimes exaggerated the complementary features of the approaches.[5] My paper explores Weber's and Marx's views of values, history, and science; it elaborates the assumptions of their approaches and explains how fundamental substantive disagreements emerge from different metatheoretic foundations. On the other hand, I argue that their differences over material interests have been exaggerated. Conventional wisdom about the incontrovertible opposition of Weberian "idealism" to Marxian "materialism" not only oversimplifies and distorts the relation of the original theories, but it also constrains dialogue between their modern offspring. Thus, my paper critically analyzes Marx's and Weber's metatheoretic assumptions in order to stimulate broader dialogue about their sociological analyses and substantive arguments about capitalism and socialism.

WEBER'S NEO-KANTIAN ROOTS:
THE FACT-VALUE DUALISM

Weber's neo-Kantian assumptions portray reality as an "infinite multiplicity"[6] of which only a small portion ("worthy of being known") can be grasped.[7] Science reflects "cultural interests":[8] "value orientations" determine the events deserving of scientific scrutiny.[9] Empirical questions are derived *ultimately* neither from pure theory nor from crude observation, but from "practical evaluations."[10] Empirical inquiry should be preceded by a "value analysis" which reviews critically the possibly relevant cultural values that determine the investigation's scope.[11] A research problem emerges from within "culturally significant" boundaries, but the *choice* of problem is drawn from a broad range of values, including less obvious ones that suggest new meanings.

After the choice of research problem, however, value judgments must be kept "unconditionally separate [from] the establishment of empirical facts."[12] Because humans are value-implementing beings, causal relations in the cultural sciences must be "understandable" in terms of configurations of meaning that express typical motives of "ideal type" actors in culturally defined situations. Sociologists should treat collectivities "as *solely* the resultants and modes of organization of the particular acts of individual persons, since these alone can be treated as agents in a course of subjectively understandable action."[13] Weber rejected organicist, functionalist, and structuralist reifications of collectivities. They omit typical motivation and, therefore, abandon the mission of the cultural sciences, which is to "understand" value-oriented action "and by means of this understanding to 'explain' it 'interpretively.' "[14]

Weber argued that nomothetic laws reduce "cultural phenomena to purely quantitative categories" and that human history "could never be deduced from" them. Such laws could not contribute to "*understanding* of those aspects of cultural reality . . . *worth knowing.*"[15] Historical knowledge of particular cultural events is a matter of "concrete causal *relationships,*" not laws.[16] Weber believed that sociological concepts should facilitate comparative and typological understanding of cultural events described by historians. Thus, rational ("one-sided") models of typical ends and means, actors and situations, replace nomothetic laws. These "ideal types" promote "understanding" by elaborating "objectively possible" motives and explaining situational constraints. Lacking the general validity of laws, these types are exclusively "heuristic" aids that portray order in limited portions of a vast empirical world.[17]

Weber believed that factual judgments and value judgments occupy different "theoretical 'provinces,'" each with its own immanent standards of evaluation ("objective" truth versus subjective conviction).[18] Following Kant, he desired to preserve the integrity of both the scientific and practical realms as autonomous but not completely separate. Value orientations are the basis for selecting scientific problems. On the other hand, science provides accurate information and "inconvenient facts" that inform and condition value decisions. But despite these interchanges, the two realms have distinct boundaries. Science cannot "save the individual the difficulty of making a choice"[19] because it can never determine the "truth" of values nor be the exclusive basis for choosing between them.

WEBER'S NIETZSCHEAN SIDE: THE WARRING GODS, DOMINATION, AND POLITICS

Weber did not concur with Kant's "categorical imperative," "kingdom of ends," or other arguments that implied moral harmony or moral progress.[20] Likewise, he broke with neo-Kantians (e.g., Rickert) who spoke of absolutely valid cultural values.[21] Weber agreed with much of Nietzsche's critique of religion, metaphysics, and Kantian ethics, particularly his pronouncement of the death of Christian morality, emphasis on the universality of power and domination, disdain for fanaticism, and aversion to metaphysical justifications. Though *not* a Nietzschean,[22] Weber agreed that the disenchanted era should be faced with "intellectual integrity." Both Nietzsche and Weber were wary of attempts to conjure up secular substitutes for Christianity and new modes of redemption. Neither could accept modern philosophies that promised restoration of organic communal ties through new intuitions of "absolute truth" nor political theories that guaranteed the creation of emancipated social orders founded on "historical truth."[23] For both thinkers, the inability of many intellectuals to accept the inherent uncertainty of life in the modern era was a sort of bad faith that caused amnesia about the stultifying stagnation of traditional societies and a weakness of spirit that blocked appreciation of the creative dynamism of modern existence.

Like Nietzsche, Weber believed that "conflict cannot be excluded from social life."[24] Moreover, disenchantment results in "a senseless hustle in the service of worthless . . . self-contradictory, and mutually antagonistic ends." Science, "representing the only possible form of a reasoned view of the world," offers no reprieve.[25] Instead, it deepens value conflict by furthering disenchantment, which permits increasingly differentiated values and interests. Weber rejected visions of harmonious, emancipated societies because freedom to pursue diverse ends widens zero-sum struggles for material and spiritual goods.

Weber stated:

Only one thing is indisputable: every type of social order, without exception, must, if one wishes to *evaluate* it, be examined with reference to the opportunities which it affords to *certain types of persons* to rise to positions of superiority through the operation of the various objective and subjective selective factors.[26]

Domination prevents omnipresent value conflict from becoming pervasive social conflict. According to Weber, "domination has played the decisive role particularly in the economically most important social structures of the past and present. . . ."[27] Structures of domination stabilize social hierarchy by containing and regulating conflicts of interest within legitimate boundaries.

Weber equated domination "with *authoritarian power of command*": the "master's" orders govern the social action of the ruled.[28] The "myth" of the "ruling minority" portrays their privileges as "'deserved'" and the disadvantages of subordinates as "the latter's 'fault.'"[29] Weber believed that "self-justification," expressed in "principles of legitimation," is necessary for stable hierarchy.[30] However, if the myths fail, masters use force to "squelch any action of the masses."[31] In Weber's view history is ubiquitous conflict and domination.

The "technical superiority" of modern bureaucracy derives from "consistently rationalized, methodically prepared and exact execution of the received order."[32] Rational components that improve productive capacities also increase the master's control over the satisfaction of material and ideal interests. Most importantly, bureaucracy "goes hand in hand with the concentration of the material means of management in the hands of the master."[33] Weber considered the "appropriation of all physical means of production" by "autonomous private industrial enterprises" and the existence of a propertyless laboring mass "under the compulsion of the whip of hunger" integral to bureaucratic capitalism.[34] He acknowledged concentrated property, elite control over it, and unequal distribution of its benefits. Capitalist accounting and formal organization are used to accumulate resources, control them, and, above all, maximize profits of property owners. "The fact that the maximum of *formal* rationality in capital accounting is possible only where the workers are subjected to domination by entrepreneurs, is a further specific element of *substantive* irrationality in the modern economic order."[35]

Weber asserted that

the "separation" of the worker from the material means of production, destruction, administration, academic research, and finance in general is the common basis of the modern state, in its political, cultural and military sphere, and of the private capitalist economy. In both cases the disposition over these means is in the hands of that power to whom the *bureaucratic apparatus* . . . directly obeys or to whom it is available in case of need.[36]

Bureaucratic centralization is not limited to capitalist enterprises, but it pervades almost all large organizations. "Mass democracy" levels "*the governed* in face of the governing and bureaucratically articulated group, which in its turn may occupy a quite autocratic position. . . ."[37] Unlike hopeful liberal or socialist thinkers, Weber portrayed an almost inevitable trend toward "crypto-plutocratic distribution of power."[38] Possible crystallization of this power in a total bureaucratic state (the "inanimate machine" or "shell of bondage") that absorbs all autonomous associations and countervailing powers imperils the existence of the "free" individual.[39]

Although Weber confronted increasing bureaucratization "without illusions," he did not pronounce the death of bourgeois society. Instead, he argued that the history of the West is still open and its fate depends in part upon the outcome of a contradiction between "democracy" and bureaucracy. Weber stressed the role of politicians who, unlike obedient bureaucratic officials, choose between ends[40] and are "the countervailing force against bureaucratic domination."[41] Politicians repel the bureaucrat's attempts to maximize organizational power and minimize external control. Democracy requires major supervisory responsibilities vested in a strong parliament with competing political parties. Furthermore, the "countervailing power of publicity" is needed to promote diffusion of power within parliament.[42]

For Weber, politics was organized "struggle" over interests, a public arena where conflicts are debated and modified by negotiation. Politicians should pursue the interests of their constituents according to the "ethic of responsibility," conditioning their value choices with a concern for consequences while maintaining an openness to compromise. Though science cannot decide political questions, it helps clarify competing values and interests, provides reliable information about consequences, and injects a degree of pacifying reason into conflicts.

Despite hopes for parliamentary "democracy," Weber was adamant that power will remain the province of the masters.[43] Furthermore, he argued that "democratization and demagogy belong together"[44] and that "democratic" leaders emerge on the basis of "who is most unscrupulous in his wooing of the masses."[45] Plebiscitary democratic leaders gain Caesaristic powers from their manipulation of mass sentiments.[46] Weber believed that large-scale, direct democracy is a fantasy and that even representative democracy is weakened by demagogic tendencies. At best "democracy" reduces coercion by establishing a sphere of limited, reasoned, and peaceful struggle between conflicting interest groups. Yet even this depends on the maintenance of countervailing powers: between state bureaucrats, professional politicians, plebiscitary leaders, unions, and capitalists. Weber's concept of democracy does not contradict his primary emphases on intensifying value conflict and expanding bureaucratic domination governed by plutocratic interests. Modern "democracy" does not overcome struggle or hierarchy; it rationalizes them through routinized, peaceful methods of mediating and limiting conflicts as well as through predictable, legal means of protecting the masters' privileges.

States pursue national goals in a conflictive world. Weber rejected pacifism and hoped that the German state would acquire and use power appropriate to its national interests. Though his views about Germany's nationalistic pursuits changed somewhat during different phases of his life, Weber generally stressed the maintenance of a strong state that unifies the populace and protects their cultural interests.[47]

Like Marx, Weber was a "realist" about modern economic, social, and political inequality; however, Weber did not herald historical trends or potential mass actions that promised to reduce substantially or eliminate inequality. There is a major difference between Marx and Weber: the thrust of Marx's approach was a critique of inequality (particularly of the economic form), while Weber had a more fateful (though not affirming) attitude about the topic. Most importantly, Weber was fearful that attempts to eliminate inequality by expanding the power of state bureaucracy would contribute to the destruction of societal dynamism and speed the trend toward greater unfreedom.

SCIENCE, POLITICS, AND SOCIALISM: MARX AND WEBER

As a student, Marx wrote his father: "Setting out from idealism . . . I hit upon seeking the Idea in the real itself. If formerly the gods had dwelt above the world, they now became its center."[48] Such a stance embraces the Hegelian view that truth is immanent in history.[49] Hegel rejected claims about ontological realms external to the subject, stressing instead knowledge as the product of self-formative labor. Truth emerges from progressive stages in the self-development of the subject.[50] Marx abandoned Hegel's idealist idiom, but he retained the view that truth is immanent and emergent in the record of human labor—history. The teleological argument is transformed from a history of "spirit," terminating in absolute knowledge, to a progression of modes of production, culminating in communist society.[51] The standard of truth, *emancipation,* unfolds partially with each developmental stage until it is realized by proletarian revolution. Valid valuative knowledge is immanent in the activity of class-conscious proletarians and is explicated rationally by the Party.

Marx's Hegelian roots conflict with the neo-Kantian and Nietzschean aspects of Weber's thought. Marx believed he overcame the Kantian dualism of fact and value and did not entertain notions of value-free science. However, he did not eschew "objective" empirical analysis and held that historical materialism captures accurately the empirical movement of history.[52] On the other hand, Marx and Weber disagreed implicitly about the value orientations that determine appropriate empirical questions. Weber stressed a plurality of values, and he made no claims about their validity. His theme of "cultural significance" is an extremely broad standard interpreted by each scientist; this contrasts with Marx's specific value of class-based emancipation. Claims about the historical validity of the emancipatory end, and the ideological nature of others, make it a collectively binding value base.[53] In contrast, Weber's view that only factual knowledge is "objective" makes individual social scientists ethically responsible for choosing among diverse cultural values. Although Marx's method implies a narrower range of potential orienting values,[54] once a problem is defined it requires an empirical phase, which, like Weber's method, should avert value bias. Finally, though it is open to knowledge with practical application, Weberian science is free to be contemplative. Validity rests exclusively on empirical accuracy. On the other hand, Marx insisted that valid knowledge contributes to emancipatory social transformation.[55] Historical materialists seek not only to interpret history but also to participate in and even regulate it rationally according to its emancipatory telos.

Marx treated emancipation as a dimension of progressive material and social evolution. In contrast to Weber's social science, which investigated pieces of an infinite reality, Marx claimed a more total understanding of the *core* features of history. The analysis of modes of production is not simply one way of organizing knowledge; rather it captures *the* determining (*real* as opposed to epiphenomenal) historical forces. The belief that emancipation is immanent in historical development is a basis for claims about transcending the Weberian dualisms between fact and value, concept and reality, and science and politics. Ultimately these emerge from Weber's emphases on a plurality of values and an infinite reality. The view that cultural science develops typologies capable of only partial understanding of social reality reflects this perspective, while Marx's objectivistic, theoretical value relation is the basis for claims of nomothetic understanding about the total historical process.

Marx's Hegelian vision of a harmonious terminus to history contradicts Weber's Nietzschean emphases on perpetual conflict and domination. Just as Hegelian spirit overcomes the subject-object dualism, Marxian communism transcends the split of individual and society. This concludes a history of struggles between ruling classes, perpetuating obsolescent property relations that fetter productive development, and victorious, subaltern, laboring classes, representing nascent property relations capable of harnessing advanced productive forces.

Marx was devoted primarily to analyzing capitalism and did not attempt to develop a systematic theory of post-capitalist society; however, he was emphatic that proletarian revolution would be the final act of the heretofore all-pervasive contradiction between owners and producers, which had shaped the historical course. Progressive advancements of productive forces and "corresponding" social relations of production, motored by class conflict, determine evolution that culminates inevitably in a harmonious, egalitarian, and rational (free) society. Under communism scientific "modes of cooperation" replace the property-based division of labor while the state and other coercive bureaucracies are supplanted gradually by neutral modes of administration and spontaneous social relations. This contrasts sharply with Weber's intensified value conflict, increased plutocracy, and pervasive bureaucracy.

Weber rejected Marx's vision of post-capitalist society and ridiculed its teleological underpinnings. He considered claims about the proletariat representing universal class interests and the historical inevitability of socialism as residua of Hegelian "emanantism" and "panlogism."[56] Marx's concepts of class and class interest were, in Weber's view, reifications that violate the tenets of interpretive sociology. For Weber, "real" class interest, which transcends the alienated consciousnesses of individuals, was a fiction that could not be "understood" sociologically.[57]

Weber believed that socialism would be another step toward total bureaucracy, rather than an emancipatory rupture with the past. The transition to socialism would produce an "expansive state," undermining parliamentary control and eliminating public supervision of state offices. He feared coercive regulation of interest groups and the destruction of the political sphere.[58] Workers would not be empowered, but control would be transferred to a unitary group of bureaucratic officials.[59] Weber stressed that *control* is far more important than whether there is capitalist or collective ownership. In either case, effective control is in the hands of an elite, workers remain wage-laborers, and management continues to maintain high prices and low wages. Moreover, socialist workers face monolithic bureaucracy that forbids strikes.[60] For Weber, socialism meant a bureaucratization of top management that forecloses interest group dynamics, destroys neutral agencies of appeal, and grants *sole* ruling power to state officials.[61]

Weber argued that socialist planning would be insensitive to mass *needs*. He could not imagine how a "consumer organization" could be generated to regulate state bureaucrats,[62] and, even if a "needs" economy were developed, it would entail an "inevitable reduction in formal, calculatory rationality which would result from the elimination of money and capital accounting." This "unavoidable element of irrationality" would hinder production, reduce administrative efficiency, and undermine technical coordination.[63] Weber did not seriously entertain the prospect of socialist decentralization because it would require a "reversion . . . to small scale organization" with unacceptable social and economic consequences.[64]

Weber believed that socialism would fail most miserably in the two areas that together constitute its reason for being—social democracy and material plenty. He thought that socialism would vastly expand bureaucracy, eliminate countervailing powers, and forcefully homogenize social life. An ironic decline in productive and distributive efficiency would accompany the brutal rationalization and centralization. Since socialist ideology is a secular theodicy that promises worldly compensation for suffering, it would become an "ethic of absolute ends" with inadequate concern for means and consequences. Weber agreed with Nietzsche that socialism would enslave the masses,[65] and political conflict would be smothered by total bureaucracy. The resulting repressive quietism is completely antithetical to Marxian emancipation. Weber's and Marx's positions about socialism were animated by contrary assumptions and fundamentally different visions of history and historical possibilities.

WEBER'S CRITIQUE OF HISTORICAL MATERIALISM

Weber believed that historical materialism was bankrupt as a "causal explanation" of history.[66] In his view Marxists "content themselves with the most threadbare hypotheses and the most general phrases since they have then satisfied their dogmatic need to believe that the economic 'factor' is the 'real' one, the only 'true' one, and the one which 'in the last instance is everywhere decisive.' " The point is that "explanation of everything by economic causes *alone* is never exhaustive . . . in *any* sphere of cultural phenomena, not even in the 'economic' sphere itself."[67] At issue is a mechanical and uncritical "one-sidedness."

According to Weber, historical materialism denies the cultural mediation of science. Its objectivistic claims about direct access to reality overlook the *hiatus irrationalis* between concept and reality. Conceptual and value impositions are conflated with empirical content, opening the way for an emanatist portrayal of mechanically unfolding "objective" conditions. Necessary stages of history were viewed, by Weber, as "evolutionary dogmatism"[68] in which individuals become "instances of *realization*" of a metaphysical concept.[69]

Weber denied that historical materialism captures the totality and truth of history, and he considered such arguments to reflect implicit values rather than "reality." Claims about understanding History propel Marxism's implicit cultural interests into hegemony over other constellations of value and, in so doing, delimit drastically the range of potential scientific questions; secondly, validation of the emancipation value on the basis of an alleged historical trend constitutes false objectivity and "pseudo-value freedom." Valuations are misrepresented as historical facts. This is the opposite of Weber's "value analysis" in which the subjective foundations of inquiry are presented for critical scrutiny, subjected to responsible choice, and demarcated clearly from empirical matters. Weber believed the confusion of fact and value destroys the integrity of both spheres.

Weber's critique of Marx was not exegetical. Weber tended to attack lesser representatives of intellectual traditions, rather than addressing the major figures directly and textually.[70] He did not dissect Marx's own position carefully, although he portrayed it as the ultimate source of his epigones' vulgar materialism.[71] Even if Weber had desired to do a textual critique, many of Marx's works (e.g., *The Economic and Philosophical Manuscripts of 1844, The German Ideology, Grundrisse,* and "Theses of Feuerbach") that might have moderated Weber's position were not yet available.[72]

The doctrinaire materialism of the "Second International" dominated Marxist thought during much of Weber's lifetime. Western Marxism, with its more voluntarist reading of Marx, had not yet emerged. Even Engels distanced Marx and himself from the reigning crude materialism and rigid determinism. Though he admitted that Marx and he, in the heat of debate, had sometimes overemphasized "the economic factor," Engels rejected emphatically the "most amazing rubbish" of younger Marxists.[73] He argued that he and Marx did not hold that the "economic element is the *only* determining one," but he explained that there are numerous irreducible, interactive elements (e.g., economic, social, political, religious) and that history reflects conflicts of "individual wills" shaped "by a host of particular conditions of life."[74] Weber would have still disagreed because Engels still contended that the material factor was "the *ultimately* determining element in history. . . ."[75] However, Engels suggested a more subtle historical materialism that demanded a more sympathetic critique.

Weber's view of historical materialism must be considered in the context of his opposition to the Social Democratic Party. Weber thought that its socialist program threatened capitalist development and the entrepreneurial class, both of which he considered essential to Germany's welfare.[76] He also felt that the Party's internationalist and anti-imperialist views could undermine German national interests.[77] Weber supported those opponents of the Social Democrats who proposed reforms to reduce class struggle (i.e., *Kathedersozialisten* and the Christian Social Movement), but who also sought to maintain capitalism and preserve a strong German state.[78]

Social Democrats espoused a theoretical line (though it was a topic of debate within the Party) that largely eliminated voluntarist elements and stressed instead material necessity, objective contradictions, and inevitable socialism. Ironically, this was combined with a moderate parliamentary political position. Since conjunctural historical conditions dimmed revolutionary hopes, Social Democrats took shelter in theory, organized, and waited for the coming capitalist collapse.[79] Karl Kautsky, an important Party theoretician, spoke of value-free "scientific socialism" that objectively derived its ends from "historical necessity."[80] He personified Weber's "pseudo-value freedom" because he saved "the individual the difficulty of making a choice." Instead, science delivered historically valid, collective ends and guaranteed their realization.

Weber's critique of historical materialism is conditioned by his limited consideration of Marx's texts and his strong reaction to the then prevailing narrow, dogmatic, and mechanistic Marxism. Weber usually treated historical materialism as a pseudo-scientific projection of political ideology, undeserving of detailed criticism. Had he been exposed to a wider range of Marx's texts and experienced the rise of western Marxism, Weber would neither have agreed with Marx nor would all of his criticisms have been rebutted; however, his view of historical materialism would probably have been modified and somewhat moderated.

WEBER AND MARX: THE CENTRALITY OF
MATERIAL INTERESTS

Some idealist portrayals overlook Weber's strong emphasis on material interests. Even his often-quoted discussion of "world images" as "switchmen" is preceded by the assertion that "not ideas, but material and ideal interests, directly govern men's conduct."[81] In another work he argued that material interests condition all aspects of cultural life, even "the finest nuances of aesthetic and religious feeling."[82] Though legitimate domination means that "*purely* material interests" alone are not an adequate basis for social structure, Weber believed that affectual and ideal factors *supplement* material interests.[83] Finally, material interests become overbearing as the capacity for calculating them advances with disenchantment, rationalization, and related technological refinements. Even in the allegedly idealist Protestant ethic thesis, modern capitalism is described as a "mechanism" that "determines" the lives of individuals with "irresistible force."[84]

Weber recognized the significance of ideal interests and that, as exemplified by charismatic outbreaks, they can be the critical factor in certain historical eruptions. However, though Weber was not a "materialist," he stressed material interests as central and systematic forces, especially in bureaucratic structures of domination. Because modern bureaucracy is managed increasingly on the basis of precise calculations of material interests, ideal interests are in a more supplemental and legitimating role than in patrimonial bureaucracy.

According to Weber's neo-Kantian epistemology, there is no direct access to material "reality" (it is always mediated by culturally structured modes of consciousness), so there is no base or superstructure. Instead, there are webs of material and ideal interests, which are expressed in systems of interconnected (by inner affinities) conceptions and values. Material interests are central because they are prerequisites for accomplishing a wide variety of human ends. This centrality is not a matter of whimsical choice, but individuals and institutional leaderships *must* realize certain material interests to effect other aspects of their agendas.

Weber's critique of historical materialism was directed more against its epistemological and teleological claims than toward its arguments about the importance of material factors for life. He asserted that Marxist laws would not be objectionable if they were employed *heuristically* as ideal types.[85]

Marianne Weber stressed this point, arguing that Weber admired Marx's approach as "an exceedingly fruitful, indeed, a specifically new heuristic principle" that opened up "previously unilluminated" areas of knowledge.[86] However, Weber felt that the approach was mired in reified and deterministic assumptions that conflated covert valuations with historical factors. Though Weber addressed these problems critically, he did not intend to provide an idealist substitute for Marx's materialism. He explicitly disavowed this goal.[87] Weber, like Marx, understood the "fatefulness" of individual lives situated in overpowering structures of domination.[88] Their valuations collide with socially structured constraints, and choices result in unintended consequences. There can be no doubt of the centrality of material interests within this world. Though Marx's and Weber's positions should not be equated, the materialism-idealism polarity is simply inadequate as a basis for distinguishing their perspectives. Despite differences in underlying values and assumptions, their analyses of material factors yield some surprising continuities.

VALUES, HISTORY, AND SCIENCE: THE MUTED WEBER-MARX DIALOGUE IN CRITICAL MARXISM

Mechanical Marxists often dismiss Weber as a "bourgeois" without discussing the differences that underlie the obvious disagreements over capitalism and socialism. On the other hand, critical Marxists explore these deeper issues incompletely. They tend to equate the pluralist and individualist value base of Weber's perspective with irrationalism.[89] They imply that Weber's value base lacks the steering capacity to preserve science's autonomy from capitalist technocracy. This is part of a broader attack on the crude positivist concept of value freedom in the modern social sciences, which means almost exclusively attempting to minimize the effect of values on research. The themes of value relevance, cultural significance, and Weber's general sensitivity to the subjective underpinnings of science have been dropped. Critical Marxists have neither analyzed precisely the relation of Weber's philosophy of science to this constricted, post-Weberian concept of value freedom nor recognized sufficiently the overlap of their own approach with that of Weber.[90] Therefore, on the basis of their criticism it is possible to confuse Weber's perspective with approaches that sever completely the connection between science and values. For example, Marcuse interpreted value freedom so narrowly that Weber appeared insensitive to the problem of values and precursive to technocratic thought.[91] Habermas treats Weber more sympathetically, but in his early work it is still a small step from Weber's decisionism to the technocratic model.[92]

Critical Marxists have neither taken adequate account of Weber's ideas about value relevance and value analysis, nor have they analyzed explicitly enough the connection of his methodological views to those of the positivists. On the other hand, they are correct that systematic reflection about values is not a methodological procedure of modern social science. Today the choice of research problem is likely to follow (nonreflectively) from the social scientist's training, taste, and opportunities for funding and publication. Weberian reflexiveness about the foundations of science is supplanted by technocratic scientism, which abandons value analysis and treats research problems as if they spring objectively from the technical process. In an age of bureaucratic rationalization and centralization the technical aspects of research production are ascendant over the concern for values. Correctly understood, Weber's approach can neither justify the uncritical acceptance of research problems produced by dominant institutions nor abandon its autonomy; such science is contradictory to Weberian methodological postulates.

Though Weber was not a technocratic thinker, his emphases on value pluralism and individual responsibility in the choice of research problems have some affinity for the modern positivist view. The Nietzschean theme of eternal value conflict, intensified by differentiation, rationalization, and disenchantment, makes the elaboration of collective value guidelines dogmatic and formalist. But how is the demand for neo-Kantian ethical reflexiveness and responsibility maintained in the face of increasingly "worthless . . . self-contradictory, and mutually antagonistic ends?"[93] Emphases on a plurality of values, cultural significance, and individual ethical responsibility were formulated in response to earlier forms of absolutism and do not address fully the threats to science posed by corporate capitalism and bureaucratic socialism.

Weberian social scientists reflect freely on culturally significant values in order to perceive, clarify, and perhaps revise initial valuations about research problems.[94] Critical Marxist contentions about irrationality focus on the lack of substantively rational guidelines for this subjective valuation. If it occurs at all, the process of reflection is influenced by the person's constellation of material and ideal interests. Critics argue that the selection of scientific problems is determined ultimately by powerful institutional interests, and, in a context that pits the bemusing conflict of values against the "objectivity" of the technical process, the individual social scientist is unlikely to reject research problems proffered by the bureaucracies that provide resources and rewards. Thus, the critical Marxist critique raises important questions: Does the neo-Kantian emphasis on ethical commitment itself become a formalism in a world of intensely conflicting values and interests? Is ethical individualism meaningful under technocratic domination? In the contemporary era will subjective reflection about research problems yield more than the constellation of interests which locate the individual in an academic bureaucracy situated in a larger, bureaucratically structured, social hierarchy?

The point is neither to expose Weber as a relativist nor to call for a revival of absolute value. His unwillingness to articulate value guidelines was not a technocratic bias, but it was a reaction to conservative as well as Marxist dogmatism. This concern remains relevant today; he emphasized the duty to reflect on and choose values rather than to succumb to slavish ties to ideologies, movements, and institutions. Weber was no relativist: his sociology reflects commitments to values such as political moderation and compromise, freedom of the individual, and rationality. However, this neither reduces the tension between his value pluralism and ethic of individual responsibility, nor does it respond fully to the critical Marxists. Portrayed fairly, Weber's methodology is not technocratic, but today it can be questioned whether it provides adequate defense of science's autonomy against technocratic encroachment and bureaucratic co-optation.

It is essential to consider critical Marxist criticism of Marx.[95] The emancipatory proletariat failed to appear, and the working class became integrated increasingly into a capitalist system characterized by heightened consumption and sophisticated modes of legitimation. Status group competition and racial, ethnic, and religious divisions deflect class consciousness. Moreover, the resilience and flexibility of corporate capital invalidate the promises of steadily intensifying contradictions and imminent collapse. On the other hand, ossified, repressive, and inefficient state socialist bureaucracies upheld Weber's projections about bureaucratic abuses, worker powerlessness, and productive inefficiency. Historical validation of emancipation is countered by advances in the means of domination, coercion, and destruction. Marx's Enlightenment optimism seems childish in the final quarter of the twentieth century. Indeed, it impedes needed reflection about the meaning of emancipation and the danger of pursuing it as an ethic of absolute ends.

The limitations of mechanical Marxism are rooted in Marx's texts and especially in the uneasy unity of science and politics. Historical materialism was a useful sociological tool when Marx applied it historically, without its teleological trappings, to analyze the production, appropriation, and distribution of necessary and surplus product and to assess the impact of these processes on the development, operation, and decline of social formations. On the other hand, Marx also invoked the approach politically to assure the proletariat of its "historical role," promise the demise of the bourgeoisie, and guarantee the rise of emancipatory communism. These teleological assertions constituted a political rhetoric urging revolutionary, working class action. However, this rhetoric conflated political values with history and consequently weakened the expressed scientific intentions of Marx's work. In mechanical Marxism teleological guarantees encourage the dismissal of disconfirming evidence and transform historical materialism into an ahistorical and even anti-empirical servant of political goals; Marx's materialist sociology is eclipsed completely by the political rhetoric. The subordination of fact to value demolishes the possibility of a unity of science and politics, and Marxism becomes a metaphysics of the concrete because it no longer reflects critically upon its ends to determine their immanent meaning and assess realistically the historical possibilities for and constraints to their realization. As a result, in advanced capitalism, materialist slogans of mechanical Marxism fail even as an ideology of working-class revolt.

Critical Marxists argue that reification of Marxism's emancipatory value base derives from the crude positivism of orthodox thinkers, and they espouse a cultural or Hegelian approach that de-emphasizes radically or rejects completely the materialist elements. Though they point correctly to ahistorical features of Marxism, critical Marxist efforts have been overly occupied with epistemological and philosophical critique. Moreover, Marx's sociological form of materialist analysis tends to be discarded along with the materialist political slogans. As in the case of the later Frankfurt School, the necessary empirical moment of Marx's approach is too often equated with scientism and positivism. Ahistorical elements cannot be eradicated by substituting philosophical critique for empirical foundations in historical materialism and political economy. A truly critical Marxism not only requires historically conditioned, philosophical reflection about the content of its political ends, but it also needs sociological means to assess accurately ''objective'' historical possibilities for and constraints to achieving these ends.[96]

CONCLUSION: THE CULTURAL MEANING OF THE WEBER-MARX DIALOGUE

Critical Marxist analyses of Weber and Marx point to problems that unfold from their respective assumptions about the relation of values, history, and science. Their divergent valuative and philosophical positions generate exceedingly complex epistemological, axiological, and hermeneutical problems unresolved by critical Marxism. Their criticism has not confronted Weber's methodological ideas or Marx's materialism directly and fully enough. Although critical Marxists have raised significant questions, their dialogue about the two theorists has been somewhat muted. Reflection upon the Weber-Marx relationship must shift to issues that the critical Marxists have not developed sufficiently.

The issue of materialism should again be considered.[97] Weber spoke of the "inexorable power" of material goods over modern life,[98] and Marx's analysis of capitalism stressed the same theme in even stronger terms. The relation of material and ideal interests and, particularly, the role of material interests in modern capitalism provide strong bases of continuity as well as strategic points of disagreement; these deserve the most careful and open-minded consideration. The aim would be to determine if critique of this issue and related meta-assumptions could clarify further the relation of Weber and Marx and perhaps provide a basis for a new approach incorporating elements from both perspectives.

The above task requires basic modifications that recast each theorist's approach. For example, a new historical materialism would be a heuristic device, albeit an important one. Engels himself suggested, in his autocritique, that "our conception of history is above all *a guide to study* [my emphasis], not a lever for construction after the manner of the Hegelian. All history must be studied afresh. . . ."[99] Though Marx and Engels did not consistently follow this prescription, it is one of the ways (and I believe the methodologically correct way) that they employed historical materialism. The new combined approach would have to abandon dogmatic adherence to a teleological conception of history and reified ideas about proletarian emancipation.

On the other hand, basic material interests (e.g., food, shelter) must be treated as more than small segments of many highly differentiated values and interests. Weber's historical analyses imply that not all values and interests are equal and that certain ones are necessary for the realization of others. He recognized that the flow of material interests is crucial to institutional existence and to the fates of individuals. Pluralities of individuals often desire similar material interests because without them their other, perhaps more random, material and ideal ends could not be achieved. The autonomy of modern social science requires a methodology that stimulates adequate awareness of these interests. Methodological recognition of human needs (material and ideal) should condition the process of value analysis and choice of research problem. Employment of such a conception would somewhat counter the tendency of science to serve nonreflectively technocratic constellations of interest. Weber's ideas about the individualistic, theoretical value relation and value pluralism would be modified somewhat.

The above sounds too simple. A Weber-Marx synthesis is a most difficult and perhaps even impossible task. There is no methodological formula for resolving the problems raised by the varying value foundations. Despite the overlap of their theories, Marx and Weber differed sharply over Enlightenment hopes about the role of reason in history and the possibilities for a rational society. Marx believed, and Weber did not. Weber's post-Enlightenment skepticism seems to have been borne out by recent history, though critical Marxists have sought new historical grounds to revive the emancipatory project. The teleological elements cannot be cut cleanly and completely from Marx's approach without vitiating its raison d'être. If historical materialism were uncoupled from the value of emancipation, or if it were no longer attributed primacy over other values, the approach would no longer be Marxism but simply another empirical, sociological method. This method already exists in some forms of academic ''Marxism'' and is a useful scientific tool. However, such an approach abandons the ethical project that Marx, mechanical Marxists, and critical Marxists all believed animated their efforts.

Dialogue about the Weber-Marx relationship concerns political and philosophical as well as scientific issues. Their views about science, values, and history raise the broader matter of the Englightenment tradition and its cultural aspirations. In the post-World War II United States, the emergence of technocratic thought and its celebration of post-industrial society produced a more narrow and naive optimism that shut down prematurely the debate over reason and rational agency. Unlike the approach of either Weber or Marx, substantive reason was seen to percolate from the technical rationality of the existing productive and administrative systems. There was a curious agreement among many on the Right and some on the Left that capitalism might have transcended its contradictions and embarked on continuous growth. In postwar American sociology Marx was seldom discussed, and Weber was often invoked in support of post-industrial views that actually contradicted his theories. Postwar abundance and optimistic beliefs about technological progress were not conducive to rethinking the critical issues raised by the two theorists. This climate also stimulated the narrow concept of value freedom that severed completely the relation of values and science. Scientific questions became objectified products of the technical process, rather than the outcome of responsible, subjective reflection.

The politically turbulent late 1960s and the multiple crises of the 1970s and early 1980s shipwrecked post-industrial optimism and reopened debate over rationality and planning. In American sociology this has been reflected in the breakdown of the functionalist-positivist consensus of the mid-1950s and early 1960s, the emergent popularity of continental approaches such as critical theory, and the resurgence of interest in classical theory, particularly Marx and Weber. Renewed dialogue about these two thinkers is timely. Social theory is not only a scientific tool, but it is also a means for talking about deeply rooted and burning cultural issues. Discussion of Marx and Weber is never ethically neutral or apolitical because their names and ideas are inextricably tied to the still-current debate over capitalism and socialism.

Two areas of dialogue are essential. Given the present crises and debates over growth, development, environment, and the economy, the issue of material constraints and possibilities is crucial; thus, materialism is an appropriate starting point for a Weber-Marx dialogue. Secondly, the materialism issue is connected to conceptions of equality, human rights, and human needs, and, therefore, cannot be extricated from reconsideration of the value foundations of science. Certainly Marx's crudest teleological claims ought to be rejected, but simple adoption of Weber's pluralist approach cannot bridge the theories. Though Marx's promise about a terminus to the prehistory of exploitation is wistful, Weber's fatalistic acceptance of inequality and even plutocracy is an equally limited foundation for later, twentieth-century sociopolitical dialogue.

The issues of decisionism and immanent critique must be considered again in the present political and historical context because they bring the matter of values to center stage in discussions about the problematic relation of history, science, and politics. The central issue concerns whether it is possible to construct a position that avoids the pitfalls of technocratic co-optation as well as dogmatic formalism. This difficult issue requires an approach that transcends both Marx and Weber. The significance of the Weber-Marx dialogue raises a deeper and broader issue concerning the contemporary relevance of the cultural heritage of the Enlightenment: the vitality or bankruptcy of the ideas of rationality and freedom. Marx and Weber addressed these issues systematically and provocatively. Any attempt to overcome the problems discussed above must exceed their efforts. This culturally important task has no easy solution, but it must begin with criticism of both Weber and Marx.

Notes

This paper was presented at the Seventy-Eighth Annual Meeting of the American Sociological Association, August 31 to September 4, 1983, in Detroit. Ira Cohen, Stephen Kalberg, David Willer, and Norman Yetman have provided generous critical comments and suggestions. Lawrence A. Scaff provided trenchant criticism of two drafts that was most helpful. Finally, thanks to Sharon Cox for typing the too numerous revisions and for detecting many editorial errors. These persons deserve my gratitude, but none of the blame for any errors.

1. Talcott Parsons, *The Structure of Social Action,* vol. 2 (New York: Free Press, 1968), 683; Parsons, *The System of Modern Societies* (Englewood Cliffs, N.J.: Prentice Hall, 1971), 1–2, 144; Parsons, *Essays in Sociological Theory: Pure and Applied* (Glencoe, Ill.: Free Press, 1949), 70; Parsons, "Capitalism in Recent German Literature," *Journal of Political Economy* 37 (1929): 40; Parsons and Neil J. Smelser, *Economy and Society* (New York: Free Press, 1956), 291–92.

2. Parsons acknowledged differences with Weber, but his claims to have extended Weber's thought sympathetically have had more impact than his textual references to disagreements. As a result, Parsons's epigones as well as some of his critics have exaggerated the harmony between his ideas and those of Weber. See Robert J. Antonio. "Parsons versus Weber: Domination or Technocratic Model of Social Organization," in *Max Weber's Political Sociology,* ed. Ronald Glassman and Vatro Murvar (Westport, Conn.: Greenwood Press, 1983), 155–74.

3. See Jere Cohen, Lawrence E. Hazelrigg, and Whitney Pope, "De-Parsonizing Weber: A Critique of Parsons' Interpretation of Weber's Sociology," *American Sociological Review* 40 (1975): 229–41.

4. Friedrich H. Tenbruck, "Das Werk Max Webers," *Kölner Zeitschrift für Soziologie und Sozialpsychologie* 27 (1975): 663–702; Tenbruck, "The Problem of Thematic Unity in the Works of Max Weber," *British Journal of Sociology* 31 (1980): 316–51; Wolfgang Schluchter, "The Paradox of Rationalization: On the Relation of Ethics and World," in Guenther Roth and Wolfgang Schluchter, *Max Weber's Vision of History: Ethics and Method* (Berkeley: University of California Press, 1979), 11–64; Schluchter, *The Rise of Western Rationalism* (Berkeley: University of California Press, 1981); Stephen Kalberg, "The Search for Thematic Orientations in a Fragmented Oeuvre: The Discussion of Max Weber in Recent German Sociological Literature," *Sociology* 13 (1979): 127–39.

5. For incisive treatment of the relationship between the approaches from a Weberian perspective see Guenther Roth, "The Historical Relationship to Marxism," in Reinhard Bendix and Guenther Roth, *Scholarship and Partisanship: Essays on Max Weber* (Berkeley:

University of California Press, 1971), 227-52; and from a Marxian perspective see Richard Ashcraft, "Marx and Weber on Liberalism," *Comparative Studies in Society and History* 14 (1972): 130-68.

6. Max Weber, *The Methodology of the Social Sciences* (Glencoe, Ill.: Free Press, 1949), 72; Martin Barker, "Kant as a Problem for Weber," *British Journal of Sociology* 31 (1980): 224-45; Thomas Burger, *Max Weber's Theory of Concept Formation* (Durham, N.C.: Duke University Press, 1976); Burger, "Max Weber, Interpretive Sociology, and the Sense of Historical Science: A Positivistic Conception of Verstehen," *The Sociological Quarterly* 18 (1977): 165-75; H. H. Bruun, *Science, Values and Politics in Max Weber's Methodology* (Copenhagen: Munksgaard, 1972).

7. Weber, *The Methodology*, 72; Burger, *Max Weber's Theory of Concept Formation*, 59-65.

8. Weber, *The Methodology*, 22.

9. Ibid., 76.

10. Ibid., 22.

11. Ibid., 145-52; Burger, *Max Weber's Theory of Concept Formation*, 96-97; Bruun, *Science, Values and Politics*, 145-200.

12. Weber, *The Methodology*, 11, 147-49.

13. Max Weber, *The Theory of Social and Economic Organization* (New York: Free Press, 1964), 101, 98-103.

14. Weber, *The Methodology*, 40.

15. Max Weber, *Roscher and Knies: The Logical Problems of Historical Economics* (New York: Free Press, 1975), 64, 217.

16. Weber, *The Methodology*, 78-79.

17. Weber, *Roscher and Knies*, 190.

18. Bruun, *Science, Values and Politics*, 16-77, 34-37; Weber, *The Methodology*, 1-47.

19. Weber, *The Methodology*, 19.

20. Immanuel Kant, *Kant on the Foundation of Morality* (Bloomington, Ind.: Indiana University Press, 1970), 156-57, 167-68; Kant, *On History* (Indianapolis, Ind.: Bobbs Merrill, 1963), 137-54; Martin Barker, "Kant as a Problem for Weber," 224-45; Bruun, *Science, Values and Politics*, 182-83.

21. Barker, "Kant as a Problem for Weber," 242; Burger, *Max Weber's Theory of Concept Formation*, 49-59.

22. For example, Weber rejected Nietzsche's central argument about the origin of religion in *ressentiment*. See Max Weber, *Economy and Society*, vol. 2 (New York: Bedminster Press, 1968), 492-500. For a sophisticated analysis of differences in Weber's and Nietzsche's views of politics and science see Robert Eden, *Political Leadership and Nihilism: A Study of Weber and Nietzsche* (Tampa: University of South Florida, 1983). For some strains in Nietzsche's thought that overlap Weber's ideas see Friedrich Nietzsche, *On the Genealogy of Morals and Ecce Homo* (New York: Vintage Books, 1969), 130-34, 148-54; Nietzsche, *Daybreak* (New York: Cambridge University Press, 1982), 66-69 (on power), 154 (the hero cult and its fanatics), 110-11 (politics, intoxication, and the feeling of power), 109 (how socialists "will put themselves in iron chains and practice a fearful discipline"). Also see William Shapiro, "The Nietzschean Roots of Max Weber's Social Science" (Ph.D. diss., Cornell University, 1978). However, Weber's thought about conflict and domination was influenced not only by Nietzsche, but also possibly by "realist" thinkers such as Marx, Machiavelli, and Burckhardt.

23. Nietzsche (*Daybreak*, 111-12) chided German philosophy for its "soft, good natured, silver-glistening idealism." Weber scolded persons too weak to "bear the fate of the times" to "return silently" to "the arms of the old churches." *From Max Weber* (New York: Oxford University Press, 1958), 155.

24. Weber, *The Methodology,* 26–27.

25. Weber, *From Max Weber,* 357, 355.

26. Weber, *The Methodology,* 27.

27. Weber, *Economy and Society,* 3: 941. Weber never provided an explicit connection between "theoretical value conflict" and "concrete struggle." Bruun, *Science, Values and Politics,* 241.

28. Weber, *Economy and Society* 3: 946. This is "domination by authority" in a chain of command. Weber also spoke of "domination by virtue of a constellation of interests," but this is less central to his analysis of domination in modern society. Ibid., 943–46. Because Marx focused on class relations rather than on bureaucracy, his analysis of capitalism attended primarily to the second type of domination. This is an important difference of emphasis in the work of Weber and Marx.

29. Ibid., 953.

30. Ibid., 954.

31. Ibid., 952.

32. Ibid., 1149.

33. Ibid., 980.

34. Max Weber, *General Economic History* (New Brunswick, N.J.: Transaction Books, 1981), 276–77.

35. Weber, *Economy and Society* 1: 138.

36. Ibid., 3: 1394.

37. Ibid., 985.

38. Ibid., 989–92, 1401–3.

39. Ibid., 1402–3. See Wolfgang J. Mommsen, *The Age of Bureaucracy* (New York: Harper Torchbooks, 1977), 47–71, 95–115; Karl Löwith, *Max Weber and Karl Marx* (Boston: George Allen and Unwin, 1982).

40. Weber, *Economy and Society* 3: 1404–5.

41. Ibid., 1417.

42. Ibid., 1423.

43. Ibid., 1439–40, 1452.

44. Ibid., 1450.

45. Ibid., 1449.

46. Ibid., 1452. See Mommsen, *The Age of Bureaucracy,* 82–94.

47. See Illse Dronberger, *The Political Thought of Max Weber* (New York: Appleton-Century-Crofts, 1971), 115–269; Mommsen, *The Age of Bureaucracy,* 22–46; Marianne Weber, *Max Weber: A Biography* (New York: John Wiley and Sons, 1975), 191–225, 391–418, 551–94, 617–58; Max Weber, *Max Weber: Selections in Translation* (Cambridge: Cambridge University Press, 1978), 263–68.

48. Karl Marx, *Writings of the Young Marx on Philosophy and Society* (Garden City, N.Y.: Anchor Books, 1967), 46.

49. Shlomo Avineri, *The Social and Political Thought of Karl Marx* (Cambridge: Cambridge University Press, 1968), 8–9.

50. G. W. F. Hegel, *The Phenomenology of Mind* (New York: Harper Torchbooks, 1967). See Robert J. Antonio, "Immanent Critique as the Core of Critical Theory: Its Origins and Development in Hegel, Marx, and Contemporary Thought," *British Journal of Sociology* 32 (1981): 330–45.

51. See Karl Marx and Frederick Engels, *The German Ideology* (Moscow: Progress Publishers, 1964), 27–95; Karl Marx, *A Contribution to the Critique of Political Economy* (New York: International Publishers, 1970), 19–23; William H. Shaw, *Marx's Theory of History* (Stanford, Calif.: Stanford University Press, 1978), 83–168.

52. See Marx and Engels, *German Ideology*, 27–95; Marx, *Writings of the Young Marx*, 151–202.

53. Antonio, "Immanent Critique as the Core of Critical Theory," 334.

54. Actual differences depend on the individual investigator. For example, a Weberian who subscribes uncritically to conventional values might be as narrow as the most rigid Marxist. Also, the meaning of emancipation is quite broad for some Marxists, encompassing a wide range of determinate value positions.

55. See Karl Marx, "Theses on Feuerbach" in Marx and Engels, *German Ideology*, 645–47.

56. Weber, *Roscher and Knies*, 55–91; Weber, *Methodology*, 68–69.

57. Weber, *Economy and Society* 2: 930.

58. Weber, *Methodology*, 46–47.

59. Weber, *Max Weber: Selections in Translation*, 251–53; Mommsen, *The Age of Bureaucracy*, 58.

60. Weber, *Max Weber: Selections in Translation*, 254–55.

61. Weber, *Economy and Society* 3: 1402.

62. Weber, *Max Weber: Selections in Translation*, 255.

63. Weber, *Economy and Society* 1: 110–12, 3: 1454.

64. Ibid., 1: 224.

65. Nietzsche, *Daybreak*, 109.

66. Weber, *Methodology*, 68–69; Guenther Roth, "Introduction," in Weber, *Economy and Society* 1: LXIV–LXV.

67. Weber, *Methodology*, 68–69, 71.

68. Weber, *Economy and Society* 2: 874.

69. Weber, *Roscher and Knies*, 66, 85.

70. Bruun, *Science, Values and Politics*, 39n.5.

71. E.g., Weber, *Methodology*, 68.

72. Bryan S. Turner, *For Weber* (Boston: Routledge and Kegan Paul, 1981), 20.

73. Friedrich Engels, "Letters on Historical Materialism," in Karl Marx and Friedrich Engels, *Marx and Engels: Basic Writings on Politics and Philosophy* (Garden City, N.Y.: Anchor Books, 1959), 399–400.

74. Ibid., 398–99, 395–412.

75. Ibid., 397–98.

76. Marianne Weber, *Max Weber*, 126–37; Dronberger, *The Political Thought of Max Weber*, 137; David Beetham, *Max Weber and the Theory of Modern Politics* (London: George Allen and Unwin, 1974), 173.

77. Marianne Weber, *Max Weber*, 224.

78. Dronberger, *The Political Thought of Max Weber*, 90–104. However, Weber was not hostile to the working class.

79. See Carl E. Schorske, *German Social Democracy* (Cambridge, Mass.: Harvard University Press, 1955), 115. Guenther Roth, *The Social Democrats in Imperial Germany* (Totowa, N.J.: The Bedminster Press, 1963), 166–71.

80. Karl Kautsky, *Ethics and the Materialist Conception of History* (Chicago: Charles H. Kerr and Company, 1907), 200–206.

81. Weber, *From Max Weber*, 280.

82. Weber, *Methodology*, 65.

83. Weber, *Economy and Society* 1: 213.

84. Weber, *The Protestant Ethic and the Spirit of Capitalism* (New York: Charles Scribner's Sons, 1958), 181, 54–55.

85. Weber, *Methodology*, 103.

86. Marianne Weber, *Max Weber,* 335.

87. E.g., Weber, *The Protestant Ethic,* 183.

88. Turner, *For Weber,* 3-28.

89. I imply here Western Marxism and, particularly, critical theory. E.g., see Georg Lukács, *The Destruction of Reason* (London: The Merlin Press, 1980), 601-19; Max Horkheimer, *Eclipse of Reason* (New York: The Seabury Press, 1974), 6; Herbert Marcuse, *Negations* (Boston: Beacon Press, 1969), 201-26; Jürgen Habermas, "Discussion on Value Freedom and Objectivity," in *Max Weber and Sociology Today,* ed. Otto Stammer (New York: Harper and Row, 1971), 59-66. "Individualist" denotes Weber's ethic of individual responsibility in the choice of values that guide research. Mommsen, *The Age of Bureaucracy,* 7, referred to "individualist decisionism" and argued that this approach reflects Weber's Nietzschean view of valuation as "the spontaneous decision of personality." Habermas spoke of Weber's "decisionism" and implied that the "scientization of politics" and modern "technocratic" thought later emerge from this type of position. See Jürgen Habermas, "Discussion on Value Freedom and Objectivity," 64; Habermas, *Toward a Rational Society* (Boston: Beacon Press, 1971), 62-66, 81-122; Habermas, "The Analytical Theory of Science and Dialectics," in Theodor W. Adorno et al., *The Positivist Dispute in German Sociology* (New York: Harper and Row, 1976), 131-62 (see the debate over this essay, ibid., 163-287). However, Habermas moderated his critical stance toward Weber in his most recent work (see the Kellner paper in this volume). See Habermas, *The Theory of Communicative Action,* vol. 1 (Boston: Beacon Press, 1983), 143-271. Also see Johannes Weiss, "Verständigungsorientierung und Kritik: Zur, Theorie Des kommunikativen Handelns' von Jürgen Habermas," *Kölner Zeitschrift für Soziologie und Sozialpsychologie* 35 (1983): 83-107; Weiss, "Rationalität als Kommunikabilität, Überlegungen zur Rolle von Rationalitätsunterstellungen in der Soziologie," in Walter M. Sprondel and Constans Seyforth, *Max Weber und die Rationalisierung sozialen Handelns* (Stuttgart: Ferdinand Enke Verlag, 1981). Also see Weiss's comments on "communicability" in his paper in this volume. For a discussion of Weber's decisionism see the Kocka essay in this volume.

90. See the Kellner essay in this volume for a discussion of how, until Habermas's most recent work, critical theorists avoided careful, textual criticism of Weber and failed to acknowledge elements they borrowed from him.

91. Marcuse, *Negations,* 201-26.

92. Habermas, *Toward a Rational Society,* 62-66.

93. Weber, *From Max Weber,* 357.

94. See Burger, *Weber's Theory of Concept Formation,* 94-102.

95. For a detailed presentation of themes in this section, see Russell Jacoby, "Towards a Critique of Automatic Marxism: The Politics of Philosophy from Lukács to the Frankfurt School," *Telos* 10 (1971): 119-46; Jacoby, *Dialectic of Defeat* (New York: Cambridge University Press, 1981); Robert J. Antonio, "The Origin, Development, and Contemporary Status of Critical Theory," *The Sociological Quarterly* 25 (1983): 325-51.

96. See Antonio, "Origin, Development, and Contemporary Status," 341-43; Antonio, "Immanent Critique as the Core of Critical Theory," 330-45.

97. Recent works of Jürgen Habermas, *Communication and the Evolution of Society* (Boston: Beacon Press, 1979), 95-177, and Anthony Giddens, *A Contemporary Critique of Historical Materialism* (Berkeley: University of California Press, 1981), express renewed critical theoretic interest in historical materialism. However, these works reflect their respective theories— "universal pragmatics" and "structuration"—and are not explicit attempts to bridge Weber and Marx.

98. Weber, *The Protestant Ethic,* 181.

99. Engels, "Letters on Historical Materialism," 396.

PART II / Theory

VMM

Stephen Kalberg	The Role of Ideal Interests in Max Weber's Comparative Historical Sociology

In a now famous passage in the "Introduction" Max Weber tells us:

Interests (material and ideal), not ideas govern men's actions directly. But, the "world views" that have been created by "ideas" have, like switchmen, very often determined the tracks within which the dynamic of interests has pushed action forward.[1]

In recent years commentators on Weber's sociology have frequently noted the centrality of this passage. It is curious, however, that scarcely an attempt has been made to define "ideal interests," one of its pivotal concepts.[2]

This lack of attention has no doubt resulted in part because Weber fails to define this term and employs it only infrequently. Nonetheless, it must be viewed as a key part of Weber's substantive writings. Indeed, as the above passage also makes clear, an understanding of this concept will enlighten his treatment of the relationship of "ideas"[3] to interests. If this relationship, which is central to the organization of Weber's entire comparative-historical sociology, can be clarified, the enduring question of his divergence from or indebtedness to Karl Marx can be approached from a more informed vantage point. Several basic features of ideal interests should be examined briefly before turning to a discussion of their sources and place within Weber's comparative-historical sociology.

BASIC FEATURES OF IDEAL INTERESTS

Ideal interests exhibit two general features. First, in respect to material interests, ideal interests, particularly as seen in the above passage, constitute, *at the analytical level,* the diametrically opposed concept. They confront material interests in a direct manner and aim to subordinate them to values. Thus, through this concept as well as his notion of value-rational action, Weber establishes conceptually the autonomous status of values. For him, values always retain a *potential* to influence action and shape the course of history, despite their regular banishment by or coalition with material interests, various types of law, sheer power, and discrete events in the empirical histories of all civilizations.[4] Secondly, ideal interests comprise one of the major bases for the formation as well as perpetuation of groups and organizations.[5] Since groups and organizations comprise the level that, to Weber, usually influences the course of history, they capture his major concern in his substantive studies. It is this level where order, or, in Weber's terms, *regularities of action,* is constituted rather than, as for Parsons, the level of society.[6]

THE SOURCES OF IDEAL INTERESTS

What are the main sources of ideal interests? Which groups and organizations both result from ideal interests and act as "carriers" of them? In what ways does this occur?

Through their beliefs and doctrines, religious groups most obviously introduce and carry specific constellations of values. In the earliest religions these values remain predominantly "this-worldly" (e.g., longevity, health, wealth, good fortune for one's progeny).[7] But salvation religions, even though values such as piety and compassion aim to insure the redemption of the soul in the hereafter *(certitudo salutis),* not only place premiums upon emotionally significant states enjoyed in the present but also upon certain kinds of action (e.g., good deeds, methodical work) and ways of life (e.g., asceticism, mysticism) *in this world.* Groups and organizations based upon ideologies and natural law philosophies[8] also introduce sets of values, and followers are expected to act consistently in their behalf. When individuals do act in good faith in reference to values, in Weber's terms they seek to fulfill their ideal interests.[9]

These are only the most self-evident sources of ideal interests. Of far greater concern in this article is a far less well-known and fully independent source: the daily activities of individuals. According to Weber, the pragmatic, everyday experiences and life chances of persons similarly situated introduce regular and even patterned social action that leads not only to the formation of groups and organizations but also to distinct configurations of values, simply as a result of this common "social condition of existence." These ideal interests, found more prominently in status groups and universal or domination organizations,[10] cannot be reduced to world views[11] or material interests. This discrete source for action-orientations in Weber's sociology has not been acknowledged in the secondary literature, despite its power to articulate a clear point of contrast with Marx and to refute all interpretations of Weber as an instrumentalist or utilitarian.[12]

In order to illustrate how, according to Weber, these ideal interests congeal and potentially orient action in patterned ways, the ideal interests in universal organizations, domination organizations, and selected status groups will be examined. Throughout, our discussion follows a double focus upon the social conditions of existence from which ideal interests crystallize and upon the ideal interests themselves. Following Weber's methodological procedure, the analytical level of essential, pure, and universal—*ideal-typical*—aspects will be accentuated rather than empirical manifestations in any particular civilization or epoch.

THE IDEAL INTERESTS OF STATUS GROUPS

Persons who share a style of life, consumption patterns, common conventions, specific notions of honor, and economic and particular status monopolies comprise a status group *(Stand)*. Status differences become apparent whenever the two major measures of social action—*commercium* (or social intercourse) and *connubium*—are restricted or lacking. Stratification by status always implies the "monopolization of ideal and material goods or opportunities" as well as social distance and exclusiveness.[13] Indeed, assuming an elevation of one's situation relative to others and a subjective sense of group affiliation, in the normal course of affairs status situation implies an even stronger bonding agent and potential for cohesion than does the objective class interest of the marketplace. Thus, while classes do not always imply the constitution of groups,[14] status situations, due to stress upon common conventions, values, and a shared style of life, normally lead to group formation.[15] This is Weber's observation, even if these groups are at times somewhat amorphous.[16]

Weber's analysis of status situation and status groups is not designed exclusively to formulate clear concepts, nor does it relate only to the goal of expanding the base for a theory of stratification beyond material interests to include style of life and social honor. Rather, he also aims to articulate the strata-specific ideal interests that originate in the pragmatic, everyday activities inherent to a status situation. A discussion of the status ethics[17] of warriors, feudal aristocrats, civic strata, and intellectuals must suffice to illustrate this concept. In each case the manners in which these strata-specific interests arise from typical social conditions of existence and potentially orient action in a distinct manner will be emphasized.[18]

Warriors. Perhaps the ideal interests of warriors, due to the extraordinary character of their activities and the intensity of their personal relationships, can be most easily understood as deriving from the social conditions of existence. These charismatic heroes gather young warriors fully dedicated to them and prove their mighty strength in marauding campaigns of plunder for booty and women. Followers emotionally surrender themselves to their permanent warriors' league and legendary leader and live together in a communistic warrior community. Since the conduct of war is their single vocation and only the cultivation of the military virtues is considered honorable, the values learned among the fraternity of warriors and in battle typically constitute their ideal interests: loyalty, bravery, and personal honor. The warrior's loyalty to friends, as praised in hymns and sagas, and his cult of personal bonds are esteemed largely as a result of the loyalty and devotion to the leader learned in warfare.

Just their pride in the military virtues inclines warriors to orient their actions to worldly matters and to scorn all metaphysical beliefs. This same pursuit of worldly interests disinclines them to ponder life's meaning through cognition alone, while their high evaluation of loyalty, bravery, and personal honor as well as their proclivity to seek mastery over events and hardship through decisive action uproot them from the immediacy to organic processes and natural events typical of peasants. Even though this distance from natural forces fails to direct them, as is the case for intellectuals, toward a search for a total understanding of the universe and its events,[19] it nonetheless predisposes warriors to scorn an immersion in emotional needs and experiences as undignified and opposed to their cult of honor.[20]

Feudal Aristocrats. Since the feudal aristocracy, according to Weber, locates its origins in the warrior stratum, its status ethic can be partially understood as a routinized form of the status ethic of these charismatic heroes. The ideal of chivalry implies all the values of military fitness: courage, personal honor, bravery in battle, valor, and loyalty to compatriots. A search for individual distinction, whether on the battlefield or in knightly games, and an active involvement in life rather than an inclination to meditate upon its higher meanings and metaphysical aspects are also typical of this stratum. As the aristocracy acquires uncontested privilege, military and knightly conventions fade in importance, and the cultivation and refinement appropriate to high status and its legitimation develop. Literature, music, and the visual arts become integral elements in their status ethic and self-glorification, convincing them of their right to rule. Yet, as is appropriate to the style of life of a leisure stratum, no systematic

attempt to master the arts is undertaken.[21] Nor are commercial relationships rationalized systematically, for to do so merely accentuates their
impersonal or perceived vulgar nature. Particularly in this respect, the
status ethic of the aristocracy diverges radically from the ethic indigenous
to civic strata.

Civic Strata. No cultivation of the military virtues characterizes the
ideal interests of civic *(bürgerliche)* strata: skilled craftsmen and artisans,
petty-bourgeoise traders and merchants. Although these strata remain just
as this-worldly in their action-orientations as warriors and feudal aristocrats, they possess distinct ideal interests. Weber considers them, as well, as
highly influenced by typical life patterns.

Uprooted from magic and taboo, detached from the bonds of nature,
and generally torn from sib and caste ties, these strata normally find their
home in urban environments. Neither the incalculable events of nature nor
the inexplicable creation involved in processes of organic reproduction
influence the work of civic strata; rather, it is characterized by a severing of
the immediate relationship to vital natural forces. Unlike agricultural
work, which is seasonal and variable and depends upon natural forces
neither known nor constant, the regular and rationally organized work of
the artisan (potter, weaver, turner, and carpenter) generally involves
essentially visible and understandable relationships between means and
ends as well as success and failure.[22]

Weber saw one of the most succinct expressions of the kernel of this
status ethic in the adage of Paul, a wandering craftsman: ''He who does not
work shall not eat.''[23] Founded in the hard necessities of workaday life, this
sober attitude endows an entire perspective toward economic transactions
with an element of calculability far more stringent than that found among
peasants, and it offers a positive evaluation of honesty, work, and the
performance of obligations.

When one compares the life of a petty-bourgeois, particularly the urban artisan or the small
trader, with the life of the peasant, it is clear that the former has far less connection with
nature. . . . At the same time, . . . it is clear that the economic foundation of the urban man's
life has a far more rational character, viz., calculability and capacity for means-end rational
influence. Furthermore, the artisan and in certain circumstances even the merchant lead
economic existences which influence them to entertain the view that honesty is the best policy,
that faithful work and a performance of obligations will find their reward and are ''deserving''
of their just compensation.[24]

This immersion in daily activities inclines civic strata away from a search
for a comprehensive meaning of the world's fragmented happenings or a
theoretical mastery of reality, away from a cultivation of military virtues,

and away from an indulgence in emotional needs and experiences. Instead, a goal-oriented pragmatism rooted in practical life situations and an unequivocal tendency toward practical rational ways of life prevail.[25]

Intellectuals. Rather than immersion in activity and in the practical tasks of everyday life, intellectuals aim to comprehend the workings of both the cosmos and their immediate surroundings through pure cognition; when this mode of understanding is given free reign, they seek to emancipate themselves from the grip of daily life.[26] Unlike merchants and artisans, who usually cultivate a practical rationalism, intellectuals repeatedly abstract generalities from the infinity of historical and natural occurrences. As contemplative thinkers who deplore the meaninglessness of empirical reality and attempt to separate themselves from the world's practical tasks, they "face life and ponder its meaning" as well as the meaning of the universe. The intellectual seeks in various ways, the casuistry of which extends into infinity, to endow his life with a pervasive meaning, and thus to find unity with himself, with his fellow men, and with the cosmos. It is the intellectual who conceives of the "world" as a problem of meaning.[27]

To Weber this proclivity to contemplate life abstractly stems not only from the typical patterns in the daily lives of intellectuals but also from their characteristic tendency to seek a comprehensive meaning for the world's fragmented and senseless happenings. This "inner need" inclines intellectuals to undertake a theoretical mastery of reality in which systematic study of the cosmos and man's place within it assumes central priority.[28] In behalf of this endeavor concepts are defined with increasing precision and knowledge, and ethical systems are ordered at ever-increasing levels of rational unity, logical construction, and inner consistency.[29] Given this inclination toward passivity, highly cognitive orientations, and theoretical rationalization, intellectuals traditionally view all forms of emotionalism as obstacles to their search for knowledge. To them, the meaning of the universe and of life can be unlocked only through theoretical thought.[30]

Accordingly, members of this status group frequently seek humanistic, philosophical, or classical educations, scorn ignorance as well as specialization as cardinal vices, and develop metaphysics as well as depersonalized systems of ethics (e.g., the Phoenicians, the Greeks, the Romans, and the Chinese).[31] Thus, a search for a comprehensive and meaningful explanation of the world, a "rationalism which . . . has been relatively theoretical . . . ," and an over-riding opposition to emotional expression distinguish the status ethic of intellectuals, regardless of their particular occupations—teachers, philosophers, theologians, legal theorists, or scientists.[32]

This reconstruction of the general status ethics and styles of life for warriors, feudal aristocrats, the civic strata, and intellectuals illustrates the way in which, for Weber, patterned social action and even values can originate solely from pragmatic daily activities, typical experiences, and life chances.[33] Now I would like to examine Weber's parallel analysis of the origin of ideal interests and their influence upon action in the universal organizations.

THE IDEAL INTERESTS OF UNIVERSAL ORGANIZATIONS

Similar to status groups, universal organizations constitute delimited orders consensually accepted by their members, uproot action from its random course, and provide a clear locus for action-orientations, including value-rational action. In Weber's view, the household, clan, and neighborhood comprise the major universal organizations.[34] As "undifferentiated forms of life," all are unequivocally endowed with an intense person-oriented, or communal, aspect.[35] Like the strata-specific interests that arise in status groups, the ideal interests of the universal organizations crystallize out of routine action, the conditions of social existence, and everyday experiences.[36]

The Household. By far the most important universal organization in Weber's analysis is the household. As the basic unit of economic maintenance and the most widespread economic organization, the household provides the locus for "very continuous and intensive social action."[37] For Weber, a house in the contemporary sense may not be required, and a household cannot be defined by its size. Unlike our own epoch in which the household has become primarily a consumption unit, in earlier times it existed as both a production and a consumption entity. With its capacity to meet daily demands for goods and labor, the household offered a certain degree of organized cultivation of the soil.[38]

The intense bond of intimacy and perpetual interaction between father, mother, and children in the household gives rise to distinct values. The sense of loyalty toward the in-group forms the basis for a strong household solidarity in dealing with the outside world and promotes an ethic of brotherhood that prohibits all financial calculation within the family. The "principle of household communism," according to which "each contributes in relation to his capacities and consumes according to his needs," expresses this sense of in-group loyalty and personal obligation. Blood bonds and continuous social action also form the basis for candor, reliability, and authority.[39]

The Clan. At those times when outsiders threaten the household, the clan *(Sippe)* consolidates itself into an organization, serves as its protective agency and even executor of blood revenge, and cultivates the household's typical values. The kin organization might even guarantee the security of members of a household against a father's authoritarianism. The organizing of the clan with clear boundaries and a head occurs only if required in order to protect social or economic monopolies. In normal situations, unlike the household, the clan remains an amorphous collectivity of people without a clear hierarchy and calls forth only discontinuous and irregular social action. Nonetheless, it constitutes, to Weber, the original locus for faithfulness.[40]

The Neighborhood. The circle of participants in the neighborhood, another universal organization, is far more fluctuating than either the clan or the household. Since based on the simple fact that people reside in close physical proximity, the social action it calls forth is far less intensive and continuous than that typical in the household. Indeed, neighborhoods very often lose their open character in which merely intermittent social action prevails and acquire firm boundaries only when they become either an economic or an economically-regulatory organization. Although they may only seldom call forth social action and vary greatly in form—scattered farms, a city street, an urban slum, a village—and cohesiveness, neighborhoods, even in the modern city, retain the potential to orient action in defined ways and to call forth values.[41]

Simply as a result of the dependence of neighbors upon one another in times of distress, the neighborhood comprises, in Weber's analysis, the original locus for an ethic of mutual assistance. Indeed, an "unsentimental ethic of brotherhood" may well arise in neighborhoods. To Weber, this ethic exists as the source of the "just price" and the prohibition against usury. It might also strengthen the household's in-group prohibition upon haggling and dickering.

The neighbor is the typical helper in need, and hence "neighborhood" is the typical carrier of "brotherhood," albeit in a somber and unpathetic, primarily economic sense. If the household is short of means, mutual help may be requested: the loans of implements and goods free of charge, and "free labor for the asking" *(Bittarbeit)* in case of urgent need. This mutual help is guided by the primeval popular ethic which is as unsentimental as it is universal: "Do unto others as you would have them do unto you." . . . If compensation is provided, it consists in feasting the helpers. . . . If an exchange takes place, the maxim applies: "Brothers do not bargain with one another." This eliminates the rational "market principle" of price determination.[42]

. . . .

The two major moral demands [the injunction against usury and the commandment to demand and give the "just price" for commodities and labor] . . . belong together and originate in the primeval ethic of the neighborhood. . . . Interest is demanded by the ruler; profit by the tribal alien, not by a brother.[43]

Thus, Weber sees the "essence of neighborly social action" as involving a "sombre economic 'brotherhood' practiced in case of need."[44] The idea of reciprocity—"as you do unto me, I shall do unto you" and "your want of today may be mine of tomorrow"—develops from this ethic of mutual assistance. Neighborliness is exercised at times, particularly when mutual dependence is clear, even in relationships of social inequality, such as those between large landowners and their helpers.

In Weber's analysis, the household, the clan, and the neighborhood comprise the major universal organizations.[45] The person-oriented values, all of which arose simply as a consequence of typical activities and life chances as well as the intense and permanent contact within these organizations, potentially orient action. Whenever they succeed in doing so, individuals act on behalf of discrete and definable ideal interests.

THE IDEAL INTERESTS
OF DOMINATION ORGANIZATIONS

Like status groups and the universal organizations, domination organizations delineate clear loci for action-orientations, including value-rational action. The manner in which the typical life experiences and pragmatic everyday activities under the patriarchal, feudal, patrimonial, and bureaucratic forms of domination lead to distinct ideal interests captures our attention, as does the potential of these ideal interests to orient action. In his discussions of legitimate domination, Weber generally refers to the constellations of values indigenous to each form as an "ethos."[46]

Patriarchal Domination. The patriarch rules over an extended family in which his dependents share food and live together in a close and permanent household. The intimate and immediate nature of rulership and the sheer strength of sib ties as a means of instilling filial loyalty and enforcing obedience keep institutionalized conflict at a minimum and preclude the rise of competing centers of independent power. Consequently, custom and the deities, acting as the guardians of traditions, remain unchallenged. Within this context orientations from time immemorial to the patriarch's authority are understood as routine and natural, as are the values of the patriarchal ethos: piety toward tradition and toward the master, and obedience and respect for authority. This belief in the domestic authority of the patriarch arises, according to Weber, as a result of piety established in the distant past and as a "natural outgrowth" of this "spiritual 'community of faith.'" Indeed, in Weber's analysis, these ideal interests remain so firmly immersed within traditions that they seldom become crystallized as conscious values in the minds of the ruler and his dependents.[47]

Feudal Domination. Both the manorial and benefice forms of feudal domination imply full appropriation of the means of administration and extreme decentralization. In both cases vassals tend to cultivate an independence from lords, and obedience remains voluntary rather than coerced. This structural context makes for endemic conflict: a situation within which customs might be called into question and both rulers and vassals attend to their self-interests.[48] On the other hand, because vassals legitimate their elevated status solely through an intact relationship with the lord, they might also purposefully set aside their drive for independence and actively cultivate this relationship.

Such high decentralization means that, according to Weber, authority depends upon whether vassals remain faithful to the *Treuebeziehung,* the fraternal relationship of allegiance rooted in a host of values.[49] This feudal ethos, which arises particularly in manorial feudalism, regulates and gives legitimacy to the precarious relationship between lords and vassals. It does so mainly through its demanding code of duties and honors, all of which provide "substantial safeguards of the vassal's interests" and stress mutual allegiance and loyalty. Consciousness of status, the privileges and duties incumbent upon status, an exalted conception of status honor, and a solidarity that precludes the imposition of arbitrary obligations upon vassals become central to this code. It is binding upon both parties and formulates, in Weber's terms, an "integrating component."

The essence of manorial feudalism is status consciousness, and it increasingly perfects this very characteristic. . . . In its fullest elaboration the feudatory relationship can only be an attribute of a ruling stratum, since it rests on emphatic notions of status honor as the basis of fealty and also of military fitness. Therefore, the requirement of seigneurial ("knightly") conduct is added everywhere.[50]

The inculcation of such an ethos based upon status honor and fealty is the subject of an elaborate special education. Military education, for example, is oriented to free camaraderie and chivalry: courage, valor, loyalty, friendship, perfection of personal military skills, and individual heroism in battle are decisive rather than discipline, drill, and adaptation of each individual to an organized operation, as in mass armies. Preparation for the way of life of the knightly stratum also entails, according to Weber, refinement, cultivation, and an orientation toward individual artistic creation.[51] In general, knightly conventions, pride of status and a high sense of aristocratic sentiment, predispose the feudal education to emphasize a heroic individualism. This opposes sharply the patrimonial official's notion of honor, based upon services and functions.[52]

Patrimonial Domination. The perpetual conflicts in patrimonialism between officials and rulers, officials and subjects, and subjects and rulers might lead to a substantial weakening of inviolable custom and an expansion of the ruler's arena of discretion. Yet he cannot enforce his decisions or expect acknowledgment of his domination as legitimate by appeals to his subjects' sense of loyalty to blood ties, as does the patriarch. Nor can he rely upon adherence to the feudal lord's knightly code of honor. At times, legitimacy is ascribed to patrimonial domination solely as a consequence of the recognition by persons in similar positions (rulers, officials, subjects) of their common self-interest.[53]

Weber views patrimonialism's ideal interests, or ethos, as also capable of legitimating domination under certain circumstances. It possesses two loci: the relationship between rulers and subjects and the particular values of officials. The relationship between rulers and subjects is characterized by a constellation of values that constitutes the social welfare ideal, or myth, of patrimonialism.

From the points of view of both rulers and subjects, the legitimacy of patrimonial domination rests largely upon the paternal character of the ruler. As a means of legitimizing his rule and consolidating his power, he seeks to portray himself as the protector of his subjects by guaranteeing their social welfare and opposing the privileged status of nobles. As in the patriarchal master's rule, humane treatment, services, social-ethical blessings, general good will, and substantive justice characterize ideally the relationship of the prince to his subjects. The legend of the good king—the guardian of his subjects' welfare and the father of the people—is the ideal glorified in patrimonial rulership rather than the warrior hero glorified in feudal domination. Not a pledge of allegiance, such as that which exists between vassal and lord, but the authoritarian relationship of father and child anchors this legend.[54]

Officials uphold the social welfare ideal, yet they also cultivate a series of values specific to their stratum. When administering large territories in a manner that efficiently protects the security and social welfare of subjects, the patrimonial staff values the dutiful execution of tasks. An ethic of personal accomplishment may increasingly emerge as the administration of patrimonial rulership becomes hierarchical and tasks within these organizations become specialized. This ethic, as well as the official's specialized training, stands in an antagonistic relationship to the feudal status system rooted in hereditary descent and status consciousness and introduces a degree of social leveling. The favorite of the patrimonial ruler is no longer a member of his family but the member of his staff who has risen simply as a result of his abundant skills and charisma "from rags, from slavery and lowly service to the ruler, to the precarious, all-powerful position of favorite."[55] The educational system for officials, Weber emphasizes, took on a corresponding form of administrative training and reward according to services; it confronted resolutely the idleness, the games, and the hero worship of the knight.[56]

The stress upon personal qualifications, administrative training, services performed, and the centrality of the office constitute the major components in the status honor of the patrimonial official. It legitimates his privileges and his exercise of the ruler's authority. This ethos and the social welfare ideal that legitimates the ruler's dominance over subjects comprise, to Weber, the ideal interests that orient action in patrimonial domination. Indeed, at times, they capture action-orientations to such an extent that traditional, affectual, and means-end rational action become suppressed.

Rational-Legal Domination: the Bureaucracy. In bureaucracies formal rationality[57] prevails: problems are resolved and decisions are made by the systematic and continuous orientation of action to abstract rules and regulations. The objective and impersonal procedures central to this organization's administration as well as its other major aspects—the division into official and private spheres, the delimitation of arenas of competence by norms and technical training, the stable distribution of labor—all tend to facilitate such patterned orientations. In the process, affectual action is suppressed, becoming a victim of the bureaucracy's demand for action oriented to abstract rules and its opposition to arbitrariness, personal favor, and all particularism. Thus, the normal functioning of the bureaucracy opposes decision making on the basis of friendship, bonds of reciprocal obligation, or the personal qualities of individuals and substitutes the maxim that impersonal prescriptions must be applied universally. On the other hand, the bureaucracy's formal rationality stands opposed to traditional action. It is not custom that legitimates or testifies to the correctness of rules, but their character as enacted through discursively analyzable procedures. Decision making and commands take place in direct reference to these rules.[58]

While these features of the bureaucracy and, in particular, its formal rationality frequently call forth means-end rationality, they might also give rise to a bureaucratic ethos, especially in light of this organization's extreme continuity and emphasis upon regularity. If this occurs, the structures of bureaucracies acquire an additional degree of stability and even efficiency: legitimacy is accorded and procedures carried out not simply as a result of expedient adaptation but also due to a value-rational belief in the legitimacy of this type of domination and correctness of its procedures.[59] What does this ethos look like?

Duty, impartiality, and discipline constitute the central attributes of the bureaucratic ethos. Employees and civil servants who uphold this ethos in good faith feel actively called and internally obligated to act in reference to these values. All orient their possessors to the action ideally found in bureaucracies: regular fulfillment of tasks, task-execution according to objective rules applied universally, and antagonism to all emotionalism, personal favoritism, and privilege. In addition, such civil servants reinforce this rulership's demand for a systematic organization of work, continuity, precision, orderliness, stability, reliability, and punctuality. The ideal of disciplined work, in particular, strengthens the bureaucracy's sober rationalism and its evaluation of order and security as absolute values. These values place premiums also upon all formal procedures that maximize calculation and minimize arbitrariness, organize tasks according to clear domains of competence and responsibility, and instill a respect for authority as well as hierarchical claims of superordination and subordination. In Weber's analysis, the notions of "duty of the office" *(Amtspflicht)* and "dutiful vocational work" *(Beruf)* incorporate many of these values. The ideal employees of bureaucracies also highly value that type of education most adapted to this type of domination's notion of competence: a specialized training oriented toward the acquisition of technical knowledge and based upon standardized tests of expertise. This knowledge, rather than the cultivated humanist or gentleman education, constitutes the ideal of the bureaucratic ethos and extends the right to hold office.[60]

Both classical Prussian civil servants and today's professional experts who fulfill their functions in the bureaucracy motivated primarily by values and a high sense of ethical duty embody the bureaucratic ethos. If this ethos becomes strong, employees of the bureaucracy feel duty-bound to implement reliably and impartially—"without scorn and without bias"—even those decisions with which they personally disagree, and those assigned tasks they find repugnant. Just such orientations of action to ideal interests enhance bureaucratic precision.[61]

The ideal interests of the patriarchal, feudal, patrimonial, and bureaucratic forms of domination have been isolated and reconstructed in their pure forms in this section. Like the ethics of status groups and the universal organizations, the ethos indigenous to each of these forms of domination crystallizes solely out of the daily experiences and regular activities of individuals over time. In all cases, these ideal interests retain the potential to influence action and even, in their perpetual confrontation with material interests, to become historically significant.

CONCLUSION: THE ROLE OF IDEAL INTERESTS IN MAX WEBER'S COMPARATIVE HISTORICAL SOCIOLOGY

In Weber's sociology, ideal interests refer not only to sets of values implied in religions, natural law philosophies, and ideologies, but also to values that arise out of pragmatic everyday activities, life chances, and the social conditions of existence. Fully neglected in the secondary literature and unexplained by Weber himself, these latter ideal interests find their sociological loci primarily in status groups, universal organizations, and domination organizations. All ideal interests are formulated as universal ideal-types, never to be found in their pure form in any particular civilization or epoch. They can be employed not only as hypotheses and heuristic models but also as yardsticks against which given historical cases can be measured and defined clearly through an assessment of their deviation. What influence, according to Weber, do the ideal interests anchored in status groups, universal organizations, and domination organizations potentially have upon the actions of individuals and upon history?

Wherever a personal dimension is clearly present, a greater likelihood exists, for Weber, that ideal interests will in fact influence action. Thus, the smaller and intimate groups and organizations—such as the household, the sib group, the patriarchal organization, and the warrior community—most effectively introduce value-rational action. Because task orientations, abstract rules, and a high component of merely functional *(sachlich)* interaction are typical, for example, in bureaucratic organizations and the status groups of civic and intellectual strata, these organizations and groups are less successful in endowing values with a strong binding element and dimension of inner obligation. Consequently, a greater possibility exists that other types of social action will hold sway in these impersonal groups and organizations, particularly the utilitarian calculations of means-end rational action.[62] The bureaucratic ethos is more likely to become a significant element in the motivation of action in bureaucracies wherever it is strengthened through the acquisition of "... an ideological halo from cultural values, such as state, church, community, party or enterprise, which appear as surrogates for a this-worldly or other-worldly personal master and which are embodied by a given group."[63]

What influence, according to Weber, do the ideal interests discussed above have in history? Far from ultimately reducible to material interests or utilitarian calculations, Weber endows the ideal interests of delimited groups and organizations with the *analytical capacity* to stand in opposition to these interests and calculations as well as, more importantly, world views, various types of law, sheer power, and discrete historical events. Frequently, in the permanent altercations between these forces in the *empirical histories* of civilizations, the ideal interests of groups and organizations lose out. Nonetheless, their autonomous thrusts *can* become manifest and even sociologically significant, as can be seen in, for example, the sib group in China, the samurai warrior stratum in Japan, and the urban civic strata and feudal aristocracy in the medieval West. To Weber, occasionally and if primarily strengthened by conducive material interests and political power, these ideal interests may exert independent influences in history.

Status groups, in particular, may become significant forces. For example, the ideal interests of clearly identifiable strata have influenced the formation of every religion's teachings and salvation notions. Indeed, whenever a world religion's carrier stratum changed, its belief system also underwent a profound alteration.[64] Similarly, the content and style of education and learning in general assumes a very different character depending upon whether court nobles, humanist literati, a feudal aristocracy, or civil servants prove decisive in its creation and proliferation.[65]

Secondly, more often than they succeed in asserting their indigenous thrusts in a pure form in history, the groups and organizations in Weber's sociology that carry ideal interests are interpenetrated by material interests, various types of laws, sheer power, historical occurrences, and the ideal conditions of world views. Even the ideal interests of groups and organizations interpenetrate and alter one another; for example, in China the ideal interests of patrimonial rulers and officials coalesced with those of intellectuals in relationships of elective affinity[66] to call forth the mandarins. On the other hand, such an alliance might lead to a decidedly different result if a third factor, such as religious doctrine, assumed a unique form; for example, in India the Brahmin priests crystallized into a coherent stratum.

Indeed, Weber frequently emphasizes the entire *context* formulated by additional discrete factors and its singular influence upon the ideal interests of coalescing groups and organizations. Far from banished, the indigenous thrusts of ideal interests are weakened in the process and in some cases suppressed for certain periods of time. Even when latent, however, the ideal interests always retain the potential, should the kaleidoscope of forces undergo just a slight shift, of becoming manifest, rooting their autonomous thrusts firmly through new alliances, and acquiring sociological significance. The ideal interests of certain strata, especially in interpenetrated forms, may even become the carriers of culture and set their stamp upon the millennia-long development of a civilization, as did two strata in particular: the Chinese mandarins and the Brahmin priests.[67] If the discussion of Weber's sociology remains confined to the amorphous and insolvable question of whether the "real Weber" was an idealist, a materialist, a decisionist, a utilitarian, or an instrumentalist, we will continue to be distracted from these fundamental dimensions and modes of procedure.

As an analytical category, ideal interests cannot be ignored if the relationship of Weber to Marx is to be fully understood. In accentuating *one* source of the more structural side of Weber's sociology—the manner in which the ideal interests typical in certain groups and organizations congeal—this brief exposition has aimed to emphasize once again that the view of Weber as an idealist in opposition to Marx as a materialist must be discarded.

Nor can ideal interests be neglected if Weber's comparative historical sociology is to be adequately reconstructed. This remains the case even if we acknowledge that, for him, material interests and other factors, which highly influence the crystallization of ideal interests and circumscribe their diffusion, often play a more powerful role in the empirical histories of civilizations. To Weber, only a *contextual sociology* capable of conceptualizing clearly ideal interests, a host of additional forces, *and the dynamic relationships between all* can begin to justify the infinite complexity of social reality. Such a sociology can greatly assist social scientists to fulfill their goal of establishing reliable causal relationships when they turn to empirical investigations.

Notes

I would like to thank Robert J. Antonio, Johannes Weiss, Guenther Roth, and R. Stephen Warner for helpful comments.

1. Max Weber, "Introduction," in *From Max Weber,* ed. Hans H. Gerth and C. Wright Mills (New York: Free Press, 1958); *Ges. Aufs. zur Religionssoziologie I* (1920; Tübingen: Mohr, 1972), 280/252. All references to Weber's texts give first the page number for the English translation, then the page number in the original German. Weber inserted this passage in the final rewriting of this essay in 1920. The translation has been altered slightly. Gerth and Mills gave this essay, the introduction to Weber's studies "The Economic Ethics of the World Religions," the somewhat misleading title of "The Social Psychology of the World Religions."

2. For the most notable and thorough effort see R. Stephen Warner, "The Methodology of Max Weber's Comparative Studies" (Ph.D. diss., University of California at Berkeley, 1972), chap. 4. Warner's approach is more psychological than mine and less focused upon groups and organizations.

3. Weber often uses quotation marks around this term both to express his reluctance to employ a concept that had been used too widely and in a vague fashion by eighteenth- and nineteenth-century historians and to defend against the widespread suspicion of this term at the turn of the century among social scientists. Despite its centrality in the secondary literature, Weber employs it only sparingly and less so in his writings after *The Protestant Ethic and the Spirit of Capitalism* (1930; New York: Scribner's, 1958) *(Ges. Aufs. zur Religionssoz. I).* To my knowledge, it does not appear at all in *Economy and Society,* 3 vols. (1921; New York: Bedminster Press, 1958; Tübingen: Mohr, 1976).

4. This fundamental Weberian axiom is visible even in the term "ideal interests" itself, allowing Weber both to side with Marx and polemicize against him and, especially, his heirs. Individuals act, for both theorists, in reference to interests; yet interests, for Weber, must not be viewed narrowly in terms of means-end rational action and the acquisition of material goods alone, as was common among the Marxists and most of the economists of Weber's day. In his view, to act in regard to interests can involve also action in behalf of values held dear. Thus, the position taken in this article stands opposed to all recent attempts to understand Weber as a neo-Marxist or utilitarian, especially the interpretation of Weber as an "instrumentalist." Cf. Jeffrey C. Alexander, *Theoretical Logic in Sociology,* vol. 3 (Berkeley: University of California Press, 1983).

5. In Weber's sociology, persons tend to knit together into groups and organizations primarily in four additional and analytically separate ways: recognition of common material

interests (as in class formation), acknowledgment of affectual feelings (as in person-oriented groups, e.g., the household, the clan, the neighborhood), awareness of relations of domination (as in the charismatic, patriarchal, feudal, patrimonial, and bureaucratic forms of domination), and the orientation to legal orders (as in primitive, traditional, natural, logical-formal, and rational particularist). Empirically, of course, all these bases for groups and organizations flow together. Organizations, to Weber, imply a greater degree of internal structure than groups. For a definition, cf. note 34.

6. It is noteworthy that Weber uses "society" *(Gesellschaft) only* on two occasions in *Economy and Society,* both times in quotation marks. In one passage he is discussing stratification variables (*Economy and Society,* 306/180), and in the other he notes his interest in the relations between the economy and society rather than the economy and culture (*Economy and Society,* 356/212).

7. Cf. *Economy and Society,* 399–439/245–68.

8. Whereas Weber sees the nineteenth century as the seedbed century for ideologies, he noted that natural law philosophies had existed since antiquity in the Occident. Cf. Weber, *Economy and Society,* 866–71/497–500.

9. The potential influence of ideal interests in history will be turned to in the conclusion. It should be emphasized that the values mentioned here do not refer to world views. Ideal interests, even in the case of religion, refer to the this-worldly values of primitive religions and, in salvation religions, the values implied in the "salvation path" or those bound up with the *certitudo salutis* question (cf. Weber, *Economy and Society,* 529–76/321–48). On this point Parsons seems to me correct in stressing that world views, even though they contain values, imply ideal conditions rather than ideal interests: they structure action and assist in defining the ends of action, but do not themselves, like interests, impel it. Cf. Talcott Parsons, *The Structure of Social Action* (1937; New York: The Free Press, 1968), 537, 668; and R. Stephen Warner, "Toward a Redefinition of Action Theory: Paying the Cognitive Element its Due," *American Journal of Sociology* 83 (1978): 1330–31. This interpretation conforms with the passage quoted at the beginning of this article. On the cognitive aspect in world views and the manner in which they become effective sociologically, cf. note 11 below.

10. Here is *one* of the major structuralist dimensions in Weber's sociology. The emphasis upon shared everyday activities and life chances naturally calls to mind the concept of class. Yet, for Weber as for Marx, classes are purely economic entities oriented to material interests. For this reason they are incapable of calling forth values. Cf. Weber, *Economy and Society,* 926–31/531–34, 302–5/177–79, 635–40/382–85, and Stephen Kalberg, "Max Weber's Universal-Historical Architectonic of Economically-Oriented Action," in *Current Perspectives in Social Theory,* ed. Scott G. McNall (Greenwood, Conn.: JAI Press, 1983), 253–88. They may, however, take over values from external sources. This commonly occurs when the disprivileged classes, for example, adopt notions of substantive justice derived from religious and political belief systems. Cf. *Economy and Society,* 893–94/512.

11. The ideal interests of these groups and organizations can be distinguished from world views not only in reference to their sources but also in reference to their composition: while values can be found in all, world views include a *cognitive aspect* that is lacking in the ideal interests of groups and organizations. On this point, cf. Parsons, *Structure,* 533–38, 668; and Warner, "Toward a Redefinition of Action Theory," 1330–31, 1344. Just this aspect, combined with their typical claim to possess a truth that is comprehensive in the sense of a capacity to explain fully the world and to form the basis for an entire way of life, enables world views to become the subject of theoretical rationalization processes. Further, whereas both ideal interests and world views contain normative aspects, the latter, if they are to become sociologically effective, must be mediated by carrier groups and organizations.

12. Schluchter and Sprondel reduce ideal interests to the arena of religion and the interest in salvation. Cf. Wolfgang Schluchter, *The Rise of Western Rationalism* (Berkeley: University of California Press, 1981), 25-27; and Walter M. Sprondel, "Sozialer Wandel, Ideen und Interessen," in *Seminar: Religion und gesellschaftliche Entwicklung*, ed. Constans Seyfarth and Walter M. Sprondel (Frankfurt: Suhrkamp, 1973), 222-23.

13. Weber, *Economy and Society*, 935/536, 927/531; Weber, "Introduction," 300/274. On the origin of status groups, cf. *Economy and Society*, 306/180, 935/536. On the translation of *Stand*, which has been often rendered as "estate," cf. *Economy and Society*, 300n.4. Alexander's reduction of status group to property and class rests on a careless reading of *Economy and Society*, 932-36/534-39 and a failure to consider Weber's later section in *Economy and Society* on the same subject (305-7/179-80) as well as "Introduction," 300/274 (the translation of this page is not precise). In the earlier text, a translation error (932/535) led him astray, and he consistently neglects statements in disagreement with the thesis he aims to prove. For example: "Status honor must not necessarily be linked with class situation; on the contrary, it normally stands in sharp opposition to the pretensions of sheer property" (932/535; trans. slightly altered). In the later discussion, property is wholly omitted from the list of possible bases for status situation (305-6/179-80), and Weber takes even greater pains to distinguish analytically the notion of status situation from class situation (306/180) than he did on 932-38/534-39 (cf. esp. 932-33/534-35, 936-37/538). Cf. Jeffrey C. Alexander, *Theoretical Logic* 3: 117-22.

14. Cf. Weber, *Economy and Society*, 927/531, 930/533, 302/177.

15. Weber defines "status situation" as "every typical component of the life of men that is determined by a specific, positive or negative, social estimation of honor." Weber, *Economy and Society*, 932/535. Cf. 305/179 for a further definition. Unfortunately, *ständische Lage* is translated on p. 932 as "status situation" and on p. 305 as "status."

16. Weber, *Economy and Society*, 932/534. Of course, the dominant mode of stratification may vary across civilizations and epochs. Class situation in the modern West has become a more central organizing principle than status situation. Cf. Weber, "Introduction," 301/274.

17. Ideal interests, status interests, and strata-specific interests are used synonymously in this section. The latter terms provide further examples of how Weber broadens *interests* over the common usage in his day. Since he devotes less attention to the character of various status ethics (cf., e.g., Weber, "Introduction," 279/251) than to the relationships of elective affinity between specific status ethics and certain world religions, I have often had to extract a stratum's *general* ideal interests from Weber's analysis of these relationships. My main sources are "Introduction," 282-84/254-57, and *Economy and Society*, 468-517/285-313.

18. In fact, for illustrative purposes, this section calls attention not only to values, but also, in keeping with Weber's broad discussion of status groups, more generally to entire "styles of life."

19. Weber notes that chivalrous warriors, as is typical of heroism in general, "have lacked . . . the desire as well as the capacity for a rational mastery of reality." This results in part from their acceptance of a notion of fate as more powerful than even heroic action. Cf. Weber, "Introduction," 283/255.

20. On the above two paragraphs, cf. Weber, *Economy and Society*, 905-8/517-18, 1142/676, 1153-54/684-85; Max Weber, *The Religion of India* (1920; New York: Free Press, 1958), 63/64-65 *(Ges. Aufs. zur Religionssoz. II);* and Weber, *The Religion of China* (1920; New York: Free Press, 1951), 24/302 *(Ges. Aufs. zur Religionsoz. I).*

21. In this respect, as opposed to the bourgeoise. This paragraph is based upon Weber, *Economy and Society*, 256/149, 1078/630, 1090/639-40, 1104-6/650-51.

22. Cf. Weber, "Introduction," 284/256; Weber, *Economy and Society*, 1178/703.

23. Max Weber, *General Economic History* (1923; New York: The Free Press, 1927), 137/128. Cf. also Weber, *Economy and Society*, 499/304; Weber, "Introduction," 279/251.

24. Weber, *Economy and Society*, 482-83/294.

25. Cf. Weber, "Introduction," 284/256. On practical rationalism, cf. Kalberg, "Max Weber's Types of Rationality," *American Journal of Sociology* 85 (1980): 1151-52; and Donald N. Levine, "Rationality and Freedom: Weber and Beyond," *Sociological Inquiry* 51 (1981): 12-13.

26. Cf. Weber, *Economy and Society*, 507/308; Weber, *India*, 177/184.

27. Weber, *Economy and Society*, 506/307-8. Cf. Further, Weber, "Introduction," 281/253.

28. Thus, unlike his analysis of the status ethics of other strata, Weber locates the sources of the typical action-orientations of intellectuals not only in the normal patterns of their ways of life, but also anthropologically. The intellectual's rationalistic compulsion to conceive the cosmos cognitively as meaningful does not originate in conditions of suffering, natural disaster, material need, or inner distress, however much it may be intensified by these factors, but from the sheer "metaphysical needs of the human mind as it is driven to reflect on ethical and religious questions." Weber, *Economy and Society*, 499/304.

29. Cf., e.g., Weber, "Introduction," 279/251, 293/266.

30. On theoretical rationalization, cf. Kalberg, "Max Weber's Types," 1152-55; and Levine, "Rationality and Freedom," 12-13.

31. Weber, "Introduction," 279/251.

32. For specific examples of the "general psychological orientation of intellectuals," cf. Weber, *India*, 352n.5/136n.1. A more complete discussion would have to focus also upon the ideal interests of the different types of intellectuals that Weber identifies, such as petty-bourgeois, proletarian, peasant, and aristocratic intellectuals (cf. Weber, *Economy and Society*, 500-518/304-14).

33. The status ethics for numerous other strata can be also reconstructed from Weber's texts. Cf. the sources in note 17.

34. Weber defines the organization *(Verband):* "A social relationship which is either closed or limits the admission of outsiders will be called an organization when its regulations are enforced by specific individuals: a chief and, possibly, an administrative staff, which normally also has representative powers." Weber, *Economy and Society*, 48/26. These social groupings—especially the clan and the neighborhood—do not always have a head and thus are not always organizations. If they are to become significant historical forces, however, they must acquire leadership and a closed character. Since it is in this form that they become of interest to Weber and for this reconstruction, *organization* is preferred here. Unfortunately, Weber did not revise the terminology of the earlier Part II in *Economy and Society* to bring it into conformity with Part I. In Part II he refers to the household, clan, and neighborhood frequently as *Gemeinschaften* (groups) rather than, in keeping with the terminology in Part I, as *Verbände*. The *Economy and Society* translators neither attempted to reconcile this teminological discrepancy, nor did they render *Gemeinschaften* uniformly: "groups" and "communities" are randomly employed. Talcott Parsons, *The Theory of Social and Economic Organization* (New York: Free Press, 1947) translates *Verband* as "corporate group," and Reinhard Bendix, *Max Weber: An Intellectual Portrait* (New York: Doubleday, 1964) prefers "formal organization." Cf. also Weber, *Economy and Society*, 61n.27 and 301n.12.

35. Weber, *Economy and Society*, 375/266.

36. Weber refers to these organizations variously as communal, traditional, primeval *(urwüchsig)*, personal, and universal.

37. Weber, *Economy and Society*, 358-59/214.

38. Cf. Weber, *Economy and Society*, 358-60/213-15. For Weber's more detailed discussion, cf. *General Economic History*, 46-50/57-60, 116-22/111-16.

39. Cf. Weber, *Economy and Society*, 359/214, 579/350.

40. Ibid., 365–66/219–20; cf. also Weber, *General Economic History*, 43–46/54–57.

41. This section is based mainly upon Weber, *Economy and Society*, 361–63/215–18.

42. Ibid., 361–62/216.

43. Ibid., 1188/710.

44. Ibid., 363/218.

45. A marginal universal organization, the ethnic organization, will be omitted. Weber is very cautious regarding the capacity of ethnicity to lead to common action-orientations, although it may facilitate their propagation whenever a "consciousness of commonality" *(Gemeinsamkeitsbewusstsein)* appears. This occurs if subjectively perceived ethnicity forms the basis for a sense of ethnic honor as well as a conviction of the superiority of one's own customs, "wherever the memory of the origin of a community . . . remains for some reason alive" (Weber, *Economy and Society*, 390/238) and wherever ties with the old community are strengthened through participation in kin and other group activities. Even more uncertain is the capacity of the ethnic factor to serve as the source for specific values. Finally, since the belief in common ethnicity is inspired by political communities, according to Weber, this belief arises artificially *(Economy and Society*, 389/237) rather than indigenously, as is the case for the other universal organizations.

46. Since Weber's definition of legitimate domination is well-known, it will not be discussed. Cf. Weber, *Economy and Society*, 215/124. For Weber's earlier formulations in Part II of *Economy and Society*, cf. 954/549–50. More generally, cf. also 262–63/153–54, 953–54/549, 947/545.

47. Cf. ibid., 1006–10/580–83.

48. On the various ways in which the ruler in manorial feudalism sought to strengthen his position against his vassals, cf. ibid., 258–59/150–51.

49. Cf. ibid., 256/149.

50. Ibid., 1081/633. Cf. also 1078/630, 1074–75/628, 1104–5/650.

51. This central aspect endows manorial feudalism with a "heroic hostility" (ibid., 1108/653) toward all commercial relationships, the impersonal and formally rational nature of which bestows upon them, from the point of view of the feudal ethos, an undignified and vulgar character. This feudal way of life exhibits a nonchalance in respect to business affairs rather than a rational economic ethos. Cf. ibid., 1106/651, 1105/650.

52. Cf. ibid., 1105–6/650–51, 1090/639–40, 1108/653.

53. Cf. ibid., 1037–38/602.

54. Cf. ibid., 844/486, 856/493, 1107/652.

55. Ibid., 1107/652.

56. Cf. ibid., 1081/633, 1107–8/652–53.

57. On this term, cf. Kalberg, "Max Weber's Types," 1158–59; and Levine, "Rationality and Freedom," 13.

58. Cf. Weber, *Economy and Society*, 217–26/125–30, 956–58/551–52.

59. On the various ways in which legitimacy can be ascribed, cf. ibid., 36/19.

60. Cf. generally ibid., 223/128, 476/290, 958–59/552–55, 998–1002/576–78.

61. On this last point, cf. ibid., 31/16.

62. If the overall emphasis in Weber's analysis of bureaucratic domination is attended to, especially the latter chapter in *Economy and Society* (cf. 217–26/125–30) and his statement that value-rational orientations become prevalent as the single basis for legitimate domination "only in extraordinary situations" *(Economy and Society*, 213/122), it seems safe to conclude that, for Weber, the bureaucracy's formal rationality is normally upheld by a predominance of means-end rational action. This conclusion, however, should not lead to an omission of the

bureaucratic ethos *as an analytical dimension* and to an understanding of Weber as an "instrumentalist," as is the case for Alexander, *Theoretical Logic,* vol. 3, or a "decisionist," as is the case for Habermas. Cf. Jürgen Habermas, *Theorie des kommunikativen Handelns* (Frankfurt: Suhrkamp, 1981), 1: 225–366, 2: 449–88. In misunderstanding Weber's aims in *Economy and Society,* both of these interpreters have recognized adequately neither the strict distinction between the analytical and empirical levels in Weber's sociology nor the manner in which Weber proceeds in reference to this distinction. *One* of Alexander's fundamental misreadings concerns his insistence that Part 2 of *Economy and Society* is "history" and that Weber is here engaged in causal analysis. Rather, and although Part 1 is far more conceptual and Part 2 is saturated with historical examples, both sections are concerned with the construction of heuristic tools rather than with the task of history as Weber views it—namely, causal analysis. Roth makes all this clear in his Introduction to *Economy and Society* (cf. pp. xxix, xxxi, lviii), and the entire German and American discussion of Weber agrees on this point.

63. Weber, *Economy and Society,* 959/553. Sources of this "ideological halo" in Germany, for example, have been Pietism and Lutheranism. Cf. 476/290, 1108/652. On the manner generally in which legitimate orders upheld by values enhance the stability of these orders, cf. 31/16.

64. For details and examples, cf. Weber, "Introduction," 268–70/239–41; Weber, *Economy and Society,* 468–518/285–314.

65. For examples, cf. Weber, *Economy and Society,* 998–1002/576–78, 1104–9/648–53.

66. Such relationships abound in *Economy and Society.* Weber's description of the relationship between Calvinism and capitalism constitutes only one example of his widespread usage of this concept.

67. Cf. Weber, "Introduction," 268–69/239–40.

✕✕✕

Alan Sica	Reasonable Science, Unreasonable Life: The Happy Fictions of Marx, Weber, and Social Theory

Theatergoers suspend skepticism as the lights dim, tolerating the magic of the stage and indulging an urge for escape, even enlightenment. Professional critics, if untransported, balk at losing a rare moment of freedom from being-in-the-world. They expected help into uncanny realms of possibility, transformation, perhaps cathartic solace. The poor play betrays them with a reminder of rationalized boundaries. They regret their trust in suspended critique and, frustrated by inept shamans, are unable to put down their private ills.

How different are students of Marx and Weber from unsettled patrons of the play? One initially comes to them for help in understanding, or perhaps ending, our Golgotha. They ask that we throw in with them by sequestering irrationality in relations of production or the throatlatch of tradition and affective outburst. But do they provide the requisite liberating tools? The standard perception, of course, views their works as agitating; they universally inspire *Aufhebung* of industrialized life and are taken as theoretical/moral firebrands (even Weber at his most measured). But this best applies to political-economic analysis in designating and disassembling macrostructures, and, indeed, for this work they are properly revered as our principal guides. But what of the other side of character and social structure, what of personality and its seat, the unholy mixture of reason and unreason? Scholars, not to mention popular writers, will not stop producing books with rationality as their theme: Cavell's *The Claim of Reason,* Gadamer's *Reason in the Age of Science,* Hollis's and Lukes's *Rationality and Relativism,* Hübner's *Critique of Scientific Reason,* Pears's *Motivated Irrationality,* Rickman's *The Adventure of Reason,* Schick's *Having*

Reasons, Simon's *Reason in Human Affairs*[1]—all recent additions to a copious literature. Each is different, but all ask the same question: how does the intellect control its objects of inquiry, including its-self?

"Rationality" figures heavily in today's social theory (despite contrary observations by a minority, e.g., Garfinkel),[2] and Parsons typifies this usage:

> . . . This rational schema of the relation of means and ends is not to be arrived at by empirical generalization from the crude facts of experience. It is not only an analytical schema, but one of a peculiar sort. What it formulates is a *norm* of rational action. Its empirical relevance rests on the view, which I believed to be factually borne out, that human beings do, in fact, strive to realize ends and to do so by the rational application of means to them. This involves what I just called a "voluntaristic" conception of human action.[3]

This is early Parsons, to be sure, but the core belief held firm throughout his career.

"Reason" is also central to Habermas's work, of course. His most recent writings, just as his earliest, include phrases that recall a previous age: "immanent rationality," "rational interpretation," "presumably universal standards of rationality," "rational reconstructions" (taken from only two pages of text).[4] Without meaning to engage Habermas's ideas contextually or for their own sake, consider this recent argument:

> To the extent that rational reconstructions explicate the conditions of validity for particular classes of expressions and performances, they can explain deviant cases and, therewith, gain a type of indirect legislative authority or *critical* stance. To the extent that rational reconstructions push differentiations between particular validity claims beyond the limits where they have been traditionally drawn, they can establish new analytical standards and therewith assume a *constructive* role. Finally, to the extent that rational reconstructions succeed in their search for very general conditions of validity, they can claim to identify universals and thus to produce a type of *theoretical* knowledge. It is on this plane that *transcendental* arguments containing the inescapability of presuppositions enter the scene.[5]

Presuppositions, indeed. It is this major organizing scheme that keeps theory's wheels spinning, with rational, orderly balance to one side and fitful, unreasoning *coupure* on the other. Germans continue to fence with the opponent on its own terms, while some of the French—Foucault's endless documentation of the "irrationality of rationality"[6] is a case in point— have tried to sidestep it altogether.

Habermas, perhaps more than he cares to remember, marches forward in the robes of an *Aufklärer.* He is subtle in the extreme but grips this legacy passionately, as do many other lacking his dialectical inventiveness. For those who find no comfort in Jung, Ouspensky, or the dark laughter of

Celine, courting reason and coaxing patterns out of movement where the naive see none become the only path toward a clearing. This is indeed a venerable mode of intellectualizing:

All intensification of being I call perfection. . . . Indeed all being consists in a certain force, and the greater this force, the higher and freer the being. Furthermore, the greater the force, the more we see *multiplicity from unity and in unity* since the one governs the many outside itself and preforms this many inside itself. Now unity in multiplicity is nothing but harmony, and because one thing agrees more nearly with this than with that, order arises, and from order beauty, and beauty awakens love. Thus it appears that happiness, joy, love, perfection, being, force, freedom, harmony, order, and beauty are all linked together, a fact which few people rightly understand. Now when the soul feels within itself a great harmony, order, freedom, force, or perfection, and is accordingly delighted, this causes joy. . . . Such joy is constant and cannot deceive and cause future sorrow if it is the result of knowledge and accompanied by light; from this joy there arises in the will an inclination toward the good, that is, virtue. . . . Thence follows that nothing serves happiness more than the light of reason and the exercise of the will to act at all times according to reason, and that such light is especially to be sought in the knowledge of these things which can bring our minds more and more toward a higher light because from this light springs an ever-enduring progress in wisdom and virtue. . . .[7]

Writing "On Wisdom" in 1693, Leibniz "in these brief characteristic sentences . . . outlined the whole development of German philosophy during the era of the Enlightenment; he defined the central concept of the Enlightenment and sketched its theoretical program."[8] Thus Ernst Cassirer. The words, the lexicon of rational liberation, are here: order, beauty, harmony, freedom, perfection, joy, wisdom, happiness, and above all, reason, bathed in its special light. It is not acceptable, after all, to celebrate an "Ent-darkenment," an ugly, nay, demonic crush of German prefix and English image of the type Mann's Adrian Leverkühn would have grinned to hear. Even Weber's sublime skepticism—"The blush of [asceticism's] laughing heir, the Enlightenment, seems also to be irretrievably fading . . ."[9]—never concealed his envy for a lost era of philosophical and moral clarity.

Social theory is now sanitized and sanctified by scientism, which has done its work on our words as on our images of truth. But though Habermas et alii do not wax freely about beauty, love, and joy—"all linked together, a fact which few people rightly understand"—the motivations for theorizing, lying squarely with these sentiments, have not changed in three hundred years. Scholars have grown afraid to step beyond the antiseptic zone, and it is precisely this fear—Freud himself shuddered at it, even in refusing to be dismayed at what he learned from "the possessed"—that began with the young Marx and received its subtle rounding out in Weber. Their undeflected sponsorship of reason as theoretical tool and societal goal is easy enough to understand in the context either of their private biographies or their intellectual and political battles. The same might be said of Habermas. But such understanding alone cannot sustain its theoretical cogency today. The struggle for "emancipatory rationality" has been the good fight that the left has fought since its birth, and the incursions of Kierkegaard, Schopenhauer, Nietzsche, and the rest (Lukács's "destroyers" of reason)[10] have been manfully repelled. Rationality is the *Grundnorm,* to borrow from legal theory,[11] the domain assumption upon which contemporary social theory pivots as it meets the opposition. Who could object? And yet, which is the play one attends again and again: *Lear* or *Pygmalion?* At what cost does the social theorist close his eyes to the "residual categories" and the "exogenous variables" that elude the rational model, no matter how ingeniously elaborated?

Two problems, then, are at hand. One might be labeled the sublimation of the unreasonable in social theory. The other, though scarcely separable, concerns the conceptualization of reason and its various Others within the thought of Marx and Weber. Neither can be pursued well in this short space, except by suggesting an outline of what might be done toward complete definition. Of the two men, Weber's work, especially the essays composed after his recovery, offers the richer vein for analysis. But the task is overwhelmingly complex and demands inordinate pains.[12] Perhaps this accounts for the minimal, half-hearted attention *das Irrationalitätsproblem* has received from Weber scholars.[13] Marx's use of reason became more of a cheer word, to quote Hodges,[14] than an important analytic term, particularly after his philosophical anthropology was left undeveloped early in life, and he had moved permanently into that temple of rationality, political-economics. Perhaps there is another route, an indirect mode of analysis, which, though not so easily defended as pure hermeneutic appraisal, might still carry the "light of reason" into the closet where our premier theorists stowed away the unreasonableness their theories could not countenance.

What I propose, in lieu of the gigantic hermeneutic struggle to specify exactly how Marx and Weber contended with the nonrational, is not some version of psychohistory, but it is somewhat speculative. Prawer[15] has blessed Marxology with a definitive study of Marx's reading beyond the confines of economics and philosophy. It is unfortunate that no such work exists for Weber. (In fact, Weber scholars seem not to have given this angle on his intellectual biography any thought at all.)[16] Perhaps one might see their theories more crisply when set beside the great fount of intellectual German-ness, particularly given the cultural atmosphere with its Pietist-Lutheran culture in which Marx and Weber were raised. Marianne Weber provides, as usual, this central datum for Weber's intellectual growth:

"The adolescent did almost no work for school, and only occasionally paid attention in class. In *Tertia,* for example, he secretly read all forty volumes of the Cotta edition of Goethe during class hours. He was always the youngest and the weakest in class. He remembers being 'lazy as sin' *(sündenfaul),* devoid of any sense of duty or ambition."[17] This does not sound like Weber as canonized in social theory. His letters from this time evidence precocious literary analyses from Virgil and Homer to Goethe's *Hermann und Dorothea.*

You asked me to report how I liked the different authors. As far as Homer is concerned I like him best of all . . . it is not only due to the beautiful sounds of the Greek language, but especially the great naturalness with which all the actions *(Handlungen)* are related. I cannot claim that reading Homer gives the same fascination one gets from the hobby of reading novels and drama . . . one can put his works down easier than a novel. When I read a novel it is always difficult to let go of it. I want to continue reading and when I stop I always have a certain feeling of being uncomfortable. With Homer one can stop anytime . . . because it is not an animated lecture . . . it is not a chain of continuous actions but the forming and quiet sequence of the action which he describes.[18]

The fourteen year old prefers Homer to Virgil because of the latter's artificial suspense, for example, surrounding Dido "in the fourth book" of the *Aeneid.* He comments on the novels of Walter Scott and the "small bourgeois epics" of Goethe, which "ought to be called 'idylls' " since they lack epic stature. The religiosity of Herodotus he dislikes, and he chastises Livy for perpetuating the former's errors though writing four hundred years later; Cicero bores him. In a detailed letter a year later he complains about writing a Latin essay for six hours, reading Wieland's poetry, and then compares Ossian and Homer at length.[19] In these schoolboy labors Weber honed his capacity for abstraction and began establishing his taste in thought, preferring Homer's pristine Greek to effusive or didactic expression, at least when he felt austere. Yet it was the novel—surely *Werther* would head the list—which Weber found irresistible, "difficult to put down." Is it too much to guess that this phenomenon among his peers, with his dreamy "reserve and aloofness,"[20] owed something to this incessant reading done when one's personality takes on the certain outline of its matured form?

There is more than speculation about Goethe's early and enduring place in Weber's life. In Marianne's "pious"[21] biography, references to Goethe outnumber all other literary figures substantially, including his other favorites Schiller, Tolstoy, and Dostoevsky. Weber scholars recall with ease Goethe's place in his work: the borrowing of "elective affinity," the detailed analysis of the von Stein letters, the *Faust* quotation ending his

"Objectivity" essay (which Bruun finds surprisingly emotional),[22] the discussion of "personality" versus scientist with Goethe as exemplar in "Science as a Vocation."[23] Perhaps the most imposing display of Weber's intellectual/moral/psychological affinity with Goethe comes during the last few pages of *The Protestant Ethic,* surely among the most impassioned and memorable he wrote. According to Mitzman,[24] this masterpiece announced Weber's recovery. Whether "Weber was identifying his compulsiveness with the most important component of the spirit of capitalism,"[25] it is clear that the essay has about it much more of the personal than most of *Economy and Society,* for instance, or, more to the point, any of his work before his collapse.

Without going fully into the bibliographical details, which is not my objective, it is interesting to note that the jeremiad which closes *The Protestant Ethic* depends solidly on Goethe's idiom:

This fundamentally ascetic trait of middle-class life, if it attempts to be a way of life at all, and not simply the absence of any, was what Goethe wanted to teach, at the height of his wisdom, in the *Wanderjahren* [*sic*], and in the end which he gave to the life of his *Faust.* For him the realization meant a renunciation, a departure from an age of full and beautiful humanity, which can no more be repeated in the course of our cultural development than can the flower of the Athenian culture of antiquity.[26]

And shortly after this comes the "iron cage" (or "casing as hard as steel")[27] metaphor, followed itself by an aphorism the like of which Weber nowhere else included in his scientific writings: " 'Specialists without spirit, sensualists without heart; this nullity imagines that it has attained a level of civilization never before achieved.' " (" '*Fachmenschen ohne Geist, Genussmenschen ohne Herz; dies Nichts bildet sich ein, eine nie vorher erreichte Stufe des Menschentums erstiegen zu haben.*' ")[28] Weber scholars (e.g., Merquior)[29] have assumed that this unforgettable line was Goethe's. It would seem by Weber's proximate reference to the great Goethe biography by Bielschowsky[30] that it is from the debate between Jarno/Montan and Wilhelm in book 1, chapter 4, of the *Wanderjahre,* regarding the most fruitful path to *Bildung,* a passage famous enough to be anthologized as part of Goethe's wisdom.[31] What is interesting is that no matter how broadly one interprets it, Goethe's meaning is contrary to Weber's. He obviously concurs with Montan's belief that specialization is the only reasonable antidote to the dilettantism then reigning in Germany, and Wilhelm offers no important resistance to this challenge. The quotation is not Goethe's so far as I can tell, not even in the conversations with Eckermann from 24 February 1824 or 20 April 1825, where Goethe rails at length against both the overly broad expectations of universities and the pointless dwelling on trivial matters which accompanies them: "He who is wise puts aside all claims which may dissipate his attention, confines himself to one branch, and excels in that."[32]

But aside from the theoretical opposition at work here between Goethe's sentiments in his last works and Weber's condemnation of bureaucratic domination, there is more direct evidence that the Goethian aphorism is Weber's own literary expression. The key words *Fachmensch* (specialist) and *Genussmensch* (hedonist), according to modern German lexica, did not exist during Goethe's life;[33] thus, it is clear that Weber exercised poetic license by mouthing Goethe's lifelong sentiments, particularly his notions about personality, in a phrase of his own fashioning. This indicates, by its rarity in Weber's work, a unique aesthetic and intellectual attachment between the social scientist and the "Proteus," as he was known during his era, of German culture. It is precisely this fellow-feeling, particularly with regard to Goethe's understanding of rationality and personality, that I will explore momentarily.

The last few pages have proposed in skeletal form two related projects, which, if done fully, would require bulky monographs. The first is Weber's response to literature, its place in his worldview, and the special role of Goethe in his theorizing and, when it suited him, in his moralizing as well. The second, both more important and more difficult, details Weber's uneasy sublation and rationalization of all the components of social life foreign to the economic model (i.e., the nonrational, irrational, and unreasonable, however defined). As one younger scholar has deftly put it, for Weber "as a radical analyst, the irrational 'exists'—and he confronted it with humility."[34] This perhaps gives him too much credit in one way and not enough in another, but resolving such a debate could spark a revaluation of attitudes toward Weber, filling another volume.

My argument has been that the two tasks can be joined and a certain measure of illumination gained by concentrating on Goethe[35] as thinker and moralist, due to his paramount role in German intellectual life. Thus far a fragmentary image of Goethe's shadow in Weber's work has emerged because so little scholarship has been done on the topic. But with S. S. Prawer's definitive *Karl Marx and World Literature,* an entirely different realm appears. Of the five hundred names in Prawer's index, only Engels accounts for more entries than Goethe. Prawer has shown conclusively that Marx spent an entire life entranced by great literature, reading Shakespeare, Homer, Cervantes, Dante, and Dickens in the original languages and dipping into his favorites "almost every day," as Liebknecht reported.[36] And, more importantly, from these literary sources he took many of his central ideas and organizing imagery, not only during his semi-bourgeois period when young and impressionable but also throughout his career as revolutionary thinker and actor. At fifty he learned Russian " 'as a diversion' [he explained to Franzisca Kugelmann] when he was suffering from carbuncles,"[37] not only to read and memorize Turgenev, Lermontov, and Pushkin but also to study politically damaging Russian Government reports that were smuggled to him; this made him "certainly the only economist in Western Europe who had knowledge of them."[38] As he liked to say, "A foreign language is a weapon in the struggle of life."[39]

The modern scholar empathizes with one of Marx's young visitors from the Spanish International: "In the presence of that great man [who had just regaled him on Spanish literature] I could not help feeling very very small."[40] By my count Weber used no less than eleven languages, though it seems he did not read literature for its own sake with the voracious cosmopolitanism of Marx.[41] Similarly, Marx wrote German, French, and English "to the admiration of language experts"[42] and read in Spanish, Italian, Russian, Greek, and Latin. This is not primarily a technical feat, like memorizing the phone book; this kind of zealotry reveals both incredible linguistic facility and talent and a dogmatic belief that great literatures in the original provide something fundamental to social thought, whether cast as aesthetics and ontology or social and economic theory. This is the prevailing conclusion that justifies Prawer's book and his portrait of Marx as having read in *Weltliteratur* (Goethe's word) not because he felt he ought to but because he could not imagine carrying out his project without doing so. For instance, when he discovered that Liebknecht had no Spanish, he sat him down with *Don Quixote* and began a series of lessons ("what a patient teacher he was")[43] which stopped when the student could translate Cervantes adequately. Eleanor Marx, imitating her father, could declaim "scene after scene from Shakespeare" by heart by the age of six.[44] This "man in love with reading who appeals to the knowledge of the German and foreign classics he shares with his educated audience, and who challenges his opponents to acquire not only better logic, but also more of the experience and insight that books can give,"[45] was as mortgaged in spirit to literature and the thoughts it provoked as was Faust to Mephistopheles. (The latter was Marx's favorite of all characters, the one he would act out for visitors, rather "grossly.")[46]

Such anecdotes put flesh on the bones of theory, but they cannot in themselves substantiate or displace more formal concerns. The general theme—the relation between Marx's aesthetic notions proper and his theories of political-economy and power—has propelled Tucker to see Marx's entire project as defining "the aesthetic life,"[47] and, in open opposition, occasioned Morawski's subtler summary and integration of

Marx's aesthetics, i.e., art as "disalienating."[48] Both approaches seem to many Marxists today more similar than not, and as such equally remote from the late, scientific (Althusserian) Marx they esteem. Prawer takes a middle course between the camps, literary/aesthetic versus scientific/ economic Marxism, by carefully examining the textual evidence of Marx's global literacy and showing where, early and late, he put to theoretical and polemical use what he had learned. It is not that Prawer disagrees with Morawski's definition of *"homo aestheticus,"* his emphasis (following Marx) on the *"inner compact structure* of the work of art," and his claim that "Marx regards aesthetic experience as synthetic in character: a mingling of the intellectual, emotional, and sensual."[49] Rather, Prawer wishes to show at the most easily secured theoretical level how impossible it is to ignore or minimize, when once pointed out, the *necessary* place of literary inspiration in Marx's most hard-edged socio-economic thinking. As he explains in one of many similar instances, "What the passage from *Towards a Critique of Political Economy* should serve to demonstrate, however, is that in the later economic works, no less than in the more obviously 'humanistic' earlier ones, the whole of Marx, with his aesthetic, literary, and linguistic interests, constantly shows itself."[50] And again, lest there be any question, it is Goethe who holds center stage, just as with Weber.[51]

From Prawer's cornucopia of examples illustrating Marx's debt to Goethe (among others), only a few can be restated here. This tie, as with Weber, was so constitutive of Marx's imagination that he could sometimes treat great writers as if they were each a Goethe manqué, for example, Aeschylus's Prometheus (a central figure for Marx) "seen through the eyes of the young Goethe"[52] or one of his two favorite Balzac stories, "Melmoth Reconciled," understood as a seriocomic variation upon *Faust.*[53] Balzac's portrait of the stock exchange as the site where the Pope manages God's properties must have satisfied him; Marx considered him the leading "historian" of the age.[54] But Balzac's entire societal dissection also connects with so much of his worldview: "Social conditions mingle elements of evil with the promptings of natural goodness of heart, and the mixture of motives underlying a man's intentions should be leniently judged"; "His relation to the world without had been entirely changed with the expansion of his faculties" [after gaining diabolic insight]; "The mechanism and the scheme of the world was apparent to him, and its working interested him no longer; he did not long disguise the profound scorn that makes of a man of extraordinary powers a sphinx who knows everything and says nothing, and sees all things in an unmoved countenance."[55]

Goethe's *Reinecke the Fox,* from which Marx borrowed repeatedly, inspired the cynical critique of "self-deception, illusion, false-consciousness"[56] that Marx unmasked among his contemporaries. This is given full vent in *The Holy Family* and *The German Ideology,* which, like *Herr Vogt* (his most "literary" polemic),[57] become impossible to appreciate without recourse to a library of literary sources. It must be emphasized—as with his motivations for learning foreign languages—that even at his most apparently ostentatious Marx used literature *and* analytic techniques of literary criticism to expedite "his self-imposed task of letting the light of reason play on heavenly and earthly authority"[58] and not to prove how "well-read" he was. This diligent attention to literature both reflected and shaped his concern for the *totalen Gestalten* (undivided self) he regarded as the pinnacle of human development, an Homeric ideal that attracted Weber as well.

The indices from the first twenty volumes of the Marx and Engels *Collected Works* (unpublished when Prawer wrote his book) yield scores of references to Goethe's works, including *Rechenschaft, Verschiedenes über Kunst, Der Zauberlehrling, Die Geheimnisse, Iphigenie auf Tauris, Die Leiden des jungen Werthers, Lilis Park, Totalität, Vanitas!, Das Veilchen, Aus meinem Leben, Belagerung von Mainz, Briefe aus der Schweiz, Der Bürgergeneral, Egmont, Götz von Berlichingen, Hermann und Dorothea, Prometheus, Venezianische Epigramme,* many references to *Faust* (over forty), *Die Wahlverwandtschaften, Wilhelm Meisters Lehrjahre, Reinecke Fuchs,* and a dozen more. Engels wrote an entire treatment of Goethe in "German Socialism in Verse and Prose," forming a critique of Karl Grün's Goethe study, all of which was then planned for inclusion in *The German Ideology.*[59] From letters of the period, and in keeping with their uniquely symbiotic intellectual relation, it is impossible to believe that Marx was any less aware than Engels of Goethe's literature and the climate of contemporary interpretations.[60] All these references appear in the first several volumes of the fifty-volume *Collected Works,* but this dependence upon "Proteus" is sustained throughout their *opera.*

In Marx's youthful novella, *Scorpion and Felix,* his character Pertini imitates Mephistopheles.[61] In an early polemic in the *Rheinische Zeitung* he skillfully distorts an obscure quotation from Goethe on the nature of artistic creation to make a strategic point, "directing into political channels energies that had previously flowed into aesthetic investigations . . . He is projecting an image of wholeness"; this recalls his love for the epigram, "Totalität"—"the artist, the lover, the fighter for freedom from political interference are one and the same persons."[62] In opening his critique of Hegel's *Philosophy of Right* he uses Goethe's *Übermensch* and *Unmensch,* "super-man" and "non-man," providing an interesting link with Nietzsche.[63] He likewise injects a visceral disgust at reification and alienation brought on by existence within a cash nexus by calling, once again, on Mephisto's black vapors: ". . . every need is an opportunity to approach one's neighbor in the semblance of the utmost amiability and to say to him: dear friend, I will give you what you require, but you know the necessary condition: you know with what kind of ink you have to sign yourself over to me; I dupe you in providing enjoyment for you."[64] And again, when surveying British rule in India for the *New York Daily Tribune,* he summons up the ideal quote from Goethe's *West-Eastern Divan* (scarcely known here) that epitomizes the "cunning of world-historical reason," a stanza he employed again, with similar but not identical ends, in an article for the *Neue Oder-Zeitung.*[65]

Two simple points have been made. Literature as a whole in the major European languages decisively helped structure Marx's (and somewhat less so, Engels's) axiological posture toward social reality—what Lukács called "social ontology."[66] And secondly, within this mass of formative reading, Goethe won a uniquely determining role. When Marx pictured money converted into capital "as if it had love in its body" *(als hätt' es Lieb' im Leibe),* he innoculated both the *Grundrisse* and *Capital* with the searing image from *Faust* of a rat, its innards burning with poison, racing in agony around the house toward its inevitable end. Such a literary device energizes Marx's "gut-feeling" that "there is something obscene about reification" and the social cost of allowing machines to suck the lifeblood from their operators.[67] If Marx did not find in high culture the actual components of his political-economy, he did "follow his occasional practice of looking to the world's great poets for economic facts and insights where other sources fail";[68] this probably understates the case.

There is a larger issue, though. Is it trivial that today's comparative social scientists do not stand a chance of rivaling Weber because of his encyclopedic awareness not only of facts but also of cognitive subtleties based on and interpretable only through different languages? Scholars hopefully rely on secondary and tertiary studies by necessity, then call it virtue. With Marx the problem is compounded, since his virtuosity encompassed not only historical or political-economic facts but a world of literary expression as well, often with philosophical intentions and conse-quence (e.g., "Prometheus Bound"). For Marx, books "are my slaves and they must serve me as I will." As Lafargue reminds us, he was truly at home only in the bibliographic world and, when needing a rest, would "lie down on the sofa and read a novel; he sometimes read two or three at a time. . . ."[69] Prawer, Demetz, Lifshitz, and others force one to consider what theoretical forms such nontheoretical labors, or pleasures, took in the work for which Marx is famous.

All of this can mean several things. If one's interest is in the quality of mind that concocted Marxism, then it pays to realize that from his earliest writings, "Marx had used men's understanding of great literature as a touchstone by which to judge their intellectual and spiritual capacity."[70] On a related level he had learned that his arsenal of hermeneutic techniques "could be used with devastating effects upon texts that were not 'literary' in any narrow sense."[71] Men who wrote works unable to withstand his critique were guilty of stupidity, "false-consciousness," or ignorance. They were estranged from Goethe's idea of "the true poet's mode of existence" revealed in *Torquato Tasso*. For Prawer, the allusion in "Wage-Labor and Capital" to this poem "added to Marx's description of alienated labor: of the way work has ceased to be that act of self-discovery and self-creation which great poetry can at once symbolize and exemplify."[72] This simultaneity, the combined symbol and exemplar, is the hallmark of Marx as a literary thinker. Clearly, he wished to join, albeit in a logically unassailable form, the truths of literature with the irresolvable facts of history into what is now called a "total science of humankind."[73] As he wrote early on, "Only through the objectively unfolded richness of man's essential being is the richness of subjective *human* sensibility—a musical ear, and eye for beauty of form . . . either cultivated or brought into being."[74] Mészáros, Prawer, and others have rightly seen in such remarks the feelings of a man valued by cosmopolites of the era as "the most cultured man in Europe." His senses, if not his literary skills (something which occasionally grieved him, but other times gave him pride),[75] had become as keenly refined as anyone's. Regarding Marx's indefinite but widely applied "laws of beauty" Prawer summarizes:

An intimate union of form and content is cleary implied in Marx's praise of man's aesthetic sense, of his ability . . . "to apply everywhere the inherent standard of the object," to keep due proportion in everything. . . . Man must be liberated from pressures that force him to appropriate objects only to satisfy his crude physical needs; he must experience aesthetic objects . . . as *relating* to him, as affirmation of his essential humanity.[76]

None of this is the least removed from Goethe's idea of the reasonable life, even if his expectations for its realization were more halting than Marx's. But the key point is that Marx's critical imagination moved with devilish skill between "broadly aesthetic antinomies, 'beauty' versus 'deformation,' 'civilization' versus 'barbarism,' "[77] prelogical values he found in great writers.

Today's social theorists, as suggested earlier, are perplexed in trying to incorporate rational action, the keystone of reasonable life, into their systems or hypotheses in such a way that they err neither in one direction (the economic model) nor the other (Romantic irrationalism). This essay suggests—quite tentatively, since tidy redaction does not benefit this sort of inquiry—that Goethe, particularly as carried into our orbit through Marx and Weber, offers a theoretically lively appreciation of rationality more robust than contemporary thinking, quite at home in *Gesellschaft,* and not as woolly or nihilistic as later German thought. I cannot hope to prove this here. Goethe scholarship is as contentious a field as Biblical hermeneutics, so the nonspecialist must nervously turn to others. But even in my choice of interpreters, Thomas Mann, Ernst Cassirer, Walter Kaufmann, Karl Löwith, and so on, there is hardly unanimity.[78] For example, a respected specialist faults Mann's political understanding of Goethe,[79] and since Mann spent a long creative life in dialogue with "Proteus," writing novels about him, imitating him, editing his works, and publishing essays about him in abundance, the outsider can only hope for the best.

Having said that, there are aspects of Goethe's thinking, and I hope the preceding has made this plausible, which were intimately known to Marx and Weber and lay as close to their hearts as to their minds; these ideas functioned as the flooring for their *Weltanschauungen* (in Mannheim's specific sense).[80] This is hardly a revelation. But the bridge between confident Enlightenment reason, its later collapse à la Schopenhauer and Nietzsche, and renewed, if tempered, hope for rationality which animates Habermas and others today, may well be behind us, not somewhere hence. Dilthey understood as much when he situated Goethe's creative achievement at the midpoint between Shakespeare and Rousseau. Goethe became the golden mean, "a balance between the inner and the outer, the subjective and objective modes of the imagination."[81]

He was able to understand by putting what was alien in relation to his own life. Once understood it became a moment of his own development. So rich was his nature, so strong his need to give his existence an unbounded scope and his insights objectivity, that he even incorporated the religious, scientific, and philosophical movements of his time in his *Erlebnis.*[82]

What is this but a vibrant ancestor of Marx's total science of humankind and Weber's *verstehende* sociology?

I have found no student of Goethe more credibly exciting, vis-à-vis reason and unreason as axial properties of his work, than Mann, unsurprising in view of *Doctor Faustus, Lotte in Weimar,* and his Goethe essays. He notes, for instance, that "it took a musician [Goethe's friend Zelter] to say the right, cheerfully critical word about the precision and elegance of

Goethe's prose, its rhythmic magic, a *rational magic,* the clearest blend of Eros and Logos.''[83] It is possible to agree with Steven Marcus that "everything within us that is not rational—our affects, our instinctual strivings, our fears, fancies, dreams, nightmares, our sexual obsessions, our uncontrollable aggression''[84]—must be faced by social theorists, particularly if personality continues to serve as a believable theoretical construct; Goethe's wisdom becomes ever more compelling. Weber was at home in such an analytic milieu, especially regarding Goethe's willingness to advance "rational magic"—an almost Weberian antinomy in itself—towards the resolution of what is and is not readily controllable in human affairs. Consider, for example, one of Weber's many philosophical moments in his comparative religion: ". . . the possibility of questioning the meaning of the world presupposes the capacity to be astonished about the course of events.''[85] Goethe states in his last letter: ". . . the best genius is that which absorbs and assimilates everything without doing the least violence to its fundamental destiny—that which we call character— . . . unite[s] the acquired with the innate *to produce a harmonious unity that astonishes the world.''*[86] And Mann, quite typically, unites both sentiments and adds something: "It is certain that with this word, the phenomenon, 'personality,' we leave the realm of the purely intellectual, rational, analyzable, and enter the sphere of the natural, the elemental, the demonic, that 'astonished the world.' ''[87]

Weber scholars know that in his polemics against Roscher, Knies, Stammler, and others, he mocked this opaque version of "personality," often identified today with Dilthey but actually closer to Schleiermacher:

. . . [R]ationality is not extrinsic to Existence as an individual being; it is rather constituted in his inward and peculiar identity. . . . [F]eeling does not stand for the irrational in the self. It is, rather, as much a part of the rational consciousness as the capacity for the most critical and scientific reflection.[88]

By 1906 when he secured his recovery, Weber would publicly have repudiated the Schleiermacherian view, augmented by Mann: Personality "is nothing but a linguistic makeshift for something that language cannot describe, for an emanation whose sources do not lie in the intellectual, but in the vital.''[89] But such a rejection, just as with Marx and now Habermas, is politically expedient, and as such understandable. They had experienced, as have we, too many joint macabre mystifications of personality and politics to permit any more within the polity. But the cunning of reason, devilishly thorough analysis, does not pause at ideological boundaries, another fact of modern life which Goethe pondered in the *Wander-*

jahre. Intellectually liberating and politically healthy ideas do not always share the same flag, as Horkheimer and Adorno explained.[90] Goethe, living, writing, and thinking in the prehysteria of our century, was more honest about these matters than we can afford to be.

The perpetual charm of *Wilhelm Meister* lies exactly here in the "pre-hystery" of the modern world. The point of Wilhelm's chronicle is "above all [to] convince him of the extraordinary interplay between resolution and fate, or between reason and the irrational" so that "he might learn the interplay of reason and emotion and might experience the essential interdependence of feeling, reflection, and discipline."[91] Is it too much to argue that we no longer sense this interdependence, largely because Marx and Weber, though knowing it well, helped banish it from polite intellectual discourse? The Dilthey scholar, H. A. Hodges, has capsulized this dilemma:

> Dilthey finds in Lessing the first formulation of such an ideal. According to him, the good life is the life of reason, a free, self-determining life, conscious of inherent worth by virtue of control exercised by reason over the passions. Goethe took over this ideal and gave it a less narrowly rational form than it had in Lessing. Goethe saw the unity of life on all levels, from the highest to the lowest. He showed that the "rational" activities of the mind are not distinct from and antithetic to the "irrational," but are a more explicit development of something which is present even on the "irrational" level. Logical thinking would be impossible if it had no basis in the life of the senses and the imagination; and here, in the keen sensibility and imaginative "genius" of the artist, Goethe finds a shaping power at work, which is the same as the power which operates in logical thinking. Art, then, and the senses, no less than science and the understanding, feelings no less than moral maxims, are essential to the completeness of the good life.[92]

From an era which knew Genius, we come to genius; from the Concept and the Absolute, we have concepts of the situational; and from the *Critique of Judgment,* we have learned mere matters of taste. Perhaps we can pay less attention now to what Marx, Weber, and other theorists wrote about Reason, reason, and "reason," and, following the dialectic, think more about why *das Irrationalitätsproblem* frightened them so. Perhaps we can look it in the face, as Goethe did.

Notes

1. Stanley Cavell, *The Claim of Reason: Wittgenstein, Skepticism, Morality, and Tragedy* (New York: Oxford University Press, 1979); Hans-Georg Gadamer, *Reason in the Age of Science* (Cambridge, Mass.: MIT Press, 1981); Martin Hollis and Stephen Lukes, eds., *Rationality and Relativism* (Cambridge, Mass.: MIT Press, 1982); Kurt Hübner, *Critique of Scientific Reason* (Chicago: University of Chicago Press, 1983); David Pears, *Motivated Irrationality* (New York: Oxford University Press, 1984); H. P. Rickman, *The Adventure of Reason: The Uses of Philosophy in Sociology* (Westport, Conn.: Greenwood Press, 1983); Frederic Schick, *Having Reasons: An Essay on Rationality and Sociality* (Princeton, N.J.: Princeton University Press, 1984); Herbert Simon, *Reason in Human Affairs* (Stanford, Calif.: Stanford University Press, 1983).

2. Harold Garfinkel wrote that sociologists "have found that the rational properties which their definitions discriminated are empirically uninteresting. They have preferred instead to study the features and conditions of nonrationality in human conduct." Garfinkel, "The Rational Properties of Scientific and Common-sense Activities," in *Positivism and Sociology*, ed. Anthony Giddens (London: Heinemann, 1974), 53. This may well be true of social research, but it does not hold for much social theory.

3. Talcott Parsons, "The Place of Ultimate Values in Sociological Theory," *International Journal of Ethics* 45 (1935): 282–300, reprinted in *Talcott Parsons on Institutions and Social Evolution*, ed. Leon H. Mayhew (Chicago: University of Chicago Press, 1983), 80. This will be the official Parsons anthology in the future and as such represents what in his thought remains "alive" for Parsonsians.

4. Jürgen Habermas, "Interpretive Social Science vs. Hermeneuticism," in *Social Science as Moral Inquiry*, ed. Norma Haan et al. (New York: Columbia University Press, 1983), 251–69.

5. Ibid., 259–60 (emphases in original).

6. Edith Kurzweil, *The Age of Structuralism: Levi-Strauss to Foucault* (New York: Columbia University Press, 1980), 195.

7. Ernst Cassirer, *The Philosophy of the Enlightenment* (Princeton, N.J.: Princeton University Press, 1951), 121–22 (emphases in original).

8. Ibid., 122.

9. Max Weber, *The Protestant Ethic and the Spirit of Capitalism*, trans. Talcott Parsons (New York: Scribner's, 1958), 182. Cf. E. Matthews's rendering: "the rosy disposition of its smiling heir"; *Max Weber: Selections in Translation*, ed. R. G. Runciman (Cambridge: Cambridge University Press, 1978), 171.

10. Georg Lukács, *The Destruction of Reason* (London: Merlin Press, 1980).

11. Hans Kelsen, *The Pure Theory of Law* (1934; reprint Berkeley: University of California Press, 1967), 3–23.

12. See Alan Sica, "The Problem of Irrationality and Meaning in the Work of Max Weber" (Ph.D. diss., University of Massachusetts, Amherst, 1978), esp. 137–351.

13. Recently Toby Huff has covered the same ground as I (see note 12), but very briefly, in several review-essays. The germane portion is Toby Huff, "On the Methodology of the Social Sciences: A Review Essay, Part II," *Philosophy of the Social Sciences* 12 (March 1982): 81–86. The essays have been reprinted with a new introduction as Toby Huff, *Max Weber and the Methodology of the Social Sciences* (New Brunswick, N.J.: Transaction Books, 1984). Another short treatment is Rogers Brubaker, *The Limits of Rationality: An Essay on The Social and Moral Thought of Max Weber* (Boston: Allen & Unwin, 1983).

14. H. A. Hodges, "Lukács on Irrationalism," in *Georg Lukács,* ed. G. H. R. Parkinson (New York: Vintage Books, 1970), 96–97.

15. S. S. Prawer, *Karl Marx and World Literature* (New York: Oxford University Press, 1976).

16. Studies which give no special attention to literature in his life or work include well-known older works—Beetham (1974), Bendix (1962), Bendix & Roth (1971), Bruun (1972), Burger (1976), Dronberger (1971), Freund (1969), Honigsheim (1968), Jaspers (1964), Lachmann (1970), Loewenstein (1966), MacRae (1974), Mommsen (1974), Rogers (1969), Runciman (1969 & 1972), Stammer (1971), Turner (1974), Weiss (1975), and Wrong (1970)—and newer studies are also consistent in ignoring this aspect of Weber scholarship, including Franco Ferrarotti, *Max Weber and the Destiny of Reason* (Armonk, N.Y.: M. E. Sharpe, 1982); Kathi Friedman, *Legitimation of Social Rights and the Western Welfare State: A Weberian Perspective* (Chapel Hill: University of North Carolina Press, 1981); Susan Hekman, *Weber, The Ideal Type, and Contemporary Social Theory* (Notre Dame, Ind.: University of Notre Dame Press, 1983); Karl Löwith, *Max Weber and Karl Marx* (Boston: Allen & Unwin, 1982); Gordon Marshall, *In Search of the Spirit of Capitalism* (New York: Columbia University Press, 1982); J. G. Merquior, *Rousseau and Weber* (Boston: Routledge & Kegan Paul, 1980); E. B. Midgley, *The Ideology of Max Weber: A Thomist Critique* (Totowa, N.J.: Barnes & Noble, 1983); Gianfranco Poggi, *Calvinism and the Capitalist Spirit* (London: Macmillan, 1983); Guenther Roth and Wolfgang Schluchter, *Max Weber's Vision of History* (Berkeley: University of California Press, 1979); Wolfgang Schluchter, *The Rise of Western Rationalism* (Berkeley: University of California Press, 1981); Bryan S. Turner, *For Weber* (Boston: Routledge & Kegan Paul, 1981). The only important study of Weber which approaches his ideas from an unusual perspective, sometimes taking sidelong glances at literature, is Arthur Mitzman's *The Iron Cage* (New York: Alfred Knopf, 1969). Reinhard Bendix, in *Max Weber: An Intellectual Portrait* (New York: Anchor, 1962), makes a rare connection between Weber and Goethe in arguing that the former's "charisma, tradition, and legality" correspond to the latter's "inspiration, custom, and faith" (389n).

17. Marianne Weber, *Max Weber: A Biography,* trans. Harry Zohn (New York: Wiley & Sons, 1975), 47–48. (*Tertia:* "The third highest class in a Gymnasium"; translator's note.)

18. Max Weber, *Jugendbriefe* (Tübingen: Mohr, [1936]), 9–11, letter 9 September 1878.

19. Ibid., 30–31, letter 19 December 1879.

20. Marianne Weber, *Max Weber,* 48.

21. Julien Freund, *The Sociology of Max Weber* (New York: Vintage, 1969), 33.

22. H. H. Bruun, *Science, Values, and Politics in Max Weber's Methodology* (Copenhagen: Munksgaard, 1972), 138: the "almost passionate last pages which end in a sweeping quotation from Goethe."

23. "Elective affinity" appears many times in Weber's work. See R. H. Howe, "Max Weber's Elective Affinities: Sociology within the Bounds of Pure Reason," *American Journal of Sociology* 84 (Sept. 1978): 366–85; the von Stein analysis occurs in *The Methodology of the Social Sciences* (New York: Free Press, 1949), 138–48; the *Faust* quote on 112; Goethe as "personality" and as scientist in Weber, *From Max Weber,* 137.

24. *The Iron Cage,* 171–75.

25. Ibid., 172.

26. Weber, *The Protestant Ethic,* 180–81.

27. Matthews's version in *Weber: Selections in Translation,* 170

28. Weber, *The Protestant Ethic,* 182; *GAzRS,* I, 204.

29. J. G. Merquior, *Rousseau and Weber,* 191.

30. Albert Bielschowsky, *Goethe: Sein Leben und Seine Werke,* 2 vols. (Munich: C. H. Beck, 1895, 1903). Bielschowsky, *Goethe,* trans. William Cooper as *The Life of Goethe,* 3 vols. (New York: G. P. Putnam's Sons, 1905–1908). Of special interest are "New sociological theories" included by Goethe in the novel, 3: 192–93, and the discussion of pedagogical theories that gave rise to the important debate between Montan and Wilhelm, 198f., 227–46, as well as "The two great fundamental ideas running through *Die Wanderjahre* are work and resignation," 195. Given Weber's use of "resignation" so frequently and in such theoretically delicate passages, this is an important connection between Goethe and him.

31. John Stuart Blackie, comp., *The Wisdom of Goethe* (New York: Charles Scribners Sons, 1883; reprint 1974), 235–36. Also Ludwig Curtius, ed., *Goethe: Wisdom and Experience,* trans. Hermann Weigand (New York: Pantheon, 1949), 155, 197.

32. Goethe, *Conversations with Eckermann* [no trans. indicated] (New York: Walter Dunne, 1901), 57.

33. My assumptions about this peculiar, if not unique, stylistic usage by Weber—a "quoted" remark that was his own—has been substantially confirmed by Professor Henry Fullenwider, German Department, University of Kansas. Neither he nor I could find in the *Wanderjahre,* nor in the *Maximen und Reflexionen* (the other work where such a remark might be found), any observation resembling Weber's. From this I assume that Weber wished to put forth his idea poetically, but with the legitimacy one might gain by presumed filiation with Goethe. The relevant texts are Goethe, *Wilhelm Meister: Apprenticeship and Travels,* trans. R. O. Moon (London: G. T. Foulis, 1947), 2: 34f. (bk. 1, chap. 4), the Jarno-Wilhelm debate; also Leonardo's long speech on citizenship and learning, 259f.(bk. 3, chap. 9); for the passages which especially interested Weber (see Weber, *Protestant Ethic,* 181), regarding the rationalization and spiritualization of time in the utopian community as given in a discussion between Wilhelm and Friedrich, 277f. (bk. 3, chap. 11), which includes these telling lines: ". . . moderation in matters of choice, diligence in what is necessary. Now let everyone in the course of his life make use of these laconic words in his own way, and he has an abundant text for unlimited performance. The greatest respect is impressed upon all for time, as the highest gift of God and Nature and the most attractive companion to existence. . . . If there is something lifeless, irrational . . . this similarly [as with miscreants] is set aside," 277–78. Also *Maximen und Reflexionen,* ed. Max Hecker (Weimar: Verlag der Goethe-Gesellschaft, 1907), vol. 21 of the *Goethe Schriften.* Professor Fullenwider notes that Goethe's celebration of specialization hardly squares with his own extraordinary diversity of experience.

34. Jürgen Zander, *Das Problem der Beziehung Max Webers zu Karl Marx* (Frankfurt: Haag u. Herchen Verlag, 1978), 151. From Gerd Schroeter, "Exploring the Marx-Weber Nexus," *Canadian Journal of Sociology* 10 (1985): 69–87.

35. Schiller would figure very importantly in any comprehensive analysis, as would Tolstoy and Shakespeare. But Goethe seems more akin to Weber if one matches Weltanschauungen, and Schiller more to Marx's, as one would imagine given their relative attitudes toward revolutionary change, self-transformation, even enlightenment.

36. Prawer, *Karl Marx and World Literature,* 208.

37. Karl Marx and Friedrich Engels, *On Literature & Art* (Moscow: Progress Publishers, 1976), 443.

38. Ibid., 439, from reports of Paul Lafargue.

39. Ibid.

40. Ibid., 444, memories of Anselmo Lorenzo.

41. Weber used Greek, Latin, medieval and modern Italian, medieval and modern Spanish, French, English, Hebrew, Russian, and his mother tongue.

42. Marx and Engels, *On Literature & Art*, 439, according to Lafargue.

43. Prawer, *Karl Marx and World Literature*, 208. Wilhelm Liebknecht, in *Marx and Engels through the Eyes of Their Contemporaries* (Moscow: Progress Publishers, 1972), 52.

44. Marx and Engels, *On Literature & Art*, 441.

45. Prawer, *Marx and World Literature*, 49.

46. Ibid., 327.

47. Robert C. Tucker, *Philosophy & Myth in Karl Marx* (London: Cambridge University Press, 1961), 157–58: "What will remain is the life of art and science in a special and vastly enlarged sense of these two terms. Marx's conception of ultimate communism is fundamentally *aesthetic* in character. His utopia is an aesthetic ideal of the future man-nature relationship, which he sees in terms of artistic creation and the appreciation of the beauty of the man-made environment by its creator. . . . The alienated world will give way to the aesthetic world."

48. Stefan Morawski, "Introduction" in *Marx & Engels on Literature & Art*, ed. Lee Baxandall and Stefan Morawski (St. Louis, Mo.: Telos Press, 1973), 6ff. 18ff.

49. Ibid., 10, 15, 17. Cf. Prawer. *Marx and World Literature*, 406, where he claims that his entire book "tends to confirm" Morawski's interpretation of Marx and Engels's aesthetics. Interpreting Marx's use of *Mass* in the *1844 MSS* and the *Grundrisse* results in Morawski's *"inner compact structure . . . "* (emphases in original), a key to Marx's undeveloped aesthetic theory. See also Stefan Morawski, *Inquiries Into the Fundamentals of Aesthetics* (Cambridge, Mass.: MIT Press, 1974), 295–308.

50. Prawer, *Marx and World Literature*, 305–6.

51. Shakespeare and Heine (a personal friend) were also central to Marx's writing, but Goethe, it seems to me, was *primus inter pares*.

52. Prawer, *Marx and World Literature*, 31.

53. Ibid., 373n.–74n., 420; Marx's letter to Engels, 25 February 1867, in Marx and Engels, *On Literature & Art*, 315.

54. Prawer, *Marx and World Literature*, 181.

55. Honoré de Balzac, *The Unknown Masterpiece*, vol. 22 of *Honoré de Balzac in Twenty-Five Volumes* (New York: Peter Fenelon Collier and Son, 1900), 86, 114, 115.

56. Prawer, *Marx and World Literature*, 130, 51.

57. Ibid., 261. Marx demolished Karl Vogt with Cicero, Virgil, Persius, Luther (a major stylistic guide for Marx throughout his life), Hartmann, Gottfried, Wolfram, Walther, Rabelais, Heine, Schiller, Samuel Butler the older, Shakespeare, Pope, Sterne, Byron, Dickens, Dante, Calderon, Cervantes, Voltaire, Hugo, Balzac, and, of course, Goethe, to name a few.

58. Ibid., 58.

59. Karl Marx and Friedrich Engels, *Collected Works* (New York: International Publishers, 1976), 6: 249–73, 677n.99.

60. In his companion volume to Prawer's, Peter Demetz, *Marx, Engels, and the Poets: Origins of Marxist Literary Criticism*, trans. Jeffrey Sammons (Chicago: University of Chicago Press, 1967), argues convincingly that Marx, "who had read and revered Goethe from his youth" (moreover, "he had always regarded [Mephistopheles] as a brother under the skin"), enjoyed a knowledge of Goethe which made the autodidact Engels's "most superficial" by comparison

(166, 165). More importantly, Engels's refutation of Grün's book is more politically instructive than intellectually reliable, for he took most of his ideas from those current at the time among liberals, especially as codified by Ludolf Wienbarg in his *Aesthetische Feldzüge* in 1834, and did not turn often enough to Goethe's works themselves. None of this, however, diminishes their mutually obsessive regard for the Promethean force in German culture; as Engels complained after buying a set of his works, "everyone was constantly chattering about Goethe" (ibid.).

61. Prawer, *Marx and World Literature,* p. 16; Marx and Engels, *Collected Works* 1: 616–32 (a fragment).

62. Prawer, *Marx and World Literature,* 36–37.

63. Ibid., 67. This connection is obscured in Marx and Engels, *Collected Works* 3: 175, where *"Uebermenschen"* is given as "superhuman being," *"Unmenschen"* as "inhuman being."

64. Prawer, *Marx and World Literature,* 83. This is his translation. Cf. other renderings, which do not make the link as clearly, in Marx and Engels, *Collected Works* 3: 307; and the older *Economic and Philosophic Manuscripts of 1844* (New York: International Publishers, 1973), 148.

65. Prawer, *Marx and World Literature,* 247–48.

66. Georg Lukács, *The Ontology of Social Being,* trans. David Fernbach, 3 vols. (London: Merlin Press, 1978–80) (various sections of Lukács unpublished German MS).

67. Karl Marx, *Grundrisse: der Kritik der Politischen Oekonomie* (Berlin: Dietz Verlag, 1953), 592; Marx and Engels, *Kapital* III, *Collected Works,* xxv, 406 (*Capital,* trans. D. Fernbach [London: New Left Review, 1981], 3: 517); and *Kapital* I, *Collected Works,* xxiii, 209 (*Capital,* trans. B. Fowkes [London: New Left Review, 1976], 1:302); see Prawer, 324–25. The range of translations of this novel passage is instructive vis-à-vis understanding the place of language and literary inspiration in Marx. Prawer's "as if it had love in its body" becomes for Fowkes, in the New Left Review edition, "as if its body were by love possessed," while in *Faust,* trans. Bayard Taylor (New York: Modern Library, 1967), 73, it is "as if he had love in his bosom," and in *Faust,* trans. Walter Kaufmann (New York: Anchor Books, 1963), 215, "As if love gnawed his vitals," the loosest but perhaps most felicitous of all. Also Fowkes expressed Marx's *"sich selbst verwertenden Wert,"* the phrase just preceding the *Faust* reference, as "value which can perform its own valorization process," which is awfully scientific and demeans the Goethe connection when compared with Prawer's "into value big with value," again, less "accurate," but much closer I think to Marx's idiom.

68. Prawer, *Marx and World Literature,* 292.

69. *Marx and Engels Through the Eyes of Their Contemporaries,* 24, 26. Prawer's commentary is on 399.

70. Prawer, *Marx and World Literature,* 374. Marx's verbal scalpel does not grow dull with time. Consider his evaluation of "French *vanité*": ". . . strutting along with new-fangled phrases, false profundity, Byzantine exaggeration, coquettish sentiment, garish irridescence, word-painting, theatricality, 'sublimity'—in short, a mishmash of lies which is unprecedented in form and in content"; in a letter, Marx to Engels, 30 November 1873, regarding a book on Chateaubriand; see Marx and Engels, *On Literature & Art,* 292; Prawer, *Marx and World Literature,* 375.

71. Prawer, *Marx and World Literature,* 356, 30.

72. Ibid., 161.

73. Cf. ibid., 217.

74. Marx and Engels, *Collected Works* 3: 301; Prawer, *Marx and World Literature,* 85.

75. Prawer, *Marx and World Literature,* 213. He admitted to Lassalle in 1858 the stylistic weakness of his work, but seven years later told Engels that "my works have the advantage

that they are an artistic whole, and this is attained only by my method of not having them printed before they are in front of me *in their entirety*"; Marx and Engels, *On Literature & Art*, 111.

76. Prawer, *Marx and World Literature*, 85.

77. Ibid., 76.

78. Indispensable studies include Ernst Cassirer, "Goethe and the Kantian Philosophy," in *Rousseau Kant Goethe* (Princeton, N.J.: Princeton University Press, 1947), 61–98; Walter Kaufmann, *From Shakespeare to Existentialism* (New York: Anchor, 1960), 35–94; Karl Löwith, *From Hegel to Nietzsche* (New York: Anchor, 1967), 2–28; Georg Lukács, *Goethe and His Age* (London: Merlin Press, 1968); Thomas Mann, *Essays* (New York: Vintage, 1957[?]), 3–179; Mann, "Goethe as Representative of the Bourgeois Age," in *Essays of Three Decades* (New York: Knopf, 1948); Mann, "Introduction" to *The Permanent Goethe* (New York: Dial Press, 1949); Friedrich Meinecke, *Historism* (London: Routledge & Kegan Paul, 1972), 373–495; Karl Viëtor, *Goethe the Thinker* (Cambridge, Mass.: Harvard University Press, 1950).

79. W. H. Bruford, *The German Tradition of Self-Cultivation: "Bildung" from Humboldt to Thomas Mann* (Cambridge: Cambridge University Press, 1975), 88ff., 246ff. This whole book relates to my themes, especially the chapter on Schleiermacher, 58–87, concerning his conception of "personality."

80. Karl Mannheim, "On the Interpretation of *Weltanschauung,*" in *Essays on the Sociology of Knowledge* (London: Routledge and Kegan Paul, 1952), 33–83, especially "Rationalism and Irrationalism" on 37–42.

81. Rudolf A. Makkreel, *Dilthey: Philosopher of the Human Studies* (Princeton, N.J.: Princeton University Press, 1975), 149.

82. Wilhelm Dilthey, *Das Erlebnis und die Dichtung*, 13th ed. (Stuttgart: B. G. Teubner, 1957 [1906]), 151.

83. Thomas Mann, "Introduction" to *The Permanent Goethe*, xl (my emphases).

84. Steven Marcus, "Introduction" to Sigmund Freud, *The Origins of Psychoanalysis* (New York: Basic Books, 1977), vi.

85. Max Weber, *Ancient Judaism*, 207.

86. Mann, *The Permanent Goethe*, xii (original emphases by Goethe).

87. Ibid., xiv.

88. Richard R. Niebuhr, *Schleiermacher on Christ and Religion* (New York: Scribner's, 1964), 109, 126.

89. Mann, *The Permanent Goethe*, xiv.

90. Max Horkheimer and Theodor W. Adorno, *The Dialectic of Enlightenment* (New York: Seabury, 1972).

91. Victor Lange, "Introduction" to Goethe, *Wilhelm Meister's Apprenticeship*, trans. Thomas Carlyle (New York: Collier Books, 1962), 10, 11.

92. H. A. Hodges, *The Philosophy of Wilhelm Dilthey* (London: Routledge & Kegan Paul, 1952), 4–5.

レ///

Douglas Kellner   **Critical Theory, Max Weber, and the Dialectics of Domination**

There are both interesting differences and little discussed similarities between Max Weber's theory of rationalization and domination and the theories of advanced industrial society developed by T. W. Adorno, Max Horkheimer, Herbert Marcuse, and other members of the Institute for Social Research.[1] During the 1930s the critical theory developed by Horkheimer and his colleagues was presented as an inter-disciplinary, neo-Marxian social theory. Critical theory was distinguished from traditional social theory by its combination of philosophy and the social sciences in a theory of contemporary society and history that was intended to be part of a practice of social transformation.[2] Although critical theory developed in its own way the Weberian themes of authority, rationalization, and domination, in the 1930s it was presented primarily as a Marxian theory and critique of capitalism and avoided direct dialogue with Weber. Moreover, although critical theory combined Marxian and Weberian themes from the 1930s to the present, it neither highlighted nor explicated Weberian elements of its theories, and did not engage in explicit reconstruction or critique of Weber's theory until Jürgen Habermas's recent work.

During the 1940s the critical theory developed by Adorno and Horkheimer, most notably in *Dialectic of Enlightenment,* turned away from the Marxian theory of history and society and developed a theory in which the Weberian themes of rationalization and domination became more prominent. In further developments of critical theory, such as Horkheimer's *Eclipse of Reason* and many of his later essays, as well as Marcuse's *Eros and Civilization* and *One-Dimensional Man,* theories of technological rationalization and domination stood at the center of their social theory. Like Weber, critical theory described the secularization of the world, the growth of bureaucracy and administration, technological rationality as a form of legitimation and domination, and threats to individual freedom in the triumphant industrial-technological society.

In this study, I trace the complex relationships between Weber and the critical theory developed by Adorno, Horkheimer, Marcuse, and Habermas from the 1930s to the present. In the first part, the similarities and differences between 1930s critical theory and Weber's theory of rationality and domination are analyzed. I indicate the turn toward Weber in 1940s and 1950s publications by Horkheimer and Adorno. Then I show how Marcuse's theories of advanced industrial society and domination are similar in many ways to Weber's theory and examine Marcuse's critique of Weber. Finally, Jürgen Habermas's systematic confrontation with Weber is discussed. The thrust is twofold: I attempt to demonstrate that the idiosyncratic version of Marxism in the central, pre-Habermasian works of critical theory has to do in part with the unacknowledged synthesis of Marx and Weber; and, secondly, I argue that although Habermas's recent work clarifies the Weberian tradition operative in critical theory from the beginning, his approach to Weber is significantly and revealingly different from that of his critical theory predecessors.

LUKÁCS, CRITICAL THEORY, AND THE DIALECTICS OF RATIONALIZATION

Since Georg Lukács introduced Weberian themes into Marxian theory and exerted a significant influence on critical theory, I begin with a brief discussion of how Lukács appropriated Weber's theory of rationalization for Marxism. Lukács was closely involved with Weber's circle in Heidelberg before World War I and knew Weber's work very well.[3] In his study of "Reification and the Consciousness of the Proletariat," Lukács uses Weber to illustrate the Marxian thesis that a socio-economic system creates social structures that fulfill the needs of the economy. This passage is worth quoting in full:

Thus capitalism has created a form for the state and a system of law corresponding to its needs and harmonising with its own structure. The structural similarity is so great that no truly perceptive historian of modern capitalism could fail to notice it. Max Weber, for instance, gives this description of the basic lines of this development: "Both are, rather, quite similar in their fundamental nature. Viewed sociologically, a 'business-concern' is the modern state; the same holds good for a factory: and this, precisely, is what is specific to it historically. And, likewise, the power relations in a business are also of the same kind. The relative independence of the artisan (or cottage craftsman), of the landowning peasant, the owner of a benefice, the knight and vassal was based on the fact that he himself owned the tools, supplies, financial resources or weapons with the aid of which he fulfilled his economic, political or military function and from which he lived while this duty was being discharged. Similarly, the hierarchic dependence of the worker, the clerk, the technical assistant, the assistant in an academic institute *and* the civil servant and soldier has a comparable basis: namely that the tools, supplies and financial resources essential both for the business-concern and for economic survival are in the hands, in the one case, of the entrepreneur and, in the other case, of the political master."[4]

This passage calls attention to certain structural similarities between classical Marxism and Weber's theory which would explain how committed Marxists, like Lukács, might be attracted to Weber's thought.

Since later, especially American, interpretations of Weber tend to sever or cover the connections with Marxism, it is useful to highlight the similarities between Marxism and Weber contained in the passages cited by Lukács. As noted, Weber, like Marx, shows structural similarities between the capitalist state and capitalist economic system. Secondly, both stress the crucial role of capitalist rationalization in eliminating previous socio-economic structures, forms of thought, and values—a point highlighted by Lukács in the following passage:

He [Weber] rounds off this account—very pertinently—with an analysis of the cause and the social implications of this phenomenon: "The modern capitalist concern is based inwardly above all on *calculation*. It requires for its survival a system of justice and an administration whose workings can be *rationally calculated*, at least in principle, according to fixed general laws, just as the probable performance of *a machine* can be calculated. It is as little able to tolerate the dispensing of justice according to the judge's sense of fair play *in individual cases* or any other irrational means or principle of administering the law . . . as it is able to endure a patriarchal administration that obeys the dictates of its own caprice, or sense of mercy and, for the rest, proceeds in accordance with an inviolable and sacrosanct, but irrational tradition. . . . What is specific to modern capitalism as distinct from the age-old capitalist forms of acquisition is that the strictly rational *organization of work* on the basis of *rational technology* did not come into being *anywhere* within such irrationally constituted political systems nor could it have done so. For these modern businesses with their fixed capital and their exact calculations are much too sensitive to legal and administrative irrationalities. They could only come into being in the bureaucratic state with its rational laws where . . . the judge is more or less an automatic statute—dispensing machine in which you insert the files together with the necessary costs and dues at the top, whereupon he will eject the judgment together with the more or less cogent reasons for it at the bottom: that is to say, where the judge's behavior is on the whole *predictable*."[5]

Here, Weber makes clear the importance of rationalization and calculation within the capitalist mode of production and stresses the homologies between the economic system and the system of law and politics—again, points similar to classical Marxism.

Building on a synthesis of Marx and Weber, Lukács develops a theory of rationalization, bureaucracy, and reification which emphasizes how these phenomena serve the interests of capital and how they produce a dehumanization of human beings, providing examples from the spheres of labor, bureaucracy, and sexuality.[6] Although Lukács appropriates Weber's theory of rationalization, he reconstructs Weber by developing a Marxian-inspired theory of *reification*. Using Marx's categories from *Capital,* Lukács argues that, within capitalist rationalization processes, "definite social relations between human beings" appear in the form of a "relation between things."[7] In addition, concrete social relations appear as a "second nature" in which social processes (subsumed by Weber under the term rationalization) have a nature-like quality beyond human control. Lukács argues that this reification is a consequence of the universalization of the commodity form in capitalist society wherein the human labor that produces commodities is devalued against their socially produced exchange values. Thus, for Lukács, reification denotes a failure to understand properly production and social processes as products of human labor which can be transformed to meet human needs.

Moreover, against Weber, Lukács stresses that the rationalization of social life subsystems can be contrasted with the "relative irrationality of the total process."[8] The lack of rationalization of the economy as a whole inevitably leads, Lukács claims, to social anarchy and crisis in a society "ruled by chance."[9] Lukács argues that in an unplanned, market economy competition between rationalized firms and economic subsectors would inevitably lead to economic crisis. For Lukács, rationalization is therefore a product of capitalist production processes which transform individuals into subjects of exploitation and administration, reduce them to abstract labor exchanged for a wage, replace qualitative aspects of people and their products with quantitative exchange values, and mystify capitalist exploitation through a veil of reification and fetishism.

Lukács interprets bureaucracy, law, and other forms of rationalization within this Marxian-Weberian framework. He criticizes both the tendency toward dehumanization within the process of capitalist production, anticipating the analysis of alienation in Marx's as yet unpublished *Economic and Philosophical Manuscripts of 1844,* and highlights the theme of the fundamental irrationality of the capitalist system as a whole, a central aspect of classical Marxism. Moreover, Lukács believes that the proletariat, with the help of Marxian theory and the party, can break the "shell of reification" and overturn capitalist rationalization in a revolutionary process that could create a new socialist society with workers' control and self-management of their own labor and social life.

Weber, of course, believed that socialism would tighten the "iron cage" of rationalization and bureaucracy and resigned himself to accepting the fate of Western industrialism as irreversible.[10] Critical theory, on the other hand, tended to share the Lukácsian perspective on capitalism, rationalization, and socialism during the 1930s, and critical theorists perceived themselves as Marxists and not Weberians. For the most part, early critical theorists perceived the triumph of fascism as a manifestation of deeply irrational tendencies within capitalism and European culture and might have believed that Weber exaggerated tendencies toward rationalization in industrial society and downplayed irrational factors. However, the main reason why they tended to neglect Weber during the 1930s was that he was perceived as *the* prototypically bourgeois thinker, a nationalist-chauvinist apologist for imperialism, an enemy of socialism, and an advocate of a model of social science which they militantly opposed.[11] Moreover, the Institute for Social Research also developed divergent theories of authority and fascism that drew more on traditional Marxian theory, contributing their own unique theories of fascism that did not really draw on Weber's theory of rationalization and authority.[12]

Fundamental divergences from Weber's theory of authority are evident in the Institute's 1930s studies of authority. Whereas Weber suggests that the "disenchantment of the world" and growing rationalization and rational-legal authority are fundamental tendencies of industrial development, the Institute argues that capitalism in its monopolistic and fascist stages actually decreased the rationality of political authority.[13] They believe that the formal-legal rationality, which Weber described, corresponds to social conditions of the liberal phase of bourgeois society and the establishment of a constitutional state *(Rechtstaat)*. In the development of monopoly capitalism, however, the earlier liberal political and legal institutions were replaced by more totalitarian ones, and political authority, in the opinion of the Institute, became increasing irrational. Fascism represents the culmination of this process in which irrational authority was institutionalized and permeated the society as a whole—the triumph of unreason as opposed to Weber's theory of growing rationalization and disenchantment as the major tendency of industrial development. Thus, rather than a "disenchantment of the world," the Institute perceives a *remystification of the world* through the spread of irrationalistic ideologies and the proliferation of fascist and other irrational forms of authority.

Examination of the Institute's theory of authority in *Autorität und Familie* reveals that the socio-psychological components of their approach are much more Freudian than Weberian. This is, in part, due to the influence of Erich Fromm, who was in the process of developing one of the first syntheses of Marx and Freud in the production of a Freudian-Marxist social psychology. In his contribution to the *Studien* Fromm argues that Freud's theory of mass psychology and the superego was the best starting point for a socio-psychological analysis of authority. He thinks that submission to irrational authority is due to both a weakened ego and fascist manipulation of sado-masochistic components of sexuality.[14] Continuing his development of a theory of social character, Fromm argues that the sado-masochistic character is the core of the authoritarian personality. Authoritarian societies, he argues, based on hierarchy and dependence, encouraged these trends and constituted a mass base for authoritarian domination.

Horkheimer and his colleagues generally accepted Fromm's perspective and the need for Freudian categories to develop an adequate theory of authority. Weber's theory of authority, on the other hand, lacked such a psychological grounding. Moreover, against Weber, critical theory began developing a theory of *critical reason,* which was sharply opposed to Weber's distinction between formal and substantial reason. Directly reversing Weber's characterization and evaluation, Horkheimer, Marcuse, and their colleagues distinguished between instrumental reason, which they described as subjective, analytical, and technical and contrasted to a more objective and substantive critical reason.[15] For Weber, however, formal reason is objective whereas substantive reason is subjective due to conflict between a diversity of individual and group ends in substantive arrangements of means and ends. The critical theory distinction, by contrast, was based on the Hegelian distinction between *Verstand* (analytical understanding) and *Vernunft* (substantive reason) where *Vernunft* (described by Hegel and critical theory as objective or critical reason) referred to rational cognition which could gain access to universal concepts, values, potentialities, and critical standards that could criticize the partiality and one-sidedness of ordinary thought and instrumental rationality.

Consequently, critical theory's reliance on Hegelian elements constitutes a fundamental difference from Weber's theory which tends to distance itself completely from idealist philosophy and to rely instead on what Weber considered properly scientific conceptions. Weber thought that substantive ends and values could be validated only subjectively and that substantive reason could never attain "historical objectivity." For Weber, only the partial reason of the measurable and calculable world of instrumental reason was "objective," and this was a modest empirical, intersubjective objectivity. Critical theory, by contrast, carried out a critique of instrumental reason and utilized a concept of substantive and critical reason to carry out social critique, to advocate socio-political transformation, and to project social alternatives.

Indeed, the critique of instrumental reason became a central aspect of Adorno's, Horkheimer's, Marcuse's, and Habermas's thought, developed in different contexts from the late 1930s to the present. These concepts were also used later to work out critiques of Weber's methodology, but I was not able to find any explicit critique of Weber's theory of science in their 1930s work. Thus, during the 1930s their *differences* from Weber's theory of rationalization and authority are most striking. In this phase critical theory generally followed Lukács's move of appropriating Weber's theory of rationalization into the Marxian theory and followed Fromm's attempt to develop a Freudian-Marxian social psychology. No systematic discussion or critiques of Weber are evident in 1930s Institute work, although there are occasional positive references to Weber's studies of religion and even to his methodological analyses.[16] During the 1940s, however, Weber's theories of rationalization and domination became even more central to critical theory, although there is still no systematic discussion of Weber's work or acknowledgment that his theory might have crucially influenced them.

MAX WEBER, TECHNOLOGICAL RATIONALITY, AND THE DIALECTIC OF ENLIGHTENMENT

The turn in critical theory toward more explicitly Weberian perspectives was first evident in Herbert Marcuse's 1941 article, "Some Social Implications of Modern Technology."[17] Marcuse argues that technological rationality is permeating contemporary industrial societies and creating new forms of social control. He claims that technological rationality is replacing autonomous, individual reason and served to adapt individuals to social domination rather than setting them critically against their society. He situates the decline of individual rationality in economic processes:

In the sphere of free competition, the tangible achievements of the individual, which made his products and performances a part of society's need, were the marks of his individuality. In the course of time, however, the process of commodity production undermined the economic basis on which individualistic rationality was built. Mechanization and rationalization forced the weaker competitor under the dominion of the giant enterprises of machine industry which, in establishing society's domination over nature, abolished the free economic subject.[18]

Individuals are forced to submit, Marcuse claims, to the *apparatus* of production and distribution and become controlled by mechanized, rationalized production and social processes.[19]

Under the impact of this apparatus, individualistic rationality has been transformed into technological rationality. It is by no means confined to the subjects and objects of large scale enterprises but characterizes the pervasive mode of thought. . . . This rationality establishes standards of judgment and fosters attitudes which make men ready to accept and even to introject the dictates of the apparatus.

Efficiency, adjustment, and matter of factness which adapt to the socio-technical apparatus and established facts, values, and behavior promoted by the expansion of technological rationality are the central factors of the emerging advanced industrial society. Marcuse concludes that in this society:

Business, technics, human needs and nature are welded together into one rational and expedient mechanism. He will fare best who follows its directions, subordinating his spontaneity to the anonymous wisdom which ordered everything for him. The decisive point is that this attitude—which dissolves all actions into a sequence of semi-spontaneous reactions to prescribed mechanical norms—is not only perfectly rational but also perfectly reasonable. All protest is senseless, and the individual who would insist on his freedom of action would become a crank. There is no personal escape from the apparatus which has mechanized and standardized the world. It is a rational apparatus, combining utmost expediency with utmost convenience, saving time and energy, removing waste, adapting all means to the end, anticipating consequences, sustaining calculability and security.[20]

Marcuse, like Weber, situates technology and technological rationality in its capitalistic context and indicates how the technological apparatus serves the purposes of capitalist profitability and social control. His theory contains a synthesis of Marx and Weber and also draws on American theorists of technology and industry such as Lewis Mumford, Thorstein Veblen, Thurman Arnold, F. W. Taylor, Henry Wallace, James Burnham, and various United States government studies.[21] I suggest that living in the United States during the period of the transition to state monopoly capitalism with the development of industrial monopoly, state planning in the New Deal, the rationalization of culture in the culture industries, rapid development of technology and mechanization, and establishment of new forms of social control and administration led the Institute theorists to conceptualize the fundamental role of technological rationality in socio-economic, political, and cultural processes and thus drew the Institute closer to Weber's theory of rationalization.

Marcuse, and to some extent other Institute colleagues, also began perceiving the rationalization processes operative in national socialism. This model is more in line with Weber's analyses of the combined rational and irrational social factors in the constitution of various societies, whereas the earlier Institute analysis of fascism tended to stress the irrationalist tendencies of fascism, rather than the unique mixture of rationality and irrationality in fascist societies. Marcuse, for example, stresses the combination of technological rationality and totalitarian oppression in the 1941 essay we are examining: "National Socialism is a striking example of the ways in which a highly rationalized and mechanized economy with the utmost efficiency in production can operate in the interest of totalitarian oppression and continued scarcity. The Third Reich is indeed a form of 'technocracy': the technical considerations of imperialistic efficiency and rationality supersede the traditional standards of profitability and general welfare.''[22]

This passage reveals a Weberian influence, but in other passages Marcuse, against some of his Institute colleagues, stresses the continuity between fascism and capitalism in an attempt to undercut the debate between Institute members who analyzed fascism as a form of state capitalism (Franz Neumann) and those who stressed the discontinuity between capitalist and fascism and therefore analyzed fascism as a new form of technocracy where political and technical factors supersede the primacy of economic factors in capitalist societies (Friedrich Pollock).[23] Avoiding these polar tendencies, Marcuse, like Weber and classical Marxism, attempts to conceptualize the reciprocal interaction of economic, political, and technical features in the constitution of contemporary industrial societies—a concept that also characterizes his later work. Thus, Marcuse's 1941 essay depicts significant similarities to Weber, although he did not, and never would, clearly signal his reconstruction of Weber and synthesis of Weber and Marx.

In *Dialectic of Enlightenment* (1947), Adorno and Horkheimer move more decisively away from classical Marxism and toward a Weberian theory of society and philosophy of history.[24] This book traces the rise of technological rationality which becomes the motor of historical development and the primary determinant of the loss of individuality and freedom in Western societies. Developing Weberian ideas in original ways, the central thesis of *Dialectic of Enlightenment* is that increasing rationalization had produced social domination on a massive scale. Unlike Lukács, who had analyzed partial social rationality and the irrationality of the whole, Adorno and Horkheimer claim that rationalization permeated Western societies (''Enlightenment is totalitarian'') and yet infused irrationality throughout the totality. Thus, like Walter Benjamin, Adorno and Horkheimer attempted to demolish the myth of history as progress.[25]

Unlike Marcuse's 1941 essay, *Dialectic of Enlightenment,* with the possible exception of the chapter on the culture industries, does not really deal with contemporary tendencies of domination and rationalization within industry or social relations; rather it focuses on the role of instrumental reason or technological rationality in the domination of nature which is then applied to domination of human beings. Instrumental reason and the domination of nature are seen as functions of both capitalist and precapitalist societies; thus, Adorno and Horkheimer's philosophical history loses the historical specificity present in both Weber's work and in Marcuse's 1941 essay. Adorno and Horkheimer's general thesis is that the domination of nature is eventually extended to the domination of human beings, both internally through reason coming to repress individual passions and desires and socially through the application of technological rationality to socio-economic, political, and cultural domains.

While Weber, and later Habermas, appraises cultural rationalization and the rationalization of various spheres of society (law, education, bureaucracy, etc.) as at least partially progressive phenomena, for Adorno and Horkheimer the extension of rationalization leads to cultural decline, the diminution of freedom and individuality, and increased societal domination. Despite the similarities to Weber's theory, Weber himself is only mentioned once in *Dialectic of Enlightenment;* instead, Hegel, Nietzsche, and Freud (but not Marx) are frequently cited.

However, in Horkheimer's *Eclipse of Reason* (1947), which presents many of the theses of *Dialectic of Enlightenment* to an American audience, there are several references to Weber. In this text Horkheimer begins more explicit criticisms of Weber's analysis of reason and social science methodology—features that characterize later Institute work. The move toward more explicit dialogue with and critique of Weber is probably due to the fact that Weber's ideas were becoming increasingly widespread in United States social science. Thus, critical theory was finally forced to confront explicitly Weber's positions; this confrontation continued in the early 1950s in Germany, where Weber's ideas were also extremely influential. Consequently, a more explicit use and criticism of Weber began in Horkheimer's *Eclipse of Reason.*

Horkheimer distinguishes between the doctrine of instrumental reason, which he describes as a subjective faculty and an instrument of adjusting means to ends, and what he calls "objective reason," which he characterizes as critical, substantive, and able to discern values, ends, and critical standards. Horkheimer argues that instrumental reason has become increasingly formalized and functions to adjust thought and behavior (i.e., means) to achieve pregiven ends. At this point, Horkheimer distinguishes his theory of reason from Weber's theory:

The difference between this connotation of reason and the objectivistic conception resembles to a certain degree the difference between functional and substantial rationality as these words are used in the Max Weber school. Max Weber, however, adhered so definitely to the subjectivistic trend that he did not conceive of any rationality—not even a "substantial" one by which man can discriminate one end from another. If our drives, intentions, and finally our ultimate decisions must *a priori* be irrational, substantial reason becomes an agency merely of correlation and is therefore itself essentially "functional." Although Weber's own and his followers' descriptions of the bureaucratization and monopolization of knowledge have illuminated much of the social aspect of the transition from objective to subjective reason . . . , Max Weber's pessimism with regard to the possibility of rational insight and action, as expressed in his philosophy . . . is itself a stepping-stone in the renunciation of philosophy and science as regards their aspiration of defining man's goal.[26]

Horkheimer characterizes accurately a fundamental and enduring difference between Weber and critical theory. Weber explicitly rejects objective reason in the sphere of value and believes that ultimately no philosophical insight or argumentation determines the rationality of values or ends important for life; for Weber, the sphere of value and activity of valuation reflects individual decisions mediated by culture. In contrast, the critical theorists, especially Marcuse, Fromm, and Habermas, attempt to elucidate and defend objective values and standards through which contemporary societies can be criticized and social transformation can be advocated and defended. Against Weber's decisionism, Horkheimer and his colleagues think that the task of philosophy is precisely to ascertain values and standards through which society can be criticized and transformed. Weber, of course, does not believe that philosophy can legitimately arbitrate value-decisions or that it can answer Tolstoy's questions: what kind of life should we lead and what should we do with our lives?[27]

In *Eclipse of Reason,* Horkheimer explicitly criticizes the Weberian separation of science and humanities, Weber's separation between fact and values, and his concept of a "value-free science," calling Weber a "positivist at heart."[28] Here, Horkheimer anticipates later Frankfurt school critiques of Weber and positivism. Yet despite the first explicit critical distancing from Weber's methodology and theory of reason within critical theory, the *themes* in Horkheimer's book are quite Weberian: the separation of means and ends, bureaucracy, industrial culture, the fundamental role of instrumental rationality within industrial societies, and the decline of the individual. Against Weber, however, Horkheimer argues sharply for the continuing importance of philosophy within social theory and social life.

Thus, *Dialectic of Enlightenment* and *Eclipse of Reason* stand in a complex relation to Weber with marked similarities in the basic themes of their social theory and with striking methodological differences in their understanding of critical social theory—differences that would be articulated in succeeding Institute work after the return of the critical theorists to Germany in 1949. Let us now examine the more explicit confrontation between Weber and critical theory in the 1950s and 1960s, focusing on Marcuse's work.

Critical Theory, Weber, and Dialectics 99

CAPITALISM, DOMINATION, AND POSITIVISM

During the 1950s, the categories of the *administered world* and *domination* became central categories of critical theory moving it toward a closer substantive affinity to Weber's social theory. However, after their return to Germany, the critical theorists distanced themselves from Weber's theory, especially his methodology and concept of social science. Although the Institute itself introduced many American techniques of social science into the German context, the members became disturbed by the growing tendencies toward uncritical empiricism that were beginning to dominate both American and German social theory. Since Weber's portrayal of a split between fact and value, his concept of objective social science, and his theory of ideal types were part of the legitimating ideology of much empiricist social science, the Institute undertook ever more frequent and detailed methodological critiques of Weberian theory.[29]

In particular, the Institute claimed that Weber's concept of value-free science and his distinction between fact and value are the philosophical basis for contemporary positivism and the critical rationalism of Karl Popper and his followers.[30] But only Habermas really carried out systematic study of Weber's methodology and his substantive social theory.[31] Moreover, Adorno and Horkheimer's critical remarks towards Weber's methodology usually conceded that Weber's social science was much more complex, more substantive, and more directed toward the real problems of contemporary social theory than the works of Weber's followers.[32]

Furthermore, Weber's theories of rationalization and domination continued to play a central role within critical theory. In Marcuse's major works of the period, *Eros and Civilization* and *One-Dimensional Man,* his central theory of rationalization and domination is quite similar to Weber's social theory; yet he still did not positively acknowledge Weber in his major works of the era, although Marcuse eventually developed a critique of Weber's social theory.[33] In *Eros and Civilization* he argues against Freud's thesis that instinctual repression is socially necessary because the fact of scarcity requires hard work and discipline. Marcuse claims that social repression is a consequence of a

> . . . specific organization of scarcity, and of a specific existential attitude enforced by this organization. . . . [T]he *distribution* of scarcity as well as the effort of overcoming it, the mode of work, have been *imposed* upon individuals—first by mere violence, subsequently by a more rational utilization of power. However, no matter how useful this rationality was for the progress of the whole, it remained the rationality of *domination,* and the gradual conquest of scarcity was inextricably bound up with and shaped by the interest of domination.

Despite progress in growing rationalization of the "distribution of scarcity," "progress" is controlled, Marcuse argues, by social groups striving to expand their economic power, thus producing "progress in domination."[34]

In *Eros and Civilization* domination emerges as the central category in Marcuse's post-1950 critical theory of contemporary society. His use of the term combines Max Weber's theory of rationalization with Marx's critique of capitalism, Lukács's theory of reification, and a Freudian-Marxist notion of repression.[35] In "Freedom and Freud's Theory of the Instincts," Marcuse claims that "domination is in effect whenever the individual's goals and purposes and the means of striving for and attaining them are prescribed to him and performed by him as something prescribed. Domination can be exercised by men, by nature, by things—it can also be internal, exercised by the individual on himself."[36] Domination is thus a process by which society controls and even shapes individual thought and behavior. Domination takes place both externally through force and institutional constraints and internally through the introjection of prohibitions, values, and restraints under which individuals discipline themselves and act out internalized social roles and behavior.

Domination has its origins in Marcuse's analysis of the organization of labor and technology in advanced industrial societies. He argues that machine-like regularities and motions in the labor process habituate individuals to submit to social authority. In this way domination takes the form of internalizing technical imperatives and mechanical behavior. Domination also occurs within the *administration* of social life through advertising, the mass media and entertainment industries, increased management and fragmentation of the labor process, socio-political control mechanisms, and new techniques of surveillance and social control. The category of domination describes a multitude of new, improved modes of social control distinguished by "voluntary servitude" and "happy submission," in which the individuals themselves follow prescribed patterns of thought and behavior. Domination thus constitutes the very "second nature" of human beings who assimilate prescribed thought, values, and forms of behavior in which they desire, feel, and think what the social powers and institutions require.

Like domination in Weber's theory, Marcuse's analysis provides a bridge between psychological and social dimensions of authority and power. He argues that the specific forms of domination in advanced industrial societies constitute "surplus repression." This repression, over and above what is rationally needed to provide for social and individual needs, operates through the "performance principle": "under its rule society is stratified according to the competitive economic performances of its members.'' The performance principle ''is that of an acquisitive and antagonistic society''; it involves compulsions toward conformity within a system of stratified roles in which one performs according to pre-established norms and rules.[37] Again, the similarities to Weber's theory are obvious, though Marcuse does not cite Weber in his text.

On the other hand, *Eros and Civilization* also clarifies the fundamental differences between Marcuse's thought and Weber's. Marcuse's reliance on Freud distances him from Weber, as does his utopian emphases on emancipation and development of a nonrepressive civilization. However, despite these striking differences, Marcuse's characterizations of advanced industrial societies, both capitalist and communist, continue to make use of Weber's theories without ever adequately citing the Weberian dimension.

In *Soviet Marxism* Marcuse describes forms of rationalization and domination in Soviet communist societies, and in *One-Dimensional Man* he creates a model of ''advanced industrial society'' and sketches growing trends toward rationalization and domination throughout capitalist, communist, and third world societies, moving closer once again to Weber's social theory and theory of history.[38] Whereas Marcuse's analyses of advanced industrial societies might seem to be similar to so-called post-industrial society theories or convergence theories which posit a growing similarity between capitalist and communist societies, he explicitly criticizes these theories, both of which were influenced by Weber.[39] Although there are certainly similarities, Marcuse differs from post-industrial society theorists by stressing the negative aspects of the rationalization process and technological development and by emphasizing the loss of individual freedom and the new forms of social control. In the face of the convergence of technology and domination Marcuse calls for a ''new technology'' and a break with previous forms of technology, social organization, and forms of domination.[40] Moreover, he stresses differences between capitalist and communist societies and throughout his writings argues that economic imperatives help constitute and shape technology.

Marcuse's clearest statement of the relationship between capitalism and technology and most forceful articulation of his differences with Weber are found in his 1964 essay, ''Industrialization and Capitalism in the Work of Max Weber.''[41] Here, Marcuse specifies the distinguishing features of the capitalist economic system that intervene in the construction of technology and in the process of rationalization. Following Weber, Marcuse argues that during the development of industrial capitalism, ''formal rationality turns into *capitalist* rationality: and appears as both the taming of the irrational ''acquisitive drive'' and the subordination of reason to a "systematic, methodical calculation, 'capital accounting.'" Capitalist reason "becomes concrete in the calculable and calculated *domination* of nature and man." Thus, capitalist reason functions as technical reason, "as the production and transformation of material (things and men) through the methodical-scientific apparatus. . . . Its rationality organizes and controls things and men, factory and bureaucracy, work and leisure." But, Marcuse asks: "*to what purpose* does it control them?" What is the driving force of this apparatus? To what ends is this "calculable efficiency" directed?[42]

Marcuse argues that capitalist rationality is conditioned and controlled by two material conditions, two unique historical facts: the provision of human needs and calculable efficiency takes place within the *private enterprise* system and is geared toward the *profit* of the individual entrepreneur or enterprise; and the means of production are private property, and the laborers must sell their wage labor to the owner of the means of production and thus must submit to servitude and domination. Marcuse next uses this Marxian analysis to critique Weber: "According to Weber, the focal reality of capitalist rationality is the *private* enterprise; the entrepreneur is a free person, responsible by and to himself for his calculations and their risks. In this function, he is *bourgeois,* and the bourgeois conduct of life finds its representative expression in innerworldly asceticism." Marcuse asks if his conception is still valid today and argues that

in the development of capitalistic rationality itself, the forms ascribed to it by Weber have disintegrated and become obsolete, and their disintegration makes the rationality of capitalistic industrialization appear in a very different light: in the light of its *ir*rationality. To mention only one aspect: "inner-worldly asceticism" is no longer a motivating force in late capitalism; it has become a fetter that serves the maintenance of the system. Keynes denounced it as such, and it is a danger to the "affluent society" whenever it could hinder the production and consumption of superfluous goods.[43]

In this presentation Marcuse creates an "ideal type Weber" which distorts Weber's thought and provides something of a straw man for Marcuse to dismiss. Weber actually stresses that Protestant asceticism no longer guides capitalist action, arguing that in the United States where capitalism was strongest, capitalist acquisition had "the character of sport."[44] Indeed, in the last pages of *The Protestant Ethic and the Spirit of Capitalism,* Weber states quite clearly that the Protestant ethic is obsolete and that capitalism is now a machine that determines our lives—precisely Marcuse's point, which he illicitly makes against Weber. Like Marcuse, Weber implies that the Protestant ethic served primitive accumulation in the early mercantile phase of capitalism but later declined in importance.[45]

Thus, Marcuse tends to ignore or to obscure similarities between his theory and Weber's regarding their characterizations of the historical trajectory of capitalism.

Although Weber, like Marcuse, was aware of tendencies toward growing irrationality in capitalist societies, Marcuse and Weber have rather different analyses of tendencies toward irrationality and different normative criteria to evaluate social processes. Marcuse, for example, criticizes "planned obsolescence," which he describes as "methodical irrationality," the production of waste, unnecessary labor for unnecessary gadgets, and the ultimate irrationality of an economy based on the production of the weapons of destruction; he concludes: "In the unfolding of capitalist rationality, *irrationality* becomes *reason:* reason as frantic development of productivity, conquest of nature, enlargement of the mass of goods . . . ; irrational because higher productivity, domination of nature, and social wealth become destructive forces. . . . [T]he struggle for existence intensifies both within national states and internationally, and pent-up aggression is discharged in the legitimation of medieval cruelty (torture) and in the scientifically organized destruction of men."[46] For Weber these tendencies might be characterized as "substantively irrational," but they are still rational instrumentally because they serve the exactly calculated pursuit of profit. Against Weber, Marcuse argues that precisely such a social order geared primarily toward profit is irrational because it contradicts human and social ends.[47] Moreover, the critique reveals Marcuse's socially critical vantage point as opposed to Weber's descriptive viewpoint: whereas increased defense spending, advertising, and so forth, may appear as irrational from the perspective of the socially critical individual, from the perspective of other social forces they are instrumentally rational.

Marcuse assumes that a critical individual can provide a standpoint from which to judge social rationality and irrationality. In his view, Weber's theory leads to the surrender of efforts at social critique and reconstruction. For example, Marcuse argues that Weber's "value-free concept of capitalist rationality" loses its force as a descriptive and critical concept by becoming apologetic as capitalism moves into ever more irrational phases. He also claims that Weber's "value-free" concept of rationality served from the beginning to legitimate political forces which used rationality claims to justify their policies and interests (i.e., imperialism, power politics, authoritarian rule, etc.). Finally, Marcuse attacks Weber for his "denunciation of the possible alternative, that is, of a qualitatively different historical rationality."[48] Here, Marcuse's fundamental difference from Weber comes to the fore. Not only was Marcuse a socialist who believed that socialism is at least potentially a more rational form of social organization than capitalism, but he was long committed to a new concept of reason, new science, new technology, and a qualitatively different form of social rationality.[49] In short, whereas Weber resigned himself to the historical necessity of capitalist rationalization, Marcuse called for, and hoped for, a break in this historical continuum and the construction of a nonrepressive society.

Thus Marcuse's crucial difference from Weber is articulated in his vision of liberation that does not ultimately capitulate to "tragic pessimism" or "resignation" concerning the inevitability of domination through the rationalization process. Interestingly, the commentators on Marcuse's 1964 Weber lecture focused their critiques on his alleged utopianism and refusal to accept historical necessity. Marcuse answers his critics arguing:

If we look at present-day intellectual and material wealth, if we look at ourselves, what we know and can do, there is actually nothing which rationally and with a good conscience we should despise and denounce as Utopian. We could actually do anything today. We could certainly have a rational society, and just *because* that is such a near possibility its actual realization is more "Utopian" than ever before; the whole force of the *status quo* is mobilized against it.[50]

Referring to his supposed "tragic reluctance to acknowledge the inevitable features of the social cultural realities of our time," Marcuse responds: "It is the reasonable willingness, not to see facts as inevitable, but to draw the conclusions of one's own capabilities. If we have gone so far as to call it 'tragic reluctance,' if one does not recognize this 'inevitability,' all thought has become meaningless; for thought which decides beforehand that facts are inevitable is not really thought at all."[51]

Marcuse rejects notions of historical inevitability, fate, necessity, and resignation, and represents a type of critical social theory that refuses to submit to existing realities and measures "social facts" and judges present realities according to their higher potentialities. Thus, from this perspective Weber presents a useful analysis of tendencies toward domination within capitalist rationality but fails both to provide an adequate critique of its irrational features and to see any higher form of social rationality, for example, in socialism. In opposition to Weber and positivism, Marcuse argues that critical social theory should posit alternatives, based on potentialities within existing society, which can be used to criticize current forms of social organization. The utopian impulse is a central aspect of Marcuse's critical theory which distinguishes him from his one-time Institute colleagues, especially Adorno and Horkheimer, who, like Weber, became increasingly resigned and pessimistic in their later years.[52]

Although there are clearly fundamental differences between Weber and Marcuse, there are also similarities which Marcuse failed to acknowledge. I attempt to show that the Weberian themes of rationalization and domination are present in various forms and degrees throughout critical theory. Moreover, I suggest that both Weberian and critical theory stress the peculiar combination of capitalist rationality and irrationality as constituents of stages in contemporary capitalist and socialist development. However, for the most part, the classical critical theorists did not utilize Weber's theory of rationality and domination either to analyze forms of *political domination* and bureaucracy or to criticize types of state socialism or capitalist states; this calls attention to a deficit of explicitly political analysis in the works of Adorno, Horkheimer, Marcuse, and their followers.

These critical theorists fail to emphasize that Max Weber located the relations of domination in advanced capitalism in the *political* relations of the state and bureaucracy and, as such, can best be used by contemporary Marxists and critical theorists both to develop theories of the state and bureaucracy and to work out critiques of state socialism—topics relatively underdeveloped in most forms of classical Marxism.[53] In fact, most critical theorists fail to note, as Jean Cohen points out, that: "For Weber, rationalization, as the extension of formal rationality, is not simply a unilinear, monolithic process immanently unfolding in all areas of modern life. Instead, as formal rationality advances, it evokes counter forces all along the way."[54] In Weber's theory, formal rationality meets resistance in its encounter with substantive rationality (i.e., various ends and goals imposed on it), traditional institutions and social practices, and human beings. Moreover, as Lukács argued, various rationalized sectors often come into conflict with each other, creating an unstable, crisis-prone capitalist society that is capable of being modified. Conflicts within the society provide the space for intervention and social change, points not adequately analyzed by many critical theorists.[55]

Most importantly, in retrospect, the peculiar version of Marxism in critical theory concerns partially a one-sided and problematic appropriation of Weber's theory of rationalization and domination. Marcuse and other critical theorists adopted Weber's analysis of the fundamental constitutive role in contemporary industrial societies of a progressively advancing technological rationality, or instrumental reason, which increasingly dominates more and more spheres of "the totally administered society" or "one-dimensional society." Unlike some Weberians, they stressed the economic constituents of advanced capitalist rationalization-domination processes and believed, as Marxists, that the social relations of production could be modified to create more democratic and rational societies with increased individual freedom and happiness. Nevertheless, their model of advanced industrial society was rather monolithic, constituted by a unitary and complementary synthesis of capital, technology, and political and cutural domination. Marcuse adopted Weberian themes in this way, especially in the 1950s and early to mid 1960s, but he failed to note that even Weber's model differentiated between spheres of rationalization and posited conflicts between various spheres and counterforces which resisted total domination. Against Marcuse, Habermas adopted a more differentiated Weberian model of rationalization and created promising new perspectives for critical theory.

HABERMAS, WEBER, AND CRITICAL THEORY

Weber's influence thus emerges from this discussion as a significant aspect of critical theory that has not been adequately appreciated or analyzed until Jürgen Habermas's recent work. Before Habermas critical theorists neither clarified the Weberian elements in their work, nor did they satisfactorily differentiate from Weber either their social theory methodology or their theory of contemporary society. During these pre-Habermasian stages of critical theory, no critical theorist really carried out a systematic and adequate critique of Weber.

Habermas began explicit dialogue with Weber's work in the early 1960s. At the 1964 Heidelberg conference where Marcuse presented his critique of Weber, Habermas discussed Weber's methodology and questioned whether Talcott Parsons, Hans Albert, and other contemporary Weberians were misinterpreting Weber's theories of understanding, value-freedom, and *Wertbeziehung*.[56] Habermas also participated in the so-called "positivism dispute in German sociology" in the 1960s and made some critical remarks on Weber's methodology, though he focused his critique more on Popper and Albert than Weber himself.[57] In his 1970 article, "Technology and Science as 'Ideology,'" Habermas took up the Weberian theme of the connections between rationality and domination, especially as they were developed by Marcuse.[58] By situating Marcuse's thought in relation to Weber, he calls attention to, for the first time, the Weberian components in critical theory. In particular, Habermas emphasizes Marcuse's critique of the supposed value-freedom of technology and his argument that substantive interests and values, which can neither be seen as politically neutral nor as objective criteria for social rationality, go into the construction of science and technology in different historical epochs. Habermas also uses this discussion and Weber's analysis of technological rationality as the starting point for his own distinction between labor and interaction; he implies that Weber provides a satisfactory analysis of instrumental rationality but that the theory cannot be applied legitimately to spheres of social interaction, politics, and the life-world.[59]

In his 1973 text, *Legitimation Crisis,* Habermas develops Weber's theories of legitimation and rationalization in original ways that enable him both to reconstruct Marxian theories of crisis and to reformulate the critical theory of society, developed by Adorno, Horkheimer, and Marcuse.[60] Against their theories of "one-dimensional society" or the "totally administered society" Habermas shows how contemporary social tendencies produce motivation, rationality, and legitimation crises. Weber's categories provide Habermas the tools with which he can both redirect critical theory to more empirical social analysis and redevelop theories of social crisis and change, heretofore ignored by the work of his more monolithic critical theory predecessors. His reconstruction of Weber's theory of legitimation into a theory of crisis enables him to overcome both the philosophical pessimism of his teachers Adorno and Horkheimer and the "tragic resignation" of Weber.

Not until his work *Theory of Communicative Action* does Habermas, or any critical theorist, undertake a systematic examination of Weber's theory of rationalization. Indeed, in this work Habermas comprehensively analyzes and criticizes Weber's theory.[61] He begins his historical and systematic analysis of contemporary social theory with discussion of Weber's theory of rationalization, which he considers the starting point for contemporary social theory and for his own "fundamental problem, namely the question of whether, and if so how, capitalist modernization can be conceived as a process of rationalization."[62] Habermas initially states:

Among the classical figures of sociology, Max Weber is the only one who broke with both the premises of philosophy of history and the basic assumptions of evolutionism, and nonetheless wanted to conceive the modernization of old-European society as the result of a universal-historical process of rationalization. He opened rationalization processes to an encompassing empirical investigation, without reinterpreting them in an empiricist manner such that precisely the rationality aspects of societal learning processes would disappear.[63]

For Habermas, Weber provides the first modernization theory of traditional society, as a result of extending to all spheres of life the processes of rationalization, which had originated in the capitalist labor process. Habermas makes clear the debt of Lukács and critical theory to Weber's analysis and suggests reading Weber within the context of Marxism and Western Marxism within the context of Weber. Habermas writes:

According to Marx, the rationalization of society takes place directly in the development of productive forces, that is, in the expansion of empirical knowledge, the improvement of production techniques, and the increasingly effective mobilization, qualification, and organization of socially useful labor power. On the other hand, productive relations, the institutions that express the distribution of social power and regulate a differential access to the means of production, are revolutionized only under the pressure of rationalization of productive forces. Max Weber views the institutional framework of the capitalist economy and the modern state in a different way—not as relations of production which fetter the potential for rationalization, but as subsystems of purposive-rational action in which Occidental rationalism develops at a societal level. Of course he is afraid that bureaucratization will lead to a reification of social relationships, which will stifle motivational incentives to a rational conduct of life. Horkheimer and Adorno, and later Marcuse, interpret Marx in this Weberian perspective. Under the sign of an instrumental rationality that has become autonomous, the rationality of mastering nature merges with the irrationality of class domination. Fettered forces of production stabilize alienated relations of production. The *Dialectic of Enlightenment* removes the ambivalence that Weber still entertained in relation to rationalization processes, and it abruptly reverses Marx's positive assessment. Science and technology, for Marx an unambiguously emancipatory potential, themselves become the medium of social repression.[64]

Thus, Habermas claims that Marx, Weber, and critical theorists like Adorno, Horkheimer, and Marcuse identify social rationalization with the expansion of instrumental rationality and share a vague but different notion of a more comprehensive social rationality: Marx in "the concept of the association of free producers," Weber in the historical model of an "ethically rational conduct of life," and Adorno and Horkheimer in the idea of "fraternal relations with a resurrected nature."[65] Against this more comprehensive concept of rationality, each measures the accomplishments of technological rationality. Habermas believes that none of these more comprehensive concepts of reason is fully developed, and he criticizes Weber for not explicitly developing a more comprehensive theory of social rationality to adequately explicate and criticize rationalization processes within the human life-world.

The key point in Habermas's critique is his claim that Weber conceives of the function, scope, and goal of reason too narrowly and fails to distinguish between instrumental reason and communicative rationality. Moreover, Habermas argues that Marx, Lukács, Adorno, Horkheimer, and Marcuse also fail to develop more comprehensive theories of social rationality; they operate within the confines of the "philosophy of consciousness" which uses a paradigm of the conscious subject representing and laboring on objects within the framework of subject-object dialectics. Habermas advocates instead a "philosophy of language" perspective oriented toward communication and "intersubjective agreement." Rather than working with a subject-object model, Habermas proposes a self-other (or *ego/alter*) model focusing on social interaction; he now calls this interaction oriented toward consensus and agreement—as opposed to goal-oriented instrumental action or success-oriented "strategic action"—"communicative action."

Habermas believes that the whole tradition of social theory from Marx through Weber through Weberian Marxism (Lukács, Adorno, Horkheimer, Marcuse) through Parsons and functionalism operates with a too narrow concept of rationalization that can neither adequately criticize the pathologies produced by modern rationalization processes nor adequately distinguish between types of rationalization to assess the positive and negative effects. In effect, Habermas believes that this entire tradition illicitly applies the concept of instrumental reason to spheres of social interaction and communication. This point restates in great detail Habermas's earlier critique that Marxism failed to distinguish properly between labor and interaction—a critique which he now extends in various ways to Weber, Lukács, critical theory, and structural functionalism. Habermas himself is attempting to overcome what he perceives as the limitations of this tradition by developing a more adequate concept of social rationality grounded in his theory of communicative action, a theme beyond the boundaries of this paper.

Yet Habermas believes that a reconstructed version of Weber's theory of rationalization offers "the most promising approach for explaining social pathologies which appear in the wake of capitalist rationalization."[66] Habermas provides, in effect, a reformulation of Weber's analysis of the "loss of meaning" *(Sinnverlust)* and "loss of freedom" *(Freiheitsverlust)* in the modern world. For Habermas, these pathologies occur due to the expansion of instrumental action into the life-world. Habermas distinguishes between instrumental and communicative action and system and life-world, and he argues that overextension of instrumental action into the life-world creates disturbances or dislocations. He construes instrumental action on the model of Weber's theory of instrumental rationality which has been the target previously of critical theory, the basis of the "critique of instrumental reason." He argues that the expansion of subsystems of instrumental rationality into the life-world prohibits rational discussion of procedures, rules, values, and so on, and denies individuals the possibility of "communicative action," that is, discussion that produces rational agreement, development of individual consciousness, and capacity for insight and rational action.

The results of extending systems of instrumental action into the life-world is "cultural impoverishment" (Weber's "loss of meaning") through expanded elitist rule of "expert cultures," which dominate cultural, familial, public, and political spheres and restrict possibilities of enhanced "communicative action" in these spheres.[67] Further, Habermas claims that the intrusion of economic and political imperatives into the life-world (i.e., money, power, etc.) helps to produce what Weber described as a loss of freedom in the modern world. Thus, Habermas concludes that "in capitalist societies, the pattern of rationalization . . . is determined by the fact that instrumental rationality wins out at the expense of practical rationality by reifying communicative conditions of life."[68]

Habermas provides a reconstructed theory of reification—deformation of the life-world through processes of the rationalization of everyday life. Unlike structuralists and right Weberians, he is able to preserve the element of social critique found in Marxism, critical theory, and Weber's own theory. Moreover, unlike his own critical theory predecessors, Habermas notes a growth of "communicative rationality" in modern societies as a positive phenomenon; he claims that there has been an evolutionary growth in the modern world of both communicative and instrumental rationality. In effect, Habermas positively valorizes Weber's differentiation of rationality into various spheres of economic, political, and cultural rationality. Whereas Habermas strongly objects to the extension of technical rationality into spheres of life (i.e., realms of communicative action) in which it is inappropriate and serves only as an instrument of domination, he also sees what Weber called "cultural rationalization" as an advance. That is, Habermas sees progressive elements in the separation of various modes of life and extension of rationalization into such spheres as law, education, and cognitive development. He believes, however, that Weber's theoretical framework does not allow him adequately to characterize spheres of cultural rationalization and communicative interaction, and he attempts to develop a more adequate conceptual framework, enabling him to articulate both regressive and emancipatory features in a theory of modernization.

The more positive valuation of progressive aspects of social rationalization thus distinguishes Habermas's version of critical theory from the classical versions of Adorno, Horkheimer, and Marcuse (at least in his *One-Dimensional Man* stage).[69] Whereas Adorno, Horkheimer, and Marcuse saw the extension of instrumental reason to more and more spheres of life as a purely negative process in which reason became totalitarian and served as an instrument of social control and legitimation, Habermas wishes to explicate certain gains in social rationalization by differentiating all spheres of life from each other and by positively appraising the extension of rationalization into at least some of these spheres. He also stresses how rationalization processes produce crises and imbalances in the life-world and may generate social protest and new social movements.[70] Thus, Habermas attempts to develop a more dialectical theory of social rationalization than the primarily negative and critical theory of his predecessors without, however, sacrificing their goals of social critique and social reconstruction.

As a result Habermas's theory is closer to that of Weber who also stresses conflicts between various spheres of life and describes both benefits and costs of the rationalization process. Indeed, Habermas's critique of Marx, Lukács, Adorno, and Horkheimer in *Theory of Communicative Action* is much sharper and more polemical than his critique of Weber. Moreover, Habermas's intense dialogue with Weber finally brings to light the long-hidden Weberian elements in critical theory and produces an explicit Weberian critical theory. It will be interesting to see if Habermas continues to attempt to synthesize Weber and critical theory or if he moves toward a more eclectic Weberian-based systems theory which attempts to subsume all spheres of social reality into one complex system—a move which would sharply differentiate his theory from that of Weber and classical critical theorists, all of whom avoided totalizing theories. In any case, Habermas's recent work shows that Max Weber's theories continue to be relevant to critical theory, which today faces the challenge of assimilating and superseding both Marx and Weber.

Notes

For helpful criticisms of earlier versions of this article and for ideas which are incorporated into this text, I am grateful to Robert Antonio, James Hammond, Donald McIntosh, and Rick Roderick.

1. On critical theory, see Martin Jay, *The Dialectical Imagination* (Boston: Little, Brown and Company, 1973); Douglas Kellner, review of Jay's book, "The Frankfurt School Revisited," *New German Critique* 4 (Winter 1975): 131–52; and Douglas Kellner and Rick Roderick, "Recent Literature on Critical Theory," *New German Critique* 23 (Spring–Summer 1981): 141–70.

2. See Max Horkheimer, "Traditional and Critical Theory," in *Critical Theory* (New York: Herder and Herder, 1972); Herbert Marcuse, "Philosophy and Critical Theory," in *Negations* (Boston: Beacon Press, 1968).

3. See Michael Lowy, *Georg Lukács—From Romanticism to Bolshevism* (London: New Left Books, 1979), esp. 37–43.

4. Georg Lukács, *History and Class Consciousness* (Cambridge, Mass.: MIT Press, 1971), 95–96. The quote is from Max Weber, *Economy and Society*, 3 vols. (New York: Bedminster Press, 1958), 3: 1394.

5. Lukács, *History*, 95–96. For discussions of similarities between Weber and Marxism, see Robert Antonio's article in this collection.

6. Lukács, *History*, 98–103. For more detailed analyses of Lukács theory of reification, see Andrew Arato and Paul Breines, *The Young Lukács and the Origins of Western Marxism* (New York: Seabury, 1979), and Andrew Feenberg, *Lukács, Marx and the Sources of Critical Theory* (Totowa, N.J.: Rowman and Littlefield, 1981).

7. Lukács, *History*, 86.

8. Ibid., 102.

9. Ibid.

10. On these themes, see Wolfgang Mommsen, *Max Weber und die deutsche Politik* (Tubingen: Mohr, 1959), and Arthur Mitzman, *The Iron Cage* (New York: Alfred Knopf, 1970).

11. See the discussion of Lukács's repulsion toward Weber's support of German nationalism and the imperialist war in the books cited in note 6; Max Horkheimer records the dismay he and others felt concerning Weber's "ideal-type" analysis of the Soviet Union after the Russian revolution in Otto Stammer, ed., *Max Weber and Sociology Today* (New York: Harper and Row, 1965), 51f.

12. On the Institute analysis of fascism, see Jay, *Dialectical Imagination*, 143–72, and the essays and discussion in Helmut Dubiel and Alfons Sollner, eds., *Wirtschaft, Recht und Staat im Nationalsozialismus* (Frankfurt: Europaische Verlagsanstalt, 1981).

13. Max Weber, *Economy and Society.* On the 1930s Institute analyses of authority, see *Studien über Autoritat und Familie* (Paris: Alcan, 1936), and Jay, *Dialectical Imagination,* 113–42.

14. See Erich Fromm, "Sozialpsychologischer Teil," in *Studien,* 77–135, and Fromm, *Escape from Freedom* (New York: Holt, Rinehart and Winston, 1941). Fromm concludes his study of the surrender to irrational religious and political authority with a characterization of Max Weber providing an "idealistic" interpretation of the rise of capitalism and modernity which exaggerated the importance of religious ideas (296). This characterization of Weber as an "idealist" overlooks the materialist elements in his theory and suggests that in the 1930s and 1940s the Institute for Social Research probably perceived Weber as *the* idealist and bourgeois thinker who was antithetical to their (at the time) Marxian materialism.

15. See Herbert Marcuse, *Reason and Revolution* (New York: Oxford University Press, 1941; Boston: Beacon Press, 1960); and Max Horkheimer, *Eclipse of Reason* (New York: Oxford University Press, 1947; New York: Seabury, 1974). Both Marcuse and Horkheimer call attention to the Hegelian heritage operative in their concepts of reason—a heritage that distinguishes their theories from that of Weber.

16. Horkheimer referred to Weber's theory of religion in "Vernunft und Selbsterhaltung," in *Kritische Theorie der Gesellschaft,* vol. 3 (Marxismus-Kollektiv: Raubdruck, 1968), 103, and his contribution to *Studien,* translated as "Authority and Family," in *Critical Theory.* Horkheimer referred to Weber's methodological analyses in "Traditional and Critical Theory," in *Critical Theory,* 193–94, 222. David Held is therefore wrong to claim that "it is not surprising, therefore, to find in the writings of many members of the Frankfurt school in the late 1930s and 1940s frequent references to Weber," as I could find few such references. Compare David Held, *Introduction to Critical Theory* (Berkeley: University of California Press, 1980), 64.

17. Herbert Marcuse, "Some Social Implications of Modern Technology," *Studies in Philosophy and Social Science* 9 (1941): 414–39. For discussion of the importance of this essay in the later development of Marcuse's theory of advanced industrial society see Douglas Kellner, *Herbert Marcuse and the Crisis of Marxism* (Berkeley: University of California Press; London: Macmillan, 1984), 230–33.

18. Marcuse, "Social Implications," 416.

19. Marcuse appropriates here a Weberian notion of a socio-technical *apparatus* (417f.) which will remain a central concept in his theory. See the study of Wolfgang Lipp, "Apparat und Gewalt: Über das Denken Herbert Marcuse," collected in *Kritik und Interpretation der Kritischen Theorie* (Raubdruck: n.p., n.d.), 210–39.

20. Marcuse, "Social Implications," 417–19.

21. This point is missed by Schoolman who claims that "Max Weber has certainly made the greatest single contribution to Marcuse's efforts" (137) and that "on the whole Weber's theoretical model of the development of formal rationality is duplicated in a striking manner by Marcuse" (197f.); see Morton Schoolman, *The Imaginary Witness* (New York: Free Press, 1980). This is completely wrong because, at most, Marcuse incorporated Weberian elements into a Marxian framework and in fact criticized Weber's theory of formal rationality. Schoolman tends to reduce Marcuse's theory to a model of technological reductionism and determinism and fails to perceive how Marcuse analyzed how economic imperatives and aspects help constitute technological rationality and advanced industrial society. See Douglas Kellner, critique of Schoolman, *New German Critique* 26 (Spring–Summer 1982): 185–201.

22. Marcuse, "Social Implications," 414.

23. See the articles in Dubiel and Sollner, *Wirtschaft.* On the debate over fascism in the Institute, see also Jay, *Dialectical Imagination,* 143f.

24. T. W. Adorno and Max Horkheimer, *Dialectic of Enlightenment* (New York: Seabury, 1972). See Kellner in "Frankfurt School Revisited," 146f., where I analyze their distance

from classical Marxism. Here the similarities are stressed, as well as some differences, in Weber's theory of society. The only explicit reference to Weber that I found in *Dialectic of Enlightenment* was a citing of his theory of "causal exchange" on p. 61. Thus, the rapprochement with Weber may or may not have been influenced by explicit study of his works.

25. See Walter Benjamin, "Theses on the Philosophy of History," in *Illuminations* (New York: Schocken, 1968); also Susan Buck-Morss, *The Origins of Negative Dialectics* (New York: Free Press, 1977). Although she makes the interesting point that *Dialectic of Enlightenment* was not for Adorno such a radical break with classical Marxism—since he never subscribed to the Marxian theory of history nor class analysis in his earlier work (61f.)—she fails to note how the book does provide rather striking departures from Horkheimer's previous theories.

26. Horkheimer, *Eclipse,* 6.

27. See the articles "Science as Vocation" and "Politics as Vocation" for Weber's ethical reflections in H. H. Gerth and C. Wright Mills, eds., *From Max Weber* (New York: Oxford University Press, 1958), 77–156.

28. Horkheimer, *Eclipse,* 81.

29. Max Weber, *The Methodology of the Social Sciences* (Glencoe, Ill.: Free Press, 1949). Institute critiques of this work are found in the texts cited in the next three notes.

30. See T. W. Adorno, et al., *The Positivist Dispute in German Sociology* (London: Heinemann, 1976).

31. See Jürgen Habermas, *Zur Logik der Sozialwissenschaften* (Frankfurt: Suhrkamp, 1970), and Habermas, *Theorie des kommunikativen Handelns,* 2 vols. (Frankfurt: Suhrkamp, 1981).

32. See, for example, the collective Institute text, *Aspects of Sociology* (Boston: Beacon Press, 1972), 119.

33. Herbert Marcuse, *Eros and Civilization* (Boston: Beacon Press, 1955), and Marcuse, *One-Dimensional Man* (Boston: Beacon Press, 1964). There are no explicit references to Weber in *Eros and Civilization* or *One-Dimensional Man,* although Marcuse's analysis of domination is quite similar to Weber's. For more details, see Kellner, *Herbert Marcuse,* and the article by Lipp cited in note 19.

34. Marcuse, *Eros,* 36.

35. See Kellner, *Herbert Marcuse.*

36. Marcuse, "Freedom and Freud's Theory of the Instincts," in *Five Lectures* (Boston: Beacon Press, 1970), 1–2.

37. Marcuse, *Eros,* 37–44.

38. Marcuse, *Soviet Marxism* (New York: Columbia University Press, 1958; reprint; New York: Vintage Press, 1961).

39. See Kellner, *Herbert Marcuse.* On "convergence theory" and theories of "post-industrial society" and the Weberian influence, see Daniel Bell, *The Coming of Post-Industrial Society* (New York: Basic Books, 1973), 11–12, 112–14; Talcott Parsons, *The System of Modern Society* (Englewood Cliffs, N.J.: Prentice-Hall, 1971), 122–37.

40. See Kellner, *Herbert Marcuse.*

41. Marcuse, "Industrialization and Capitalism in the Work of Max Weber," in *Negations,* 201–26. The article is printed in a shorter form with commentary and a reply by Marcuse in Stammer, *Max Weber and Sociology Today,* 133–86.

42. Marcuse, "Industrialization," 204–5.

43. Ibid., 206–7.

44. Max Weber, *The Protestant Ethic and the Spirit of Capitalism* (New York: Charles Scribner's Sons, 1958), 182.

45. Weber, *The Protestant Ethic.*

46. Marcuse, "Industrialization," 207.

47. Ibid., and Kellner, *Herbert Marcuse.*

48. Marcuse, "Industrialization," 208.

49. Kellner, *Herbert Marcuse.*

50. Marcuse, in Stammer, *Max Weber,* 185.

51. Marcuse, in Stammer, *Max Weber,* 186.

52. See Kellner, "Frankfurt School Revisited" and *Herbert Marcuse.*

53. In recent years there has been some work on developing Marxist theories of the state that have been influenced by Weber. See studies by Claus Offe, *Strukturprobleme des kapitalistischen Staates* (Frankfurt: Suhrkamp, 1972); Rudolf Bahro, *The Alternative in Eastern Europe* (London: NLB, 1978); and many articles by Eastern European theorists, Andrew Arato, Jean Cohen and others in *Telos.*

54. Jean Cohen, "Max Weber and the Dynamics of Domination," *Telos* 14 (Winter 1972): 65.

55. This point is stressed in a review of critical theory by Robert Antonio, "The Origin, Development, and Contemporary Status of Critical Theory," *The Sociological Quarterly* 24 (Summer 1983).

56. Jürgen Habermas, in Stammer, *Max Weber,* 59–66.

57. Jürgen Habermas, in Adorno, *Positivism Dispute,* 131–62, 198–225.

58. Jürgen Habermas, "Technology and Science as 'Ideology,'" in *Toward a Rational Society* (Boston: Beacon Press, 1970), 81–122.

59. Habermas, "Technology," 91f.

60. Jürgen Habermas, *Legitimation Crisis* (Boston: Beacon Press, 1975).

61. Jürgen Habermas, *Theorie des kommunikativen Handelns* 1: 207–366, 455–88, passim. My reading of this text is indebted to Rick Roderick's Ph.D. dissertation on Habermas and to discussions with Roderick.

62. Habermas, *Theorie* 1: 202.

63. Ibid., 207.

64. Ibid., 208.

65. Ibid., 209.

66. Ibid. 2: 449.

67. Ibid., 481, 488. This theme reprises Habermas's earlier critiques of the decline of the public sphere and the scientization of politics. See Jürgen Habermas, *Structurwandel der Offentlichkeit* (Neuwied and Berlin: Luchterhand, 1962), and Habermas, *Toward a Rational Society.*

68. Habermas, *Theorie* 1: 485.

69. He makes this point explicit in an article. Jürgen Habermas, "The Entwinement of Myth and Enlightenment," *New German Critique* 26 (Spring–Summer 1982), 13–30.

70. Habermas, *Legitimation Crisis,* and Habermas, *Theorie,* vol. 1 passim.

⅃/ℳⅣ\

Johannes Weiss | **On the Marxist Reception and Critique of Max Weber in Eastern Europe**

A SHORT OUTLINE OF THE MARXIST RECEPTION AND CRITIQUE OF WEBER

It is a well-known fact that during the Stalinist period there existed almost no reception of non-Marxist, or even divergent Marxist, conceptions of social science in the Soviet Union. And there is no discussion of Weber's work from the early 1930s until the late 1950s. Clear proof of the political-ideological ban on this author can be found, at least in a semi-official though anonymous form, in the 1951 edition of the *Great Soviet Encyclopedia* (Bolšaja sovjetskaja enciklopedija). This article, in fact, seems to be the only reference of note to Weber's work from within the socialist countries during that period. However, this isolated reference provides a possible explanation of his exclusion: Weber is presented and dismissed as "a reactionary German sociologist, historian and economist, a Neo-Kantian, a most malicious enemy of Marxism" and "an apologist of capitalism." Of Weber's works only the books in Russian translations, *The General Economic History, The City,* and *The Agrarian Sociology of Ancient Civilizations,* are mentioned; no reference is made to the Russian translations of parts of Weber's studies in the sociology of religion, published by the journal *Ateist* in 1928. The only interpretation of Weber mentioned and quoted is Lenin's polemical remark on the "professorial wisdom of the cowardly bourgeoisie," as expressed in Professor Weber's articles on the Russian events of 1905.

That the above treatment of Weber has to be explained by reference to the special nature and needs of Stalinistic rule can be seen most clearly in the articles on Weber in the first and third editions of the same encyclopedia published before and after this period. Moreover, a comparison of these articles indicates that the standard of scholarly criticism accepted in 1928 had not yet been reestablished in 1970. As a matter of fact, the quite remarkable pre-Stalinist-Marxist reception of Weber has not been taken up, discussed, or carried on by Marxist scholars until now. Even the translations of Weber's work published in the Soviet Union between 1923 and 1928 have not been listed completely and correctly. Alexander Neusychin's studies,[1] representing beyond any doubt the most important and broadest Marxist discussion of Weber's work to emerge out of this pre-Stalinist period (and most probably until now),[2] are examined only very hesitantly. Other pre- or non-Stalinist attempts at a critical examination of Weber's sociology from a Marxist point of view are not mentioned. It is obvious that the restraint derives from political-ideological factors, particularly in the case of theorists classified as revisionists (e.g., Max Adler, Lukács, Wittfogel, Kofler, and the Frankfurt School, including Marcuse). But, of course, reasons of this sort are not convincing scientifically—not even in cases where the deviation from genuine historical materialism is seen to consist in the acceptance of Weberian categories or arguments.

Yet there is one exception that has been stated above: the reception of Weber's work in Polish sociology. This cannot be explained satisfactorily by the special political and cultural conditions in this socialist country, but only by the existence of the particular, important Polish tradition of theory construction and research in sociology. The affinity between the "humanistic" theory tradition, dominated by F. Znaniecki, and Weber's concept of interpretative and action sociology is of very great importance.

The number of publications discussing Weber's work from a Marxist point of view has grown constantly during the last twenty years, especially in the socialist countries.[3] It has become so great that an exhaustive quantitative assessment would be impossible even if there were no language problems. My only hope is that my knowledge of the Weber literature (especially in the Soviet Union, Poland, and the German Democratic Republic) is a sufficient basis for an adequate discussion of the arguments put forward by the Marxist scholars.

CHARACTERIZATION OF WEBER'S EPISTEMOLOGICAL POSITION

The most general characterizations of Weber's epistemological position in almost every Marxist critique are: "subjectivism," "subjective idealism," but also—often at the same time—"objectivism," even "positivism," and finally "nihilism" and "agnosticism." All these reservations are summed up in the expression: "Kantianism" or "neo-Kantianism." These characterizations are used in order to consign Weber to that special tradition of bourgeois or revisionistic philosophy and epistemology which is widely accepted among Marxist authors as having received its definite destruction in Lenin's "Materialism and Empiriocriticism." And, as a matter of fact, all the arguments which are put forward against Weber's epistemological conceptions have already been formulated clearly by Lenin.[4]

Viewed from the perspective of a clear and decisive political standpoint, the hoary, bewildering conflict among epistemologists can, as Lenin puts it, be resolved by reducing it to a simple alternative: idealism or materialism.[5] All modifications and intermediate positions (Kantianism, Humeanism, and also realism; positivism as well as pragmatism; and, of course, Machism) can only have one function, namely to mask this decisive opposition of idealism and materialism and thus to weaken the power of the materialistic position. The common characteristic of all subjectivism or idealism is seen to lie in a denial of the fact that reality in general, and social reality in particular, is subject to immutable laws. Lenin gives an "objective, class-related"[6] appraisal of all epistemological positions which are not strictly materialistic: objectively they must be associated with bourgeois class interests. If there exist tendencies "to Kant, to Neo-Kantianism, to critical philosophy" within the Social Democratic movement, these have to be understood (and opposed) as "petit bourgeois trends."[7]

The general arguments put forward against Weber's epistemological or methodological position by his Marxist critics are consistent with Lenin's principles. Weber's neo-Kantianism or subjective idealism is seen to reside in the fact that he: (a) is unable to grasp social reality in its objective materiality and is therefore forced to conceive of knowledge as an activity of the knowing subject and not as a reflection of objective reality; (b) intends to produce "formalistic analyses," typologies, and "empty analogies" instead of discovering "real causal relationships" and "laws";[8] and (c) refuses to recognize a necessary development within society, thus destroying the one firm foundation of political action[9] and consigning society to irrationalism and nihilism.[10] It is somewhat puzzling to see the adherents of a "dialectical" philosophy criticize Weber's idea of a specific subject-object relation in the cultural and social sciences by defining knowledge (*all* knowledge) as reflection of objective reality. It might well be that with his conception of a materialistic epistemology Lenin, who once proposed the foundation of a "society for the materialistic friends of Hegelian dialectic," has prevented more detailed investigation in this field—above all, that concerning the subject-object relation in social research. If knowledge is defined as a copy or photograph of objective reality on the basis of immediate sensations,[11] one will not be able to understand adequately the complicated and highly productive mental operations leading to an elaborate scientific theory, such as is represented in the political economy of Marx. To say that there is no empirical knowledge without sensations is one thing, fully accepted by both Kant and Weber; for Lenin, however, it is obviously this aspect of sensation alone that brings about objectivity and truth: "To consider our sensations to be copies of the external world, to acknowledge objective truth, to stand on the standpoint of materialistic epistemology: this all means exactly the same."[12]

Contrary to Lenin's reflection theory of knowledge, both Weber and Marx have stated that knowledge always involves a great deal of activity on the part of the knowing subject.[13] Regarding the social world in particular, sociological research obtains its objects of enquiry by starting from the views and interests which constitute our practical social life, not by going back to immediate sensations. Immediate sensations cannot define, or even constitute, social reality—neither for everyday life, nor for scientific experience, neither as discovery, nor verification. Up to this point, there seems to be no difference between Marx's and Weber's views. Weber's remarks on the "chaotic" nature of reality "as such," which in fact sometimes sound rather Kantian, should not be considered as being metaphysical or ontological statements but rather as indicating the perspectivity of all knowledge and the necessity of selection and formation *(Auswahl und Formung)*[14] on the part of the knowing subject. Reality is not chaotic *as such* (this would not be a reasonable assumption for any science aiming at causal explanation), but merely *for us,* as long as we persist in looking at it without any structuring viewpoint. Only such an interpretation is in accordance with Weber's concept of value-relevance *(Wertbeziehung) as well as* with the idea of a concrete reality science *(Wirklichkeitswissenschaft)* as he understood it.[15]

The convergence between Marx and Weber also extends to the insight that the interests or values determining the "selection and formation of an object of empirical investigation" are, at least in the case of historical social science, themselves historical. That is why they are transformed in the process of epochal socio-cultural change. Otherwise the social sciences could not respond to the dominant problems of their time, as, again, both Marx and Weber demand of them. A really decisive difference between Weber's and Marx's conception of historical-social knowledge does however exist, due to Marx's assumption that the perspectival and the historical nature of social science does not prevent it from detecting the very substance of social reality, that is, in the last analysis the overall determining factors of social life. It is the idea of social progress making its way objectively and according to brazen laws which justifies the ascription to historical-political knowledge of at once a historically determined point of view *and* the capacity to detect the substance of social reality. For Weber, it was impossible to retain the idea of objective, historical progress.[16] Except for mere technological progress (e.g., concerning the development of the means of production as such), there are no objective (i.e., empirical or ontological) criteria of social progress. The conception of progress depends totally on values or aims that must be defined, accepted, and accounted for by man. Thus, reference to anything valued as progress does not provide a direct and infallible guide to what is here *causally* essential to implement it.

I conclude these reflections with a short remark about ideal-types and idealism. Weber's views have nothing in common with subjective idealism. This term, accurately used, refers to an epistemological position which interprets the universal and necessary elements in human knowledge, not its material content, as produced by the knowing subject. Despite his reference to "modern epistemology, which originates with Kant,"[17] Weber never advocated such a conception, although it is of course worthy of discussion. Value-relevances in general and ideal type constructions in particular do not in Weber's view have an epistemological status that could be paralleled to Kant's categories of pure reason.[18] Ideal types are purely conceptual, even utopian, constructions which do not serve as a priori forms of all possible experience but as a means of detecting relations existing in the real world. Because of this status, they cannot be wrong, but only more or less useful; needless to say they are by no means "universal" or "necessary."

VALUE FREEDOM AND HISTORICAL DETERMINISM

Weber's central argument concerning the logical heterogeneity of scientific (i.e., logical, hermeneutic, and empirical) statements on the one hand and value judgments on the other is *not* opposed by the majority of his Marxist critics. It is, indeed, not always made sufficiently clear that this *is* the decisive point in Weber's thinking on value freedom, but there are Marxist authors who state explicitly their full agreement with Weber as far as this question of logical heterogeneity is concerned. Thus Hofmann, who provides the most detailed discussion of this issue from a Marxist perspective, remarks that the assumption that "factual propositions and value judgments are essentially different from each other" cannot be denied.[19] Similarly, even though not quite as clearly, others (e.g.,

Kuczynski and Kon)[20] insist that actual value judgments have to be kept apart from scientific analysis. With regard to confusions (Weber's expression) of this sort, Kon refers to a corresponding Marxian evaluation: "He who tries to accommodate science to a standpoint which does not emerge (however erroneously) from its own immediate scientific necessities, but instead from external, extraneous interests, is to be called 'vulgar.' "[21]

In spite of this acknowledgment of the logical heterogeneity of factual judgments and value judgments, Marxist theorists believe that value judgments can be justified scientifically. Insofar as they allude to objective historical progress, the brief remarks made in the last paragraph will have to suffice. However, some further reflections are called for on a more general version of that idea, referring namely to the deterministic nature of the historical process as such. A typical and fairly clear formulation of this argument is the following: "The decisive refutation of this conception (of Weber's) derives from insight into the clearly recognizable determinism and law-conforming nature of class struggle, which underlies the conflict of value systems. This practical, empirically verifiable context is discounted by Weber in an artificial way."[22]

In order to forestall misplaced opposition, it should be said at the outset that Weber attached great weight to class interests in connection with furnishing an explanation of the "struggle of value systems."[23] The question is, however, whether it is artificial or in fact logically compelling to distinguish between the causality and the validity problem. Let us assume for this purpose that class struggle is the fundamental dimension in all historical-social processes and that its development in accordance with an objective determinism can be empirically ascertained. These are, indeed, highly problematic assumptions, but they do not surpass the limits of empirical science, at least in principle. This is also true of the further assumption that the struggle of value systems can be explained exclusively and completely by class struggle proceeding deterministically. But even if all these assumptions are accepted, what has been demonstrated by them? Only that the problem of the right value system proves to be a classical case of a pseudo-problem: with regard to objective necessity it would be quite senseless to ask the value question (i.e., the question, what *ought* one to do). Whenever this question is asked, it is assumed that something could be different from how it actually is now or has come to be. It would be rather unconvincing to trace back such obscure argumentation on the relation of historical determinism and ethical-political decision to the venerable concept of the dialectic. Nevertheless it would be interesting to ascertain how Hegel's and Marx's idea of necessity in history, combined with a renunciation of every genuine method of justifying practical norms rationally, could come to suffer from such a flaw. A detailed investigation might lead to the result that Marx had already overestimated the scope of a theory of history which renounces all nonempirical, idealistic presuppositions. Maybe it is of much greater weight than Marx himself believed if one replaces the category of logic or reason (as used in Marx's early writings) by the category of law or determinism. Above all, it is the Marxian assumption that a radical critique of the status quo is nothing but the reverse of a strictly empirical analysis which very probably would not stand up to closer examination.[24]

IDEAL TYPE CONCEPTS AND HISTORICAL-SOCIAL ACTION

No other part of Weber's methodology has attracted so much interest among his Marxist critics as his conception of ideal types.[25] Here, only one aspect of this very complex problem can be discussed. It is recognized, however, that this particular aspect is of great importance, especially for Marxist theorists. The question concerns the affinity of ideal type concepts to the orientation characteristic of historical-social action.

It is Weber's principal reference to historical patterns of meaning and the criterion of adequacy according to meaning *(Sinnadäquatheit)* which connect the ideal types of social sciences with the orientational and communicational needs of social action. Orientation with regard to practical social aims means orientation within the context of social meaning patterns with an eye on distinct meaning or value dimensions. A very important point is the following one: ideal types reconstruct historical-social reality according to objective possibility. But the same category of objective possibility also specifies the perspective of social actors as long as they strive for a rational clarification of the actual historical situation. If objective laws of the global historical process existed, there would be no basis for social action guided by rational consideration and examination of the different possibilities.

This interpretation of ideal type methodology cannot be traced to explicit statements by Weber. It is, however, in complete conformity with a fundamental intention imbedded in Weber's programmatic conception of social science, namely the intention of undercutting all misleading and, in practice, dangerous tendencies to hypostatize theoretical concepts, and indeed all such confusion of concepts and reality in the social sciences.[26] Insofar as ideal type conceptions reconstruct historical-social reality according to objective possibility, they tend to counteract the danger of reification of sociological concepts and theorems. This critical function of ideal type constructions, as opposed to a rash use of nomological or even deterministic propositions, should be perceived and specially examined by

Marxist theoreticians. It is very questionable, indeed, whether Marxist sociologists can continue to maintain a socio-technological conception of social and political practice defined as "domination and guidance"[27] of societal processes and grounded in theoretical assumptions that are held to be deterministic.

Further objections, of the sort above, can be raised against a rather widespread interpretation of Marxist theorists,[28] which considers Weber's ideal type conception acceptable insomuch as it can be identified with the model concept in physics. Such an interpretation is not wrong in every respect, but there is an obvious risk of obscuring the decisive difference. In physics, models are used in order to provide a representation of the world as it really is under certain ideal conditions; with regard to this function it is by no means accidental that models conform to the postulate of "universality, formalism, and permanence" (S. K. Langer) or that they are related to factors which can be measured quantitatively. Ideal types, on the contrary, refer to reality only to the extent that it is meaningful and thus historical.[29] This is why the status of objective *possibility* is essential to them: socio-cultural reality is neither universal, nor permanent, nor necessary. Weber's reflections on ideal types are meant to demonstrate that, despite this fact, historical social science does not have to renounce concepts and theorems which are clear, precise, and at the same time more or less general.

INDIVIDUALISM AND THE PROBLEM OF ALIENATION

Some remarks of Karl Marx merit quoting as a starting point to this section. Despite the fact that Marxists, as well as many non-Marxists, oppose his holistic view of society to Weber's individualistic, action-related perspective, Marx's texts contain references that undoubtedly imply some sort of individualism. Some of the most important of Marx's statements in this connection are the following: "The circumstances of the individuals can, at all events, be nothing other than their mutual behavior";[30] "What is society, whatever be its form? The product of the mutual action of men";[31] the "economic categories" too (private property, commodity, etc.) are merely conceptual abstractions and do not express anything other than "the social behavior of men to each other."[32] Not only does Marx agree with Weber that social circumstances or institutions, including society as a whole, in reality can only be interrelated human action, but he also states that real action can only be ascribed to individuals: it is "the personal, individual behavior of individuals, their behavior towards each other as individuals, which has created the existing conditions and is creating them anew every day."[33] With regard to these very clear Marxian statements I assert that there is in fact no divergence, at least none in principle, between Marx and Weber on the problem of individualism.

In order to substantiate this assertion, however, some clarifications of Weber's view have to be made. First of all, a very common misunderstanding exists: the assumption that action can only be ascribed to individuals by no means carries the implication that those individuals are subjects consciously pursuing egoistic aims.[34] To be sure, actions of this special kind very often also produce results which are not intended by any individual actor but may, nevertheless, most pointedly determine the way they act: "Thus the collisions of numberless singular wills and singular actors in the realm of history lead to a situation which is completely analogous to that characteristic of unconscious nature. The aims of the actions are intended, but the outcomes actually resulting from these actions are not."[35] This fact is of particular importance for an understanding of capitalist society, especially as emphasized by A. Smith, and is obviously one of the basic insights to be built into *any* theory of social action; of course these nonintended consequences of actions can be explained only by going back to the actions themselves.

But what about social behavior which is neither determined by egoistic motives nor indeed performed consciously at all, but instead derives from, and is explained by, intersubjectively established values and norms? Why then is it only possible to ascribe this to individual actors? Weber's answer to this question is to point to meaningfulness as the decisive characteristic of social action per se. Meaning can be constituted and experienced by individual subjects only, even though meaning thus constituted and understood is always related to the complementary perspectives of other actors.

There is one obvious objection to this view of Weber which is especially characteristic of Marxist critics; this objection derives from the fact that individuals are confronted with social conditions and institutions, in the creation and maintenance of which they are not participating in any real sense. But Weber's argument is not that all possible social conditions of human action are created and maintained by *all* possible individuals involved in, or determined by, these conditions. Certain institutions may, on the contrary, oppose certain individuals or groups of them as being, according to Marx, a genuinely "external force" to which they have no meaningful relationship. At the same time, however, these institutions exist only within the meaningfully interrelated actions of other individuals.

It is hard to understand why Marxist theorists confine themselves to criticizing Weber's view instead of recognizing and developing the specific form of individualism underlying the thinking of Marx. It is even worth discussing whether the reasons Weber gives for his individualistic perspective cannot be transferred to Marx. The individual Marx refers to cannot possibly be understood as the individual organism, involving a particular psychic constitution; he/she must be understood, on the contrary, as the subject of historical-social, and hence meaningful, action, work, and interaction. Moreover, such an interpretation seems to be the only one which is in accordance with Marx's view of the aim of political action: the elimination of all alienation and the establishment of society as an association of free men.

It is appropriate to reflect on this very problem of alienation. Any analysis of this fact, so fundamental for a Marxist view of social reality, will fail if it does not renounce any hypostatization of the products of human action. A Marxist analysis cannot fulfill its critical function without exposing systematically the action-relatedness of *all* social conditions. To insist on a materiality of social relations, supposedly beyond the reach of human action, is just as anticritical as the assertion put forward against Weber's individualism that it is the task of a materialistic analysis "to reduce individual behavior to the behavior of masses, groups, and classes in particular, 'the individual to the social.' "[36] The inclination of many Marxists to ascribe a higher form of existence and a higher legitimacy to collective being rather than to individuals may be founded on good reasons, but these reasons are of a political-ideological nature at best and without any scientific relevance.

RATIONALITY AND DOMINATION

There is little dissension among followers as well as critics of Weber that the most general frame of reference of his sociological and historical work is defined by the concepts of rationality and rationalization respectively. This has also been stated quite explicitly by Weber himself. It is both Weber's concrete-historical and own personal experience of the specific process of rationalization characteristic of the history of modern Occidental society which becomes, on the level of his scientific work, a comprehensive and highly elaborate program of sociological research. It is this transformation of a most pressing social and personal problem into a basic guideline for sociological research which seems to be a classical example of what Weber called value relevance.

Thus it is quite understandable, and also wholly legitimate, that Marxist critics of Weber show a predilection for devoting themselves to the basis of interests which is revealed, or maybe concealed, by the selection of this special frame of reference in Weber's work. Furthermore, it is quite admissible to work with the assumption that those interests are class or domination interests, at least in the last instance. In order to make such an assumption still more plausible, one can finally point to the fact that there exists a close and seemingly positive relationship between the concepts of rationality on the one hand and of domination on the other. Almost all Marxist critics of Weber on the problem of rationality are operating with an assumption of this sort. This is why they discuss rationality in its relation to social power and domination in a double sense: first, they try to determine the class or power interests underlying such a rationality perspective in sociological theory and research; and, secondly, their intention is to demonstrate the ideological basis of Weber's analysis of domination in general and of bureaucracy in particular. Some provisional remarks are called for against one particular criticism of this sort.

The assertion that Weber's *idée directrice* of rationality is ideological per se has been put forward in an especially decisive and influential way by Marcuse.[37] The main steps of his argumentation follow. Rationality, as Weber understands it, is either technological, instrumental, or formal; this is quite obvious if one looks at Weber's use of this category in his analysis on modern Occidental capitalism. Technological rationality is supposed to be value-neutral, and it is this seeming value-neutrality which explains the great ideological utility of this rationality concept. In fact, however, technological rationality in Marcuse's view is related to one and only one aim, the aim of domination. Thus it is technological reason or technology as such, and not any specific use of it, which implies "domination (over nature and man), methodical, scientific, calculated and calculating domination."[38] Weber binds "his own reason to that of the bourgeoisie": that is to say, to "the formal rationality of capitalism."[39] Therefore, when investigating modern Occidental capitalism for its ultimate value basis, he cannot avoid considering it the embodiment of the highest possible rationality and thus justifying it as being without any reasonable alternative.[40] At least two objections must be raised against this interpretation of Weber's conception of rationality.

It is true that Weber wanted to confine empirical social science to the boundaries of formal and technological rationality. This, however, does not at all mean that this specific kind of rationality is the only one to be the object of a sociological enquiry. A glance at Weber's conceptual-theoretical as well as his historical analyses shows that there is no restriction of this sort. Besides the distinction of formal versus substantive rationality, also mentioned by Marcuse, a great variety of types and dimensions of rationalization can be found. It would be difficult enough to provide an all-inclusive systematization of these types and dimensions, but without any doubt it would be impossible to subsume them all under the heading of formal rationality.[41] If there is one fundamental meaning of rationality in Weber, it is what he occasionally called communicability, which pertains to meaningful social action as such.[42] This, and by no means formal or technological rationality, is the dimension that must be implied when one speaks of a fundamental rationality assumption or rationality bias characteristic of Weber's conception of social action. Obviously it is much more difficult to demonstrate the ideological nature of such a basic assumption than it would be with regard to either formal or technological rationality.

The second objection refers to the role of technological rationality in the development of capitalist and also socialist society. Marcuse's criticism concerning this matter is somewhat puzzling, if it is to be regarded as Marxist criticism. It is Marx who explained the development of capitalist society as being most decidedly a product of economic-technological rationalization. Marx, to be sure, also assumed that the capitalist mode of production would become economically and technologically irrational in the end, which would necessarily lead to the termination of capitalist relations of production. For Marx the transition to socialism is above all a question of technological rationality, and not of ethical-political, substantively rational, considerations. Neither Weber nor Marcuse share the above-mentioned assumption of Marx. On the contrary, both of them state that the process of advanced, technological rationalization does not stimulate radical change in the realm of socio-political institutions or of domination, but it serves rather as a powerful means of legitimization and stabilization (if indeed not petrifaction) of the social and political status quo.

Marcuse and many other Marxists assert that in view of such a situation Weber's restricted conception of rationality could only produce resignation and fatalism or escape into irrationalism.[43] This assertion is not valid. It has been said already that Weber conceded explicitly a genuine legitimacy to nontechnological and nonformal modes of rationality. But this general concession is much less important than the fact that with regard to the given historical situation he pointed to the possibility and even necessity of opposing a substantively rational idea, namely the idea of human and civil rights, to the processes of depersonalization and reification.[44] Whether or not this idea will be successful against the force of technological rationality is an empirical and, above all, practical question. In this respect, it is a question well worth discussing—whether the use of charismatic leadership as a means of preventing, or of escaping, the technological-bureaucratic "cage of serfdom" would not endanger the very content of the substantively rational value idea just mentioned.

Notes

This paper results from a larger work which offers a detailed exposition and examination of the critique of Weber's thinking provided by Marxist scholars, particularly those from the socialist countries. See J. Weiss, *Das Werk Max Webers in der marxistischen Rezeption und Kritik* (Opladen: Westdeutscher Verlag, 1981); forthcoming in English translation (London: Routledge and Kegan Paul).

1. A. I. Neusychin, "Sociologičeskoe issledovanie M. Vebera o gorode" ("Max Weber's Sociological Studies on the City"), *Pod znamenem Marksizma* 6 (1923): 219–50; Neusychin, "Novyi opyt postrojennija sistematičeskoj istorii chozjajstva" ("A New Attempt at the Foundation of a Systematic Economic History"), *Archiv Marksa i Engel's* 1 (1924): 425–35; Neusychin, " 'Empiričeskaja sociologija' Maksa Vebera i logika istoričeskoj nauk" ("The Empirical Sociology Max Weber's and the Logic of the Historical Sciences"), *Pod znamenem Marksizma* 9 (1927): 113–43 and 12: 111–37. This unfinished article as well as "Sociologičeskoe issledovanie . . ." can also be found in Neusychin, *Problemy jevropejskogo feodalizma. Izbranie trudy* ("Problems of European Feudalism") (Moscow: Nauka, 1974).

2. This is also Kon's view. See I. S. Kon, *Die Geschichtsphilosophie des 20. Jahrhunderts,* 2 vols. (Berlin: Akademie, 1964), 150.

3. The present author's larger work refers to a bibliography of about two hundred books and articles which is not exhaustive.

4. Quotations are from the German edition V. I. Lenin, vol. 14 of *Werke* (Berlin: Dietz, 1970).

5. Lenin, *Werke* 14: 339.

6. Ibid., 363.

7. Ibid., 34: 375.

8. G. Lukács, *Die Zerstörung der Vernunft,* Werke (Neuwied: Luchterhand, 1962), 9: 530; Lukács, "Marx und das Problem des ideologischen Verfalls," *Einheit* 1 (1946): 111.

9. Lukács, "Marx und das Problem des ideologischen Verfalls," 112.

10. Lukács, *Die Zerstörung der Vernunft,* 533.

11. Lenin, *Werke* 14: 124.

12. Ibid., 125.

13. In this respect Marx's "Thesen über Feuerbach" is of special importance.

14. M. Weber, *Gesammelte Aufsätze zur Wissenschaftslehre,* 3rd ed. (Tübingen: Mohr, 1968), 511. Further citations to this work are indicated by *WL*.

15. Cf. J. Kocka, "Karl Marx und Max Weber im Vergleich. Sozialwissenschaften zwischen Dogmatismus und Dezisionismus," in H. U. Wehler, ed., *Geschichte und Ökonomie*

(Köln: Kiepenheuer und Witsch, 1973), 60. There is an enlarged version in J. Kocka, *Sozialgeschichte* (Göttingen: Vandenhoeck und Ruprecht, 1977), 9–47. Kocka's essay appears in translation in this volume. Cf. D. Henrich, *Die Einheit der Wissenschaftslehre Max Webers* (Tübingen: Mohr, 1952).

16. Weber's most important remarks on this topic are *WL*, 518.

17. Ibid., 208.

18. Cf. R. P. Devjatkova, *Nekotorye aspekty sociologii M. Vebera: Kritičeskij analiz*, Avtoreferat Diss. (Leningrad, 1969), 8; Iu. Fojtik, *Kritika sub'jektivizma sociologii M. Vebera i ego posledovatelej*, Avtoreferat Diss. (Moscow, 1962), 8; W. Korf, *Die Kategorien 'kausale Zurechnung' und 'Idealtypus' in der Methodologie Max Webers: Darstellung und Kritik*, Phil. Diss. (Berlin, 1968), 98, 112; I. S. Kon, *Der Postivismus in der Soziologie: Geschichtlicher Abriß* (Berlin: Akademie, 1973), 48; and H. Kramer, *Philosophische Aspekte der Soziologie Max Webers*, Phil. Diss. (Leipzig, 1968), 140. Kon's and Kramer's discussions of this point are more refined and adequate.

19. W. Hofmann, *Gesellschaftslehre als Ordnungsmacht: Die Werturteilsfrage—heute* (Berlin: Duncker und Humblot, 1961), 18.

20. J. Kuczynski, *Studien zur Wissenschaft von den Gesellschaftswissenschaften* (Berlin: Deutscher Verlagder Wissenschaften, 1972), 192; Kon, *Positivismus in der Soziologie*, 153.

21. K. Marx, *Theorien über den Mehrwert* (Berlin: Dietz, 1959), 108. Quoted, Kon, *Positivismus in der Soziologie*, 156. As to further Marxian remarks on scientific "impartiality" (Marx's expression) see U. Steinvorth, "Wertfreiheit der Wissenschaften bei Marx, Weber und Adorno," *Zeitschrift für allgemeine Wissenschaftstheorie* 9 (1978): 294.

22. *Wörterbuch der marxistisch-leninistischen Soziologie*, 2nd. ed. (Opladen: Westdeutscher Verlag, 1971), 207.

23. See, e.g., M. Weber, "Gutachten zur Werturteilsdiskussion" (1913), published in E. Baumgarten, *Max Weber, Werk und Person* (Tübingen: Mohr, 1974), 111, 131, 133 (quoted, Gutachten). The assertion that the use of the concept of "class struggle" had to be "rejected as being nothing but a value judgment" by Weber is quite obviously made without the slightest knowledge of Weber's work. See G. Assmann and R. Stollberg, *Grundlagen der marxistisch-leninistischen Soziologie* (Frankfurt: Marxistische Blätter, 1977), 356.

24. See, above all, Marx's remarks in the epilogue to the second edition of *Capital.*

25. Cf. Devjatkova, *Nekotorye aspekty sociologii M. Vebera;* Fojtik, *Kritika sub'jektivizma sociologii M. Vebera;* L. V. Korablev, *Koncepcija "ideal'nych tipov" "social'nogo dejstvija" M. Vebera i ego teoretičeskaja nesostojatel'nost'*, Avtoreferat Kand. Diss. (Moscow, 1969); W. Korf, "Der Idealtypus Max Webers und die historisch-gesellschaftlichen Gesetzmäßigkeiten," *Deutsche Zeitschrift für Philosophie* 11 (1964): 1328–43, and *Die Kategorien 'kausale Zurechnung' und 'Idealtypus' in der Methodologie M. Webers;* Kramer, *Philosophische Aspekte der Soziologie M. Webers;* Neusychin, "Sociologičeskoe issledovanie" and "'Empiricčeskaja sociologija'"; L. Nowak, "Social Action versus Individual Action," *Polish Sociological Bulletin* 23 (1971): 84–93; J. Kmita and L. Nowak, "The Rationality Assumption in Human Sciences," *Polish Sociological Bulletin* 21 (1970): 43–68.

26. Cf. Weber's remark on the anticritical function of all "collective concepts," in *WL*, 212.

27. Korf, "Der Idealtypus Max Webers," 1334.

28. See, e.g., Korf, "Der Idealtypus Max Webers," 1335, and "Die Kategorien 'kausale Zurechnung' und 'Idealtypus' in der Methodologie M. Webers," 204; Korablev, *Koncepcija*, 528.

29. This objection must also be raised about L. Nowak's reflections on ideal types and "idealized laws," although these reflections seem to be very useful in filling the "gap" between Marx's and Weber's view of concept and theory formation in historical social science.

30. Marx and Engels, *Werke* (Berlin: Dietz, 1956), 3: 423.

31. Marx and Engels, *Ausgewählte Briefe* (Berlin: Dietz, 1953), 42 (letter to Annenkow).

32. "Heilige Familie," quoted in W. Tuchscherer, *Bevor das Kapital entstand* (Berlin: Akademie, 1973), 224; see also *Ausgewählte Briefe,* 47.

33. Marx and Engels, *Werke* 3: 423.

34. V.-W. Bader et al., *Einführung in die Gesellschaftstheorie. Gesellschaft: Wirtschaft und Staat bei Marx und Weber,* 2 vols. (Frankfurt: Campus, 1976), 25, 226, 345, 492, too, still maintain this misunderstanding although their book generally shows a comparatively high degree of discriminative capability.

35. Engels, "Ludwig Feuerbach und der Ausgang der klassischen deutschen Philosophie"; Marx and Engels, *Werke* 21: 296.

36. B. F. Bakurkin, "Koncepcija social'nogo dejstvija M. Vebera—Osnova povedenčeskogo podchoda v sociologičeskom funkcionalizma," *Kritika sovremennoj buržuaznoj ideologii* (Moscow: Izdatel'stvo Moskovskojo Universiteta, 1975), 22, is here referring to Lenin's critique of "subjectivistic" sociology.

37. H. Marcuse, "Industrialisierung und Kapitalismus im Werk Max Webers," *Kultur und Gesellschaft* (Frankfurt: Suhrkamp, 1965), 2: 107.

38. Ibid., 127.

39. Ibid., 129.

40. Similar argumentation can be found, e.g., in P. P. Gajdenko, "Sociologičeskie aspekty analiza nauki," *Očenye o nauke i ego razvitii* (Moscow, 1971), 238.

41. Korablev's *Koncepcija,* 9, 14, view of the status of "formal rationality" in Weber's work, must be objected to for the same reason.

42. For a more detailed discussion of this point see J. Weiss, *Max Webers Grundlegung der Soziologie* (München: Dokümentation, 1975), 51.

43. See, e.g., R. P. Devjatkova, "M. Veber i problema 'zapadnoj racional'nosti," *Vestnik Leningr. Universiteta. Serija ykonomiki, filosofii i pravo* 17 (1968): 129; W. Korf, *Ausbruch aus dem 'Gehäuse der Hörigkeit'? Kritik der Kulturtheorien Max Webers und Herbert Marcuses* (Frankfurt: Marxistische Blätter, 1971), passim; A. A. Kuznecov, *Kritika sociologija religii M. Vebera,* Avtoreferat Diss. (Leningrad, 1975), 9; Bader et al., *Einführung in die Gesellschaftstheorie,* 316.

44. Cf. M. Weber, *Gesammelte politische Schriften,* 3rd. ed. (Tübingen: Mohr, 1971), 62.

FURTHER PUBLICATIONS

R. P. Devjatkova, "Max Weber und Karl Marx," *Deutsche Zeitschrift für Philosophie* 16 (1968): 1356–61.

L. Nowak, "Historical Generalizations and Problems of Historicism and Idiographism," *Polish Sociological Bulletin* 20 (1969): 48–55.

A. S. Seregin, "Metodologičeskaja nesostojatel'nost' i social'naja suščnost' buržuaznoj koncepcii racional'nosti," *Kritika sovremennoj buržuaznoj i revizicnistkoj ideologii* (Moscow, 1975), 68–83.

PART III / Method

I/ÄÜ/I

Jürgen Kocka	**The Social Sciences between Dogmatism and Decisionism: A Comparison of Karl Marx and Max Weber** *Translated by Charles Lawrence*

Weber has been called the "bourgeois Marx,"[1] but this controversial comparison refers to much more than can be treated here.[2] Marx and Weber "give a critical analysis of contemporary man within bourgeois society in the context of the bourgeois-capitalist economy."[3] What Weber described as the autonomous and, ultimately, the irrational character of the rationality of modern society, Marx had a half a century earlier analyzed as alienation. While Weber accepted this inversion of the means-ends relationship as an inescapable "cage," and simultaneously as the locus for the possibility of individual freedom, Marx sought to encourage transformation by demonstrating the possibilities of societal change. For Marx, rational consciousness mediated through interests leads necessarily to praxis; for Weber some forms of adequate understanding tend to impede action, though Weber also demanded that action occur with an awareness of its conditions and possible effects.

The present essay investigates systematically[4] the relationship of Marx to Weber with reference to one of the fundamental problems in the philosophy of the social sciences: namely, the relationship between the object of inquiry and the process of acquiring knowledge of that object. It has been addressed in two extremely different ways: in Marx's theory, which is oriented toward Hegel, and in Weber's philosophy of science *(Wissenschaftslehre)*. Both approaches are too important to ignore each other, and they represent two contrary, but fundamental, positions in the philosophy of science. Marxists frequently accuse "bourgeois" scientists of irrational decisionism, arbitrariness, vagueness, and agnosticism in the determination of the relationship between concepts and reality and often mention Max Weber as the witness for the prosecution.[5] Conversely, many Marxists claim to be the only ones who have adequately formulated the problem, concepts, and theories whose identity with the structures of reality to be analyzed is assured in principle and which alone make scientific knowledge of societal regularities possible; to those who are not strong adherents of Hegelian-Marxian epistemology, these claims appear as not only unjustified and uncritical but also as antipluralist and dogmatic.[6] The purpose of the following comparison is to create a frame of reference for understanding some of the conditions, implications, and perspectives, which will lead to resolution of this theoretical and practical argument.

The confrontation of Marx's and Weber's philosophies of science and methodological conceptions will reveal their respective limitations and biases. Sharpened awareness of their deficiencies can lead to advances, which encourage and support partial mediation of the positions and which decrease their respective one-sidedness. An attempt should be made to elaborate aspects of the interpretations of Marx and Weber which have been neglected. We should try to identify those elements in both frameworks which are indispensible for any new philosophy of science, which can be defended against *both* the charge of authoritarian dogmatism *and* the charge of non-committal decisionism, and which has either abandoned truth claims for its results or can only claim them methodologically. In addition, it will be shown that a continuing problem in the philosophy of social science (i.e., the relationship of the object of inquiry to knowledge of that object) is most closely connected with a separate issue in the philosophy of history concerning the relation of historical reality to the norms of political action (i.e., the relationship of science to politics).

This undertaking confronts certain difficulties.

1. Weber rarely dealt with Marx explicitly. Whenever he focused on Marxism, he criticized a particular elaboration of Marx's theory but essentially missed Marx's own position, from which the contemporary historical materialists had regressed.

2. Marx scarcely explained his methodology, just as those who base their approach on him have hardly produced more than a few sketches toward a methodology. An explanation for this failure must be found. In order to ascertain Marx's methodological position, it will be necessary to draw on his philosophical and economic works and to develop his position from his concept of history.

3. Consequently, the logic of comparison requires an investigation of Weber's concept of history, underlying his theory of science.[7] A perspective has to be developed to make the difference between Marx and Weber clear; such a perspective would have become manifest if Weber had interpreted Marx more adequately.

WEBER'S CRITIQUE OF MARX

Weber cannot be understood merely on the basis of his opposition to Marx.[8] Frequently, and especially in his major work, *Economy and Society,* Weber followed a method, similar to Marx's approach: that is, relating forms of social organization and consciousness to economic processes. For example, Weber deduced the formation of communities and development of a value-related societal structure from the primacy of economic competition,[9] and in his sociology of religion he established the significance of the premise of a God for a particular economic development.[10] Even Weber's critique of historical materialism is indebted to the method of Marx: "Under the impression of the profound significance of modern economic transformation and especially the far-reaching ramification of the 'labor question,'" historical materialism gained its monistic character (WL, 167).[11] By relating Marxist monocausality to its socio-economic basis, Weber placed it under suspicion as being an ideology.

On the other hand, in *The Protestant Ethic and the Spirit of Capitalism,* Weber consciously rejected Marx;[12] his method reversed Marx's approach by setting forth the spiritual-religious origins of capitalist relations of production.[13] In order to explain Weber's ambivalent attitude towards Marx, Weber's statements regarding Marxism must first be considered.

"The so-called 'materialist conception of history' with the crude elements of genius of the early form which appeared, for instance, in the *Communist Manifesto* still prevails only in the minds of laymen and dilettantes" (WL, 167/68). Weber rejected this as a *Weltanschauung.* He argued that this concept of history implies the naive belief "that all cultural phenomena can be *deduced* as a product or a function of the constellation of material interests" (WL, 166/68). Weber defined "materialistic" as "the unequivocal dependence of 'historical' processes on the respective type of acquisition and utilization of material, that is economic commodities and especially, the unequivocal determination of 'historical' acts of men by 'material,' that is economic interests" (WL, 314). Objections to this type of historical materialism can be found throughout Weber's work.[14]

Nevertheless, Weber believed "*that the analysis of social phenomena and cultural processes* with special reference to their *economic* conditioning and ramifications was a scientific principle of creative fruitfulness and with careful application and freedom from dogmatic restriction, will remain so for the forseeable future" (WL, 166/68). Weber even considered the danger that the Marxist method might be undervalued in the contemporary era. "The eminent, indeed unique, heuristic significance of these ideal types [i.e., Marxist categories] when they are used for making a comparison between them and reality is known to everyone who has ever employed Marxist concepts. Similarly, their perniciousness as soon as they are thought of as empirically valid or real (i.e., truly metaphysical), 'effective forces,' 'tendencies,' etc., is likewise known to those who have used them'' (WL, 205/103).

Weber attempted to preserve the Marxist interpretation of history, as he understood it, for his own definition of science. He accepted historical materialism as a heuristic principle and freed it from its claims to absolute truth and therewith from its revolutionary potential. He viewed it as one of many methods of scientifically interpreting reality—insofar as this is possible at all. Thus, Weber could benefit from Marx's models without allowing them to diminish the eclectic character of his own methodology. This point necessitates consideration of Weber's critique of Marx's interpretation of history. Two aspects must be distinguished. First, Weber took historical materialism to task for mistaking the tendencies, forces, and regularities, which it ascertained for reality, rather than characterizing them as ideal types, which are distanced from reality. According to him, historical materialism naively identifies empirical scientific knowledge with objective reality.[15] Secondly, Weber believed that causal explanations of a historical materialist type deduce individual historical phenomena from a ''law'' which is, in the final analysis, ahistorical; this law of causal dependence of societal consciousness and action on economic relations is held to be the unique cause of all development. This second reproach does not do justice to Marx's understanding of a ''law.''

Concerning the relationship between the writing of history and the philosophy of history, Marx stated:

With the description of reality, independent philosophy loses its medium of existence. At best, a summary of the most general results, abstractions derived from observation of the historical development of men, can take its place. Apart from actual history, these abstractions have in themselves no value whatsoever. They can only serve to facilitate the arrangement of historical material and to indicate the sequence of its particular strata. By no means do they give us a recipe or schema, as philosophy does, for trimming the epochs of history.

The premises guiding the arrangement and description of material are found only through ''the study of the real life-process and activity of the individuals of any given epoch.''[16]

Marx rejected expressly philosophical laws beyond the writing of practical history; he had three major reasons. First, for Marx, history, which is a ''process between man and nature''[17] mediated through labor, is not an automatic, fully determined product of the ''material base.'' To be sure, some of Marx's formulations make such an interpretation possible, but these are contradicted by the dominant thrust of his approach, which is thoroughly historical. Though this is not as strongly emphasized in his major economic work as in his early writings, the historical dimension can still be detected in his later works, as well.[18] For Marx, history cannot develop without consciousness which has become practical. Consciousness is not to be understood as an effect of "material existence," where human action is nothing more than an unequivocal, deterministic effect of laws dictated by "the base." "The [undialectical] materialistic doctrine[19] concerning the change of circumstances and education forgets that circumstances are changed by men and that the educator himself must be educated. Hence this doctrine must divide society into two parts."[20] This is just what Marx did not want. On the contrary Marx contends that societal being and consciousness are reciprocally changing elements of an intertwined relationship. At every historical stage there is an ensemble of established social relations which "on the one hand is modified by the new generation but on the other hand also prescribes its conditions of life, giving it a definite development and a special character. It shows, therefore, that circumstances make men just as much as men make circumstances."[21] After insight into his dialectical mediation of being and consciousness—of conditions of existence and human beings—it is obvious that Marx was not speaking of ahistorical, deterministic natural laws.

Second, if Marx had formulated laws of history, he would have committed the same errors of which he accused Feuerbach. According to Marx, Feuerbach was wrong when he spoke of "man" rather than referring to "actual historical individuals" in all their variability.[22] Marx would have had to abstract from history, state a natural law, and thereby depart from his own approach, which argues that the nature of man is his history and that this could not be grasped in the form of laws.[23] The objective possibilities for man in society are limited only by his previous history and by inherent natural laws insofar as nature is not fully absorbed by the mode of its historical appropriation.[24] These inherent laws of nature, which are not wholly at man's disposal, can only be described in the context of a particular historical situation in which men struggle with them. Therefore, they do not provide the basis for the formulation of an essence of man, even one negatively defined.[25]

Finally, in 1870 Marx engaged in sharp polemics against the attempt "to subsume" the whole of history "under one great natural law," the principle of survival of the fittest.[26] He frequently used the concept *natural law* to characterize the developmental tendencies of society. He spoke of the natural laws of capitalist production, which "act with firm necessity and have the tendency to prevail."[27] Natural law is to be understood in a double sense.

Marx used the term critically to explain the self-reproduction of the capitalist system: "because the cohesion of the aggregate production imposes itself as a blind law upon the agents of production, and not as a law which, being understood and hence controlled by their common mind, brings the production process under their joint control."[28] Societal or economic processes proceed according to natural laws in this sense as long as men have not yet become subjects who can determine their own conditions of existence.[29] By referring the natural laws to a particular historical situation from which they originated and within which they operate, Marx tried to show that the notion of natural laws was itself historically relative and changeable. At the same time, he criticized their rigid, repressive, naturalistic character, with the intention of overcoming it.[30]

Marx also believed that all historical stages of production have *certain* common characteristics. "Insofar as the labor process is only a simple process between man and nature, then its simple elements remain common to all forms of societal development."[31] Such constants, within Marx's conceptualization, are not astonishing when one reflects on the relationship of man and nature in Marx. While young Marx characterized the goal of historical development in utopian fashion as "the complete unification of man with nature,"[32] he observed later that nature is not fully absorbed in the historical manner of its practical appropriation. Even in socialist society man will still have to struggle with nature to satisfy his needs, because, even then, it will not be fully stripped of its capacity for resistance.[33] In 1868, he wrote: "Natural laws cannot be suspended. What can be changed is only the *form* in which the laws prevail in historically different circumstances."[34] It is evident that, here, natural law means the ever present conditions of existence and eternal necessity of nature, independent of all societal forms.[35] Nevertheless, it is not these formal and abstract natural laws which, in the opinion of Marx, are the objects of inquiry of historians and political economists; they study only the forms wherein these laws prevail.[36]

Such ambivalent formulations may suggest contradictions in Marx's analysis. But they should not obscure the fact that, for Marx, natural laws are not ahistorical, transcendental laws abstracted from historical, concrete, individual cases or rules to interpret historical phenomena; instead, Marx's natural laws are universals found only in the particular.[37]

It is true, for Marx, that history did not have an unlimited plasticity. However, the "eternal laws" which Weber ascribed to him are not in Marx's thought. When Weber accused the historical materialists of having an ahistorical and monocausal notion of law, he was not criticizing Marx, but rather those who interpreted him rigidly and nondialectically. Of course, Marx didn't always follow his own historical-dialectical approach, and above all Marx's concept of the relation of the universal and particular in history can be understood only on the basis of its origins in Hegelian logic. By the turn of the century and especially in the decades following, such concepts were interpreted by a public which no longer shared the assumptions and insights of Hegelian logic; even Weber may have succumbed to this type of misunderstanding.

Nevertheless, understanding the one-sidedness of Weber's views does not remove the differences between Weber's and Marx's methodological positions. Marx did not formulate ahistorical laws of historical process but nevertheless maintained the claim of analyzing scientifically the "core structure" of capitalist society (i.e., to reach a true understanding of the substance of reality) which Weber considered to be impossible and which he rejected as "metaphysics." Even if Weber had interpreted Marx more adequately, Marx's premise would still have been unacceptable to him.

REALITY AND METHOD: WEBER

Weber believed in a strict separation between the scientist and the reality under investigation. Certainly it is incorrect to maintain that Weber held that this reality is unstructured before it is observed scientifically. "The *choice* of the object of investigation and how far this investigation extends into the infinite causal web" is determined by the evaluative values *(Wertideen)* of the researcher (WL, 184/84). This formulation implies that causal connections into which the investigation can extend do exist. In other words, the investigation *follows* preexisting structures of reality; it does not create them from thin air.[38] Furthermore, this reality, which is pregiven in the *Geisteswissenschaften,* is social-historical reality. For Weber, the objects of social scientific inquiry have already come into being on an "ontic"[39] dimension through value-related action and to this extent are related to, and also structured through, meaning. This special character of the object makes, according to Weber, historical "understanding" possible, which likewise can only proceed through reference to values (WL, 180f.).

On the other hand, Weber made some statements suggesting that reality is chaotic. "The light which emanates from those highest evaluative ideas always falls on an ever-changing finite segment of the vast chaotic stream of events, which flows away through time."[40] From these quotations, many interpreters have concluded that Weber meant reality had absolutely no objective structure.[41]

This contradiction between conceptions of reality as structured and as chaotic can be resolved. Even though the reality of the "heterogeneous continuum"[42] is structured through and determined by causal relations and value relations, this does not mean that the scientist discerns this reality *in these relations*. In fact, the pregiven structures of the "continuum" could be irrelevant to those structures sought and in part constituted by scientific inquiry. This would be the case if the pregiven causal relations are infinite in number while simultaneously each element stands in an ambiguous relationship to the others. One can speak of a chaos of causal relationships and of a mass of individual value-related elements,[43] of "an amorphous detritus" even though the elements are individually structured. Culture is merely a slice of reality, arranged and constituted according to the analyst's specific values and standpoints. Though it is certainly structured, reality nevertheless appears chaotic to the observer.[44]

If reality is presented as infinitely complex and diverse, then empirical scientific knowledge can only be partial knowledge. "All the analysis of infinite reality which the finite human mind can conduct rests on the tacit assumption that only a finite *part* of this reality constitutes the object of scientific investigation *(Erfassung)* and that only it is 'important' in the sense of 'being worthy of being known'" (WL, 171/72). The choice of what is "important" proceeds from value ideas and viewpoints derived from the interests of the researcher. These interests cannot be taken "from the material itself" (WL, 181). Again and again Weber denied the possibility of deriving the standpoint which makes scientific inquiry possible from the object itself.[45] The criterion for judging the correctness of a research perspective or the possibility of choosing among several standpoints cannot be derived sufficiently from the object to be investigated.[46] Although the reality in the "hetereogeneous continuum" is structured, Weber had to stress the independence of the standpoint of the inquiry and construction of categories from the object of investigation because the "ontic" structures in the "heterogeneous continuum" are largely indifferent to the causal connections and interdependent structures which the scholar tries to establish. To be sure, the "ontic" structure of reality is *not completely* indifferent to the formulation of a scientific framework (the formulation of concepts, models and explanations). The scientist cannot approach every object with each interest and each concept and cannot contrive randomly "a historical individual."[47] At the very least, the richness of empirical data which allows for many, though not all, interpretations provides discretionary limits.[48] But, as long as scientific concept formation does not contradict this elementary fact (and for Weber the degree of latitude appears to be quite large), reality remains indifferent to the construction of categories.

Weber's effort to demarcate clearly the world of objects as a value-free facticity from the sphere of values and the standpoints dependent on them is understandable on the basis of his notion of reality, and it is a constitutive and indispensable dimension of his philosophy of science *(Wissenschaftslehre)* and ethics. However, this separation drew accusations of decisionism. In fact, it does appear as if the choice of research perspectives *(Erkenntnisgesichtspunkte)* is a decision which cannot be rationally grounded or criticized, if the matter to be investigated (i.e., historical reality) is eliminated as a criterion for this choice.[49] Weber stated that the choice of standpoint is not arbitrary as long as it is successful (WL, 170), but this success is judged according to the same standpoints for which it in turn is supposed to be the criterion.

On the basis of Weber's methodological essays summarized thus far, there remains a deep gulf between reality and understanding. Objectivity can only be achieved methodologically, not on the basis of content. This disavowal justifies Weber's further claim that the value-relevant standpoint be exempted from rational discussion. Reason and decision seem to go their separate ways. From this viewpoint, Weber's ambivalent attitude towards Marx is easier to understand. Weber could accept Marx's perspectives and categories as one set of possibilities among many, and he gave Marx neither preference nor derision relative to others. Thus, he criticized both historical materialism and racial theories, placing them formally on the same level, deserving of equal consideration (WL, 167). For Weber, there could be no knowledge of the substance of reality in itself *(Substanzeinsicht)*, and, therefore, he had to contest the claim that Marx's theory was more than a rational ordering of an ultimately chaotic reality.

REALITY AND METHOD: MARX

Marx rejected the comprehension of reality solely as "a form of the object" and, instead, conceived it as "sensuous human activity," as praxis.[50] Thus, historical reality is a process in which human labor and human consciousness are objectified continuously and to an ever-increasing extent. In turn, historical reality acts as a limiting condition on the thinking and acting subject. Marx would have rejected the Weberian demand for a clear demarcation between the knowing subject and object of inquiry as too abstract. He could have argued that on the one hand, we can always find a significant degree of human consciousness in the limiting conditions on every level of historical process; on the other, in any situation human consciousness can be described as historical in form and content, that is, determined by the historical process. (As Marx wrote: "Der Mensch, das ist die Welt des Menschen.")[51]

Two points follow logically. First, reality is not in principle estranged from rational human understanding insofar as it is mediated increasingly through labor and constituted through consciousness transformed into praxis. Marx adhered to this position contra Feuerbach even for the objects of natural sciences; "even this 'pure' natural science is provided with an aim, as with its materials through trade and industry, through the sensuous activity of men."[52] This applies all the more to the social sciences. Second, human consciousness does not approach reality with categories alien to the subject matter. "The essence of man is not an abstraction inhering in each individual. In its actuality it is the ensemble of social relations."[53] Therefore, in form and content human consciousness is "a historical existence in its conceptual form, an area of experience and range of ideas determined by society."[54] This implies that values and points of view must be incorporated as features of the total social and historical process and not, as in Weber, remain unrelated to the object of investigation.

Within Marx's approach it does not follow, however, that human consciousness is always adequate to its objects. According to Marx, conceptual elements, which enter into reality, can and must appear inverted in the consciousness of the carriers and agents of alienated economic relations.[55] When private producers in capitalist exchange combine their social labor in an abstract way, "they are not aware of it, but they do it."[56] Marx was convinced that the task of science is to clear up this necessarily false consciousness. However, he thought that this can be mediated only through proletarian class interests and, likewise, can only be successful if connected with actual changes in social conditions.

What are the methodological consequences of this implied inseparability of consciousness and world? It definitely does not entail the dissolution of the object in the knowing subject. The "concrete subject [i.e., the object of inquiry] remains outside the intellect and independent of it—that is so long as the intellect adopts a purely speculative, purely theoretical attitude. The subject, society, must always be envisaged therefore as the pre-condition of comprehension even when the theoretical method is employed."[57] Thus, inquiry can hardly be described as an agreement of the intellect with external objects, in the sense of a mimetic theory of knowledge. This theory would presuppose the duality of subject and object which Marx attempted to overcome.[58]

Nor can inquiry be described outside the practical relations of man and reality. On the one hand, Marx's reflection on objects of the external world began with the significance of those objects for satisfying human needs;[59] on the other, labor itself is objectified in the historical reality under study through the progressive practical appropriation of these objects. Accordingly, human praxis enters into the definition of this reality which it has in part constituted, and in this way praxis becomes a criterion for truth. "The question as to whether human thinking can reach objective truth is not a question of theory, but a *practical* question."[60] Without entering further into the problems encompassed by this statement,[61] it is clear that, in Marx's view, even scientific thought is already preformed by a practical relation between world and man. Scientific thinking focuses on a world which is incomplete in the sense that it needs further evolution through praxis, insofar as it always already contains objectified human praxis. Historical reality is structured: scientists can determine structures through the praxis operant in that context. Weber's distinction between "objective" and "historical" (e.g., constituted through the application of scientific concepts) realities is irrelevant to this mode of thought. Marx stated: "The dispute about the actuality or non-actuality of thinking—thinking isolated from practice—is a purely *scholastic* question."[62]

This way of referring to praxis as ever present and also continually changing excludes two inferences. First, such an approach does not permit formulation of a general *system* of economics or sociology. Such a system would be detached from its historical context and rendered abstractly independent. Thus, it is once again clear that the general law of history, criticized by *Weber,* found little room in Marx's thinking. But there is a limited agreement between Marx and Weber, since Weber argued on the basis of the constantly changing research interests *(Erkenntnisinteressen)* a definitive system in the cultural sciences was impossible (WL, 184). Second, within such an approach, a methodology in Weber's sense is impossible to perfect. Every methodology must complete the break, which Marx rejected, between the knowing subject and object of analysis. Moreover, it can be argued that a methodology is always required to abstract from concrete historical cases; in other words, it must provide a schema, under which it subsumes all processes of inquiry.[63]

From Marx's perspective, therefore, a critique of Weber's methodological position proceeds in the following manner.[64] Social reproduction has attained such independence that the human world confronts humanity as something completely alien. The historical process cannot be fathomed by the isolated individual for reasons specified by Marx; this is reflected in Weber's characterization of reality as an incomprehensible chaos. One can no longer think in terms of progress. Rationality shrinks to efficient means-ends relations, so that goal-setting no longer needs to be related to reason. Marxist critique of Weberian methodology strives to interpret the latter's ahistorical formulations of cognitive processes of the empirical sciences by reflecting on their social-historical presuppositions; and in this way the critique relativizes them historically and socially, thereby negating them as a general methodology. One step of this critique involves clarifying Weber's notion of reality, a presupposition on which he never reflected. Such a critique locates Weber in his social and historical context. Thus, the critique of abstract categories proceeds to the critique of abstract relations, the former being a pseudo-approximation of the latter. Ahistorical categories, separated from their objects, are shown to be indicative of alienated thought, and thereby relative.

HISTORICAL TOTALITY VS. "HETEROGENEOUS CONTINUUM"

It follows from the above that Marx, in contrast to Weber, had a notion of historical totality *(Gesamtgeschichte)* and thought of society as a specific and specifiable totality. The whole determines its individual, interrelated elements, just as it is determined by them. Marx applied the method which he briefly delineated in the introduction to the "Critique of Political Economy."[65] He proceeded from the "actual and the concrete, the real preconditions," thus, in the study of political economy, from the people. This "true and concrete" proves to be an empty abstraction, if its structure of classes and their basic elements, capital, wage labor, and so forth, are not penetrated. The conception of the whole remains chaotic and completely unspecified as long as one does not proceed analytically from what is believed to be concrete to always thinner abstractions and simpler definitions. "From there the journey should be made once again in the opposite direction, until one arrived once more at the concept of the populace, which this time is not a vague notion of a whole, but a rich totality comprising numerous definitions and interrelationships." Therefore, what is concrete for Marx is not immediate perception, but "the concrete concept is concrete, because it is a synthesis of many definitions, thus representing a unity of diverse elements."[66] This concrete totality encompasses the entire social relations of a historical period.

The whole can only be found in its parts. "The presupposition for the existence of the whole lies in the nature of its parts, and so it is only through the study of these parts that the whole is constituted. But even this is not enough for it must be shown how the parts interrelate with one another and mutually determine one another in order to appear as a whole."[67] Conversely, because of their interconnections, each part can be grasped only if, at the same time, the whole is investigated. Marx condemned indirectly any approach that viewed the object of inquiry as one example, which in turn is subsumed under a context of meaning *(Sinnzusammenhang).*

The implicit basis for this methodology is a conception of reality that requires appearance to be distinguished from essence and surface from core. "The final pattern of economic relations as seen on the surface, in their real existence and consequently in the conceptions by which the bearers and agents of these relations seek to understand them, is very different from, and indeed quite the reverse of, their inner but concealed essential pattern and the conception corresponding to it."[68] Although in an alienated society the existing form of social relations more often disguises than reveals its true character, social scientists must nevertheless begin with one of the surface manifestations, for they can only locate the core structure in its concrete historical manifestation. The task of science is to define the concept of this "core structure,"[69] that is, "to reveal the economic laws of motion of modern society."[70] However, this does not imply a general law in the sense of a universal formula. Rather, it is a matter of formulating a concept which cannot be severed from its forms of existence. Therefore, Marx demanded simultaneously "the beginning of the journey in the opposite direction"; that is, the uncovering of the relations between the core structure and surface phenomena. Only then can the core structure be adequately grasped (i.e., concretely).[71] At the same time, "the conceptions by which the barriers and agents of these relations seek to understand them" are questioned.[72] Thereby, the possibility arises of altering these ideas. This possibility is not limited to the theory but must proceed toward practical changes of those relations that shaped false consciousness.

According to Marx, and in contrast to Weber, understanding of the substance of reality is in principle possible for science on the basis of the aforementioned dialectical relation between consciousness and reality. However, this can only be reached by consciousness which is no longer constrained by class relations or warped by the pressures of alienated economic conditions. The possibility of such knowledge cannot be reflected on abstractly, since the content and form of knowing consciousness are determined by the outcomes and moments of particular historical situations.

Marx's demand that science provide insight into the essence of historical relations, which means a grasp of the totality, is made possible by a materialist reformulation of Hegel's notion of reality.[73] This notion encompasses a structural unity in all its diversity as well as a core structure in all its appearances. In contrast, Weber's neo-Kantian position conceives of reality as a "heterogeneous continuum" and must be satisfied with partial knowledge. Weber condemned every distinction between essence and appearance as bad metaphysics and every intention of conceptualizing the whole as a presumptuous self-deception. Conversely, the persuasive power and consistency of Marx's propositions are extraordinarily dependent on their Hegelian premises.

Weber's method proceeds from a conception of historical reality as a "heterogeneous continuum." Above all, it is distinguished from Marx's emphasis on the whole by the isolation of *one* "causal chain" from the richness of reality according to *one* heuristic standpoint. Weber did not think of reality as a structured totality. In addition, even though he could pursue supplementary "causal chains" in further investigations, it is very difficult, using Weber's method, to reflect continually on the relation and significance of one moment of reality in relation to others.

This abstraction, required by Weber's methodology, results in difficulties, as in *The Protestant Ethic and the Spirit of Capitalism*. For example, Weber was unable to explain adequately the phenomenon of Pietism within his limited approach. Pietism, though resting on the same religious foundation as Puritanism, hardly led to the same sober asceticism and work ethic. To explain this difference, Weber would have had to portray the other conditions that led to the transformation of Calvinistic religiosity into secular efficiency. These conditions are probably of a social, economic, geographic, or other character and have the effect that similar religious contents led in one case to an active worldliness and in another to an inner piety.[74] Weber would have had to reflect on the interwoven character and reciprocal influence on different conditioning elements and weigh their significance relative to one another.[75]

Weber had similar difficulties by limiting, to *one* causal chain, his explanation of how early capitalist manufacturing grew out of traditional cottage industries in the eighteenth century.[76] He presented the new Calvinist spirit as the motivating force that effected an intensification of controls over work, planning, the search for customers, and so on, and also destroyed the prevailing forms of industry. However, it is questionable whether the impetus and effects of this new spirit can explain adequately why manufacturing required a central workplace separate from one's living quarters. It is at least conceivable that the planning, canvassing for customers, and increased rationality of labor could also have been guaranteed in a decentralized form of operation. The explanation of the origin of the centralized enterprise requires reference: to the development of the means of production, the tools and early machines, whose purchase and use demanded centralization; to the work process whose future technical development clearly demanded a centralized administration; and to the connection of these elements with the new capitalist spirit. Weber's approach does not spur investigation of these questions and connections.

Marx, in contrast, attempted to grasp reality with all its diverse, reciprocally conditioning elements, including scientific research itself. As seen in his elaboration of "labor," even the most abstract categories are historical. It could only be thought of as "labor in general" in a "well developed totality of actual types of labor, where none dominates the others." This presupposes a societal form "in which individuals easily pass from one type of labor to another, and are indifferent to the particular kind of labor which befalls them." That was less the case at the time of the physiocrats than in modern bourgeois society. Marx demonstrated convincingly "how even the most abstract categories, despite their validity for all epochs, precisely because they are abstractions, are equally a product of historical conditions even in the specific form of abstractions and they retain their full validity only for and within the framework of these conditions."[77] In this way, the above mentioned thesis—the inquiring subject does not approach an object with alien categories—takes on concrete form. However, subjects must continually reflect on their position within the totality of the historical process and on the origins of their categories within this process.[78] Categories and perspectives can be criticized only insofar as they are placed within the context of conditions under which they originated and are applied.

Marx justified the dominant position of the categories of work, production, and exchange on the basis of their great importance in capitalist society. For Marx, categories were also categories of being *(Seinskategorien)*. To use Weber's language, for Marx, scientific standpoints were likewise dominant elements of the reality to be investigated.

Here, a question should be addressed to Marx the historian: can categories, which are purportedly applicable to contemporary society, also be applied to the past? For example, can class and class struggle, categories which according to Marx are historically relative, be equally well applied in investigations of the Middle Ages? Marx was sufficiently historical and aware of the heterogeneity of historical particularities so as not to contend naively that contemporary concepts are automatically applicable to previous historical periods. "Thus, although it is true that the categories of bourgeois economy are valid for all other social formations, this has to be taken *cum grano salis*."[79] Nevertheless, he believed that insight into the structure and relations of past societies is possible only on the basis of the present form of social organization, since this has attained the highest level of development. The earlier forms are looked upon by the latest "as stages in the development of itself." "In this way the bourgeois economy provides the key to antiquity, etc.,"[80] although the historical differences must not be overlooked. Marx's position indirectly implies that only in the present do individual elements come to light as what they were, in disguised form, in the past. The present is the developed form of the past, and contemporary categories, related to past forms, can grasp the essence of those forms better than categories which were known and used during the period under investigation.

In other words, Marx conceded that historical observation always occurs from the specific horizon of the observer. However, for Marx, the present conditions, which constitute that horizon, are the more developed and more adequate form of the conditions under study. Here, there is a certain justification for Weber's criticism that the "laws" of historical materialism are a universal historical method in which the relations of production have an almost metaphysical preponderance. There are, indeed, some elements within Marx's thought which make it easy to mistake his portrayal of the anatomy of bourgeois society for a maxim of the philosophy of history or a "materialist conception of history."

The above peculiarity of Marx's method follows necessarily from his modified appropriation of Hegel's concept of development. With this goes the presupposition that is fundamental to Marx—namely, that history can be grasped as a rational process, at least in principle, and to which man belongs unconditionally as an active mediating agent. For Hegel, true history is the way to self-liberation of the spirit, which moves to manifest the reality of its essence though initially existing only in itself. The materialist Marx no longer held this position. Nevertheless, he conceived every historical epoch as a structured totality, whose contradictions already contain within themselves the demand and promise of their dissolution. Accordingly, the present is "restricted future."[81] The future is only the realization of developmental tendencies which are already established and fixed in the present.

In the final analysis the above presupposition explains the antagonism of Marx's thought to Weber's position. Weber's rejection of any concept of development (Entwicklung) follows necessarily from an understanding of reality as a "heterogeneous continuum."[82] This difference is highlighted clearly through a comparison of what Marx and Weber understood as critique. Weber stated: "The fate of a cultural epoch which has eaten from the tree of knowledge is that it must know that we cannot learn the *meaning* of the world from the results of its analysis, be it ever so perfect; it must rather be in a position to create meaning itself. It must be recognized that general views of life and universe can never be products of increasing empirical knowledge, and that the highest ideas, which move us most forcefully, are always formed only in the struggle with other ideals which are just as sacred to others as ours are to us" (WL, 154/57). "Every meaningful value judgment about someone else's *aspirations* must be a criticism from the standpoint of one's own Weltanschauung. It must be a struggle against *another's* ideals from the standpoint of one's own" (WL, 157/60).

In contrast, Marx asserted: "Reason has always existed, but not always in rational form. The critic therefore can start with any form of theoretical and practical consciousness and develop the true actuality out of the forms *inherent* in existing actuality as its ought-to-be and goal."[83] While for Weber, an individual acting autonomously creates meaning in a world which is ultimately meaningless, Marx believed that the meaning of new social relations could be found through a critique of past relations, which already embody them implicitly.

CRITIQUE AND ATTEMPTS AT MEDIATION

In Marx's theory the reality to be investigated is a criterion for the suitability of the categories of investigation. Since the issue is knowledge of essential structures, of "laws" of a particular reality and not partial knowledge, the categories of investigation cannot be derived arbitrarily. Instead, the object of inquiry compels researchers, who immerse themselves in the object, to accept standpoints and categories adequate to the investigation. This also applies to the relation of values (norms and criteria of action) to reality. Pushed to its limits, the position is that norms of action are deducible from the correct analysis of historical reality.[84] In contrast to Weber's value freedom, decisions are clearly open to examination and are thereby simultaneously eliminated. In a " 'scientific civilization' where politicians would no longer be 'decision makers' or 'rulers,' but rather analyzers . . ." politics would consist of drawing consequences from the constraints of the social mechanisms that determined societal development.[85] Similarly, in a world that rendered an analysis of itself and its "objective potentialities" possible, to the extent that understanding of what was "socially desirable" could be derived from them,[86] value decisions would be replaced by deductions from an analysis of reality. In both instances, from the consequent elimination of decisions, there emerge the dangers of illiberalism, authoritarian antipluralism, and dogmatism. In science, this is manifested as intolerance towards other propositions. From the confines of this approach, such propositions appear only as errors or ideological deviations from true reality. Socio-politically, this approach provides an ideological justification of its own goals as general and absolute because they are based on supposedly scientific insights (though, in fact, its goals are thoroughly one-sided).

Weber's philosophy of science postulates a contrary position, holding fast to the impossibility of deriving prescriptive knowledge from the object of inquiry. For Weber, knowledge is always fragmentary: its direction is determined by the initial choice of one standpoint from several alternatives. Weber hardly mentioned the interdependence of this choice with one's knowledge of reality, even though he claimed that the origin of the inquiry and the manner and aim of its proceedings is determined by these standpoints.

Above all, this radical separation is applicable to the relationship between historical reality and values, between empirical science and life decisions. Knowledge of values and goals of action do not follow from empirical scientific analysis. According to Weber, science can contribute something to the formulation of goals of action,[87] but it cannot justify the preference of one value over its opposite (WL, 149ff.). Even if science were able to establish a developmental tendency in history, this still would not provide actors with clues as to whether they should support or oppose its realization (WL, 474f.). Since a variety of possible actions derived from contrasting values is left open, the origin and choice of values appear closed to rational discussion (WL, 469f.). In the arena of action (the process of inquiry), goals and norms (cognitive standpoints and goals respectively) are constituted ultimately by a choice on whose essential rationality it is impossible to comment.[88]

Up to the point, Marx and Weber represent alternative and radically opposed ways of thinking. This confrontation points to shortcomings and pitfalls of their paradigms and provides a basis for alternating critique and attempts at mediation. This gives rise to the question whether there are perhaps certain elements within both Marx's and Weber's approaches, elements which require going beyond the pattern reconstructed so far in this article. I have tried to show that an approach, where the cognitive standpoint can be derived clearly from the reality under investigation, necessarily presupposes a concept of history, which, though modified in the direction of praxis, depends heavily on Hegel. Norms of action can be oriented towards the objective possibilities of a specific reality only if that reality in its historical form is such that it can be mediated through correct practical consciousness towards the realization of that which existed heretofore only as potentiality (i.e., a type of reality which, for becoming itself, needs human praxis and, hence, practical knowledge). This reality is neither external nor alien to understanding, but rather, as Hegel stated, "it is the nature of the content and that alone which lives and stirs in philosophic *[wissenschaftlichen]* cognition, while it is this very reflection of the content which itself originates and determines the nature of philosophy."[89] The presupposition is certainly of the initial identity of the object of inquiry and the knowing subject, which is anchored in Hegel's philosophy.

If history is an act, "by which the absolute final aim of the world is realized in it and the merely implicit mind achieves consciousness and self-consciousness,"[90] then—and only then—can critique consist of the confrontation of a particular reality with its potentiality or its "claims," thereby ensuring historical progress. This concept of history guarantees, in principle, the unproblematical adequacy of contemporary categories in historical investigations, for these categories arise from a present which is the true and developed form of the past. For Hegel, the identity of subjective and objective spirit, of human consciousness and historical actuality, which becomes manifest in morality *(Sittlichkeit)*, is marked out and present (if only implicitly) from the beginning.

But the question must be posed whether Marx, in his historical materialist rejection of Hegel's premise of a universal, historically unfolding reason,[91] did not also deny the foundation for conceiving the relationship between humanity and history in an Hegelian manner, as an identity that is already existent and merely needs to be realized. Certainly from Marx's position it can be argued that, since historical reality is always formed and mediated by human reason, it needs neither to be alien to human understanding nor "a vast chaotic flow" in Weber's sense. But it is less clear from Marx's premises why the particular level of metabolic process between man and nature[92] should always carry implicitly within itself its own future design or its own critique in the sense of an Hegelian objective possibility, which enables one to state without question—"What is valuable for society is always what has become possible historically."[93] For in Marx's view the material of the historical process is not identical with a notion of nature, which could be described as idea in its otherness[94] and whose implicit truth would be embodied in history from its beginning. Just as nature, for Marx, does not unfold fully in history, neither does it *demand* its meaningful cultivation through historical labor; at best it *permits* it and leaves open alternatives (e.g., destructive utilization). However much each historical situation is mediated through concepts, it does not fully and unambiguously contain the goal of its future. The goal of humanity is the concept of its previous development only if this concept as self-actualizing reason already precedes its own development. However, Marx rejected this premise.[95] Thereby, the deducibility of goals of political action from an appropriate analysis of previous history becomes objectively highly questionable within any Marxian approach (although Marx did not see this).

The same objection applies to the deducibility of cognitive standpoints and conceptual categories from the object of inquiry. As shown above,[96] Marx's social and historical analysis proceeds from a specific historically determined and practical horizon. Since, on the basis of his methodological remarks, Marx claimed to proceed from "the actual and concrete elements of real preconditions" and took "the people" as the point of departure for his research in order to arrive at their organization (classes) and the fundamental elements of the latter,[97] then at this point, he already had an implicit preunderstanding *(Vorverständnis)*. For example, he did not start with one nation-state as opposed to other nation-states. And his theory enabled him to arrive at economically defined classes as organizational elements but not, for example, religious or ethnic groups. This theoretical preunderstanding is neither self-evident, nor is it the only one possible. But Marx wrote as if this preunderstanding, these categories, and theoretical statements would be imposed on the researcher by the object of inquiry, as if they would emerge naturally from immersion in the object. But, in fact, this belief does not follow from his own premises.[98]

In the preceding section, I tried to show that within Marx's approach (but in some contrast to what Marx himself wrote): (1) the object of inquiry is itself not a wholly sufficient criterion, not a fully sufficient "empirical referent" for clear determination of appropriate concepts and cognitive approaches; and (2) the problem of the fit of concept and object (which Weber stated clearly, though he solved it in too decisionistic a fashion) cannot be passed over simply by referring to Marx. The same objection applies to praxis as a second possible mode of control over the formulation of scientific concepts, categories, and theories. Certainly, Marx's theory convincingly shows that scientific research always stands in a multireferential practical context, and hence, can and must find criteria for its procedures.[99] However, even if research must always be oriented to praxis, it is impossible for this praxis to provide a fixed objective measure, either for evaluation of norms or for the choice of cognitive approach. Man is always a constitutive element in the midst of this praxis, just as cognition is a dimension of the very process that it desires to understand. Cognition is unable to objectify praxis as a comprehensible totality. Therefore, the problem of the "hermeneutical circle," of which Marx was unaware, has to be addressed.[100] This is especially pertinent for a mode of thought that considers itself as part of the totality to be known. In addition, praxis is continually changing, among other ways through the progress of research, the guidelines for which it is supposed to provide. And historically, praxis never attains a definitive form; it can always be interpreted differently.

If correctly interpreted, in Marx's thought there persists the unresolved problem of how values and cognitive approaches and categories can be controlled. Neither the historical reality to be investigated nor the specific historical praxis of the investigator provides a sufficiently clear criterion for such choice. However, this does not require a return to the decisionistic alternative discussed above.

The following points must be retained: (1) the cognitive standpoint is reflective of the object of inquiry and the specific form of societal praxis, although it is not unequivocally deducible from them; and (2) individual historical phenomena, per Marx's claim, are not grasped outside of a notion of totality, despite the fact that totality cannot be fully or directly conceptualized. How do these points relate to Max Weber's philosophy of science?

To be more compatible with these two elements of Marx's theory, an interpretation of Weber's philosophy of science must (1) maintain Weber's primacy of the cognitive standpoint in empirical research, while holding to the impossibility of simply deriving it from criteria based on the subject matter or the existing culture, and (2) find, within Weber's theory, possibilities for control of the choice of standpoint so as to free it from the charge of decisionism.

Weber has been criticized for presenting science with an object that does not exist in historical reality. Because of the absence of structure in the "heterogeneous continuum," knowledge can only—according to this criticism—be validated methodologically and not through a confrontation with reality. Culture is merely a "subjective concept" and history only "our composition." Weber's reality, "an amorphous detritus of appearances," supplies no criterion for choice, evaluation, and control of those perspectives which make knowledge possible.[101]

This criticism, supported by Weber's statements, remains valid even if, as shown above, the "heterogeneous continuum" is not wholly without structure, for these "ontic" structures cannot prevent reality from appearing first and foremost as a "chaotic stream." Nevertheless, such a radical critique, according to which Weber's methodological position must appear paradoxical,[102] cannot explain sufficiently numerous other elements and passages within his philosophy of science. Weber indicated, at least implicitly, that although cognitive standpoints are deducible from the object of inquiry, they can be questioned and controlled. Thus, he hoped to determine, with more research, "the *extent* of the cultural significance of ascetic Protestantism" for modern capitalism.[103] This would mean that, at a later point, a rational decision can be reached concerning the importance of one perspective and causal chain (e.g., the socio-economic) relative to others.

Weber considered the scientist's principle value premises *(Wertideen)* to be the criterion for the choice of cognitive standpoint (WL, 259f.). He believed that a "scientific genius" would gear his inquiry to values that determine "the 'conception' of a whole epoch" (WL, 182). Weber also implied that the researchers' cognitive interests and standpoints are mediated by the practical needs of their time (WL, 148, 158, 165). Certainly, Weber's intertwining of the standpoints with social conditions is not a sufficient basis for control of a standpoint. For if practical, cultural problems are introduced as a criterion of appropriate correspondence for the formulation of the standpoint and concepts, there arises the question as to how it is possible to achieve an unequivocal understanding of those very problems. The same difficulty reappears because, according to Weber's position, the practical, cultural concerns vary according to the interests, values, and standpoints of the individual, whereas these standpoints are supposed to be measured against the problems.

Nevertheless, Weber's awareness of the close relation between standpoints and social conditions can justify, within his own theoretical framework, the demand that the formulation of scientific standpoints and theories be reflected on from the perspective of the societal context, one element of which is the research itself.[104] Weber does not expressly make this demand, but it has a place within his philosophy of science. Moreover, Weber's repeated demand for clarity and intellectual integrity can, within the confines of his position, justify sufficiently the demand that scientists reflect on the intertwining of their cognitive standpoints with their social situations; this Weber acknowledged (WL, 259f.). If this is a correct interpretation of Weber's philosophy of science, it is somewhat protected against the charge of irrational decisionism.

In Weber's theory both the social reality of the investigator and the object of inquiry offer possibilities of limiting subjective arbitrariness. "If, however, I wish to grasp the concept of 'sect' genetically, e.g., with reference to certain important effects *(Kulturbedeutungen),* which the 'sectarian spirit' has had for modern culture, certain characteristics of both [church and sect] become *essential,* because they stand in adequate causal relation to those effects" (WL, 194/93-94). For Weber, the concept of cultural meaning *(Kulturbedeutung)* usually indicated the basis for the interest with which the researcher turns to a particular historical object, a methodical procedure, according to which "a segment of the meaningless infinity of world events" is bestowed with "meaning" and thus becomes "culture."[105] In the above quoted case (WL, 194/93-94), however, *Kulturbedeutung* denoted the connection through which a cultural phenomenon of the past has influenced modern culture. Thus, though *Kulturbedeutung* usually belongs to those concepts which bind scientific knowledge to the researcher's value decisions, here the term denotes an objective structure.[106] In Weber's view, culture not only represented a slice of chaos ordered by a methodical relationship with the scientist's values and viewpoints, but he also recognized something similar to a "material concept of culture," culture on the "ontic" level, whose structure and meaning, at least initially, are not constituted by the researcher's standpoint.[107]

This is evidence for something like an "ontic" turn in Weber's work; this can help to defend against the charge of decisionism. But how does it fit into the framework of his theory? How can freedom of choice of the research perspective, which Weber insisted on so frequently, be reconciled with the assumption of a "material" culture? If such a "material" culture exists, scientific investigations cannot confront it as a subordinate, amorphous stuff; rather, it demands that researchers adequately reconstruct the object (the "ontic" structure) of their investigations. At any rate, "material" culture is, within Weber's approach, part of a reality of which only partial knowledge is possible, and it cannot be thought of such that cognitive standpoints are *unequivocally* deducible from it. Nevertheless, it represents a *real* context which controls retroactively whether the perspectives from which the research proceeds are appropriate to the structures for which they have been constituted. Though the subject matter does *not impose* standpoints on the researcher, it *nevertheless influences* their choice and application. Moreover, it requires continuous reflection on the relationship between standpoint and object. In this way the subject matter limits arbitrariness of the choice of standpoint.

Weber never made this premise of his arguments explicit and thus did not justify it in the context of his other concepts. Discourse in the philosophy of science, at that time, occasioned Weber to stress the nondeducibility of evaluative standpoints against the attacks of the nomothetical and historical schools.[108] Putting this aside, an explication of such a premise would have had to include a theory of material culture, which Weber was not prepared to undertake. The goal of such a theory would have been to reconcile the tension between it and reality viewed as a "heterogeneous continuum." Possibly this would have led to irresolvable contradictions and the need to examine a notion which Weber supported exclusively through appeals to empirical evidence.

For Weber as well as Marx, subject matter exercised a control function over the application of the previously constituted standpoint, a process whose explication might not be possible without modification of Weber's whole theory. The question arises: through which mechanism does the research object influence and direct the choice of cognitive standpoint? Attention is drawn to the prescientific preunderstanding of the object *(Vorverständnis)*, which steers the formulation of categories.

"All historical 'valuation' includes, so to speak, a 'contemplative' element, it contains not only and not primarily the immediate value judgement of the assessing person, but rather its essential content is . . . a 'knowledge' of the object's 'relations to value.' It therefore presupposes the capacity for a change in the attitude towards the object, at least theoretically" (WL, 260/158). Even if historical research, namely the search for historical causes, is preceded and constituted by the choice of certain values, this constitutive act always presupposes some "knowledge" of the various possibilities through which the object can be related to values: "the 'objectification' and analysis of concrete reality is thereby taken for granted" (WL, 86). Here, Weber emphasized that another form of knowledge of reality must have preceded the constitution of scientific standpoints and concepts. He designated this prescientific preunderstanding as "objectification" and "analysis":[109] it makes possible the formulation of scientific concepts and limits their arbitrariness.

It appears that Weber knew of a—to him, self-evident—regulator of the choice of perspectives and concept-formation which inhered in the subject matter; however, its explication would have entangled his theory in contradictions. The notion of "heterogeneous continuum" forced Weber to describe the cognitive process as a process of abstracting and isolating factors. In contrast, a preunderstanding, which informs the analyst of the different possible value relations, must include a notion of the whole. For only on this basis can a preunderstanding exclude the fortuitousness of the choice of standpoints and provide, though not in wholly adequate fashion, a presupposition for the critical examination of the "essential" in the sense of "worthy of being known." Weber was aware of this when he acknowledged a "*functional* analysis of the relation between the 'parts' and the 'whole'" as a requisite "preliminary orientation to problems" (WL, 515, 518; *Economy and Society*, 15, 17). Weber noted: ". . . in certain circumstances, this is the only available way of determining just what processes of social action it is important to understand in order to explain a given phenomenon" (WL, 515; *Economy and Society*, 15) and to enable us to carry out the task of interpretive *(verstehende)* sociology. A question arises as to whether a concept of the whole is meaningful and practicable within a reality conceived of as a "heterogeneous continuum." Once again, Weber would have run into difficulties in further explication of his theory, as this would have called into question the "heterogeneous continuum."

Confronting Marx's thought with Weber's theory revealed tensions, dogmatic tendencies and deficiencies within the former, but also showed that Weber's approach in no way resolved the problem of Marx's thinking. The confrontation of Weber's philosophy of science with Marx's position likewise entailed critique and offered simultaneously the opportunity to free Weber's theory from some of its decisionistic consequences (i.e., interpreting it so that it is less closed to some of the indispensable elements of Marx's teachings). This attempted mediation found its clearest limits in the two authors' notions of reality, namely in the residue of Hegelian historical speculation in Marx and in the concept of an "heterogeneous continuum" in Weber. It has been argued that revisions of these notions, though leading to new problems and tensions, would eliminate certain extreme and unacceptable aspects of both Marx's and Weber's philosophies of science, specifically the danger of dogmatism in the former's epistemology and the danger of decisionism in the latter's methodology.

The outlines of a practical position in the philosophy of science are indicated clearly. Naturally, its elaboration could rest on numerous contributions which can neither be considered nor further investigated here.[110] The outlines are as follows: on the one hand, neither the structures of the object of inquiry nor the practical mediatory context within which investigators find themselves are able to prescribe unequivocally the researcher's cognitive standpoint, statement of the problem, categories, explanatory models, and theories; on the other hand, they are not indifferent to these matters. Therefore, researchers must justify continually, via argumentation and as part of the research procedure, their decisions concerning theories, concepts, and procedures in categories appropriate to the subject matter and congruent with societal rationality (which, to be sure, is open within limits to different interpretations). This position would *establish* a context for discussion, be open to a plurality of research perspectives, and, yet, simultaneously *circumscribe* this context through indicating points of control: the object itself, the relation to praxis, and the rational, critical, open, and to the greatest extent possible, autonomous communication among the investigators. Only in this way can a position in the philosophy of science escape both the charge of authoritarian dogmatism and the verdict of decisionistic arbitrariness.

Notes

This essay developed out of a seminar given by Professor D. Henrich at the Free University of Berlin during the winter of 1963–64. It was first published under the title "Karl Marx und Max Weber: Ein methodologischer Vergleich," in *Zeitschrift für die gesamte Staatswissenschaft* 122 (1966): 328–57. It was then revised and published in H. U. Wehler, ed., *Geschichte und Ökonomie* (Cologne, 1973), 54–84; and was revised once more and published for a third time in Jürgen Kocka, *Sozialgeschichte: Begriff—Entwicklung—Probleme* (Göttingen, 1977), 9–40; in addition, a Japanese translation of it appeared in 1976.

Translator's note: I would like to thank the following individuals for their generous assistance: Charles Cudney, José Casanova, Stephen Kalberg, and Brunhild Kring-Lawrence. Gerd Schroeter and Robert Antonio also contributed to work on this translation.

1. See E. Topitsch, "Max Weber's Geschichtsauffassung," *Wissenschaft und Weltbild* 3 (1950): 262.

2. Throughout the essay, "Wissenschaft" has been translated as "science" and "Wissenschaftler" as "scientist." However, "Wissenschaft" is a broader concept including disciplines that, in the Anglo-American tradition, are usually considered to be part of the "humanities" rather than the "sciences."

3. K. Löwith, "Max Weber und Karl Marx," in K. Löwith, *Gesammelte Abhandlungen* (Stuttgart, 1960), 7. Cf. Löwith, *Max Weber and Karl Marx* (London, 1982), 25.

4. However, the historical aspect of the relationship between Marx and Weber is not treated here. See G. Roth, "Das Historische Verhältnis der Weberschen Soziologie zum Marxismus," *Kölner Zeitschrift für Soziologie* 20 (1968): 429–47.

5. Cf. W. Lefèvre, *Zum historischen Charakter und zur historischen Methode bürgerlicher Soziologie. Untersuchungen am Werk Max Webers* (Frankfurt, 1971), 6–23 passim.

6. For examples of such Marxist argumentation see: F. Tomberg, "Was heisst bürgerliche Wissenschaft?" *Das Argument* 66 (1971): 470–75; W. Eckermann and H. Mohr, *Einführung in das Studium der Geschichte,* 2nd ed. (Berlin, 1969), 33, 40f., 47f., 69f.; E. Hahn, *Soziale Wirklichkeit u. soziologische Erkenntnis: Philosophisch-methodologische Aspekte der soziologischen Theorie* (Berlin, 1965). For criticisms see: H. Albert, *Traktat über kritische Vernunft,* 2nd ed. (Tübingen, 1969), 7, 47–54; H. Seiffert, *Marxismus und bürgerliche Wissenschaft* (Munich, 1971), esp. 85–104.

7. On Weber's philosophy of science, see A. V. Schelting, *Max Webers Wissenschaftslehre* (Tübingen, 1934). J. J. Schaaf, *Geschichte und Begriff: Eine kritische Studie zur Geschichtsmethodologie von Ernst Troeltsch und Max Weber* (Tübingen, 1946); D. Henrich, *Die Einheit der*

Wissenschaftslehre (Tübingen, 1952); F. H. Tenbruck, "Die Genesis der Methodologie Max Webers," *Kölner Zeitschrift für Soziologie* 11 (1959): 573–630; J. Janoska-Bendl, *Methodologische Aspekte des Idealtypus: Max Weber und die Soziologie der Geschichte* (Berlin, 1965); and most recently, G. Hufnagel, *Kritik als Beruf: Der kritische Gehalt im Werk Max Webers* (Frankfurt, 1971), including a detailed bibliography.

8. For example, K. Braunreuther wrote "Max Weber's true vocation was to be an anti-Marxist" (116) in "Bemerkungen über Max Weber und die bürgerliche Soziologie," *Wissenschaftliche Zeitschrift der Humboldt-Universität, Gesellschafts- und Sprachwissenschaftliche Reihe* (1958/59), 115–23.

9. Max Weber, *Wirtschaft und Gesellschaft*, 4th ed. (Tübingen, 1956), 199–207.

10. Ibid., 212 (for example, the connection between Chthonian dieties and agriculture). See also 352.

11. From Max Weber, *Gesammelte Aufsätze zur Wissenschaftslehre*, 3rd ed. (Tübingen, 1968). This is referred to in the text as (WL . . .). However, the pagination is from the first edition (1922) since the second and third editions list the page numbers from the first edition in brackets on their inside margins (insofar as these differ from the third edition). This makes possible the use of all three editions. Translation: Max Weber, *The Methodology of the Social Sciences*, trans. and ed. Edward A. Shils and Henry A. Finch (New York, 1949), 69. The second page number refers to this translation: e.g., WL 167/69.

12. See Max Weber, *Die protestantische Ethik und der Geist des Kapitalismus*, in *Gesammelte Aufsätze zur Religionssoziologie*, vol. 1 (Tübingen, 1920), 38/P.E. (Parsons trans.) 56. The realization that in the United States the spirit of capitalism existed prior to capitalist economic development was used by Weber in his polemic against "naive" historical materialists: "In this case the causal relationship is just the reverse of what would be postulated from a 'materialist' standpoint. But the 'youth' of such ideas is generally more difficult than the theorists of the 'superstructure' assume and their development never comes to fruition like that of a flower." Also ibid., 60.

13. However, Weber himself acknowledged that this approach is not sufficient to explain *mature* capitalism: "The [victorious capitalism] force of the norms of economic action on the individual, insofar as he is enmeshed in the market-nexus." Ibid., 37/P.E. 54. Therefore, in *mature* capitalism (which is what Marx investigated in *Das Kapital*), the *spirit of capitalism* must, to a significant extent, be conceived as a function of conditions which, according to Weber, it had initially helped to bring about. These conditions have since developed into a self-reproducing system (cage). But this insight was not part of Max Weber's methodological reflections. See also ibid., 203f.

14. See, for example, ibid., 37f., 60, 83, 205f., and Weber, *Wirtschaft und Gesellschaft*, 228–352.

15. In this connection, Janoska-Bendl, *Methodologische Aspekte des Idealtypus*, 89–114.

16. Karl Marx and Frederick Engels, *Die Deutsche Ideologie;* Karl Marx and Frederick Engels, *Werke* (Berlin, 1977), 3: 27. Hereafter volume abbreviated as *MEW*. Translation: Loyd D. Easton and Kurt H. Guddat, *Writings of the Young Marx on Philosophy and Society* (New York, 1967), 415–16. Henceforth: Easton and Guddat, *Writings of the Young Marx*.

17. Marx, *Das Kapital*, I, *MEW* 23: 57.

18. In the foreword to *An Introduction to a Critique of Political Economy* (1859), Marx provided a schematic compilation of his previous studies. In this summary, he seemed to argue in favor of a thorough-going separation between social being and consciousness; this has led to an undialectical interpretation of his own work. K. Marx, *Zur Kritik der politischen Ökonomie*, *MEW* 13: 18ff. Such mechanistic statements in Marx's writings were adopted and emphasized by later theoreticians such as Karl Kautsky and Max Adler, in part already by Frederick Engels,

and in still another way by the Stalinists. A. Wellmer has demonstrated this in *Kritische Gesellschaftstheorie und Positivismus,* 3rd ed. (Frankfurt, 1971), 45–127.

19. Referred to here is the doctrine of materialism which was current during Marx's time and which he criticized, i.e, Feuerbach's formulation among others.

20. Marx, *Dritte These über Feuerbach, MEW* 3: 5f. Trans. Easton and Guddat, *Writings of the Young Marx,* 401.

21. Marx, *Die Deutsche Ideologie, MEW* 3: 38. Trans. Easton and Guddat, *Writings of the Young Marx,* 432.

22. Ibid., 42. Trans. Easton and Guddat, *Writings of the Young Marx,* 432.

23. See Marx, *Ökonomisch-philosophische Manuskripte aus dem Jahre 1844, MEW,* Sup. Vol., Part 1, 479: "Neither objective nature nor subjective nature is immediately present—adequately—in human nature. And so everything natural must come into being, likewise man also has his act of creation, *history.* . . . History is the true natural history of man."

24. See A. Schmidt, *Der Begriff der Natur in der Lehre von Marx* (Frankfurt, 1962), 51ff.

25. As to the historical character of Marx's approach in general, with further references: A. Schmidt, "Über Geschichte und Geschichtsschreibung in der materialistischen Dialektik," in: *Folgen einer Theorie, Essays über 'Das Kapital'* (Frankfurt, 1967), 103–9; and H. Fleischer, *Marxismus und Geschichte* (Frankfurt, 1969).

26. Marx's letter to L. Kugelmann, 27 June 1870, *MEW* 32: 685, *Letters to Dr. Kugelmann by Karl Marx* (London, [1934]), 111.

27. Marx, *Das Kapital,* I, *MEW* 23: 12.

28. Ibid., III, *MEW* 25: 267. Translation: Karl Marx, *Capital,* III (Moscow, 1959), 251–52.

29. See ibid., I, *MEW,* 89, 511: " . . . with blind destructive effect of a natural law . . . ," " . . . as for example the law of gravity, when a house collapses on your head." See also R. Rosdolsky, "Ein Neomarxistisches Lehrbuch der politischen Ökonomie," *Kyklos* 16 (1963): 631f.

30. See also A. Schmidt, *Über Geschichte,* 128f.

31. Marx, *Das Kapital,* III, *MEW* 25: 890f.

32. Marx, *Ökonomisch-philosophische Manuscripte, MEW,* Sup. Vol., Part I, 538.

33. See Marx, *Das Kapital,* III, *MEW* 25: 829, and Schmidt, *Begriff,* 57, 109, 115ff.

34. Marx's letter to L. Kugelmann, 11 July 1868, *MEW* 32: 553.

35. Marx, *Das Kapital,* I, *MEW* 23: 57.

36. As an example, Marx points to the necessity of the social division of labor as a prevailing natural law which assumes the form of exchange value in capitalist society. "The task of science is to explain *how* the law of exchange prevails" (letter to Kugelmann, 11 July 1868). See R. Rosdolsky, "Der Gebrauchswert bei Karl Marx," *Kyklos* 12 (1959): 31ff.

37. See also Marx's letter to Engels, 9 December 1861, *MEW* 30: 207: "Hegel never referred to the dialectic as a subsumption of a mass of 'cases' under a general principle."

38. See Henrich, *Die Einheit der Wissenschaftslehre,* 14.

39. The adjective *ontic* refers to reality as it is pregiven to scientific analysis, a reality which has not yet been constituted through the scientific-methodological reference to values and standpoints. (In contrast, Weber used the term *historical individual* to refer to a unity of elements of reality, which are tied to one another partly through an act of the investigator, an act which is related to the investigator's values and interests.) Just as Weber avoided epistemological reflections concerning the appearance of reality to the scientist, so the term *ontic* is used here in an epistemologically unproblematical fashion. (See Henrich, *Die Einheit der Wissenschaftslehre,* 17ff.)

40. *WL,* 213/111, 180/81: " 'Culture' is a finite segment of the meaningless infinity of the world process, a segment on which *human beings* confer meaning and significance"; *WL,* 177/78: "The number and type of causes which have influenced any given event are always *infinite* and there is nothing in the things themselves to set them apart as alone meriting attention. A chaos of external judgements. . . ."; *WL,* 184/84: "The stream of immeasurable events flows unendingly towards eternity." There are numerous other passages in the same vein.

41. Tenbruck, "Die Genesis der Methodologie Max Webers," 601, and also, e.g., S. Landshut, "Kritik der Soziologie," in S. Landshut, *Kritik der Soziologie und andere Schriften zur Politik* (Neuwied, 1967), 37ff.; Hufnagel, *Kritik als Beruf,* 139, 211.

42. This is Rickert's term; Weber did not use it. It signifies an incalculable, manifold, and differentiated reality which is characterized by an immense number of features in its space-time determinations as well as in its quantitative aspects. Every concrete object stands in a total context, its determining elements are just as complex and in principle as inexhaustible as its own characteristics.

43. Such a value referent constitutes a common structure for all acting individuals. However, this remains purely formal since nothing binding or anything in the way of regularities can be stated concerning the content of the values which function as points of reference. Though this reference to values, which is conceived as a specifically human "rationality," constitutes a structure at the level of the individual (the "personality"), it is not suitable for the establishment of a supra-individual structure in the sense of material culture. This is due to the fact that the content of its rationality can consist of an incalculable number of different combinations. Thus it is clear that the objects of interpretive sociology *(verstehende Soziologie)* are "solely the resultants and modes of organization of the particular acts of *individual* persons, since these alone can be treated as agents in a course of subjectively understandable action." See *WL,* 514; trans. Weber, *Economy and Society,* ed. Guenther Roth and Claus Wittich (New York, 1968), 13. Therefore, within a sociology of understanding it is hardly possible to have a concept (either dialectical or functional) of the social whole.

44. Cf. Tenbruck, "Die Genesis der Methodologie Max Webers," 600. On the question of Weber's view of the structure of reality, see the modifications of this interpretation below, pp. 154–56.

45. Standpoints are tied to "evaluative ideas . . . [whose] . . . validity can *not* be deduced from empirical data as such," *WL,* 213/111. "We cannot discover, however, what is meaningful to us by means of a 'presuppositionless' investigation of empirical data. Rather perception of its meaningfulness to us is the presupposition of its becoming an *object* of investigation," *WL,* 175f./76. See also note 40.

46. Similarly, Weber had to deny the deducibility of norms of action from the knowledge of the context in which the action is to take place. See *WL,* 154 and 475.

47. See Henrich, *Die Einheit der Wissenschaftslehre,* 19.

48. For further criteria which from Weber's theoretical perspective can serve to limit the arbitrariness of the choice of concepts and categories, see below pp. 154–57.

49. See also *WL,* 151f. and 469ff.

50. Marx, "Erste These über Feuerbach," *MEW* 3: 5.

51. Marx, *Zur Kritik der Hegelschen Rechtsphilosophie,* Einleitung, *MEW* 21: 378. Bottomore translates this as "Man is *the human world,* the state, society," in *Karl Marx: Early Writings,* trans. Bottomore (New York, 1964), 43.

52. Marx, *Die Deutsche Ideologie, MEW* 3: 44; trans. ibid. (New York, 1947), 36.

53. Marx, "Sechste These über Feuerbach," *MEW* 3: 6; trans. Easton and Guddat, *Writings of the Young Marx,* 402.

54. O. Morf, *Geschichte und Dialektik in der politischen Ökonomie: Zum Verhältnis von Wirtschaftstheorie und Wirtschaftsgeschichte bei K. Marx,* 2nd ed. (Frankfurt, 1970), 114.

55. Marx, *Das Kapital,* III, *MEW* 25: 219.

56. Ibid., I, *MEW* 23: 88.

57. Marx, *Einleitung zur Kritik der politischen Ökonomie, MEW* 13: 633; trans. Karl Marx, *A Contribution to the Critique of Political Economy* (New York, 1970), 207.

58. Lenin's mimetic theory was criticized in this respect by Marxists. See K. Korsch, *Marxismus und Philosophie* (Leipzig, 1930), 25ff.

59. See Marx, "Randglossen zu Adolph Wagners' 'Lehrbuch der politischen Ökonomie,'" quoted in Schmidt, *Begriff,* 93.

60. Marx, "Zweite These über Feuerbach," *MEW* 3: 5; trans. Easton and Guddat, *Writings of the Young Marx,* 401. See also Schmidt, *Begriff,* 101.

61. See E. Bloch, *Das Prinzip Hoffnung* (Berlin, 1960), 1: 214ff.

62. Marx, "Zweite These über Feuerbach," *MEW* 3: 5; trans. Easton and Guddat, *Writings of the Young Marx,* 401.

63. See Schmidt, *Begriff,* 94; Marx, *MEW* 3: 5.

64. See G. Lukács, *Die Zerstörung der Vernunft* (*Werke* 9) (Neuwied, 1961), 521-37; for a more differentiated and relatively, positive view, see the Marxist analysis of I. S. Kon, *Die Geschichtsphilosophie des 20. Jahrhunderts* (Berlin, 1964), 1: 136-57.

65. Marx, *Einleitung zur Kritik der politischen Ökonomie, MEW* 13: 631ff.; trans. (New York, 1970), 206.

66. Ibid. Also see Morf, *Geschichte und Dialektik,* 36ff.; and A. Schmidt, *Geschichte und Struktur: Fragen einer marxistischen Historik* (Munich, 1971), 41ff.

67. Morf, *Geschichte und Dialektik,* 128.

68. Marx, *Das Kapital,* III, *MEW* 25: 219; trans. Karl Marx, *Capital* (Moscow, 1959; London, 1960), 3: 205.

69. Ibid., 825: "all science would be superfluous if the outward forms of appearance of objects were identical with their essence. . . ."

70. This is Marx's own formulation of his "goal." *Das Kapital,* 1, *MEW* 23: 15f.

71. See Rosdolsky, *Lehrbuch,* 645ff.

72. See note 68 above.

73. One must agree with G. Lukács, *Geschichte und Klassenbewusstsein: Studien über marxistische Dialektik* (1923; reprint, Neuwied, 1970), 255-355; H. Marcuse, *Vernunft und Revolution* (1941; reprint, Neuwied, 1962), 241ff.; K. Bekker, *Marx' Philosophische Entwicklung: Sein Verhältnis zu Hegel* (Zurich, 1940); S. Avineri, *The Social and Political Thought of Karl Marx* (Cambridge, 1968), 3 passim; Schmidt, *Geschichte und Struktur,* 47-51 passim; and many others who argue for the immense and continuous influence of Hegel's philosophy on Marx, a philosophy which Marx himself had radically transformed. For an unconvincing contrary position, see L. Althusser, *Für Marx* (Frankfurt, 1968), 130-35, 142-45.

74. Weber, *Die Protestantische Ethik,* 134ff., 192.

75. Probably, Weber saw this himself. He characterized this work of his as preliminary and expected supplementation from future research carried out from other perspectives. Ibid., 205ff.

76. Ibid., 52f.

77. Marx, *Einleitung zur Kritik der politischen Ökonomie, MEW* 13: 634; trans. Marx, *A Contribution to the Critique,* 210.

78. These demands are only implied by Marx, ibid., 617f.; they can be inferred from the context. Weber does not make these demands because he completely separates the researcher's standpoints from the object of inquiry. See below pp. 150-51.

79. Marx, *Zur Kritik der politischen Ökonomie, MEW* 13: 636; trans. Marx, *A Contribution to the Critique,* 211.

80. Ibid., 636.

81. E. Bloch, *Subjekt-Objekt, Erläuterungen zu Hegel* (Berlin, 1951), 221ff.

82. E. Troeltsch, *Der Historismus und seine Probleme* (1922; reprint, Aalen, 1961), 1: 367.

83. Marx's letter to A. Ruge, September 1843, in *Die Frühschriften,* ed. S. Landshut (Stuttgart, 1953), 169; trans. Easton and Guddat, *Writings of the Young Marx,* 213. See Wellmer, *Kritische Gesellschaftstheorie,* 59–61, 78–92, as to the possibility of reconstructing this immanent critique in Marx's work in connection with the transition from Hegel to Marx (a theme which I have not extensively treated).

84. As a modern representative of this position, see M. Horkheimer, "Zum Begriff der Vernunft," in Adorno and Horkheimer, *Sociologica* 2 (Frankfurt, 1962), esp. 204, and W. Hofmann, *Gesellschaftslehre als Ordnungsmacht: Die Werturteilsfrage heute* (Berlin, 1961), 29.

85. This "technocratic" perspective, from a non-Marxist position, is formulated in H. Schelsky, *Der Mensch in der wissenschaftlichen Zivilisation* (Cologne, 1961), 25 and passim.

86. In the context of Marxist thought see Hofmann: "The idea that social facts can be judged according to their value gains a general validity when those social facts objectively correspond to the level of the potentials of a given historical formation. That which is socially valuable is always that which has become historically possible." *Gesellschaftslehre als Ordnungsmacht,* 32.

87. These functions of science are listed briefly, but succinctly, in *WL,* 427f.

88. As a decisionist, in this sense, Weber is categorized with some modifications and often contradictory evaluations by Tenbruck, "Die Genesis der Methodologie Max Webers," 600ff.; Lukács, *Die Zerstörung der Vernunft,* 532ff.; L. Strauss, *Naturrecht und Geschichte* (Stuttgart, 1956), 107ff.; J. Habermas, *Technik und Wissenschaft als Ideologie* (Frankfurt, 1968), 121f.; H. Marcuse, *Kultur und Gesellschaft* (Frankfurt, 1965), 2: 107 ff. Also see the overview in G. Roth, "Political Critiques of Max Weber. Some Implications for Political Sociology," *American Sociological Review* 30 (1965): 213–23.

89. G. W. F. Hegel, *Wissenschaft der Logik* (Leipzig, 1923), pt. 1, 6; trans. G. W. F. Hegel, *Logic I* (London, 1929), 36. Morf, *Geschichte und Dialektik,* 77, claims this statement for the Marxist method. As to the close relationship between Marx's method and Hegel's logic, see Schmidt, *Geschichte und Struktur.*

90. G. W. F. Hegel, *Enzyklopädie der philosophischen Wissenschaften im Grundriss,* 6th ed. (Hamburg, 1959), 426 (section 549); trans. G. W. F. Hegel, *Philosophy of Mind* (London, 1971), 277.

91. See Marx and Engels, *Die Deutsche Ideologie, MEW* 3: 13ff.

92. See above pp. 137–38, and Marx, *Das Kapital,* I, *MEW* 23: 57.

93. See note 86 above.

94. This is Hegel's notion: Hegel, *Enzyklopädie,* 197 (section 244).

95. Recently Wellmer elaborated on the remnants of this Hegelian, speculative logic of history in Marx's thought, even though it no longer has a proper place or justification for being there. Welmer saw in these remnants the basis for Marx's tendency to assume that social-historical contradictions would be overcome, almost out of necessity, in a progressive revolutionary manner. *Kritische Gesellschaftstheorie und Positivismus,* 56ff., 64f., 77, 93f., 126ff. This assumption has "proven itself to be false, in a fatal fashion," ibid., 28. See also M. Theunissen, *Gesellschaft und Geschichte: Zur Kritik der kristischen Theorie* (Berlin, 1969), 30, 33–38. He shows that even though "Critical Theory" explicitly rejects Hegelian premises (the presupposition of an absolute, though historically developed, Objectivity), in the final analysis "Critical Theorists," e.g., Habermas, act as if they could still proceed on the basis of the

presupposition of a philosophy of identity. It is at this juncture that Theunissen locates in "Critical Theory" certain tendencies towards an intolerant dogmatism and absolute claim of an epistemological-political character.

96. See above, p. 148.

97. Marx, *Einleitung zur Kritik der politischen Ökonomie, MEW* 13: 631f.

98. Habermas demonstrates convincingly the tremendous significance of such a preunderstanding for scientific inquiry, a prescientific understanding which is historically changeable and heterogeneous even within the same society and epoch. Habermas turns this insight against certain representatives of neopositivism who fail to take it sufficiently into account. "Analytische Wissenschaftstheorie und Dialektik: Ein Nachtrag zur Kontroverse zwischen Popper und Adorno," in *Zeugnisse, Th. W. Adorno zum 60. Gerburtstag,* ed. M. Horkheimer (Frankfurt, 1963), 473–501, esp. 476. Reprinted in T. W. Adorno, ed., *Der Positivismus-streit in der deutschen Soziologie* (1969; reprint, Neuwied, 1972), 151–91; trans. T. Adorno et al., *The Positivist Dispute in German Sociology* (New York, 1976), 131–62, and in J. Habermas, *Zur Logik der Sozialwissenschaften,* 2nd ed. (Frankfurt, 1970), 9–38. These critical reflections must also be addressed to Marxist approaches insofar as they suppress their own historicity and skip over hermeneutical issues in epistemology.

99. See above, pp. 143–44.

100. Theunissen, *Gesellschaft und Geschichte,* 34, showed that even "Critical Theory," which relies on Marx, cannot solve this problem and that the possibility of Critical Theory's dogmatism, in relation to other theories, results from its claim to knowledge of the totality, a claim which neglects the problematic of the hermeneutic circle, but does not solve it.

101. See, e.g., Tenbruck, "Die Genesis der Methodologie Max Webers," 600, 602; and similarly Landshut, see note 41; Lefèvre, *Zum historischen Charakter,* 16ff.

102. Finally, on the basis of such an interpretation of Weber's methodology, no sufficient reason can be found for *not* interpreting the origin of British capitalism from the high frequency of fog in England. In contrast to this interpretation, it must be remembered that Weber produced not only a philosophy of science, but also practical research projects, whose results can hardly be understood against the background of such a paradoxical methodology.

103. Weber, *Die Protestantische Ethik,* 205f.

104. This interrelatedness between science and society is analyzed in: Habermas, "Analytische Wissenschaftstheorie," 473f.

105. *WL,* 180. Also Henrich, *Die Einheit der Wissenschaftslehre,* 74ff., and Henrich, "Diskussionsbeitrag," in *Max Weber und die Soziologie heute: Verhandlungen des 15. deutschen Soziologentages,* ed. O. Stammer (Tübingen, 1965), 81–87. This argumentation will neither be accepted nor disapproved for these making, in my opinion unsuccessful, attempts to categorize Weber as an epistemological decisionist. See above all Lefèvre, *Zum historischen Charakter,* 16–29, and esp. 20f. and 115f. Lefèvre referred, as have many before him, to the problems and limits of Weber's approach. What is striking is the high degree of uncritical self-confidence with which he suggested that Weber's difficulties can in principle be overcome along with bourgeois society, without demonstrating how this could be accomplished, either on the level of the philosophy of science or in scientific practice. A few allusions to the solvability of the problem through participation in the anticapitalist "struggle of the laboring masses for the control over the objectivities produced by them" remain mere affirmations. Hufnagel, *Kritik als Beruf,* 139 n.2, 211, 213 passim, also attempted to retain a decisionistic interpretation of Weber's approach. Much more convincing is W. Schluchter, *Wertfreiheit und Verantwortungsethik: Zum Verhältnis von Wissenschaft und Politik bei Max Weber* (Tübingen, 1971), who placed Weber in the context of Habermas's pragmatic model.

106. "The *Kulturbedeutung* of unfree labor was finally re-enforced significantly through the inclusion of large inland areas." Max Weber, "Die sozialen Gründe des Untergangs der antiken Kultur," in *Max Weber—Soziologie, Weltgeschichtliche Analysen, Politik,* ed. J. Winckelmann, 2nd ed. (Stuttgart, 1956), 8; trans. "The Social Causes of the Decay of Ancient Civilization," I, *The Journal of General Education* 5 (1950): 79. Here *"Kulturbedeutung"* denotes the decisive force that radiates from a specific cultural content to the culture as a whole, thus an objective reality.

107. Janoska-Bendl speaks of a "minimum of philosophy of history" in Weber, and certainly the character of Weber's ideal-types is "conceptual," i.e., they are neither mere representations of reality nor fully autonomous thought constructs. *Methodologische Aspekte des Idealtypus,* 33f. The attempt to identify "the fundamentals of a philosophy of history" in Weber implies the assumption that Weber presupposed implicitly something like structures of socio-historical reality, which are pregiven to scientific inquiry. See above all W. J. Mommsen, "Universalgeschichtliches und politisches Denken bei Max Weber," *Historische Zeitschrift* 201 (1965): 557–612. However, Mommsen overlooked this consequence and sketched the relationship of reality and scientific knowledge in a way (569f.) that can only be maintained logically by those who simultaneously deny all elements of a theory of material culture in Weber. Mommsen lacked any insight into the connection between "the fundamentals of a philosophy of history" (which he treated extensively) and the question of the relation between socio-historical reality and scientific knowledge in Weber's works. Similarly flawed is his critique in *Historische Zeitschrift,* 211 (1970), 623f.

108. See Tenbruck, "Die Genesis der Methodologie Max Webers," 590ff. The relationship of Weber's methodological position to his critique of the Wilhelmine bureaucracy cannot be discussed, though it is possible to find historical causes for the pointed statements in his philosophy of science. Important references are found in G. Schmidt, *Deutscher Historismus und der Übergang zur parlamentarischen Demokratie: Untersuchungen zu den politischen Gedanken von Meinecke, Troeltsch, Max Weber* (Lübeck, 1964), 226–305.

109. Other passages demonstrate that Weber generally used the term "analysis" to characterize a nonempirical scientific approach to an object. See, for example, *WL,* 262f.; trans. in essay.

110. Of special importance are the relevant statements by Habermas. See the brief summation: J. Habermas, "Einleitung," in Habermas, *Theorie und Praxis: Sozialphilosophische Studien,* 2nd ed. (Frankfurt, 1971), 9–47. Also, see the work of H. Albert. His "Critical Rationalism," based on Karl Popper, doubtless escapes a significant portion of the intense critique of positivism launched by Adorno, Habermas, etc. In this debate, the gap between "Critical Theory" and "Critical Rationalism" has been made to appear greater than it actually is. Albert stresses the differences between his position and positivism (which has been criticized strongly by the Frankfurt School). See Albert, *Traktat über kritische Vernunft,* 6f., 54, 59f., 61f., 75f. The possible mediation of his argument, which navigates between dogmatism and decisionism, with certain positions found in "Critical Theory" would have to be addressed separately.

⊿⊿⊿

Stephen P. Turner   **Explaining Capitalism: Weber on and against Marx**

$\mathbf{W}$eber's dispute with his predecessors over the problem of the origins of capitalism is both methodological and historical. The historical issues are obscure because references to the problem are scattered, the "problem" itself is complex, and it is often unclear who Weber is discussing. When he addressed Marx explicitly, he characteristically did so in restricted ways or dealt with relatively minor points of dispute.[1] The methodological issues are obscure because of the difficulty of the methodological writings. But the difficulties are unavoidable: to make *any* sense of Weber's explanation of capitalism one must proceed from some sort of answer to the questions of what constitutes a causal explanation for Weber and what do historical concepts mean for him.

Weber discussed the latter question in terms of the ideal-type, and his account in "The Protestant Ethic and the 'Spirit' of Capitalism" is presented as an application of the method of historical ideal-type construction. The question of cause is dealt with less directly in the text. Nevertheless it is central to both his methodological writings and the problem of the origins of capitalism. The centrality of these questions is reflected in the literature interpreting Weber's argument. For example, Gordon Marshall explains Weber's account in terms of the concepts of necessary and sufficient cause, MacIntyre in terms of Mill's Method of Difference, and Louch through a comparison with the ideal gas laws.[2] Other interpreters construe his account of capitalism in terms of other noncausal explanatory forms, such as the "immanence" of the market,[3] or as incidental to his thesis of immanent rationalization.[4] Yet these interpretations do not fit Weber's extensive writings on the subject of causality and explanation, which reject—unequivocally in the case of Millian cause, perhaps equivocally in the case of immanence—all of these forms of causal or explanatory narration. This chapter explores the problem of Weber's account of early capitalism and his critique of Marx as it is illuminated by the methodological writings on cause and discusses in particular the question of the development of Weber's views and the bearing of this development on his relationship with Marx.

THE TECHNICAL BACKGROUND TO THE 1903–1907 ESSAYS

Weber published a closely related set of methodological essays in the middle of the first decade of the century, at the same time the Protestant ethic essay was published. Two of these papers were published in the *Archiv für Sozialwissenschaft und Sozialpolitik,* in 1904 and 1906, as was "The Protestant Ethic," in 1905. The first paper, which contained the most extensive discussion of causality as it relates to the Protestant ethic thesis and to Marxism, was Weber's introductory statement on assuming editorship of the journal. This and all Weber's methodological papers of this period appeal to a particular doctrine of probabilistic causation. They use the technical terms of this doctrine and draw conclusions about the character of historical knowledge on the basis of the doctrine's technical features. Some of these conclusions have direct bearing on the problem of capitalism. The doctrine was derived from the work of Johannes von Kries, and Weber's own testimony on his reliance on it is quite unambiguous: "I find the extent to which, here as in many previous discussions, I have 'plundered' von Kries' ideas almost embarrassing, especially since the formulation must often fall short in precision of von Kries'."[5] This is a curiously lavish statement, given that von Kries proved to be an insignificant figure in the history of the interpretation of probability theory, but the attractions of his doctrines for Weber are understandable.

The reason for von Kries's insignificance is also understandable. Philosophical probability theory has been an enterprise of combining standard conceptual elements to give solutions to a set of standard puzzles. Von Kries developed a particular combination of elements, which contained a flaw: he posited a "true" probability of events, such as the results of a horse race, and treated empirical averages (e.g., the proportion of favorites that won horse races in a given season) as the combination of all of the individual true probabilities of winning a given race for each favorite; the flaw in this doctrine was that these true individual probabilities were unknowable, which led to the epistemologically paradoxical and philosophically unhelpful result that the known was to be explained by the unknowable.

Weber had some significant reasons for being undaunted by this result. One was connected to the neo-Kantian epistemology of the time, the basic structure of which paralleled the von Kriesian notion of true probabilities: the unknowability of true probabilities was easily accepted, once one accepted, as Weber did, a doctrine of the unknowability of the world. Another followed from this. Von Kriesian probabilities were propensities. Hence it is intelligible to speak, in von Kriesian terms, of the probability of a "historical individual" (i.e., of an event whose meaning cannot be captured by an enumeration of the classes or types of which it is a member). It is also possible, in von Kriesian terms, to give an interpretation for the notion of degree of contribution to an outcome event which is a "historical individual." This merit was connected to the flaw, for the interpretation of "contribution" depends on the notion that events have an inherent probability.

According to the von Kriesian theory, *each* of the various events that stand in a *sine qua non* relationship to a given event in its full particularity may be said to have a relation of conditionality to the outcome event. This relation can be numerically assessed in a two-stage process. First, one estimates the dependent probability of the outcome event on the particular condition considered apart from the various other conditions. For example, if I wish to assess the efficacy of the condition of low brake fluid in producing an automobile accident, I estimate the dependent probability A that a particular level of brake fluid is likely to be followed by an accident a given proportion of the time. If I wish to assess the efficacy of drunkenness in producing accidents, I estimate the dependent probability B. The second stage is to weigh the relative contribution of various conditions to an accident which involves a drunk with low brake fluid. If I calculate the probability C of drunks with low brake fluid having accidents, I may subtract from C the probability of either the low brake fluid A alone or the drunkenness B alone producing the accident and determine which of these conditions was the more efficacious. If $C - A > C - B$, the causal contribution of B would be considered the more efficacious. The true inherent probability of the event would correspond to the combined (inherent) dependent probabilities of all the conditions of the event. This probability is, in von Kriesian language, the "objective possibility" of an event. An event that increases an outcome probability is called an "adequate cause" as opposed to a "mere condition."

Adequate cause, thus construed, corresponds—more or less—to our intuitive notion of responsibility, and this correspondence is the basis of the most significant applications of the doctrine, in the context of law. Weber was impressed with this correspondence. He took the view that the legal "problem of the conditions under which it is possible to assert that someone's action was 'responsible' for a certain overt consequence . . . is obviously of the same logical structure as the question of historical causality."[6] This claim in itself places Weber in a particular relation to the received doctrine of nineteenth-century philosophy of social science, for, as Weber was aware, these writings were explicitly opposed to Mill and to those theories of legal causality in the German tradition that derived from Mill.[7]

This opposition concerns primarily the problems with the concepts of necessary and sufficient cause. In experimental contexts these notions are readily applicable: a necessary condition is one without which an experimental outcome will not occur; a sufficient condition is one that assures the occurrence of the outcome. In historical contexts, which are reconstructed rather than experimental, matters are not so simple. For any historical event there is an infinity of actual conditions, stretching to the beginning of time, without which the event in its full particularity (i.e., as a historical individual) would not have occurred. The procedures of an experiment amount to an implicit selection of a set of conditions. The selection is not arbitrary because it is checked by the fact of the success or failure of the experiment. In the case of historical explanation, selection is also necessary, but there are no checks on the selection of conditions.

The problem takes a particular form. The immediate difficulty is that the probabilities relevant to the sort of subtraction described in the auto accident example cannot be readily estimated. To produce any estimate at all it is necessary first to "isolate"[8] certain of the "*infinity* of causal factors [that] have conditioned the occurrence of the individual event"[9] because one can obtain the dependent probability of the outcome only for the particular class of events that has equivalent conditions, and one can do this only if one considers a limited set of conditions, such as the complex of conditions "a drunk driver with low brake fluid." This selection, or isolation in the von Kriesian technical language Weber used, is arbitrary. In the case of the accident, the question of driver error or mechanical malfunction delimits the range of causal factors to be considered, but it does so in a nonarbitrary way only because this question represents the implicit interest of the court in assessing liability. The point of Weber's constant references to the infinity of causal factors for any event was that generally no such nonarbitrary delimitation is possible. The invention of the automobile and the building of the road on which the accident happened are also preconditions. This technical consideration has direct bearing on the problem of explaining capitalism.

Another, related consideration also has bearing. The arbitrary selection of conditions is one kind of abstraction from the flow of events. A different kind of abstraction in von Kriesian probabilistic explanations occurs in redescribing the individual event in terms of general categories. Such categories as "drunk" or "low brake fluid" are perhaps relatively uncontroversial because they are susceptible of quantitative definition, but such theoretical categories as capitalism are idealizations which fit actual states of affairs imperfectly. This problem of abstraction, called generalization in von Kriesian terms, is distinct from the problem of ideal-types.[10]

METHODS AND PRACTICE

Weber did not make explicit appeals to von Kriesian language or considerations in the body of the essay "The Protestant Ethic." The primary evidence in Weber's own writings for connections between the thesis of the Protestant ethic essay and the methodological essays comes from the methodological essays themselves. In particular, when he discussed the methodological problems of explaining capitalism in "Objectivity" he seemed to be indicating how he regarded the explanation in "The Protestant Ethic."[11] The strongest common strand in "Objectivity" and "The Protestant Ethic" is the theme of one-sidedness of explanation, a theme that involves both the concept of ideal-types and the von Kriesian notion of causality. The theme also places Weber's account in a particular relationship with Marx, but it is a peculiarity of "Objectivity" as a text that the antagonists are masked: it is not Marx but dilettantish materialists that Weber attacked, and when he did so he gave as grounds for these attacks extremely general methodological formulations involving the notion of infinitude. In part these are glosses on von Kries.

Infinitude figures in the von Kriesian framework in a specific way. Any assessment of causality depends on an arbitrary selection or isolation of a few conceptually distinct factors among the infinity of events that are *sine qua non* for a given historical outcome. As we have seen, the method begins with the estimation of the probability of an outcome on a given class of causes and subtracts from this an estimation of the probability of the outcome on a given subclass of these causes. Hence the assessment depends on the *selection* of the class of causes, the "condition complex," from this infinity of conditions. It should be noticed that this concept of condition includes, as conditions, much more than the experimental or nomic prerequisites included by traditional usage[12] and that this highly extended usage is not shared with conventional accounts of causality or with the Anglo-Saxon theory of legal causality. Yet Weber was impressed with this notion of conditionality and took seriously the infinitude of causal factors it implied.[13] However, his discussions of it are confusing, for they mix this problem of infinitude with epistemological issues. The treatment of the subject in "Objectivity" exemplifies both the confusion created by his attempt to give von Kriesian notions general significance and his tendency to run disparate issues together in explicating the concept of the ideal-type. In this context that which has been run together may be separated.

There are at least two kinds of selectivity or one-sidedness at stake in Weber's account. The first is epistemological and relates to the ideal-type. The second is explanatory and relates to the procedures of causal imputation in the adequate cause–objective possibility theory, in particular to its two processes of abstraction: isolation, the selection of a limited set of possible causes dictated by the fact of the infinity of causes influencing a given event; and generalization, which epistemologically is equivalent to the selectivity which any construct has in relation to concrete individuals or to the infinitude of the world process. For Weber, epistemological and ontological considerations were prior to, and took precedence over, considerations of causality and methodology. In part this reflected the neo-Kantian idea of epistemology as a foundational discipline; in part it was simply a matter of polemical tactics dictated by the fact that many of his methodological opponents denied a place in history to causality. And in a highly general methodological essay such as "Objectivity" he needed arguments that applied to these opponents. Moreover, he wished to suggest that the deficiencies he was forced to concede, with respect to his kind of causal account, are shared, at least on the epistemological level, with the historical methods of his opponents who rejected his causal aims. Sometimes the issues arise successively, in the epistemological form and then in the causal form, as in the case of one conceptual device, the genetic ideal-type. These are "constructs in terms of which we formulate relationships by the application of the category of objective possibility. By means of this category, the adequacy of our imagination, oriented and disciplined by reality, is *judged.*"[14] In short, they have the logical form of adequate cause–objective possibility accounts and may be assessed accordingly for their intelligibility and factual adequacy.

Although Weber did not say so explicitly, presumably the ideal-type presented in "The Protestant Ethic" is genetic, and hence to be understood as an objective possibility construction. Presumably he also believed that the cause he identified increases the probability of the outcome sufficiently to be considered an adequate cause. This notion is signaled in "The Protestant Ethic" by his reference to the technical problem of showing "the quantitative cultural significance of ascetic Protestantism."[15]

Weber also considered the materialist explanation of history to be a genetic ideal-type; this suggests the possibility of assessing the relative adequacy of the materialist account against Weber's, since the whole point of the adequate cause–objective possibility doctrine in law is that it provides a means of dealing with the question of *degree* of contribution. Moreover, much of what Weber said, in "The Protestant Ethic" and in "Objectivity," would lead to the same expectation. But constructing an ideal-type and showing its applicability is not the same as showing the quantitative significance of a factor. Weber believed that he had done the former without doing the latter. In the conclusion to "The Protestant Ethic" he explained that the next step would be parallel studies. These would show the significance of other, *independent* cultural influences (e.g., "humanistic rationalism, . . . philosophical and scientific" development, and "technical development")[16] since "The Protestant Ethic" was a study of certain cultural effects of ascetic religion. He would then show other consequences of ascetic Protestantism, such as its influence on forms of social organization "from the conventicle to the State,"[17] and place Protestantism in the larger process of the development of ascetic religiosity from its medieval origin to its current diminished form.

In the final paragraph he cautioned that "it is, of course, not my aim to substitute for a one-sided materialistic an equally one-sided spiritualistic causal interpretation of culture and history" and explained that he had "only attempted to trace the fact and the direction" of the influence of Protestant ascetic religious "motives in one, though a very important, point." He added that it would also "be necessary to investigate how Protestant Asceticism was in turn influenced in its development and its character by the totality of social conditions, especially economic."[18]

The one-sidedness in question in this passage is the causal kind, rather than the kind generic to all ideal-typical constructions. Weber's point is not that he was, himself, giving anything other than a one-sided explanation, but rather that his account and the materialist account are both equally one-sided. His materialist opponents (Marx, again, is not mentioned by name) make the error of turning a causal interpretation into a philosophy of history, which Weber had warned his readers *not* to do with the interpretation in "The Protestant Ethic." Weber said nothing about the question of the relative *weight* of spiritual and material conditions in producing the outcome, in spite of what one might plausibly expect on the basis of his contemporaneous methodological discussions of the adequate cause–objective possibility theory, with its stress on the problem of weighing contributions. What is to be made of this?

One *reason* Weber did not attempt to replace these intentionally one-sided explanations[19] of capitalism with a comprehensive explanation of capitalism is that such an explanation was precluded by the logic of causation in the von Kries-Radbruch theory. The theory precludes any general confrontation between culturalist and materialist explanations as well. The technical reasons for this are straightforward. As long as a putative causal factor has some degree of adequacy (i.e., a sufficient difference in the probability of an outcome results from subtracting a factor from a given constellation of factors), it must be accredited as an adequate cause of the outcome. The weight of the cause, the *degree* of adequacy, depends on the selection of the constellation. There are, however, no general grounds for the selection of the set of background factors: in present jargon, selections are interest-relative. The interest of the courts serves, more or less, as a de facto device for selection. There are some analogues to the interest of the court in scholarly contexts. Thus, in "Objectivity" Weber suggested that comparing the causal influence of economic factors only to other economic factors is warranted by considerations of convenience: "training in the observation of the effects of qualitatively similar categories of causes [e.g., economic causes], . . . offers all the advantages of the division of labor,"[20] and at the close of "The Protestant Ethic," the list of suggestions of other influences to be investigated is a list of *cultural* influences.[21] This is a choice dictated *only* by convenience.

"MATERIALISM" IN THE EARLY WRITINGS

If the goal of the explanation of capitalism was to construct a truly comprehensive theory, these specialized investigations, including "The Protestant Ethic," could be regarded as preliminary. But Weber did not hold this as a meaningful goal. A truly comprehensive theory would include the *infinity* of conditions for the outcome, and any account that included this infinity of factors would be *eo ipso* a meaningless chaos itself. In the face of infinity *both* the Marxian and the Protestant ethic explanations pale. In other words, any explanation can be made to seem significant only by a self-willed restriction of one's point of view.[22] So both explanations are equivalent in this respect. The error that one might commit in the face of this is to forget that these explanations depend on one-sided selection. In "The Protestant Ethic" Weber remarked that one might "proceed beyond" his deliberately restricted account "to a regular construction which logically deduced everything characteristic of modern culture from Protestant rationalism." He then said that this "may be left to the type of dilettante who believes in the unity of the group mind and its reducibility to a single formula.''[23] An analogous comment on who follow the materialism of the *Manifesto* is made in "Objectivity." There such materialists are compared to single-minded racialist theorists who believe that " 'in the last analysis' all historical events are results of the interplay of innate 'racial qualities.' ''[24]

The bad legacy of Marx is the "peculiar condition" that the "need for a causal explanation of an historical event is never satisfied until somewhere or somehow economic causes are shown (or seem) to be operative.''[25] Any such stopping point is necessarily arbitrary. The "dogmatic need to believe that the economic 'factor' is the 'real' one, the only 'true' one, and the one which 'in the last instance is everywhere decisive' ''[26] results from the erroneous thought of these dilettantes that "they could contribute something different and better to our knowledge of culture than the broadening of the possibility" of imputing concrete historical causes to concrete cultural events "through the study of precise empirical data which have been selected from specific points of view." The error, in short, is the wish to go beyond self-critical historical knowledge,[27] which concedes its cognitive limitations, to a *Weltanschauung* or a formula. Thus the bad Marx forgets the irreducible arbitrariness inherent in explanation and transforms one-sided explanations into a metaphysical commitment to the economic factor as an explanatory ultimate or hypostatizes them as effective forces, tendencies, and so on. The good Marx is the heuristic Marx, who uses the materialist scheme of explanations as an ideal-type.[28]

If Weber had intended a debate with the ghost of Marx, this line of argument would have represented a strangely formalistic resolution. Not only did Weber not use "The Protestant Ethic" directly against Marx, but, in the discussions of causal one-sidedness, he showed that it *cannot* be used against Marx. To be sure, Weber scored points against a kind of materialist metaphysics. But he labeled it as the view of laymen and dilettantes—the better to dismiss it, but also the better to mark a legitimate place for appropriate "materialist" hypotheses. It is possible that Weber believed that the metaphysical materialism he rejected was in fact Marx's own view or that Marxism as a serious intellectual enterprise (e.g., as a universal history) was itself inseparable from these metaphysical elements.

THE PROBLEM OF THE LISTS

The program of future research sketched, however diffidently, at the end of "The Protestant Ethic" was never followed up. A quite different program of research was pursued, in which the religious factor retained a significant role. But this research program was completed only in part, and its nature and aims have been a matter of continuous dispute. Neither the early methodological essays nor the suggestions for research found in "The Protestant Ethic" illuminate the project Weber actually pursued, and this raises the question whether Weber in later work significantly altered the account of capitalism found in "The Protestant Ethic." Moreover, the later methodological essays and various remarks in the research corpus itself appear to revise some of the central notions of the early methodological essays.[29]

In the *General Economic History,* based on notes for his final series of academic lectures, Weber reiterated what can be found scattered throughout his later writings on "the distinguishing characteristics of Western capitalism and its causes" by listing explanatory factors, including rational law, the rational organization of labor, rational technology, rational accounting, free labor, the use of stock shares, the rational spirit, and a rationalistic economic ethic. The status of these lists is left vague: "distinguishing characteristics" and "causes" are never distinguished. The rational organization of labor is at one moment produced by Western capitalism, at another its primary cause, at another its distinctive feature. This ambiguity makes it difficult to treat the lists as explanations at all, and it creates a puzzle about Weber's intent in producing them. The lists are not so much an answer to the question of the origin of *homo economicus modernus* as a restatement of it at the institutional level, radically broadened into the question of the origin of *homo rationalis modernus.* This new historical question, of the character of the break between what Weber thought of as the traditional and the rational, comes close to the Marxist problem of the transition between feudalism and capitalism.[30]

READINGS OF THE LATER TEXTS

Weber spoke of a " 'rationalization' process" in "The Protestant Ethic," and his later formulations of traditional and rational as ideal-types together with his rejection of the theory of the *Überbau* suggest an interpretation of his later work that treats capitalism as incidental to, and a by-product of, a larger process of rationalization.[31] Weber was never explicit about this. Yet he said some things highly congenial to this kind of interpretation, especially in the *General Economic History;* for example, he remarked that the reason various distinguishing features of modern capitalism, such as the rational organization of work, appeared *only* in the West must be found in the special features of its general cultural evolution.[32] Some writers think that substituting the notion of evolutionary rationalization for the problem set of the earlier essays was wholly intentional on Weber's part, and that his premature death prevented his articulation of a fully developed universal history with rationalization as its core concept. Two such revisionist interpretations, one causal and one teleological, may be briefly considered here.

In the first revision Tenbruck, Schluchter, Luethy, and others view the thematic center of Weber's work as the historical process of rationalization. One merit of this account as an interpretation is that it enables one to make sense of the lists of the distinguishing features of modern capitalism: the lists (of rational this and rational that) become the *explananda* of Weber's universal history, and economic development can be left as incidental to the achievement of rationality in these realms. The market, it may be conceded, hastens the process of rationalization by coercing laggards to rationalize to survive, and bureaucratic structures serve the cause of rational discipline. But the framework of rational institutions is a precondition for these processes, which are thus secondary to rationalization, the primary historical process. The primary difficulty with this line of interpretation is the generic conflict between Weber's methodological writings (causalist, anti-essentialist, and anti-teleological) and any construal of Weber as a teleological historicist.

Tenbruck comes to terms with the issue by locating the inconsistency in what he calls the "methodological shock" of Weber's use of a "real" type instead of an "ideal" type in dealing with the influence of religious ideas. He locates this shock in the early pages of a short paper written to integrate parts of what was to become the *Religionssoziologie*. [33] Here Weber said "[T]he rationality, in the sense of logical or teleological 'consistency,' of an intellectual theoretical or practical-theoretical attitude has and always has had power over man. . . ." [34] Thus rationality is not merely in the eye of the ideal-type constructing beholder: it is also a force, real apart from the ideal-typical constructions one places on it. Since this is the conceptual sin Weber attributed to Marxists in "Objectivity," this statement is indeed an interesting departure.

Weber remarked that "religious interpretations of the world and ethics of religion created by intellectuals and meant to be rational have been strongly exposed to the imperative of consistency" (which is the case with Christianity), but he went on to say that "the effect of the *ratio*, especially of the teleological deduction of practical postulates, is in some way, and often very strongly, noticeable among all religious ethics." [35] This is universality enough for Tenbruck, who goes on to treat it as a candidate for the role of key universal historical force. Perhaps it is too much universality, for consistency in this broad sense is such a general notion. Similarly for meaning: to say that everyone seeks it once in a while is not to say much at all. Tenbruck is aware of this, so he stresses the *distinctiveness* of the mechanism of rationalization in the religious sphere, namely the process of rendering theodicies consistent, a process he treats as immanent. "Religion advances according to its own laws," he says. "A rational development of religious images of the world proceeds apace with the rational logic specific to religion."[36]

Historical circumstance provides openings in which this universal, but ordinarily weak, force may have dramatic effects, and this was the case with Protestantism. This accounts for *one* of the kinds of rationality on the lists in the lectures. Tenbruck treats the others as more or less fortuitous. "The world, for Weber, is made of partial rationalizations which are called into being according to the interests of the moment—economic, technical, military and administrative."[37] He distinguishes these rationalizations from the religious one, and singles it out as key: "the modern economy originated from the pressure of discipline and not from the gratification of interests,"[38] and the source of discipline was Protestantism. As Weber said in the lectures, "Such a powerful, unconsciously refined organization for the production of capitalistic individuals as the Protestant sects has never existed in history."[39]

One difficulty in this line of interpretation is that Weber did not make the sharp distinction between adventitious rationalization produced by the interests of the moment and rationalization that proceeds according to an inner logic which Tenbruck's account relies on, nor did he give discipline the primacy Tenbruck gives it in producing modern capitalism. In one of the lists of rational factors, Weber called discipline complementary to the permanent rational enterprise, the factor which "in the last resort" produced capitalism.[40]

The language of factors, produces, and so on suggests a causal rather than teleological interpretation of Weber's account of the origins of capitalism. Yet the attempts to overcome, by a causalist interpretation, the ambiguity and obscure purport of such things as the lists of factors in the lectures have faced difficulties as well. These are well illustrated by the late Benjamin Nelson's argument that Weber's later work, especially the *Religionssoziologie,* was an attempt to interpret the "sociological experiment" left us by history.[41] Weber, he said,

tells us plainly that he is applying Mill's "Method of Difference" and, therefore, looking for the factor or chain of circumstances which helped to explain some unique outcome of a given experiment. The unique outcome, as he saw it, in the Protestant ethic was the spread of a rationalized sociocultural order based on the assumption of vocational asceticism.[42]

The "master clue to his aims," Nelson suggested, is the "Introduction" to the *Religionssoziologie,* in which the break between the noncomparativist "Protestant Ethic" and the comparativist, "universal historical," later work is most evident. Nelson agreed with Tenbruck that the "Introduction" shows that rationalization had become Weber's central concern and that the change alters "The Protestant Ethic" by placing it in a different explanatory structure. But Nelson's notion was that the new explanatory structure is Mill's Method of Difference.

Contrary to Nelson's claim,[43] which he failed to support by a specific citation, there is no place in which Weber "tells us plainly" that he was using the method of difference. Indeed, Weber had embraced an anti-Millian doctrine of cause in the 1903–1907 essays and subsequently wrote on methodology without explicitly embracing a doctrine congenial to large-scale civilizational causal comparisons of a distinctively Millian variety. The peculiarity of this might be overlooked if one could use Millian terms to construe Weber's texts into an explanation that was significantly coherent or lent coherence to the *Religionssoziologie.* But the explanation, construed in Millian terms, turns out to be a disappointment.

There is again the problem of distinguishing "distinguishing features," the *explana-dum,* from differentiative causes, the *explanans.* Nelson's solution was to treat Protestantism as a differentiating element *not* found elsewhere, the "spur" which, together with the spirit of capitalism, promotes rationalization. To argue thus Nelson must say that "in his [Weber's] later work, his comparative work, he sought to show that all other components which were involved in the Western fusion could be found separately and in combination in other places."[44] If the other components could *not* be found elsewhere, the method of difference would fail to distinguish the cause from the mere conditions on the list. But this line of interpretation is belied by the "Introduction" itself, which stresses the uniqueness to the Occident not *only* of the spur of Protestantism but of rational art and architecture, rational science, bureaucratic state organization, constitutionalism, the rational enterprise, the rational organization of formally free labor, rational bookkeeping, and the separation of enterprise and *oikos.*[45]

THE PURPOSE OF THE LISTS

The lists thus remain an enigma. In themselves they are uncharacteristically schematic and mechanical, vague as to the causal mechanisms by which the effects are produced, and lacking a framework of logic that would give sense to a notion of them as causes. As explanations, they appear to conflict with Weber's opinions on method: to the extent that they weigh factors, they conflict with the discussions of objective possibility in the early writings. Because they are explicitly *culturalist* schema, they conflict with the caution about culturalism, as well as with the disdain for historical formulae expressed in *Economy and Society*.[46] Methodological considerations aside, the sheer opacity of these lists as explanations leads one to believe that Weber never intended them as causal explanations in any strict sense.

But what did he intend? The clues in the "Introduction" to the *Religionssoziologie* are sparse, but there are clues. And there are clues in the methodological "Introduction" to *Economy and Society* as well. A contemporary described Weber's views as follows: "Max Weber sets himself the task of understanding the nature of a society in terms of the psychological motivation of individual actions. He allows organic explanations derived from the nature and function of sociological structures to serve only as preliminary orientations and aids to analysis."[47] This is the explicit theme of the methodological "Introduction" to *Economy and Society*. In Weber's time, "large scale comparative explanation" typically took the form of appeals to collective entities. Lukács took Weber's most systematic attack on collective entities, in "On Some Categories of Interpretive Sociology," as the key document for Weber's anti-Marxism, for the paper rejects the explanatory autonomy of the state and attempts to show that even this supra-individual entity is reducible to individual expectations and beliefs.

In historical explanation this commitment to individual explanation implies that such *explanans* and *explananda* as the Protestant ethic and the spirit of capitalism, rational law, rational accounting, the rational organization of labor, and so on must be treated in a particular way: they cannot be treated as effective forces; their causal and explanatory adequacy depends on the possibility of our "cashing them in" for individual explanations. To disaggregate historical explanations framed in terms of these concepts into individual patterns of motivation and conduct one must normally use idealtypes. Thus in disaggregating the state one identifies repeated patterns of individual belief and action, namely belief in the legitimacy of commands and action in obedience to them. In disaggregating large-scale historical explanations the same principles apply, but where the explanations are genetic the focus changes from conduct and belief to motive.[48] That is, if one explains belief by the immediate circumstantial plausibility of a belief, and conduct by the immediate circumstances of belief and interest, the long-term transformation of belief and interest must be explained by some element of individual meaningful action that is deeper and more permanent. Genetic historical explanations characteristically make these appeals. Thus, in theology a pattern of conduct motivated by a desire to make doctrine consistent will produce one and then another pattern of belief; likewise, the creation of new doctrines makes possible their systematization, refinement, and supplanting by more new doctrines which overcome the flaws of previous doctrinal inventions. Similarly in law, long-term underlying motivations, such as internal considerations of legal technique in a particular legal tradition or the professional interests of lawyers, produce successive changes in conduct which in turn change the circumstances under which successors choose and act.[49]

The most interesting historical genetic processes are those which interact and transform the conditions under which they and others develop. The Protestant ethic, as a *genetic* ideal-type, is an account of an underlying motivation with respect to the ethical conduct of life, from the original reformers to the succeeding generations of preachers, to Franklin, to "victorious capitalism," which "rests on mechanical foundations" and "needs its support no longer" so that "the idea of duty in one's calling prowls about in our lives like the ghost of dead religious beliefs."[50] Two points must be noticed about this genetic ideal-type. First, the fact that Weber could trace this genetic process in terms of intelligible individual motivations—for pragmatic historiographic reasons, necessarily "typified"—warrants his use of Protestantism as a historical variable. Second, any list of the "distinctive features" of a phenomenon for which genetic types of this sort may be provided is *itself* a causal explanation of the features, simply because the genetic types are themselves causal. Thus, taken by themselves, the lists are not meaningful as causal explanations. They *are*, however, meaningful as preliminaries, aids to analysis, and summaries of arguments. But the genuine explanatory work is done on the level of the individual acts that make up the genetic ideal-type patterns, not on the level of factors.

In the "Introduction" to the *Religionssoziologie*, Weber characterized the Protestant ethic thesis as a genetic ideal-type. In "Objectivity," the Marxist account is characterized as one. Weber's account of the rise of a centralized administrative bureaucracy out of the struggles between monarchs and their enfeoffed vassals is presumably a genetic ideal-type as well. *Economy and Society* is a compilation of ideal-types, which makes frequent reference to their genetic aspects and to the interactions between developmental processes. The primary theme is interaction between various processes and economic interests, but there are other kinds of interaction as well, in particular the mental affinities arguments of which Weber was so fond.

The *interaction* between distinct genetic processes of rationalization suggests a different approach to the question raised by Kronman as to the relation between the various forms of rationality. The origins and internal development of various forms of rationality (e.g., accounting, law, administration, the disenchantment of the world, science, theodicy, asceticism, and canon law) are proper subjects for genetic typifications. Changes in belief and conduct in these various spheres are successive. Weber stressed with respect to science, for example, that it is always in the business of surpassing itself. Similarly for theodicy, law, and the other forms; the pursuit of the activity itself changes the subject of the activity and the conditions under which successors pursue the activity. Weber pointed out that one consequence of asceticism was worldly success, a consequence with evident implications for the practices and beliefs of successors in this tradition. And asceticism had other implications as well, particularly for the possibility of certain forms of work discipline, which altered the conditions under which other activities developed. In the case of modern rationalism, there arose a dynamic of interactions between various genetic processes in which intelligible changes in one reinforced, hastened, and encouraged changes in others. The mental affinity between business practice and disenchanted religion is a simple instance of this: hard-bitten businessmen had little interest in religions with magical elements; ascetic religionists proved to be successful in business and to be assiduous, disciplined workers; asceticism encouraged business; and the rise of a business class served to expand the base of ascetic religion.

If one traces the interactions between changes in law, ethics, administration, religion, and so on, one finds a powerful dynamic of interactions. The dynamic is the explanation of modern rationality, and incidentally of modern capitalism, which is part of the dynamic. But there is no more to the explanatory force of this dynamic than that which comes from explaining the intelligible actions of individuals and their consequences. So the explanation is to be a work of tessellation, the composition of a pattern of actions. Ideal-types were a shorthand means of describing patterns in this mosaic, but no more—not Millian causes made up of institutional facts and not the immanent universal historical forces of rationalization. Each act in the mosaic was to be intelligible, and each step in these genetic processes was to be construed as contingent in the way human action is contingent. This, at least, was Weber's methodological ideal at the time he wrote the methodological "Introduction" to *Economy and Society,* and he never repudiated it.

THE INCORPORATION OF THE MARXIAN ACCOUNT

We are left with the question of the relation between Weber's mosaic and Marx's account. One might expect to find the parts of Marx's explanation

Weber regarded as acceptable among the patterns in the mosaic Weber constructed. Marx formulated the problem of the origins of capitalism in various ways. The most elaborately developed discussion is of the "primitive accumulation" of capital, and this discussion overlaps with Weber. The problem is dictated by the logical structure of standard accounts of the accumulation of capital, Marx's included:

> The accumulation of capital pre-supposes surplus-value; surplus-value pre-supposes capitalistic production; capitalistic production pre-supposes the pre-existence of considerable masses of capital and of labour—power in the hands of producers of commodities. The whole movement, therefore, seems to turn in a vicious circle, out of which we can only get by supposing a primitive accumulation (previous accumulation of Adam Smith) preceding capitalistic accumulation; an accumulation not the result of the capitalist mode of production, but its starting point.[51]

The puzzle is how one arrives at this starting point.

Marx's own account of the transformation has struck many readers as question-begging.[52] One might hope for an explanatory account that showed capitalism as a natural outgrowth of the inherent conflicts of feudal development. One receives an approximation of this—an explanation of the ways in which the dissolution of feudalism removed obstacles to the expropriation of the surplus value of free labor. This does not explain the transformation of money into capital (i.e., the initial use of money or values for the purpose of additional accumulation, the origin of capitalistic *purposes*); it only explains how the transformation, once begun, proceeded when the impediments were removed. For a Marxist holding to the doctrine of the historical specificity of human motivation, this is a special embarrassment because the form of Marx's explanation seems to presuppose *homo economicus* and thus appears implicitly to concede the naturalness of a type Marx had earlier stigmatized as "alienated."

In classical economics the problem of the origin of purposeful accumulation was resolved by what Marx rightly regarded as a legend that "in times long gone by there were two sorts of people; one, the diligent, intelligent, and, above all, frugal elite; the other, lazy rascals, spending their substance, and more, in riotous living."[53] Frugality explains the transformation by suggesting that money in the hands of the frugal is capital, while money in the hands of the profligate is not. "The Protestant Ethic" echoes this distinction, while supplying an alternative account of the underlying motivation for accumulation. Indeed, in the older form of the essay, accumulation in the form of "a peculiarly calculating sort of profit-seeking"[54] is stressed above all else as Protestantism's significant consequence for economic conduct. But there is little suggesting that Weber considered this to bear on the Marxian problem of primitive accumulation. In Weber's later work the heavy stress on accumulation disappears; it is replaced by the rationalization of life, the rational spirit, and the rational organization of labor.[55] This last concern represented a more direct confrontation with Marx, for Weber's account of it challenged the historical specifics of the Marxian account of the rise of wage labor while preserving the narrative centrality of Protestantism. According to Weber's later work, especially the "Introduction" to the *Religionssoziologie* and the lectures on general economic history, the relation between Protestantism and the rational organization of work was that Protestantism produced the persons who had the psychological and ethical capacity to be the participants in rational work organizations. This Weber took to be the differentiating feature between true modern capitalism and the trade capitalism of the Jews, a differentiation which Sombart's analysis emphasizes. As he put it, "the contrast may be formulated by saying that Jewish capitalism was speculative pariah-capitalism, while Puritan capitalism consisted in the organization of citizen labor."[56]

Marx spoke in detail of the development of rational work organizations in connection with the problem of primitive accumulation,[57] and Weber specifically rejected this account. The Marxian version of the development of organizations that used free labor "rationally" considered a rather different aspect of the "organization of citizen labor." Marx pointed out that bourgeois economists emphasize that the persons who worked for these new organizations were persons who had been emancipated from serfdom and "the fetters of the guilds." But, Marx said, most of these persons became sellers of their own labor because in their emancipation they lost their feudal rights to the soil, their means of subsistence. They were thus forced into the labor market. The expropriation of the peasantry gave capitalism a ready-made proletariat whose labor could be, and was, ruthlessly exploited.

The organizations employing the impoverished labor that had thus been "freed" differed from those of earlier times. Under the guilds and with cottage industry, the capital requirements of a productive unit were largely requirements for operating funds. The new organizations were simply much larger workshops, which brought together spindles and looms and located them in the same place. A single owner thus had a much larger requirement for fixed investment. This investment enabled the owner to exploit labor. It was thus profitable; the profits were the value extracted from the laborer. Marx called this "the period of manufacture properly so-called"[58] to distinguish it from the period of machine industry. The productive units of the period of manufacture were the predecessors of the units that took advantage of the Industrial Revolution; they served to concentrate capital in the hands of those who could pay for inventions like the power-loom. These later organizations exploited labor even more ruthlessly.

Weber recapitulated the Marxian account of the development of capitalistic labor in *General Economic History*, including the central notion of the Marxian account, the origin of English free labor in peasant eviction.[59] Weber made one significant modification. He rejected the distinction between "factory" and "manufactory," the crux of chapter 30 of *Capital*, as "casuistical and of doubtful value." Both, according to Weber, involved fixed capital and rational organization of labor. This is an important difference, since Marx was concerned to show that these organizations are not more productive than cottage industries but merely more exploitative.[60] Hence, Marx would deny that they *were* more rational in the organization of work. Weber insisted that these new work organizations were more rational and that the "centralization of the material implements of organization in the hands of the master" was part and parcel of the process of rationalization,[61] a process Weber considered to be paralleled in the state by bureaucratization.

Marx's causal factors were retained in Weber's account but were transformed by being given new roles in the argument. For Weber, the availability of free labor was one prerequisite among others for the development of the factory system, such as inexpensive techniques of production and a steady mass market: in short, the prerequisites for the development of rational work discipline of the modern kind. An ideal-type of this kind of discipline, with genetic implications, is given in *Economy and Society*. Thus the elements of the Marxian account are retained, as members of the supporting cast in a story Weber regarded as more significant—the story of the rise of rational organization and the inexorability of its dominance of the modern life-world.

Notes

1. E.g., in Max Weber, *The Methodology of the Social Sciences* (New York: Free Press, 1949), 68, and Max Weber, *General Economic History* (New York: Collier Books, 1961), 128–29.

2. Gordon Marshall, *In Search of the Spirit of Capitalism: An Essay on Max Weber's Protestant Ethic Thesis* (London: Hutchinson, 1982); Alasdair MacIntyre, "A Mistake about Causality in Social Science," in *Politics and Society,* ed. W. G. Runciman and Peter Laslett, 2nd series (New York: Barnes & Noble, 1962), 48–70; A. R. Louch, *Explanation and Human Action* (Berkeley: University of California Press, 1966).

3. Jean Baechler, *The Origins of Capitalism* (Oxford: Basil Blackwell, 1975).

4. Wolfgang Schluchter, *The Rise of Western Rationalism: Max Weber's Developmental History* (Berkeley and Los Angeles: University of California Press, 1981).

5. Max Weber, *Selections in Translation* (Cambridge: Cambridge University Press, 1978), 128n.

6. Weber, *Selections in Translation,* 114.

7. H. L. A. Hart and A. M. Honoré, *Causation in the Law* (Oxford: Oxford University Press, 1959), 393. Cf. Weber, *Selections in Translation,* 114n.

8. Weber, *Methodology,* 173.

9. Ibid., 169 (emphases in original).

10. Ibid., 103.

11. Ibid., 93–94; Max Weber, *The Protestant Ethic and the Spirit of Capitalism* (New York: Free Press, 1958), 200. Marshall, in *In Search of the Spirit of Capitalism* (33), suggests that the "Protestant ethic" was itself an intervention into the *methodenstreit.*

12. Cf. Hart and Honoré, *Causation in the Law.*

13. Weber, *Methodology,* 78.

14. Ibid., 93.

15. Weber, *Protestant Ethic,* 183.

16. Ibid.

17. Ibid., 182.

18. Ibid., 183.

19. Weber, *Methodology,* 67.

20. Ibid., 71.

21. Weber, *Protestant Ethic,* 182–83.

22. Weber, *Methodology,* 71.

23. Weber, *Protestant Ethic,* 283–84.

24. Weber, *Methodology,* 69.

25. Ibid., 68.

26. Ibid., 69.

27. Ibid.

28. Ibid., 103.

29. Cf. Stephen P. Turner and Regis A. Factor, "Objective Possibility and Adequate Causation in Weber's Methodological Writings," *Sociological Review* 29 (1981): 5-28, and Stephen P. Turner, "Weber on Action," *American Sociological Review* 48 (1983): 506-19.

30. Cf. Alan Macfarlane, *The Origins of English Individualism: The Family, Property, and Social Transition* (New York: Cambridge University Press, 1979), 34-52.

31. Max Weber, "Die protestantische Ethik und der 'Geist' des Kapitalismus," *Archiv für Sozialwissenschaft und Sozialpolitik* 20 (1905): 29. Cf. Wolfgang J. Mommsen, "Max Weber as a Critic of Marxism," *Canadian Journal of Sociology* 2 (1977): 378.

32. Weber, *General Economic History,* 232.

33. Translated by Gerth and Mills under its original subtitle "Religious Rejections of the World and Their Directions."

34. Max Weber, *From Max Weber: Essays in Sociology* (New York: Oxford University Press, 1946), 324.

35. Ibid.

36. Friedrich H. Tenbruck, "The Problem of Thematic Unity in the Works of Max Weber," *British Journal of Sociology* 31 (1980): 334.

37. Ibid., 341.

38. Ibid.

39. Weber, *General Economic History,* 270.

40. Ibid., 260.

41. Benjamin Nelson, "Max Weber's 'Author's Introduction' (1920): A Master Clue to His Main Aims," *Sociological Inquiry* 44 (1974): 275.

42. Benjamin Nelson, "Weber's Protestant Ethic: Its Origins, Wanderings, and Foreseeable Futures," in *Beyond the Classics? Essays in the Scientific Study of Religion,* ed. Charles Y. Glock and Phillip E. Hammond (New York: Harper & Row, 1973), 71-130, esp. 111-12.

43. Ibid., 111.

44. Ibid., 111-12.

45. Weber, *Protestant Ethic,* 13-24.

46. E.g., "It is not possible to enunciate any general formula that will summarize the comparative substantive powers of the various factors involved in such a transformation or will summarize the manner of their accommodation." *Economy and Society: An Outline of Interpretive Sociology* (Berkeley and Los Angeles: University of California Press, 1978), 577.

47. Otto Hintze, *The Historical Essays of Otto Hintze* (New York: Oxford University Press, 1975), 380.

48. Weber, *Economy and Society,* 10.

49. E.g., ibid., 688, 709, 853, 855, 874, 884, 886.

50. Weber, *Protestant Ethic,* 181-82.

51. Karl Marx, *Capital: A Critical Analysis of Capitalist Production* (Moscow: Progress Publishers, 1954), 1: 667.

52. Baechler, *Origins of Capitalism,* 10-25.

53. Marx, *Capital* 1: 667.

54. Weber, *Protestant Ethic,* 55.

55. The shift is striking when the original essay and the later "Introduction" to the *Religionssoziologie* are compared. The "Introduction" never mentions accumulation, but discusses the rational organization of labor repeatedly. The original text of "The Protestant

Ethic'' mentions the rational organization of labor only in passing. One may speculate that Weber's industrial studies impressed him with the importance of the organization of work.

56. Weber, *General Economic History*, 276.

57. Marx, *Capital* 1: 702–15.

58. Ibid., 700.

59. Weber, *General Economic History*, 128–30.

60. Marx, *Capital* 1: 698.

61. Weber, *Economy and Society*, 1156.

PART IV / History

I/XX/I

Lawrence A.
Scaff & Thomas
Clay Arnold

Class and the Theory of History: Marx on France and Weber on Russia

If any section of history has been painted grey on grey, it is this. —*Karl Marx (1852)*
But in present-day Russia what actually is "historical?" —*Max Weber (1906)*

When Max Weber resumed teaching in 1918, after an absence of two decades, he chose to entitle his first lecture series "Economy and Society: Positive Critique of the Materialist Conception of History." The subtitle was an indication of Weber's long-standing dialogue with Marx and "history." In fact, no topic was more central to this dialogue than the theory of history and Marx's part in developing the theory.

Recent studies of both Marx and Weber converge on the problem suggested by a theory of history. In a characteristic attribution, Marx has been credited with having "not only a *philosophy* of history, but also what deserves to be called a *theory* of history, which is not a reflective construal, from a distance, of what happens, but a contribution to understanding its inner dynamic."[1] In this conception what distinguishes a theory of history is the analysis of material production and socio-economic structure (in contrast to consciousness and culture) as forces of historical change. The terms "rigorous" and "scientific" are often used to characterize such a view, typically ascribed to Marx—so much so that for some "there is no real rival theory of history" to Marx's.[2] However, there is precisely such a rival in Weber's work, as writers approaching the issue from the perspective of Weberian categories have sought to show.[3] Weber's is a construal of history similarly concerned with inner dynamics or with the complex interplay between society and consciousness, economy and culture.

It is often assumed that Marx and Weber stand for opposed theories of history. The view associated with Marx, still tied to its Hegelian origins, is said to conceive of history as a step-like progression, a dialectical movement through stages that are ultimately continuous, cumulative, and subject to real and necessary laws of evolutionary progress. A theory of history from this perspective is, in effect, always a "stage theory" in which opposition, cancellation, repetition, and emergence form the essential images for the laws of motion. The second view, associated with Weber and revealing something of Nietzsche's assault on Hegelianism, is thought to conceive of history as a plurality of histories proceeding through contingent, hypothetical phases which may be noncontinuous and incommensurate. This "developmental history" is assumed to reveal little more than rationalizing tendencies, in different spheres of action, grasped through heuristic ideal-types. A naturalistic assumption underlies the first view, a hermeneutic assumption the second: the belief in an ontology to history which can be grasped by the rational mind and recorded with precision as the real and the actual is countered by a belief in history as an invented record of paradox (unintended consequences and irrationalities) and thus recorded through an act of interpretation informed by a particular and interested perspective.

This essential contrast may serve as a useful point of departure for the contemporary analysis of the theory of history, but it also conceals a number of difficulties. First, for Marx the use of evolutionary language suggests a more rigid approach to the historical process than he at times wanted to employ. Second, in Weber's usage the terminology of "developmental history," appearing notably in the Russia essays of 1906, is always employed with a strong measure of critical distance. (In fact, in the Russian context "developmental theorists" become for Weber precisely those thinkers, swayed by a reductionist Marxism, who attach themselves to "historical laws" of the kind Marx himself sometimes rejected!) Third, this contrasting language tends to overlook a common meeting ground in history for Marx and Weber, already anticipated in Löwith's striking comparison between Weber's treatment of rationalization under conditions of modern disenchantment and Marx's analysis of self-alienation under conditions of capitalist appropriation.[4] Finally, articulation of the opposed theories of history remains at the level of a general or abstract universal history. What seems odd, given the understandable and perhaps unavoidable distancing from a history of events, is that the theory of history continues to be philosophical, that is, "a reflective construal, from a distance."

There does not yet exist a discussion of the respective dynamics of the two rival theories as revealed in the writing of *actual* history, writing which is itself a historical act, a depicting of what Löwith aptly calls "this history of the present, which is however itself merely a 'segment of the process of human destiny.' "[5] If Marx and Weber did indeed have theories of history, then we should expect to find those theories at work in their specific and detailed writings on episodes of consequence—fateful and revolutionary episodes—in the societies of their time. Did a theory of history make a difference, and did it gain in depth and sophistication as it was brought from heaven to earth and abolished cosmic tragedy with human comedy?

In this paper we propose to test the logic of the theory of history by analyzing and comparing Marx's historical writings on revolutions in France, particularly in *The Eighteenth Brumaire of Louis Bonaparte* (1852), and Weber's writings on the Russian Revolution, especially in *Zur Lage der bürgerlichen Demokratie in Russland* (1906). This analysis starts from the conviction that both Marx and Weber employ three modes for understanding history—dramatic, scientific, and prophetic—which both displace and subsume the distinction between evolutionary and developmental schemes. Beginning with Marx's attempt to explain class conflict and the outcome of events in France from 1848 to 1851, we wish to show that Marx, notwithstanding his brilliant insights on the ironies of history, was reluctantly driven to transcend the evolutionary postulates of historical materialism in favor of a dramatic or rhetorical understanding of history. Weber, on the other hand, in analyzing classes and revolution in Russia half a century later, was able to assemble Marx's dramatic history as a coherent explanation within a scientific scheme. What had perplexed Marx as irrational and paradoxical in the history of the present was then seen by Weber as part of the very nature of the process of transformation itself. In other words, what Marx had understood as a unitary process driven by class conflict was seen by Weber as a fragmented process driven by rationalization; as class failed to occupy its theoretically assigned role *in* history, the theory *of* history had to change. Thus, Weber not only criticized historical materialism, but he comprehended and completed its aspirations to be a science, that is, to be something more solid than dramatic metaphor or prophetic prediction. It is then precisely in Weber's twentieth-century writings on revolution, not in Marx's nineteenth-century productions, that we find a distinctively modern, post-Hegelian view of class and the *meaning* of history—a meaning that has now become, using Weber's word, "provisional."[6]

MARX'S FRANCE AND WEBER'S RUSSIA

Karl Marx published three works on French politics and society: *Class Struggles in France,* a report covering events from the 1848 February revolution to signs of the denouement in 1850; *The Eighteenth Brumaire of*

Louis Bonaparte, a continuation of the story to the "Staatsstreich" or "trick of state" of 1851; and finally *The Civil War in France,* an analysis of the short-lived Paris Commune of 1871, a harbinger for Marx and Engels of the revolutionary "dictatorship of the proletariat." The *Eighteenth Brumaire* contains Marx's most penetrating and brilliant writing, linked backward to the comedy of Bonaparte's first appearance as the peasantry's savior and forward to the tragedy of the proletarian revolution's shattered hopes; it becomes the centerpiece of Marx's contribution to contemporary history or a "history of the present."[7]

Max Weber is not often remembered for his practical commentaries and interests, much less his thinking about revolution, and yet there are remarkable similarities between his relation to Russia and Marx's to France. Like Marx's writings, Weber's form a series: the two essays of 1906, *Zur Lage der bürgerlichen Demokratie in Russland* (On the Situation of Bourgeois Democracy in Russia) and *Russlands Uebergang zum Scheinkonstitutionalismus* (Russia's Transition to Pseudo-Constitutionalism), published as supplements to the *Archiv für Sozialwissenschaft und Sozialpolitik* at Weber's personal expense (and with the added investment of learning Russian); and "Russlands Uebergang zur Scheindemokratie" (Russia's Transition to Pseudo-Democracy), published in April 1917 in the pages of Naumann's reformist journal, *Die Hilfe.* In Weber's case the second essay resembles Marx's *Civil War in France,* for in both texts history is represented as a linear chronicle with minimal intrusion of restructuring categories and emphases; historical time is conceived as a chronology. Like the *Eighteenth Brumaire,* the decisive shift in the reworking of a history of crisis comes in Weber's first essay, a reading of revolutionary tragi-comedy alluding back to the experience of 1848 and forward to the leap out of chronological "history" of 1917.

Marx's *Eighteenth Brumaire* and Weber's *Bourgeois Democracy in Russia* stand at the center of our discussion because both deal with extraordinary political episodes—one as the apparent culmination of a revolutionary movement, the other as the apparent beginning. But in both cases there is undisguised ambivalence: the culmination is also a reversal, the beginning a continuation. Lack of resolution becomes for Marx and Weber a crisis of double significance: an epoch of social change and a precise instant which marks a limit. The epoch receives its imprint as that transitional phase between traditionalism and modernity, while the instant simply is December 2, 1851, in France (Louis Bonaparte's *coup d'état*), and October 17, 1905, in Russia (Nicholas II's October Manifesto). The task Marx and Weber set themselves is to separate appearance from actuality in the epochal phantasmagoria of transition and then to judge what is an ending, what is a beginning?

We note parallels in the form of questioning for Marx and Weber, given their respective political interests. Marx initially pursues one specific question, namely what are the prospects for proletarian revolution; the obverse of which is Weber's beginning question, namely what are the prospects for bourgeois liberal democracy? One prospect is invariably haunted by the other: for Marx there is the specter of failed revolution— "Why did the Paris proletariat not rise in revolt after December 2?"[8] The question can be restated in more general terms: given the alignment of social and economic forces in history, how was Napoleon III possible at all? For Weber, on the other hand, the specter looms of a failed liberalism, of an ideological movement that belongs to history and can be revived only in memory but never again in fact. Inside Russia liberalism seems doomed. Beyond Russia the question assumes a general form: given capitalism's commanding position, "how in the long run are all these things [i.e., 'democracy,' 'freedom'] 'possible' at all?"[9]

The urgency of Marx's inquiry is called forth by impending disconfirmation of the evolutionary laws of motion and by a threatened denial of closely guarded historical expectations. What begins as a specific question opens out to an inquiry about a regime, then about the nature of the state as such, and finally about a "riddle of history."[10] Marx evokes a profound puzzlement about the meaning of France's modern experience: "The revolution thus moves along an ascending line," but later "the revolution thus moves in a descending line."[11] It is small wonder that Marx proposes to reconcile both movements in history's "grey on grey" amidst promises of a new Hegelian flight by Minerva's owl.

But for Weber when the "falling of the dusk" comes to *Russia,* then "what actually is 'historical'?"[12] Setting aside the church and peasant communism, which present special problems, his answer is unequivocal: "absolutely nothing" (and certainly not liberalism) "except the absolute power of the Tsar, taken over from the age of the Tartars, which today is suspended in midair in completely unhistorical 'freedom,' following the crumbling of all those 'organic' images that gave seventeenth and eighteenth century Russia its peculiar stamp."[13] "Suspended in midair," the old autocracy has lifted itself out of "history," its connection with the social order severed. Tsarist autocracy has become impossible. However, Weber proposes that it may be replaced by more modern autocratic forms, such as the "dictatorship of the proletariat."

The inquiry into Russia is thus linked to Weber's concern with the historical fate of Western culture, a connection formed through the medium of Marx or, more specifically, Marx's analysis of capitalist development, class, and revolution. For Weber also, what begins as a specific, time-bound question explodes into an inquiry about a regime, the modern state, and finally the movement of history. Toward the end of his essay Weber puts the problem on a contemporary basis, reminiscent of Tocqueville's formulations, by arguing that Russia is "finally entering the path of specifically European development . . . just as conversely the enormous influx of European immigrants . . . into the United States is in the process of shredding the old democratic traditions—and in both cases in alliance with the forces of capitalism. . . . However—and this is the more important point—both developments reveal in a certain sense that this is the 'last' chance for building 'free' cultures 'from the foundations upward.' "[14] Weber is clear about what awaits the complacent: "all *economic* weather vanes point in the direction of increasing unfreedom," and in one of his most famous images, "everywhere the cage for the new serfdom is ready."[15]

What intervenes between the *Eighteenth Brumaire* and *Bourgeois Democracy*, between 1852 and 1906, is of course Marx himself, the form of consciousness ahead of its time. Marx's ghostly presence in Russia, like the serialized social revolution in France, creates the dramatic tension and complexity so evident in Weber's account. In what form will Marx next appear? when? where? to whom? are the ideological questions Weber must incorporate with a socio-economic analysis in order to render history intelligible. Marx's ideological stranglehold over the revolutionary movement becomes the surest demonstration of the limits to a rigid historical materialism. Yet since the effect of Marx cannot be unambiguously predicted, Weber's analysis takes on a shifting, layered, kaleidoscopic quality. Events in a history of crisis conceal endless possibilities and meanings; in Russia's case Weber is willing to rest on just one certainty: even given Marx's revolutionary presence, "Only an unsuccessful *European* war would conclusively smash the autocracy."[16] In contrast to Weber's recording of crisis (i.e., of concealments and qualifications) Marx's *Eighteenth Brumaire* seems almost straightforward and undialectical. It has the clean lines of nineteenth-century vision. With *Bourgeois Democracy* we have entered the convoluted world of the twentieth century, the century of mass movements, revolutionary vanguards, bureaucratic domination, and total war.

For Weber, not only Marx but also Marxism is felt on every page of *Bourgeois Democracy in Russia*. The reason lies in the rationalization of economic life in the context of Russian intellectual culture: "The further development of capitalism will complete the disintegration of 'populist' romanticism," Weber is convinced, "which will no doubt be succeeded for the most part by Marxism."[17] But Marxism will come as a revolutionary ideology having different forms and different audiences: as the fastidious stage theory justifying the view that conditions are not yet ripe for proletarian revolution, as a defense for the eschatological politics of the Narodniki, or as a flexible rationalization for the creative act of imposing "socialisation of the means of production" and the "dictatorship of the masses."[18] Weber is thus able to pose as both interpreter and defender of Marx against Marxism. Complaining about the romantic revolutionaries, Weber notes that "for their knowledge about the nature of capitalism they have generally read no one except Marx and have misunderstood even him, since they leaf through his work with the incessant question about 'the moral lessons of history.' "[19] Here is the beginning of an opportunity to rescue Marx from his epigones, if not from himself.

Just as Weber incorporates Marx(ism), so Marx in the *Eighteenth Brumaire* anticipates Weber. Anticipations come in the form of doubt and reassurance—doubt that the laws of motion are continuing to drive history forward, reassurance that "the most motley mixture of crying contradictions" is the precondition for progressive evolution; doubt that the centralized state has become an autonomous power even for the social revolution, reassurance that "the state power is not suspended in midair"; doubt that the peasantry can be accommodated within a "materialist" analysis of the "relations of production," reassurance that the peasantry's political interest "finds its final expression in the executive power subordinating society to itself."[20] But what if the doubts are justified by the course of events; what if the reassurances are overstated? Weber enters, carrying his suggestions that the laws of motion are ideal-types, that the Russian state power has already been "suspended in midair," that the peasantry is not a modern class that can be expected to conform to developmental laws. At these points the dialectic can be unwound and used against itself, a project already present in Marx and adopted by Weber for his own purposes.

THE GENEALOGY OF REVOLUTION: HISTORY AS DRAMA

It was Marx who announced the concept of "modern revolution," a concept that could only be made intelligible in relation to a remembered past. This past contains two "moments," to speak with Hegel: the "old regime" and the "periods of revolutionary crisis." Thus, the history of Europe can be conceived as interrupted and segmented by 1789, and before that by 1688, 1640, 1517, and so forth, back to Old Testament prophecy. The prophecies of 1848 were only the latest additions to a sequence. Marx chose to view the revolutionary breakthroughs as a repeated parody ("Hegel remarks somewhere that all facts and personages of great importance in world history occur, as it were, twice. He forgot to add: the first time as tragedy, the second as farce'') and as a collective exercise in learning ''to present the new scene of world history in this time-honored disguise and this borrowed language.''[21] But the telescoping record was not one of continuous and evenly paced evolution of social forces and consciousness. By 1852 Marx observed France both making up for lost time with ''an abbreviated because revolutionary method'' and reversing the prescribed ''textbook course of development'': ''Society now seems to have fallen back behind its point of departure; it has in truth first to create for itself the revolutionary point of departure, the situation, the relations, the conditions under which modern revolution becomes serious.''[22] But how can Marx make sense of a process characterized by both acceleration and reversal? How can serious modern drama be made to replace classical farce?

The answer is found in Marx's distinction between eighteenth-century bourgeois revolutions and nineteenth-century proletarian revolutions and in his left Hegelian-Trotskyite battlecry: *''Hic Rhodus, hic salta''*—that is, show here and now what can be done, without waiting for the ''maturation'' of history. As if to prove Marx's insight into the grip of revolutionary memories, Trotsky himself borrowed these passages from the *Eighteenth Brumaire* in order to point toward the meaning of the ''new'' revolutionary experience of 1905:

> Bourgeois revolutions, like those of the eighteenth century, storm swiftly from success to success . . . but they are short-lived; soon they have attained their zenith, and a long crapulent depression lays hold of society before it learns soberly to assimilate the results of its storm-and-stress period. On the other hand proletarian revolutions, like those of the nineteenth century, criticize themselves continually in their own course, come back to the apparently accomplished in order to begin it afresh, deride with unmerciful thoroughness the inadequacies, weaknesses, and paltrinesses of their first attempts . . . until a situation has been created which makes all turning back impossible.[23]

In this view revolution as a category of action is lifted out of the natural world of events and into the human world of intentional action: from spirited intoxication to cool self-consciousness. But 1905 is already the twentieth century, Trotsky's century of ''permanent revolution'' and the ''law of combined development.'' Marx's modern revolution is restated as a synthesis of bourgeois and proletarian forms, intoxication and self-consciousness, parody and seriousness, comedy and tragedy. To see this change is to see what both unites and separates Weber and Marx.

For Weber also to write a history of revolutionary crisis is to reform events as a text, encapsulating predecessors and telescoping present into past in search of familiar categories and languages. Thus Marx reappears in Weber's Russian drama as the "ghost" of modern revolutionary self-consciousness, the *Urtext* cast as the determined "old mole" to Weber's aloof Hamlet, burrowing from within the foundations of Russian society.[24] To be more precise, Marx is visible for Weber as the father of Russia's revolutionary intelligentsia, of the ideological and fraternal struggle between Martov and Lenin, who then represent, according to Weber, the "Girondin" and "Jacobin" possibilities already surfacing as the foundations dissolve.[25] The year 1905 is thus situated within the revolutionary tradition: the autocracy doubles for the *ancien régime,* Nicholas II for Louis XVI and Charles I, Russian radicals for the French Convention, Bolshevism and Leninism for Jacobinism, Count Witte for Guizot, Struve for Lafayette, Petrunkevich for Carnot, the Zemstvos for the 1848 Frankfurt Parliament, the Russian gentry for the Prussian royalists in 1848, soviets for revolutionary committees.[26] In proceeding analogically Weber follows not simply Marx's lead but also that of his Russian subjects, who, as in Dostoevsky's novels, constantly borrow Paris, 1789, and *la langue du citoyen du monde* as symbols of authentic revolutionary accomplishment.

Of course, Marx substitutes "the Nephew for the Uncle" in the "second edition of the eighteenth Brumaire" in order to amend Hegel's version of world history, to parody the present. For Weber, however, revolution's "bloody tragi-comedy"[27] prohibits such extravagance:

Like the modern military battle, stripped of the romantic charm of knightly combat, so it is also with modern "revolution": it represents itself as a mechanical operation between the products of mental labor in laboratories and industrial plants, objectified as instrumental things, and the cold power of money; also as a frightful, perpetual stress placed on the strength of *nerve* of the leader as well as hundreds of thousands of followers. Everything is—at least for the eye of the observer—"technique" and a question of iron steadfastness of nerves.[28]

Weber's formula for revolutionary success might read, mastery of technique (including the social technique of organization) plus strength of ideological commitment; the formula already represents a purposive rationalization of spontaneous consciousness and an overcoming of all "developmental laws." The genealogy of revolution after Marx leads to the instrumentalization or scientization of revolution or, in the Hegelian terms borrowed by Weber, "the return of Spirit to itself," that is, the rationalization of revolutionary technique through deliberate self-reflection.[29]

Now self-reflection requires a language, and in their dramatic histories Marx and Weber appropriate that language from the underworld of human affairs: a Faustian language of dissolution, suspension, sorcery, conjuring, and subversion accounts for the emergence of modern forms. It is introduced with Marx's purloined line from Mephistopheles, "For all that comes to be, deserves to perish wretchedly," although here Marx forgot to add, "especially bourgeois liberalism."[30] But wearing the cloak of the "Spirit who negates," Marx does encounter the European liberals soon enough: "I need not relate the ignominious history of their dissolution. . . . Their history has come to an end forever," or so it seems in France.[31] For Weber the encounter is repeated a few generations later in the East: "No one knows today how many of the liberals' hopes for a liberating reform capable of breaking bureaucratic centralism still remain, and how many of them have dissolved into nothingness, like a Fata Morgana."[32] Like Marx, Weber suspects that such hopes are indeed following Marx's lead and "dissolving into nothingness," assisted by the hovering presence of the sorceress of history.

The one thing that remains from these present encounters is *human* sorcery, the conjuring of images, the sly Faustian art of pure politics. Here is Marx's seriousness with a vengeance: thus, according to Weber's juxtaposition of 1789 and 1905, "as Louis XVI wanted under no circumstances to be 'rescued' by Lafayette, so nothing appears more certain than that Court circles of officialdom would rather make a pact with the devil than with Zemstvo liberalism."[33] And there are similar possibilities set forth by Marx earlier: on the one hand revolutionists may "anxiously conjure up the spirits of the past," but on the other hand "Revolution is conjured away by a cardsharper's trick," and in either case "the enemy . . . was only conjured away in imagination" but not in fact.[34] Just as, for Marx, Louis Bonaparte is "like a conjurer *[Taschenspieler]* . . . springing constant surprises . . . under the necessity of executing a *coup d'état en miniature* every day," so in Weber's view Nicholas II must 'dance on a tightrope" in order to preserve the illusion of mastery over fate.[35] But Bonaparte's art is revealed only by Marx's unmasking, while the tsarist system has already been undone by events, including the forceful presence of Marxist ideology. In the final paragraph of *Bourgeois Democracy* Weber alludes to "that shocking poverty of 'spirit' " revealed to the public: "the illusions and the aura with which the system surrounded itself . . . are completely destroyed. . . . Far too great is the number of those who saw the system in its nakedness and had to laugh in its face: 'conjurer *[Taschenspieler]*! You will call forth no more spirit.' "[36] Here on the negative side the "developmental theorists" are correct; Weber acknowledges: "the existing Russian autocracy . . . has no choice but to dig its own grave," a fine confirmation of Marx's encouragement to "let the dead bury their dead" in order to free revolution from its fetters to the past.[37] Both represent definitive endings.

But the crucial difference emerges at this point: whereas the second Bonaparte and his regime signify repetition and interruption on the way toward a tragi-comic completion, the tsarist *Selbstherrschaft* or autocracy represents emptiness and collapse as elements in an endless cycle. Marx surely wants tragi-comedy as the next *Aufhebung,* a final act in which Faust is redeemed, Prometheus unbound. Viewing Marx's creations, Weber instead sees a tragi-comedy gone awry—"bloody," rationalized, endless. The desired happy transcendence, the final act, retreats in the distance as a mirage. The idea of finality, of completion, is itself an illusion. There is no "end" to history, no meaning derived from our moment's relation to a hypothetical end. This difference, stated in dramatic form, reverberates throughout Marx's and Weber's thought and affects even their applications of science to history.

CLASS, SOCIETY, STATE: HISTORY AS SCIENCE

Dramatological language forms one part of Marx's and Weber's account of the growth of revolution, but it is supplemented by a sociological language which uncovers the inner dynamics of revolutionary change. It is here that we encounter what is typically called "class analysis," that is, in its simplest terms an identification and explanation of the social relations among bourgeoisie, proletariat, peasantry, gentry, and aristocracy in an attempt to account for the mechanisms and direction of social development. Both Marx and Weber employ this kind of analysis, albeit with rather different assumptions about its standing in science and with different specifications of relevant subject matter, particularly with respect to strata omitted above: the intelligentsia and the bureaucracy.

For Marx the analysis of class falls under the headings of "material interest" and "contradiction." In one of the few places where a definition appears, class is said to exist when "millions of families live under economic conditions of existence that separate their mode of life, their interests, and their culture *[Bildung]* from those of other classes, and put them in hostile opposition to the latter."[38] In this phrasing, class is essentially an economic category, conceived in relation to property and exchange, although *Bildung* suggests a qualification which Weber will elaborate in the concept of status group. From the conception of class, according to Marx, a complete social world can be envisioned: "upon the social conditions of existence rises an entire superstructure of distinct and peculiarly formed sentiments, illusions, modes of thought, and views of life. The entire class creates and forms them out of its material foundations and out of the corresponding social relations."[39] Once these material foundations and dependent superstructure are set in motion by productive forces, encompassing oppositions among class interests, the pattern of history will begin to unfold.

One problem among many posed by Marx's formulation (and the one we want to address) concerns the postulated dynamic relationship between class, capitalism, and political outcomes. What becomes problematic for Marx (and Weber) is the role played by class in the scheme of historical development. There can be no doubt that at least Marx himself thought he had traced Louis Bonaparte's "success" to France's "class struggle." The first step toward the December 2 *coup d'état* was taken by the bourgeoisie's suppression in the "June days" of the modern, proletarian, social revolution of February 1848. The second was taken by the struggle for power within the middle class itself between commercial, financial, industrial, and land-owning interests, thereby subverting the social bases of support for the parliamentary republic. The third was taken by the trade crisis of 1851, a crisis of overproduction and overspeculation, combined with an unheroic bourgeoisie and a parallel antiparliamentary movement for order among the *lumpenproletariat* and the peasantry.[40]

Two important and peculiar assumptions underlie this explanation, one regarding the bourgeoisie as a class and a second concerning the peasantry. Marx must assume the bourgeoisie can be politically divided against itself, and he must assume a distinction between class and class interest (or the means and ability of a class to act on its true collective interest). In his words, while bourgeois parliamentary representatives "declared the political rule of the bourgeoisie to be incompatible with the safety and existence of the bourgeoisie," the class they represented "invited Bonaparte to suppress and annihilate its speaking and writing section, its politicians and its literati, its platform and its press, in order that it might then be able . . . to get rid of its own political rule in order to get rid of the troubles and dangers of ruling."[41] This is an extraordinary admission; borrowing a line from Marx, the turning of a class against itself appears to be a case of the content (the bourgeoisie's actions) going beyond the phrase (the theory of historical materialism). Marx sensibly sides with content over phrases, but the results are confusion in the concept of class and doubts that class struggle really is the motive force of history.

The conclusion Marx should have drawn from these twists and turns of class-based politics is the one Weber in fact reaches in his assessment of Russian conditions: succinctly put, "Political antagonism within the same social stratum or between socially competing strata are often subjectively the most intense."[42] There may be objective class interests, defined within a particular *Weltanschauung* masked as a theory of history, but in the scheme of historical events such interests are often replaced by subjective or ideal interests as primary causes. Weber does not want to suggest by this line of thought that class is unimportant, but he does mean to stress that other factors, particularly those relating to political domination and its ideological imperatives, are often more crucial for understanding the dynamics of conflict. Consequently, from Weber's standpoint there is hardly a precise a priori fit between material foundations and "modes of thought and views of life." Society is composed not only of class, however defined, but of other units and organized spheres of influence that form and act quite independently of class as such.

The details of Weber's reply to Marx are found in revisions of the concept of class and in the comparisons he sketched between the class struggles and revolutionary movements of Western Europe, especially France, and those of Russia. Recognizing on the one hand that "the development of an urban middle class in the Western European sense is very weak" in Russia,[43] and on the other that a particularly virulent form of state-sponsored capitalism had reacted with unique nativist popular traditions to produce an especially aggressive and intransigent revolutionary movement, Weber proposed to use class flexibly in order to identify transitional social formations lying between agrarian-traditional society and urban-industrial civilization. For example, when analyzing Zemstvo membership, Weber found that the second element "mainly represent 'bourgeois' intelligentsia, if one takes this word not in the sense of economic class, but rather in the sense of the general standard of life *[Lebenshaltung]* and level of culture or education *[Bildungsstufe]*."[44] The bourgeoisie, in other words, had to be subdivided into *Besitz-* and *Bildungsbürgertum,* the former representing large-scale commercial and industrial interests and the latter the unattached intelligentsia, "carriers of a political and socio-political idealism" who were "without material interests."[45] Lacking a secure economic foundation, this stratum was more like a status group than a class. In Russia it also shaded into the third element of technically trained specialists employed locally by the Zemstvos, a "proletarian intelligentsia" in Weber's terms, and finally into the "revolutionary intelligentsia," overwhelmingly with bourgeois backgrounds, from the *Narodnaia Volia* (People's Will) to the Leninists.

Comparative generalizations led not simply to analogies but rather to the heart of Russia's differences and dilemma: "The unique aspect of the situation in Russia," Weber argued in one key summation, "appears to be that an intensification of 'capitalist' development, coincident with rising value of land and its products, alongside further development of the industrial proletariat and thus a 'modern' socialism, can also lead to an increase of 'unmodern' *agrarian* communism.''[46] Whereas in France, given Marx's theory, continued capitalist expansion might be expected to return eventually after Louis Bonaparte's detour to the historic path of class struggle, in Russia nothing of the sort could occur. Instead, Weber reasoned, the growth of capitalism in Russia would insure the growth of urban and agrarian radicalism, whether socialist or communist, but without proportionately strengthening the bourgeoisie. This was one lesson to draw from 1905, a year when an apparently bourgeois revolution was conducted with an absent bourgeoisie. The liberal program, as Weber judged, could only be negative: "opposition to Jacobin centralism."[47] Every other aspect of its program was riddled with contradictions: support for economic modernization, electoral reform, agrarian reform, and civil liberties based upon "inalienable human rights" would all have adverse consequences from the liberal point of view among a mass population, unlike the French, that was already opposed to modern individualism. Here was Weber's equivalent to Marx's "crying contradictions," a society caught between modern and unmodern forms, often attempting to combine the two even within the same movement (as with the Narodniki) in heterodox ways.

In this setting Weber saw that the course of revolution depended less on modern class conflict—bourgeoisie versus proletariat—than on the peasantry's allegiances. "Concerning the possibility of a free 'development' in the Western European sense," he pointed out, "the decisive question surely is and remains the position of the *peasantry.*"[48] Observing nineteenth-century France, Marx had actually arrived, albeit with greater reluctance, at a similar conclusion concerning the possibility for revolutionary development. Here we turn to the second assumption in his explanation of events leading to 1851.

The analysis of Weber (and the Russian Marxists) contains traces of Marx's own depiction of the quixotic peasantry on the stage of the world history, a depiction formed around a double image: on the one hand, having run through a sequence of class-related explanations of the *coup d'état* of December 2, Marx in the end hit upon the peasantry as the last solution to his riddle: "Bonaparte represents a class," he concluded, "and the most numerous class of French society at that, the *small-holding peasants.*"[49] But who are these survivors of an earlier era, and what can their modern role be? According to Marx, they "form a vast mass," yet their "mode of production isolates them from one another instead of bringing them into mutual intercourse." Moreover, "in so far as there is merely a local interconnection among these small-holding peasants, and the identity of their interests begets no community, no national bond and no political organization among them, they do not form a class.''[50] So the peasantry both is a class and is not a class—that is, a "mass," incapable of identifying its interest, let alone acting upon it. Even if the peasantry were a class, it would still inhabit a world removed from the economic forces necessary for social transformations, for (as Marx admits elsewhere) it is "not directly involved in the struggle of capital and labour.''[51] Yet since it apparently is not a class, what sense can it make to base Bonaparte's rule on its support? Marx's only answer is an early sketch of the theory of mass society: since the peasantry cannot form and represent its own interests, it must find a power that can, a representative who appears "as an unlimited governmental power that protects them against the other classes. . . . The political influence of the small-holding peasants, therefore, finds its final expression in the executive power subordinating society to itself.''[52]

There is a second possibility, however: lurking beneath the unsettled surface of this paradoxical analysis is Marx's conviction that the actual, material problems of the peasantry—burdensome taxes, mortgages, debts—cannot be solved by the bourgeois state, but instead they require a revolutionary reform of the system of small-holding itself, which is necessarily enslaved by finance capital. "Hence the peasants find their natural ally and leader in the urban proletariat," Marx hopefully concludes, announcing a position that is taken up by the Bolsheviks in 1905, when it is encountered by Weber with fascinating results.[53]

In fact, Weber agreed with Trotsky that the Russian peasantry was "an aid to the revolutionary party," at least in the short run, even if conditions could be expected to improve.[54] In Weber's words "communistic radicalism is . . . bound clearly to *increase* precisely *if* the lot of the peasants is improved—that is, if their burdens are lightened and the disposable land of the communes increased.''[55] Nevertheless, Weber's reaction to Marxist class analysis of the peasantry was characteristically blunt: "Marxist orthodoxy has no more of a definitive agrarian program here than anywhere in the world," Weber insisted; moreover, he was convinced that "the intellectual resources of Marxism are simply not adequate for work on the massive and fundamental agrarian problem.''[56] The *Eighteenth Brumaire* could be taken as a case in point: none of Marx's expectations for the French peasantry was satisfied. In Russia one encountered similar attempts to find a solution, none of which would succeed. Why not? What was amiss from Weber's point of view?

The answer must be sought initially in a fundamental socio-historical distinction. While Marx's small-holding peasants exhibit a kind of stubborn, autarchic individualism, associated only like "potatoes in a sack," Weber's Russian peasantry was stoutly collectivist from the start, emerging as it did from the communal traditions of the *mir* and the *Feldgemeinschaft*. Put succinctly, "in opposition to his Western European counterpart, the Russian peasant is not anti-collectivist," and he "cannot in any circumstances be won over to an 'individualist' agrarian program in the Western European sense."[57] His communal orientation presupposes opposition to private ownership of land and indifference to private property generally, which suggested to Weber a particularly significant divergence from the classic case of 1789, where property was still included in the "rights of man."[58] Thus, whereas in France the peasantry could support bourgeois radicalism, in Russia it could latch onto the cultural appeal of communist radicalism. It was as if Marx's hopes for the peasantry in France could be fulfilled in Russia, but only temporarily and for the wrong reasons. For Russian agrarian communism was traditionalist and precapitalist—Tolstoyan rather than Marxist. It was not a modernizing force, and it would side with revolution essentially for cultural reasons rather than class interests. To see this distinction is to see why Weber can say the Russian peasantry perceived the revolution as something quite specific and concrete and would one day wake up astonished to hear of the intelligentsia's theoretical and Marxist designs, which would call for an end to *all* forms of traditionalism.[59]

Furthermore, even if the French or Russian peasantry possessed a single material interest, it was most likely defined in terms of traditional "land hunger," whose satisfaction led typically to the doorstep of the state. In this last respect Marx was correct. However, for Weber the peasantry had no natural class ally and no consistent ideological orientation: "In modern European revolutions the peasants have generally swung from the most thorough-going radicalism imaginable either to apathy or all the way to political reaction, depending on the way in which their immediate economic demands have been satisfied."[60] This material feature of peasant politics can account for Marx's double imagery of the peasantry both as a class and not as a class, as a pillar of reaction and a force for revolution. But even more significantly, one can say that with this pattern of dialectical reasoning Marx had inadvertently shifted the entire discussion from class to the relationship between society and state or more specifically to the problem of the potential *opposition* between society and state bureaucracy (the "executive power"). The question simply became, to what extent can the "state" be considered "autonomous"?

With this question Weber's analysis comes into its own; Marx's riddle is solved by clues Weber provided. In other words, what Marx explains as an ironic historical deviation in 1852 reappears to Weber in 1906 as the fully comprehensible rationalization of the modern monopolistic bureaucratic state.

Marx's judgments about the state tend to vacillate. First, he follows his own advice and dusts off a familiar category: despotism. "Instead of *society* having conquered a new content for itself, it seems that the *state* only returned to its oldest form, to the shamelessly simple domination of the sabre and the cowl," causing "all classes, equally impotent and equally mute, [to] fall on their knees before the rifle butt."[61] Next, Marx chooses to see the state bureaucracy embedded in a class system, either as "the means of preparing the class rule of the bourgeoisie" or as "the instrument of the ruling class."[62] Finally, he abandons class analysis for political analysis and conceives bureaucracy to be "an artificial caste" created "alongside the actual classes of society" in order to dominate them.[63] This last and most thorough form of domination—rule by bureaucracy rather than class, one of the subversively anomalous *idées napoléoniennes*—is, of course, supposed to wither away in the coming victory of society and its universal representative, the proletariat. Until now "all revolutions perfected this [state] machine instead of smashing it," Marx grants, but the tragi-comic revolution will effect a reversal.[64]

Weber reassembled these elements from Marx in a precise and refutative juxtaposition. In Weber's science the second edition of the *Eighteenth Brumaire* represents bureaucratic domination with a plebiscitary component, which is merely an extension of the centralization and bureaucratization of the state apparatus encouraged by radical theory stemming from 1789, Robespierre, and the first Napoleon.[65] Marx himself, despite denials, stands within this developmental trend. The modern "socialisation of the means of production" in Russia and elsewhere will lead either to greater administrative centralization, taking France as the model, or more generally to what Weber calls "the rationalization of bureaucratism" which will in turn trigger a Trotskyesque "war in permanence of 'society' against bureaucracy."[66] What does such rationalization entail? Weber provides the list: "the slowing down of technological and economic 'progress' and the victory of loan interest *[Rente]* over commercial profit *[Gewinn]*, in conjunction with the exhaustion of the remaining 'free' land and 'free' markets" assisted by "mounting complexity of the economy, by partial nationalisation or 'municipalisation,' by the territorial extent of nations, by constantly increasing paper work, and by increasing occupational specialisation and formalised administrative training—in other words, by caste."[67]

In his concept of "caste" Marx also glimpsed the coming rule of the "new mandarins," but he should have concluded with Weber that by this point the state had become fully autonomous, regardless of who controlled it. Revolutionary policies in this context served not the universal class but rather the state's interest; differences between capitalism and state socialism scarcely mattered. The new "conflict zone" was defined not by class struggles but rather by a social struggle against the omnivorous state bureaucratic apparatus. In the real world of historical development, bureaucratization had led to the final displacement of the old "laws of motion" as a science.

ESCHATOLOGICAL POLITICS AND MODERNITY: HISTORY AS PROPHECY

A discussion of the theory of history is incomplete without considering, as a final step, the crisis of the present in relation to history's putative end, a crisis whose very meaning is established by that relation. But here we press against the boundaries of our inquiry for now it becomes not simply a question of the theory of history but (in Nietzsche's terms) of the "use and abuse" of history, a far more serious affair.

Weber's appreciation of Marx's penetration of Russia was no doubt conditioned by his understanding of the "two-souled character" of Marxism as a dispassionate, realistic, and historical analysis of society and as an impassioned, rationalistic, and universal call to action. According to Weber, "even the reasons for the split" between Lenin and Plekhanov "generally coincide with the 'two-souled' character that Marxism already revealed in Marx's own relationship to the Paris commune and on other occasions."[68] Weber adapted this language from Sombart, where it was used to refer to the clash between scientific and utopian schemata within Marx's thought and within the Marxist movement.[69] But Weber now used the language to align the heroic myth of 1871, created in part by Marx himself, with the Leninism of 1905. In Weber's view Marx had forecast this dual emphasis, for the *Manifesto* epitomized both "scholarship of the highest order" promising a new historical science and a "prophetic document" promising redemption from history.[70] Similarly, in his own terms in the *Eighteenth Brumaire* Marx thought he had unfolded the historical laws of class struggle with methodical precision, but at the same time he claimed to have proved "that the class struggle necessarily leads to the dictatorship of the proletariat" which in turn "constitutes the transition to the abolition of all classes and to a classless society."[71]

Thus, Marx could be interpreted as offering two different views of historical evolution—one emphasizing inevitability and necessity, the other volition and contingency—even though Marx himself might have envisioned them as a synthetic unity, a continuous process of transition "mediated through consciousness and will," using Hegel's words.[72] As

Marx avowed, "Men make their own history, but . . . they do not make it under circumstances chosen by themselves."[73] Such formulations suggest the problem of clarifying the sense in which circumstances in history "determined" choice, a clarification that remained uncompleted. Nevertheless, we must not miss the compelling nature of Marx's most audacious claim: the reality of the "transitional stages" leading to the "future society," an "association of individuals" free from domination, is said to be grounded in *history*. It was as if the flight of Minerva's owl begins only with the breaking of the dawn.

Significantly, Weber employed the distinction between science and prophecy not to castigate Marx for abandoning the scientific analysis of society in favor of a more spectacular road to fame but rather both to admit Marx's work to the realm of scientific criticism and to consider the political reception of Marxism after Marx. On the first level Löwith's assessment is surely correct: "Weber's objection to Marxism as 'scientific socialism' is not that it rests upon scientifically unprovable ideas and ideals, but that the subjectivity of its fundamental premises is presented with the appearance of 'objective,' universal validity," thus encouraging the conclusion that "Marxism is not too little committed to a belief in science, but far too much."[74] In brief, Weber's argument seems to be that Marx participates in constructing the "cage for the new serfdom" by reifying science and solidifying its dogmatic core.

But Weber also employed the distinction to raise a question about the politics of Marx and the reception of Marxism. In this respect, for Weber, Russia rather than France served as the ultimate test case, "the great experiment" in the practical application of the modern revolutionary idea.[75] Ironically, Marx himself had already envisioned the fate of Marxism among the revolutionary audience: the expected dawn of revolution became, as among the French democrats, "a fixed idea, a dogma, like the day on which Christ should reappear and the millennium begin, in the minds of the Chiliasts."[76] And the content of this newly revealed dogma was, of course, Marxist science itself. In Weber's view, however, by 1905 such millenarian hopes had fallen into disrepute in the West, as Marx's future society retreated into the distance, while nevertheless flourishing in the East. The question became, why in Russia did the "prophetic" Marx gain such ascendancy as a guide to the politics of "last things"?

For Weber the answer was found in history itself—Russian social and intellectual history—and specifically in the "pragmatic rationalism" which "naturally found its strongest support in the actually existing communism of the Russian village-community."[77] Weber conceived a subtle distinction between the "naturalistic rationalism" of the Enlightenment in the West, an orientation expressed in conceptions of inevitable progress and natural law which still flourished in the scientific evolutionism of Marx, and the "pragmatic rationalism" of a defiant commitment to achieving specific results in the world. It was the latter that had already been incorporated in the thought of Herzen, Lavrov, and even in Lenin's attacks on economism. In politics it served as the foundation for the view that revolution could happen through "creative action," which built upon "revolutionary consciousness," in spite of (or against) allegedly objective evolutionary conditions, a view that "lay deep in the blood of a specifically Russian socialism" and could be rationalized with reference to the millenial line of Hegelian thought read into Marx.[78] In this case, "the return of spirit to itself" meant the return of modern revolutionary enthusiasms to traditional communal foundations.

In Russia there was another setting in which pragmatic rationalism found a home: bureaucracy. Weber discovered an intriguing affinity between revolutionary and bureaucratic action and organization, as well as between ideological radicalism and authoritarianism among the intelligentsia. He noted "the relative frequency of the 'transformation' of extremely radical students into highly 'authoritarian' officials . . . [and] the reverse occurrence—a sudden conversion from a convinced supporter of bureaucracy, as represented by the pragmatic rationalism of Plehve and Pobedonostsev, to the extreme social-revolutionary camp." What united the apparent extremes was substantively their "state socialist character" and formally their "thirst for the 'deed' that stands in the service of the absolute social-ethical norm, and . . . oscillates back and forth between the 'creative' deed from 'above' and from 'below.' "[79] It is as if in this world the Faustian starting point—"In the beginning was the deed"—had become the highest expression of the political art.

The remarkable novelty in pragmatic rationalism was its ability to assimilate romanticism (the romance of the deed) to a pragmatic politics. It was pragmatic and political precisely because it embodied an *Erfolgsethik,* an ethic oriented toward success and therefore a form of action shaped by means-ends calculations. For Weber, the antithetical apolitical position was Tolstoy's, represented in works like *Resurrection* and in an absolutist ethics of *"fiat justitia, pereat mundus"* for which means became sacred.[80] Pragmatic rationalism, however, could be flexible about means, including the use of violence, while ends (e.g., achieving Marx's future society) were given; pragmatic means could be used to promote romantic ends. The novel combining of pragmatism and romanticism accounted for the special reception accorded a prophetic Marx. The Marxist politics of revolution was not ideological in the sense that it was capable of making infinite adjustments to Russian socio-political realities; yet it was ideological in the sense that it had embraced Marx's design for the course of history and was pledged to making predicted outcomes "real."

If Marx is assigned authorship of the concept of modern revolution, then Weber must be credited with first perceiving the inner connection between the new eschatological politics of Marx*ism* and bureaucratization. Revolution now became the rhetorical expression for a politics concerned with achieving immortality against the mechanistic laws of motion in history, just as bureaucratization became the specific replacement for class-formation as the rationalizing force of history.

But did Weber himself reveal a personal attitude toward this new synthesis? Lacking any fixed points in history or final categories for historical knowledge from which to "triangulate" the future, Weber should have remained content to speak of "the impenetrable mist of the future of human history." However, the temptation to say something more could not be suppressed at the end of *Bourgeois Democracy:* "On this sterile ground only spiritual indifference can grow," Weber writes of the authoritarian discipline of new mass parties, "once the 'eschatological' epoch of the movement has passed and generation after generation has vainly clenched its fists in its pockets or bared its teeth toward heaven." For Weber the politics of last things must undermine its own motives and purposes: it cannot persist and afterwards will come the routinized politics of an "economically 'satiated' and intellectually 'content' world"—a bleak world suited only for bureaucracy. After this warning, Weber's singular and ambivalent message, following Goethe's, is "to work while it is still day," a statement whose true force is felt only in the latter essays of the First World War and thus leads beyond the boundaries of this study.[81]

CONCLUSION: HISTORY RECONSIDERED

In the *Philosophy of History* Hegel distinguishes between change as it occurs in nature and as it occurs in the "realm of the mind" or "spirit," that is, in human affairs. The former shows only a "cycle of constant repetition," but the latter exhibits "novelty" that is "based on an inner determination . . . which brings itself into existence." Development *(Entwicklung)* for Hegel is thus a process, mediated by consciousness, of the objectification and realization of *Geist,* or the movement through stages toward completion of free, absolute, and universal self-consciousness.[82] Development possesses an internal dynamic that leads somewhere, to ever-new syntheses of historical experience; whereas change in nature leads nowhere, constantly turning back on itself in endless cycles. For Hegel this discovery becomes a way of identifying the origins and distinctive mechanisms presupposed by the very idea of history.

For Marx, on the other hand, the Hegelian distinction provides the basic categories for comprehending any "history of the present." In this respect the *Eighteenth Brumaire* is far more revealing than Marx's more explicitly theoretical work about the assumptions and dilemmas of a theory of history, for in mid-nineteenth-century France, Marx believes he has encountered an anomalous "history without events," or a sequence of "development, whose sole driving forces seems to be the calendar."[83] One is thus thrown back from history to nature. In this stretch of time the Hegelian *Entwicklunglehre* seems not to apply; one is left with a natural form, a kind of anti-history envisaged as a smooth treadmill of repetitions. Marx in fact senses that the dynamics of a historical materialist account have been outpaced by events, and thus he resorts to both dramatic irony and prophetic substitutions as a supplement to materialist science. His logical problem is to combine these three analyses into a coherent whole. But the more fundamental problem transcends mere logic; the actual subject matter of Marx's reflections simply *is* human affairs, not nature, and it therefore requires an understanding appropriate to the realm of history.

If the theory of history begins in Hegel's philosophy, then surely it is brought to completion in Weber's history of the present. Against the background of the Hegelian and Marxist problematic, Weber must be said "to return history to itself." Since he repudiates the metaphysical distinction between nature and mind, Weber argues that in the human invention of history "the structuring of the empirically given data is determined by the theoretical and metatheoretical presuppositions and requirements of the autonomous intellect."[84] Or in Weber's more prosaic declaration, "There are no 'finally valid' historical concepts"[85]—none, that is, which are grounded in history and thereby thought to be transhistorical or placed beyond history. From Weber's historical point of view the European revolutions from 1789 to 1905 enter the course of history as episodes in the rationalization of the modern state. What these episodes show is the rise and fall of class as the motive force of history, the differentiation of bureaucratic forms of control as "mind objectified,"[86] the continuing grip of authority, and the human-all-too-human propensity for self-deception. "All experience suggests that 'history' continues inexorably to bring forth new 'aristocracies' and 'authorities,'" Weber concludes, adding the biting reminder, "to which anyone can cling who finds it necessary for himself— or for the 'people.'"[87] Weber hoped such necessities would wither away. We cannot say that the history of the twentieth century has treated his hopes with kindness.

Notes

1. G. A. Cohen, *Karl Marx's Theory of History: A Defence* (Princeton: Princeton University Press, 1978), 27.

2. William H. Shaw, *Marx's Theory of History* (Stanford, Calif.: Stanford University Press, 1978), 167.

3. See Guenther Roth and Wolfgang Schluchter, *Max Weber's Vision of History, Ethics, and Methods* (Berkeley: University of California Press, 1979); and Wolfgang Schluchter, *The Rise of Western Rationalism: Max Weber's Developmental History,* trans. Guenther Roth (Berkeley: University of California Press, 1981).

4. Karl Löwith, *Max Weber and Karl Marx,* ed. T. Bottomore and W. Outhwaite (1932; trans., London: Allen and Unwin, 1982).

5. Ibid., 29.

6. Weber, "Zur Lage der bürgerlichen Demokratie in Russland," *Archiv für Sozialwissenschaft und Sozialpolitik* 22 (1906): 6; hereafter cited as *Bourgeoise Democracy.*

7. The first phrase is from Engels's introduction to Marx, *The Class Struggles in France, 1848-1850* (New York: International Publishers, 1964), 9.

8. Marx, *The Eighteenth Brumaire of Louis Bonaparte* (New York: International Publishers, 1963), 119; hereafter cited as *Eighteenth Brumaire.*

9. *Bourgeois Democracy,* 118, 119.

10. *Eighteenth Brumaire,* 21.

11. Ibid., 42-43.

12. *Bourgeois Democracy,* 18; the reference is to Hegel's lines in the *Philosophy of Right* (London: Oxford University Press, 1952), 13, using an image of "philosophy's grey in grey" borrowed from Goethe's *Faust.*

13. *Bourgeois Democracy,* 18.

14. Ibid., 121; see Tocqueville's comparison of America and Russia in *Democracy in America,* ed. J. P. Mayer (Garden City, N.Y.: Anchor Books, 1969), 412-13.

15. *Bourgeois Democracy,* 119; cf. Max Weber, *The Protestant Ethic and the Spirit of Capitalism,* trans. Talcott Parsons (New York: Scribner's, 1958), 181-82.

16. *Bourgeois Democracy,* 110.

17. Ibid., 118.

18. Ibid., 63, 86.

19. Ibid., 85.

20. *Eighteenth Brumaire,* 43, 123-24.

21. Ibid., 15.

22. Ibid., 19.

23. Ibid.; Leon Trotsky, *1905* (New York: Random House, 1971), 56.

24. For this language see *Eighteenth Brumaire,* 121.

25. *Bourgeois Democracy,* 53.

26. Ibid., 15, 20, 51, 62, 88, 94, 111, 114, 116, 118, 120; and Weber, "Russlands Uebergang zum Scheinkonstitutionalismus," *Archiv für Sozialwissenschaft und Sozialpolitik* 22 (1906): 232. The latter article is cited below as *Russia's Transition to Pseudo-Constitutionalism.*

27. *Russia's Transition to Pseudo-Constitutionalism,* 7.

28. Ibid., 232.

29. *Bourgeois Democracy,* 55, 120.

30. Goethe, *Faust,* trans. W. Kaufmann (New York: Anchor Books, 1963), 1: 1339–40; *Eighteenth Brumaire,* 21.

31. *Eighteenth Brumaire,* 37.

32. *Bourgeois Democracy,* 122.

33. Ibid., 116.

34. *Eighteenth Brumaire,* 15, 18, 20.

35. Ibid., 135; *Bourgeois Democracy,* 125.

36. *Bourgeois Democracy,* 125.

37. *Eighteenth Brumaire,* 18.

38. Ibid., 124.

39. Ibid., 47.

40. Ibid., 47, 107.

41. Ibid., 106.

42. *Bourgeois Democracy,* 116.

43. Ibid., 23.

44. Ibid., 16.

45. Ibid.

46. Ibid., 93.

47. Ibid., 118.

48. Ibid., 65–66.

49. *Eighteenth Brumaire,* 123.

50. Ibid., 123–24.

51. Marx, *The Civil War in France,* in *Political Writings,* ed. David Fernbach (New York: Vintage Books, 1974), 3: 208.

52. *Eighteenth Brumaire,* 124.

53. Ibid., 128; Trotsky, *1905,* ch. 3; V. I. Lenin, *Selected Works* (New York: International Publishers, 1943), 3: 8–9, 92–101, 262–66.

54. Trotsky, *1905,* 35.

55. *Bourgeois Democracy,* 89; Matthews trans., in W. G. Runciman, ed., *Max Weber, Selections in Translation* (Cambridge: Cambridge University Press, 1978), 269.

56. *Bourgeois Democracy,* 99, 118.

57. Ibid., 75, 89.

58. *Russia's Transition to Pseudo-Constitutionalism,* 233.

59. *Bourgeois Democracy,* 56–57.

60. Ibid., 105; Matthews trans., in Runciman, *Max Weber,* 272–73.

61. *Eighteenth Brumaire,* 18, 121.

62. Ibid., 122.

63. Ibid., 129.

64. Ibid., 122.

65. *Bourgeois Democracy,* 88.

66. Ibid., 28, 86, 88; *Russia's Transition to Pseudo-Constitutionalism*, 67.

67. *Bourgeois Democracy*, 119; Matthews trans., in Runciman, *Max Weber*, 281.

68. *Bourgeois Democracy*, 54.

69. Werner Sombart, *Socialism and the Social Movement* (London: Dent, 1909), 69.

70. Weber, "Socialism," in *Max Weber: The Interpretation of Social Reality*, ed. J. E. T. Eldridge (London: Michael Joseph, 1970), 205.

71. Marx, letter to Weydemeyer, 5 March 1852, reprinted in *Eighteenth Brumaire*, 139.

72. Hegel, *The Philosophy of History*, trans. J. Sibree (New York: Dover, 1956), 55.

73. *Eighteenth Brumaire*, 15.

74. Löwith, *Max Weber and Karl Marx*, 31.

75. Weber, "Socialism," 215.

76. *Eighteenth Brumaire*, 20.

77. *Bourgeois Democracy*, 55.

78. Ibid., 55, 94.

79. Ibid., 94.

80. Ibid., 103, 106; *Russia's Transition to Pseudo-Constitutionalism*, 233.

81. *Bourgeois Democracy*, 121; Matthews trans., in Runciman, *Max Weber*, 283–84.

82. *The Philosophy of History*, 54–5.

83. *Eighteenth Brumaire*, 43.

84. Georg Simmel, *The Problems of the Philosophy of History: An Epistemological Essay*, trans. G. Oakes (New York: Free Press, 1977), 186.

85. *Bourgeois Democracy*, 120.

86. The phrase appears in Weber, *Gesammelte Politische Schriften*, 2nd ed. (Tübingen: Mohr, 1958), 320.

87. *Bourgeois Democracy*, 119.

VXXVI

Guenther Roth	**Marx and Weber on the United States—Today**

The hundredth anniversary of the death of Karl Marx can serve as an occasion to consider how much the world has changed in a century, whether we think such a time span long or short. For me, the first lesson is that Marx and Engels, and also the generation of 1890, which began its work soon after Marx died, were poor forecasters. Lack of foresight is part of the human condition. In some ways the world always changes more slowly than expected, and in others more dramatically. Marx and Engels fully recognized that industrial civilization would radically transform the world, but they simply could not imagine that anything could derail history as a story of spiritual liberation and material abundance. They did not anticipate that technological breakthroughs, the exhaustion of resources, and ecological deterioration would combine to threaten human survival. Weber's generation, though more skeptical in many respects, also did not foresee how quickly a double energy crisis would change the outlook: that there would be too little energy for production and too much for self-destruction and the destruction of nature.

But in contrast to Marx and Engels, Weber saw much more clearly the dangers to history as the progress of freedom, although he still expected a period of material saturation. On the occasion of the first Russian revolution he warned:

Only the much maligned "anarchy of production" and the equally maligned "subjectivism" have made masses of people self-reliant and independent. If an "inalienable" sphere of personal freedom cannot be won for the masses during the next few generations, so long as this economic and intellectual "revolution" has not yet exhausted itself—and once the world has become economically satiated and intellectually sated—then this task will perhaps never be accomplished.[1]

I would like to compare our contemporary situation with some of the prognoses and expectations of Marx, Engels, and Weber, not to confront them with the wisdom of hindsight, but for the sake of a better understanding of the present. I focus on some economic and political changes that they failed to perceive clearly enough or misperceived outright but that can be interpreted in their terms. Today, we live with the Marxist paradox that capitalism did not only expand much more slowly than expected, but that it has not been vanquished in its old and new centers, whereas socialism (as a command economy) has prevailed in Russia and China, two vast areas in which capitalism had never established itself. The core capitalist countries, however, have not only become welfare and garrison states in different degrees, they have also retained or gained democratic constitutions with different articulations.

As an institutionalist and constitutionalist Weber studied democratic arrangements intensively. He tried to identify the distinctiveness of American democracy in contrast to the European development, yet he could not shake the belief that in the near future the developmental dynamics of the modern state and of modern party organization would prevail in the United States, and here lay a major error of prediction.[2] Public administration, both civilian and military, has become bureaucratized to a significant extent, but the bureaucratic party system has not emerged, contrary to Weber's expectations. Thus, we have a Weberian paradox in addition to the Marxian: in contrast to most other democracies, public bureaucracy in the United States is today more than ever juxtaposed to a highly decentralized, personalist system of political representation and governance. It is a personalism with a universalist, not a clientelist, foundation. It appears that the aspect of political modernity most crucial to both Marx and Weber will not arrive in most of the world—the decline of personal rulership and personal subservience. In a world-historical perspective and in contemporary comparison, the constituency politics of the American political system is a remarkable counterpoint to the clientelism, neotraditionalism and neopatrimonialism that pervades most of the world. Insofar as bureaucratic party organization is a typical feature of Weber's concept of modern mass democracy, the United States does not share it. This is another side of American exceptionalism, and it will be elaborated in the second half of my essay.

American exceptionalism has usually been addressed as the question of why there has been no socialism in the United States. I will not rehash the often repeated historical answers.[3] The question arose from the theory of class conflict in *The Communist Manifesto*. The most comprehensive response was already given by Werner Sombart, who made the query the title of his famous pamphlet of 1906. It is not well known, however, that it first appeared in 1905 under a different title in the *Archiv für Sozialwissenschaft und Sozialpolitik,* which Sombart edited with Weber and Edgar Jaffé: "Studies in the Developmental History of the North American Proletariat."[4] The concept of developmental history refers in the older literature of the time to the evolutionary stages in the progress of humankind and in the newer literature primarily to scientific laws of development, as in the works of Karl Lamprecht and Kurt Breysig. By and large, Sombart was close to Weber's notion of developmental history as the movement of a "historical individual" toward a characteristic configuration, which is not historically inevitable and which has different articulations, including paradoxical consequences. Sombart too answered his question paradoxically—all factors which retarded the development of socialism in the United States "are at the point of disappearing or of being turned into their opposite, so that socialism will in all probability reach its full flowering in the next generation."[5] In spite of some agreement with Weber's open-ended conception, Sombart could not give up the idea of historical necessity, as indeed Weber himself did not manage in the case of the United States. It is even less surprising to read that Karl Kautsky, who replied to Sombart at length in his *Neue Zeit,* remained wedded to the older notion of developmental history. "Everybody who looks at the facts I presented here will very likely not be able to avoid the conclusion that the flowering of socialism must necessarily be expected, not for the next generation, but much earlier. Everything in America moves faster and more violently than in Europe."[6]

Sombart's and Kautsky's expectations of a dramatic aggravation of class struggle between proletariat and bourgeoisie were as much disappointed as twenty years earlier were those of Eleanor Marx and Edward Aveling after their American journey. They had no inkling of the new middle classes that today are a crucial component of American social structure. They remained attached to father Marx's theory of class struggle and minimized the difference between America and Europe, insofar as the conditions for victorious class struggle did not appear even better here than there.[7] This part of the historical prognosis derived from *The Communist Manifesto* was fundamental for the self-interpretation and propaganda of the socialist labor movement, but it proved to be a tremendous misperception and self-deception. There is, however, another perspective from the *Manifesto* that was farsighted and put the United States in the developmental context of the world economy. In fact, it anticipates loosely the so-called world-systems approach pursued by Immanuel Wallerstein and others. The prognoses of Marx and Engels apply in the present to the extent that they deal equally with the staying power of capitalism and the chances for a socialist revolution; and their predictions are off by about a century.

In their London exile Marx and Engels wrote a series of articles in 1850 for their short-lived journal *Neue Rheinische Zeitung—Politisch-ökonomische Revue,* which appeared in Hamburg. Applying for the first time the insights of the *Manifesto,* as Engels later explained, they made little known predictions about the development of the capitalist world economy, especially the United States, that have surprising contemporary relevance. In 1850 Marx and Engels were still extremely confident the revolution would soon triumph in Europe. They expected the next English panic for July or August and were convinced that this time the crisis "would mark the beginning of the modern English revolution."[8] But in the next sentence Marx and Engels addressed American events they viewed as "even more important than the February revolution" of 1848, that is, the discovery of gold in California. On this basis, they predicted a crucial shift in the center of the capitalist world economy, with far-reaching negative consequences for Europe. The "world history of Europe" passes before our eyes in the authors' exciting vision of the future:

Even now, hardly eighteen months later, it can be foreseen that this discovery will have much grander results than the discovery of America itself. . . . [T]he Yankees have already started a railroad, a great highway, and a canal from the Mexican Gulf; steamers from New York to Chagres, from Panama to San Francisco, are already in regular service; trade with the Pacific Ocean is already concentrating in Panama, and the trip around Cape Horn is obsolete. A coast of 30 degrees longitude, one of the most beautiful and fertile in the world, hitherto practically uninhabited, is being visibly transformed into a rich and civilized land, thickly populated with people of all races, from Yankees to Chinese, from Negroes to Indians and Malays, from Creoles and mestizos to Europeans. California gold is flowing in streams over America and the Asian coast of the Pacific Ocean, drawing the most recalcitrant barbaric peoples into world commerce, into civilization. For the second time, world trade acquires a new direction. New York, San Francisco, San Juan de Nicaragua, Chagres, Leon and Panama are now becoming what Tyre, Carthage, and Alexandria were in antiquity, what Genoa and Venice were in the Middle Ages, and what London and Liverpool have been hitherto—the emporia of world commerce. The center of gravity of world trade—in Italy in the Middle Ages and in England in modern times—is now the southern half of the North American hemisphere. . . . Thanks to Californian gold and the untiring energy of the Yankees, both coasts of the Pacific Ocean will soon be as populated, as open to commerce and as industrialized as the coast from Boston to New Orleans is now. Then the Pacific Ocean will play the same role as the Atlantic Ocean does now and as the Mediterranean did in antiquity and in the Middle Ages—the role of a great water highway of world commerce—and the Atlantic Ocean will decline to the level of an inland sea, as the Mediterranean is now.[9]

Marx and Engels were carried away by their own vision and showed openly their admiration for capitalist enterprise. As good Europeans, however, they were also worried about the competitive chances for European industry and sounded similar to current businessmen and economists who admonish the Europeans not to lose the race with the most advanced sectors of the world economy:

The industry and commerce of Old Europe must make a mighty effort not to fall into the same decline as the industry and commerce of Italy have since the sixteenth century, if England and France are to avoid becoming what Venice, Genoa and Holland are today. . . . The one chance the civilized European countries have of not falling into the same dependency as Italy, Spain and Portugal today lies in a social revolution which, while there is still time, revolutionizes the mode of production and trade on the basis of the production needs that arise out of the modern productive forces and thereby makes possible the creation of new productive forces in turn that can insure the superiority of European industry and thus compensate for the geographic disadvantages.[10]

Marx and Engels, then, considered social revolution necessary in order to maintain the competitiveness of European industry. They also stressed the dependence of German prosperity on the world economy.[11] They did not dream of abolishing world trade in contrast to some of their successors, who consider the development of a poor country feasible only if it is uncoupled from the world market. On the contrary, as Marx wrote Engels in 1858, "the proper task of bourgeois society . . . [is] the creation of the world market, at least in its basic structure, and of production founded on it. Since the world is round, this task seems to have been accomplished with the colonization of California and Australia and the opening up of China and Japan."[12] But capitalist engulfment of the world threatened the chances for a successful social revolution in Europe. By 1858 Marx was plagued by strong doubts about his historical timetable. He questioned whether a revolution in little Europe could succeed. In his anglicized German he confessed to Engels: *"Die schwierige question für uns ist die: auf dem Kontinent ist die Revolution imminent und wird auch sofort einen sozialistischen Charakter annehmen. Wird sie in diesem kleinen Winkel nicht notwendig gecrushed werden, da auf viel grösserem Terrain das movement der bürgerlichen Gesellschaft noch ascendant ist?"*[13]

The revolution never came in western Europe, but Marx was correct in anticipating a time when European industry would be falling behind. What strikes me strongest in retrospect, however, is the delay of capitalist expansion. Everything took much longer than these impatient revolutionaries imagined. The Panama Canal was not opened by the United States until 1914, after the French project had been abandoned. California did not become the most populous state until the 1960s. Only recently can it be argued accurately that the countries around the Pacific are the new center of the world economy with its "global factory." Next to the highly developed countries of Australia, New Zealand, Japan, and the United States are South Korea, Taiwan, Hong Kong, Singapore, and even Mexico, all of which have advanced rapidly in the last twenty-five years. California's "Silicon Valley" competes with Japanese microelectronics for technological leadership, and even Communist China attempts to gain access to the world market through privileged production zones.

Thus, with much delay, history took the course prophesied by Marx and Engels, and yet so much is different today. Missing outright in their vision is any sense for the inherent limitations of the forces of production. After the world was drawn into the capitalist economy and its resources were made available for systematic exploitation—when would this age of plenty be exhausted? That question did not burden Marx and Engels. It was familiar to the generation of 1890 but without yet evoking a sense of urgency. At the end of the "Protestant Ethic" Weber remarked that the "mighty cosmos of the modern economic order, which is bound to the technological and economic conditions of machine production . . . shapes the life style of all individuals born into this machinery . . . with irresistible force and will perhaps continue to condition it until the last ton of fossil fuel has been burned up."[14]

Sombart tells us in his *The Economy in the Age of High Capitalism:* "When I once talked to Max Weber about the future and raised the question of how long the witches' Sabbath might last that humanity has been performing in the capitalist countries since the beginning of the 19th century, he replied: 'Until the last ton of ore has been smelted with the last ton of coal.' " Sombart considered Weber mistaken: "Weber's view is erroneous, unfortunately, some will say, happily others."[15] Sombart believed neither in the practical finiteness of raw materials nor in the exhaustibility of energy. He put his trust in solar energy, just as the Nobel prize-winning chemist Wilhelm Ostwald did, whose tract on the "Energetic Foundations of the Cultural Sciences" Weber demolished in 1909.[16] The theologian Ernst Troeltsch, however, appears to have sided with Weber:

The metaphor, which [Emil] Du Bois-Reymond [1818–96] liked to dwell on, of the last human who bakes the last potato with the last lump of coal cannot be rejected completely. This state of affairs is much more likely to happen than the fulfilment of socialism or the second coming of Christ or the breeding of superman. . . . The prospect of a [civilizational] decline, intelligible enough as an analogy with organic life, cannot discourage us. We are not frightened by [Du Bois-Reymond's image] because human beings have been in that situation innumerable times before.[17]

Of course, Troeltsch was not advocating the Christian ideal of poverty, but denying that the idea of a development of humanity—either in analogy with the organic life-cycle or with the endless movement of logical thought—could help us work out the synthesis of values required for our spiritual and material survival. In contrast to Marx and Engels, Weber and Troeltsch gave some thought to the limits of industrialization, but the exhaustion of resources, especially coal and oil, seemed to be a thousand years away. Like almost all of their contemporaries, they did not anticipate how soon the ecological ravages would be felt. Indicative of the rapidity of change is the fact that Weber's brother Alfred and Karl Jaspers, who was born a hundred years ago, lived long enough to gaze at the dawn of the atomic age and to fear the twilight of civilization.[18]

If Marx was right in foreseeing the economic ascendancy of America and the shift of the center of the capitalist world economy to the Pacific but mistaken about the intensification of class struggle in the most developed countries and about its cataclysmic conclusion, Weber was right in foreseeing the bureaucratization of the United States as a welfare and garrison state, but quite wrong about the American status structure. He suspected that a hierarchy of status groups with exclusivist tendencies, in the mode of Thorstein Veblen's *Theory of the Leisure Class,* was being established. The status issue will be mentioned only very briefly, insofar as it affects the political system. I will then suggest that Weber's sociology of domination can help illuminate the latter, even though he failed to see the direction in which party organization would move. Substantively, the issue is important for all of us, since the maximization of political democracy in the United States has been combined with a personalist fragmentation that often collides with strategic and organizational rationality.

As early as 1949 Reinhard Bendix argued that the higher civil service in the United States did not constitute a status group like their older German counterparts.[19] Weber's generalization was that "bureaucracy is the carrier of a specific 'status' development in business as well as public service, just as had been the completely different office-holders of the past" (1001).* But he also generalized about American exceptionalism: "Usually the social esteem of the officials is especially low where the demand for expert administration and the hold of status conventions are weak. This is often the case in new settlements by virtue of the great economic opportunities and the great instability of their social stratification: witness

* All bracketed numbers are page references to Max Weber, *Economy and Society,* ed. Guenther Roth and Claus Wittich (Berkeley: University of California Press, 1978). The translation has sometimes been made more accurate.

the United States" (960). But he hedged this qualification immediately with the observation that "the demand for professionally trained administrators is now becoming important in the U.S." (961). Parallel to these bureaucratic status trends, Weber also claimed to discover aristocratic tendencies which he considered "characteristic of the present American development in addition to, and partly in opposition to naked plutocracy. . . . American political democracy, which knows no status barriers, prevents neither the rise of a raw plutocracy . . . nor the slow emergence of an aristocratic status group, which will be just as important for its cultural history." Weber overestimated the long-range significance of these aristocratic tendencies, but saw clearly that American democracy was no "sand heap"—a charge levelled by German literati: "In the past and up to the present, it has been a characteristic precisely of the specifically American democracy that it did not constitute a formless sand heap of individuals, but rather a buzzing complex of strictly exclusive yet voluntary associations."[20]

Prior to World War I there were indeed tendencies toward a conspicuous leisure class, and the direction of party organization was not yet clear. The reform movement of the Progressive Era was certainly a good demonstration of the power of voluntary association and civic spirit. The movement fought for more "direct democracy," including the direct election of senators, the referendum, and the recall, but it also demanded the professionalization of the civil service. The reforms were directed not against an entrenched status group of bureaucrats but against the political machines and their corrupting ways.

Before contrasting Weber's social and political prognoses with the actual development, I would like to put the United States in the framework of his casuistry, which permits its typological placement irrespective of the accuracy of his historical predictions. In Weber's developmental history, democracy is an anti-authoritarian transformation of the charismatic principle of legitimation. Recognition by the ruled turns from a duty into the very grounds of legitimacy. Weber specified the United States as a particular case of constitutional government, as "the juxtaposition of plebiscitary presidency and representative parliament," hence as a "plebiscitary-representative" combination (295). The principle of representation, which developed only in the West, had "completely left behind its charismatic basis" (1128). Only in the United States had there occurred, at the level of the "formally highest ruler," a "development from charismatic acclamation of the ruler to his genuine election by the community of the ruled" (1127). Every discussion of presidential charisma in the United States should preserve this institutional transformation.

As sociologists should know, charisma exists only if it is accepted, but in the American case this acceptance has been institutionalized. The nominating process is formally charismatic because every candidate must make a personal claim without legitimation from any organization. There are no longer any party leaders who can impose a candidate on the convention, and after a convention has selected a candidate, the charismatic process is repeated: the candidates still must justify what is primarily a personal claim. But after election by "the people," which consists only of a minority of those entitled to vote and sometimes of a minority of those voting, the candidate acquires legal authority, the ideological and institutional bedrock of the political system. Elements of material charisma, if measured by the emotional intensity of the hopes attached to a president, may persist, and an incumbent can also lean to some extent on the aura of institutional charisma that traditionally surrounds the office. But the Constitution irrevocably transforms the formally charismatic claim of a successful candidate into the legal authority of one person, another aspect of universalist personalism in the United States. Repudiation of a president at reelection time is usually a judgment of his personal record rather than that of a party.

Whereas the presidential election involves the selection of a temporary ruler, who through this plebiscitary act also establishes his authority vis-à-vis Congress, many American state constitutions have gone far in the direction of populist "direct democracy." Thinking of these state constitutions in his definitions of the various forms of representation, Weber wrote "that the governing powers of representative bodies may be both limited and legitimated by the direct canvassing of the ruled: the referendum" (295). Moreover, many elected officials are "strictly limited by an imperative mandate and a right of recall and thus dependent on the approval of the voters. These 'representatives' are in truth the agents of those they represent" (293).

This was a definition, not a historical description. In his theory of democratization Weber made a crucial distinction that has often been overlooked. It is embedded in the open-ended, paradoxical, or, if you wish, dialectical logic of his developmental history:

We must remember the fact which we have encountered several times and which we shall have to discuss repeatedly: that "democracy" as such is opposed to the "rule" of bureaucracy, in spite and perhaps because of its unavoidable yet unintended promotion of bureaucratization. . . . Hence, one must in every individual historical case analyze the special direction in which bureaucratization developed. For this reason, it must also remain an open question whether the power of bureaucracy is increasing in the modern states in which it is spreading (991).[21]

My suggestion is that the power of American parties, which Weber labeled bureaucratic in an imprecise manner, has declined in favor of what I call universalist personalism. In principle, every candidate for electoral office— from the lowest to the highest in the land—must personally face the voters. Because of the primary system, a product of the reform periods, the rudimentary parties cannot control who will bear their label. To an extent unknown and often unimaginable in Western European democracies, elected officials are viewed by the voters as their personal representatives. The typical American member of a legislature is a lawyer, in Weber's sense a vocation economically available for full-time politics. In English usage, and also in German, those who employ the services of lawyers are called clients—a complete reversal of the sociological concept of clientelism that is applicable around the globe. Whereas in many countries the people are at the mercy of political patrons or at least need them as go-betweens with the government, in the United States elected office-holders have become dependent on the voters to a politically significant extent.

Weber believed that "a bureaucracy of the European kind would inescapably arise" in the United States (1398) because "purely technical, irrefragable needs of the administration determine this development."[22] He was not wrong on this score, but the dictate of these needs took a long time to become effective. The great expansion of the federal bureaucracy began only with the New Deal, often ad hoc, outside the civil service, and partly in deliberate circumvention of it. World War II brought forth a large military bureaucracy, which by now has become unwieldy and inefficient. What strikes me today is the observation that the federal bureaucracy is so firmly under political control: the civilian agencies are on the defensive in an era of budget-cutting, and the opinions of the Joint Chiefs of Staff apparently are disregarded by the political decision-makers at the Pentagon.

Weber's major misperception concerned the course of American party organization. He tried too hard to squeeze the American case into the developmental model. He acknowledged that

the United States still bears the character of a polity which, at least in the technical sense, is not fully bureaucratized. But the greater the zones of friction with the outside and the more urgent the needs for administrative unity at home become, the more this character is inevitably and gradually giving way formally to the bureaucratic structure. Moreover, the partly unbureaucratic form of the state is materially balanced by the strictly bureaucratic structures of those formations which, in truth, dominate politically, namely the parties under the leadership of "professionals" or experts in organization and election tactics (971).

In applying the term "bureaucratic" to the United States civil service and the political parties, Weber used inconsistent terminology. His own description demonstrated clearly that the urban machines were not bureaucratic but patrimonial; they were a political business which offered services in return for voter loyalty and manipulated the dependencies of immigrant populations. Weber considered countertrends to the political machines, but he recognized primarily charismatic challenges. The example of the Bull Moose movement of 1912 even seemed to point to an interplay between party bureaucracy and charisma: "Since all emotional mass appeals have certain charismatic features, the bureaucratization of the parties and of electioneering may at its very height suddenly be forced into the service of charismatic hero worship. In this case a conflict arises between charismatic heroism and the mundane power of the party organization, as Roosevelt's campaign demonstrated" (1130). Weber assumed that party machines would prevail over reformist tendencies and contain charismatic eruptions: "As a rule, the party organization easily succeeds in [the] castration of charisma. This will also happen time and again in the United States, even if the plebiscitary presidential primaries are introduced, since in the long run the continuity of professional operations is tactically superior to emotional worship" (1132). We may be willing to accept the very broad generalization that "professional operations" will in the long run win over "emotional worship," but the old political machines and patronage parties disappeared, supplanted successfully by extended popular primaries, so that we now have extremely long election campaigns.

It is true that the Progressive movement alone was not strong enough to destroy the machines and the bosses. It took the rapid expansion of the welfare state and the economic prosperity after World War II to bring about their demise. New interest aggregations emerged on both federal and state levels. Better educational and vocational opportunities promoted social and geographical mobility. The great exodus to the suburbs, especially California, led people into areas in which there were no organized parties. The massive enlargement of the civil service opened up many positions to college graduates. Only in Chicago is there still a major machine which employs thousands of loyal members in "temporary" jobs that circumvent civil service rules—and even this machine has been in serious trouble for several years.

The new personalism has changed and accelerated the manner in which interests are articulated and mediated, and thus has brought about more direct democracy. Of course, as long as the country is capitalist, money will talk, and more political action committees will be organized. As in the medieval city, which Weber described as an oath-bound confraternity of free citizens, the *popolo grasso* usually has more power than the *popolo minuto*. Since the 437 members of the House of Representatives and hundreds of representatives in the state legislatures have only two years before another election, they must conduct a permanent campaign and accede to as many personal and group wishes as possible. The two-year rotation, which the "Greens" advocate in the Federal Republic of Germany, is an ever-present possibility for many American representatives. In the last fifteen years, there has been so much unintended rotation that the number of experienced parliamentarians has shrunk. The older form of patrimonial appropriation has largely disappeared, with the exception of archaic states such as Massachusetts. There are now situations in which almost no representative knows how a legislature is supposed to act in certain cases. It is also important to note that there have been six presidents in twenty years.

The imperative mandate, demanded so vehemently in the Federal Republic of Germany, also plays a greater role in the United States. Since the old majorities have disintegrated in many districts, very small groups of two to three percent, whether right or left, can topple representatives in the next election, if they do not accept their single issue. Under these circumstances small, ideologically or materially motivated groups can have disproportionate power. New movements can quickly make their influence felt. In several states the will of the people has recently been imposed effectively through propositions and referenda, although it was sometimes manipulated by special interests. When Weber observed the reforms of the Progressive Era, he commented that "the mistrust against the powerless and, therefore, corrupt parliaments of the individual states has led to an expansion of direct popular legislation." He preferred parliamentarism to the plebiscite, both "as a means of election and of legislation," because the latter makes compromise difficult and enforces dichotomous decisions (1455). "It is hard to imagine how in a mass state with severe class tensions tax laws other than progressive income taxation, property confiscations and 'nationalizations' can be adopted through popular vote" (1455). Today, however, plebiscites have become important in taxation matters. State legislatures often turn to the voters, if they do not want to, or cannot, make difficult decisions on their own. Whereas Weber saw the dangers primarily in confiscatory taxation from below in states ridden with class tensions, much was revealed about the lack of class tension even in the recession-ridden America of the early 1980s where voters tried to force the legislatures to forgo tax hikes because these appear as confiscation from above.[23]

Another new element of personalism is the need for presidential negotiation, at least in theory, with all 537 members of Congress about every law. The situation is similar for many governors and legislatures. Also, in theory, every representative can insist on reciprocity toward every colleague. After the decline of the imperial presidency, the chief executive must now come to terms with a strengthened Congress, which, however, has been weakened internally. Not only have inflation and recession accelerated the turnover of members, but the liberal reforms of the 1960s have destroyed or reduced the authoritarian powers of the majority leader, the minority leader, the speaker, and especially of the committee chairmen. The time has long passed since a Johnson and a Rayburn could make binding agreements with an Eisenhower outside the public limelight.[24]

The ability of elected representatives to satisfy the articulated needs of their constituents and to pursue their own goals depends largely on the efficiency of their personal staffs, and this brings me finally to the neopatrimonial elements of American personalism. These staffs establish a loyalty relation with their masters which rests primarily on material and ideal interests. Though they were in existence in Weber's time, the staffs were not highly developed. He contrasted the old clientelist patronage staffs, which reward loyal followers, with the Caesaristic system of reform mayors: "Viewed technically, as an organized form of domination, the efficiency of 'caesarism,' which often grows out of democracy, rests upon the position of the 'caesar' as a free trustee of the masses . . . , who is unfettered by tradition. The 'caesar' is thus the free master of a body of highly qualified . . . officials whom he selects freely and personally without regard to tradition or to any other impediments" (961). Today, under conditions of vastly increased technological and economic complexity, intellectual and technical competence are highly desirable in personal staffs, but personal loyalty remains the basic condition of employment. Therefore, I prefer neopatrimonial to Caesaristic. (In the newer version of *Economy and Society,* Weber replaced the term "caesarist" with "plebiscitary"—cf. 555 with 156f.) Famous staffs of this kind were the apparatus of the Kennedys—a kind of nationalization of the old Bostonian, Irish machine—and the Rockefeller apparatus, out of which Henry Kissinger emerged.[25]

Today the president has a very large personal staff. As the federal bureaucracy grew and the role of the United States on the world stage could not be reversed in the wake of World War II (in contrast to World War I), the White House staff had to grow by leaps and bounds, from the few dozen members in Weber's time to approximately 1,500 at present. It is organized bureaucratically but remains inspired patrimonially; this can lead to great frustration, as James Fallows explained, on the part of those down the ladder who want to serve their president with particular avidity.[26] At the very top a president's effectiveness depends largely on the staff's degree of success in linking unswerving loyalty with the articulation and balancing of divergent political views and policy options. If the top staff is too parochial, as in the case of Carter's "Georgia Mafia," they cannot serve the president well; if they are too ideological, as in Reagan's case, they may lose the capacity for balanced judgment.

The political appointees in the federal agencies, too, are part of the neopatrimonial apparatus of a president. They number roughly 6,000 and constitute the so-called "in-and-outers"; they are the temporary personnel, which Richard Neustadt long ago declared to be more efficient than the English system of a permanent high-ranking civil service.[27] The American mode of operation can indeed be flexible and efficient in the absence of bureaucratized parties, but it also creates great difficulties. I refer only to three.

First, it can take too much time to fill the top positions. The Reagan administration too has had great difficulties here, in part because the right wing of Congress has insisted on strict ideological screening. Also, there is always the danger of returning to the old "amateur administration by booty politicians."[28] The appointment of top personnel requires confirmation by Congress in order to reduce patrimonial dependency on the president and to maintain the principle of the separation of powers. The result, however, is frequently that the directors of an agency must serve two masters. All members of Congress claim the right to intervene with the federal bureaucracy for the sake of their constituents or clients and for their own reelection. Since the agencies must account for their operation before congressional committees, they are particularly receptive to the wishes of committee members. Under these circumstances it is often extremely difficult to draw the fine line between service to the citizens and corruption. Of course, some regulatory agencies have for a long time been coopted by the industries they are supposed to regulate and have in practice become their corporate representatives.

Second, great tensions arise when the president's patrimonial officials have the more or less veiled mission to sabotage the laws passed by Congress and earlier presidents and to paralyze federal agencies. These are the "hatchet men" and, now, also the "hatchet women." Nixon tested their loyalty first in the White House before sending them out to cripple agencies such as those created during the "War on Poverty." The Watergate affair, which led to the first resignation of a president for breaking the law, was an extreme case of patrimonial domination in which loyalty to the president was unequivocally extended above the law. Compared to it, the bribes paid by construction firms to Nixon's vice-president were only an old-fashioned form of personal enrichment. At least in the first two years of the Reagan administration, the top personnel in the

EPA, the Department of Energy, the Department of Education, the Legal Services Corporation, and some sections of the Attorney General's Office had been assigned to prepare for their agencies' dissolution or at least to undermine their morale and effectiveness. Only public pressures forced the White House to mitigate this drive.

Third, because of the nuclear armament race between the superpowers and the troubled world economy, American foreign policy needs more than ever inventiveness combined with steadiness and predictability. These are sorely lacking. The difficulty does not lie only in the tendency of each administration to repudiate its predecessors and make a new beginning which soon gets bogged down nor primarily in the turnover of a large patrimonial apparatus, but it also lies in the fact that the presidential system itself, which for a long time has been significantly more person-than-party-centered, has become more unpredictable with Washington outsiders, from Carter to Reagan, capturing the White House. This accounts for the extreme difficulty of president and Congress to develop long-range policies, whether reforms of social security or consistent policies of economic support for the world economy and of pragmatic relations with the Soviet Union.

The Marxist prophecy of an increasing class polarization between proletariat and bourgeoisie has not been fulfilled in highly developed countries, in part because of the inherent strength of capitalism and democracy and because the socialist dreams turned into nightmares. Before the First World War, the class struggle was harsher and bloodier in the United States than in western Europe, but this did not lead to long-range polarization. Instead, the class basis of politics largely dissolved. The Roosevelt coalition had been a class movement to a considerable extent, but after three decades it lost its economic basis with the growing prosperity and expansion of the welfare state. Paradoxically, the recent era of stagflation and its aftermath have further weakened class-based action. The majority of voters acts in terms of short-range interests and makes "highly personalist judgments about the costs and benefits of the welfare state," as Morris Janowitz has claimed.[29] He did not have in mind the political personalism with which I am concerned, but the utilitarian calculus of the "rational actor," who wants to have others pay the public costs while he is a "free rider." Today, the welfare state has become expensive also for the lower income strata and therefore does not appear attractive if there are no visible personal advantages. As election results and opinion surveys demonstrate, many voters seem to be for and against the welfare state, for and against the raising of taxes, and for and against the reduction of armaments.

The utilitarian personalism in Janowitz's sense and the political personalism in my sense support one another. Socially, American democracy is still no sand heap: people effectively organize on short notice for all kinds of interests and causes, especially on the local, but also on the national, levels, as we see now with the peace movement. There seems to be a considerable danger, however, that the political system may turn into a sand heap. The vulnerable spot of the United States, then, would not be class conflict or clientelist fragmentation but a personalism that weakens and undermines institutional efficiency and rationalization. In many respects the country has fared quite well with its peculiar personalist form of "direct democracy" and may be able to live with it for some time to come, unless political and economic events in the world require another institutional solution. I have no prophecy to make about the possible shape of such reforms. The present state of the European party system, especially the condition of its left parties, does not encourage me to recommend its imitation.

Notes

1. Max Weber, "Zur Lage der bürgerlichen Demokratie in Russland," in *Gesammelte politische Schriften,* ed. Johannes Winckelmann, 3rd ed. (Tübingen: Mohr, 1971), 65. For a quite different rendering, see W. G. Runciman, ed., and E. Matthews, trans., *Max Weber: Selections in Translation* (Cambridge: Cambridge University Press, 1978), 283f.

2. For an overview of Weber's views on the United States, see Wolfgang Mommsen, "Die Vereinigten Staaten von Amerika im politischen Denken Max Webers," *Historische Zeitschrift* 213 (1971): 358-81; reprinted in Mommsen, *Max Weber: Gesellschaft, Politik und Geschichte* (Frankfurt: Suhrkamp, 1974), 72-96.

3. See S. M. Lipset, "American 'Exceptionalism' in North American Perspective," in *The Idea of America,* ed. E. M. Adams (Cambridge: Ballinger, 1977), 107-61; Lipset, "Why No Socialism in the United States?" in *Sources of Contemporary Radicalism,* ed. Seweryn Bialer and Sophia Sluzar (Boulder, Colo.: Westview Press, 1977), 31-149, 346-63. See also R. Laurence Moore, *European Socialists and the American Promised Land* (New York: Oxford University Press, 1970).

4. See Werner Sombart, *Warum gibt es in den Vereinigten Staaten keinen Sozialismus?* (Tübingen: Mohr, 1906); Sombart, *Why Is There No Socialism in the United States?,* trans. Patricia Hocking and C. T. Husbands (White Plains, N.Y.: International Arts and Sciences Press, 1976).

5. Sombart, *Warum,* 142.

6. Karl Kautsky, "Der amerikanische Arbeiter," *Neue Zeit* 24 (1906): 787.

7. Edward Aveling and Eleonore Marx-Aveling, "Die Lage der Arbeiterklasse in Amerika," *Neue Zeit* 5 (1887): 312f. The two reported at the time: "In its industrial development America has reached the same point as Europe. Here too the consequence is the increasing recognition of the class conflict between capital and proletariat. . . . Wherever the American masses become conscious of this class antagonism, it quickly takes on threatening proportions." Insofar as the United States was an exception, this only seemed to add force to Marx's predictions, since "the class antagonism in America is much more immediate than in Europe. There are no transitional stages and transitional classes. There is no middle class, not even in ideological *(geistige)* respects. Economically the class conflict is equally unmediated. There is a much deeper abyss between capitalist and worker than in Europe, an abyss that is not bridged and veiled by the middle classes. . . . The actual division of society into two classes, capitalists and workers, is obvious [to the people], and not hidden by feudal remnants. In America the capitalist mode of production did not emerge from the feudal one. It was taken over from Europe, and with all its recklessness it broadcasts the fact that there are only two classes in American society and they are enemies."

8. Karl Marx and Friedrich Engels, "Revue," from "Neue Rheinische Zeitung—Politisch-ökonomische Revue" [Jan./Feb. 1850], in Karl Marx and Friedrich Engels, *Werke* (Berlin: Dietz, 1969), 7: 220f.

9. From Karl Marx, *On America and the Civil War,* ed. Saul Padover (New York: McGraw Hill, 1972), 14f. The Californian sociologist Stanford M. Lyman called attention to these views of Marx, without mentioning Engels's coauthorship, in *The Seven Deadly Sins: Society and Evil* (New York: St. Martin's Press, 1978), 255ff.

10. Marx, *On America,* 14f. (Translation altered.)

11. Marx and Engels, *Werke* 7: 437.

12. Marx and Engels, *Der Briefwechsel* (Munich: DTV, 1983), 2: 342; Karl Marx, *On Revolution,* ed. Saul Padover (New York: McGraw Hill, 1971), 139.

13. Marx and Engels, *Briefwechsel,* 342: "The difficult question for us is this: the revolution is imminent on the Continent and will immediately take on a socialist character. But won't it be necessarily crushed in this little corner of the world, since the movement of bourgeois society is still ascendant in much larger areas?"

14. Weber, *The Protestant Ethic and the Spirit of Capitalism,* trans. Talcott Parsons (New York: Scribner's, 1958), 181. (Translation altered.)

15. Werner Sombart, *Das Wirtschaftsleben im Zeitalter des Hochkapitalismus* (Munich: Duncker und Humblot, 1927), Zweiter Halbband, 1010.

16. For Weber's critique of Wilhelm Ostwald's belief that there will be no scarcity of energy resources in the future and his own view that our energy resources could be exhausted "in little more than a thousand years if exploitation increases at its present rate," see his last untranslated "methodological" critique, " 'Energetische' Kulturtheorien" [1909], in Max Weber, *Wissenschaftslehre,* ed. J. Winckelmann (Tübingen: Mohr, 1951), 409.

17. Ernst Troeltsch, *Der Historismus und seine Probleme* (Tübingen: Mohr, 1922), 101, 188.

18. Karl Jaspers, *Die Atombombe und die Zukunft des Menschen* (Munich: Piper, 1958).

19. Reinhard Bendix, *Higher Civil Servants in American Society* (Boulder: University of Colorado Press, 1949).

20. Hans Gerth and C. W. Mills, eds., *From Max Weber* (New York: Oxford University Press, 1946), 310, 392.

21. Weber always emphasized the power distribution. He made a similar point about the power of the priesthood in history: "The intellectual influence upon religion of the priesthood, even where it was the chief carrier of literature, was of quite varied scope, depending on which non-priestly strata opposed the priesthood and on the power position of the priesthood itself" (501).

22. *From Max Weber,* 88.

23. Late in 1983, in a grassroots tax rebellion, two Democratic state senators in Michigan became the first legislators ever to be recalled from office in the state's history. See *New York Times,* 2 Dec. 1983, 11.

24. For the latest but rather descriptive account of changes in the American political system, see Michael Nelson, ed., *The President and the Political System* (Washington, D.C.: Congressional Quarterly Press, 1984), esp. contributions by Jack L. Walker and Roger G. Brown.

25. For a long time the Rockefellers fought unsuccessfully the legendary Robert Moses, who wrote his own person into the constitution of New York State and made himself the irremovable chief of an authority, thereby controlling, for decades, billions of dollars for the construction of bridges, parks, freeways, and housing. This was an extraordinary case of personal rulership which violated the constitutional norm of universalist personalism. See Robert Caro, *The Power Broker: Robert Moses and the Fall of New York* (New York: Knopf, 1974).

26. See James Fallows, "The Passionless Presidency," in *How the System Really Works,* ed. Herbert M. Levine (Glenview, Ill.: Scott, Foresman, 1982), 201ff.

27. See Richard Neustadt, "White House and Whitehall," *The Public Interest* 1 (1966): 55–69.

28. *From Max Weber,* 88.

29. Morris Janowitz, *The Last Half-Century: Societal Change and Politics in America* (Chicago: University of Chicago Press, 1978), 154.

WMW

| Wolfgang J. Mommsen | Capitalism and Socialism: Weber's Dialogue with Marx |

Translated by David Herr

The advance of modern industrial capitalism and consequent social developments are the dominant themes of Max Weber's sociological work. As early as 1893, Weber predicted that, within a few generations, capitalism would destroy all tradition-bound social structures, and that this process was irreversible. He described modern capitalism as an essentially revolutionary force and believed that it was not possible to arrest, by any means, its triumphal march. Much of his scholarly work was concerned with investigating the societal and cultural effects of industrial capitalism from the standpoint of their meaning for the future of western liberal societies. Consequently, it was inevitable that Max Weber would confront Karl Marx's analysis of modern capitalism and his ideas about a future socialist society. Weber's sociology can be viewed as an attempt to formulate an alternative position standing in harmony with his own bourgeois-liberal ideals, but one that does not simply dismiss the socialist critique of bourgeois society as being without foundation.

Weber belonged to a generation that stood midway between the generation of Marx and our own. His socio-political views were formed under the influence of the extraordinarily rapid growth of modern industrial capitalism in the last decades before 1914. The development of large industrial combinations, trusts, and monopolies, all typical of a maturing capitalist system, took place before his eyes, and he could not but note how this new reality conflicted with classical political economy's ideal image of capitalism. Although Weber did not ignore these developments, he remained throughout his life a passionate champion of a liberal brand of dynamic capitalism. Weber was perhaps Marx's greatest theoretical opponent; given the range of his sociological work he has been rightly called a "bourgeois Marx."[1]

Weber occasionally referred to himself as "a member of the bourgeois class" who was "educated in their views and ideals."[2] In 1907, in an argument concerning German Social Democracy, he requested expressly that Robert Michels simply regard him as a "class-conscious bourgeois," adding that his wife was now a factory shareholder.[3] Nevertheless, one hesitates, in light of Weber's constant striving for critical self-examination, to call him a bourgeois in the ordinary sense of the word. Rather, to use his own terminology, he is better located in the intelligentsia, a social group that cannot be assigned to any of the economic classes. Weber was less a "bourgeois" than a resolute liberal, for whom the autonomy of the individual was an indispensable principle, and it was from this perspective that he approached the nature of capitalism and Marxism. As a result, Weber's attitude toward capitalism as a total societal configuration proved to be thoroughly ambivalent; this will be shown in greater detail. Although he vigorously defended the capitalist system against its critics on the Left (whether they were from the workers' movement or from those intellectuals whom he described as having succumbed to "the romanticism of the general strike" or to "revolutionary hope"), he did not hesitate to criticize the system's inhuman consequences.

The starting point of Weber's analysis of modern capitalism was not as far removed from Marx as Weber himself assumed. His concern for the preservation of human dignity under the societal conditions created by and typical for mature capitalism (particularly, the severe discipline of work and exclusion of all principles of personal ethical responsibility from industrial labor) is entirely consistent with Marx's effort to find a way of overcoming the social alienation of the proletariat under industrial capitalism.[4] But Weber's sociological analyses of industrial societies led him to conclusions that were, in many respects, opposed to those of Marx.

It is hardly necessary to point out that Weber always took Marx's theoretical work seriously. Weber labeled the *Communist Manifesto* "a pathetic prophecy," but at the same time, despite his decidedly different views, he considered it "a scholarly work of the highest order."[5] Eduard Baumgarten reported that, in the last years of his life, Weber told one of his students:

One can measure the integrity of a modern scholar, and especially of a modern philosopher, by how he sees his own relationship to Nietzsche and Marx. Whoever does not admit that he could not accomplish very important aspects of his own work without the work that these two have performed, deceives both himself and others. The world in which we ourselves exist intellectually is largely a world stamped by Marx and Nietzsche.[6]

Weber achieved his own intellectual position through constant grappling with these two completely opposite thinkers. Weber's pronounced aristocratic individualism can be traced largely to Nietzsche. This was held in check, of course, not only by Weber's liberal convictions, but also by the insight that the fate of the individual is determined extensively by material and economic factors and to a very great degree is dependent upon anonymous socio-economic processes—an insight which is ultimately traceable to Marx.[7]

Nevertheless, it seems that during the early stage of his scholarly career Weber paid little attention to the original writings of Marx and Engels.[8] At least until 1906 he referred exclusively to vulgar-Marxist interpretations; direct references to Marx were almost totally absent. During these years he confronted Marx and Marxism primarily in his methodological writings. There, Weber distanced himself sharply and repeatedly from what was then called "historical materialism." In principle, Weber rejected all material philosophies of history. He considered these and other approaches that claimed to discover objective historical laws or even an inner meaning to history, "charlatanism."[9] From his own standpoint, perhaps best characterized as a neo-Kantianism fleshed out with Nietzschean principles, there could be no objective ordering of the historical process. In Weber's opinion the Marxist theory of history, which described historical change as a determinate sequence of social formations with each characterized by its respective mode of economic production and propelled by class conflict, lacked any scientific basis. For Weber, there were no objective laws of social reality. At best, it might be possible, with the aid of ideal-types, to construct law-like theories of societal processes. These can serve as criteria for determining the degree to which certain segments of social reality depart from such nomological models.

Weber's radical position followed unavoidably from the fundamental premise that history is meaningless in itself and that, at least from the standpoint of a random observer, it appears as more or less chaotic. Only when specific concepts and categories, formulated from the perspective of ultimate cultural values, are applied to a limited segment of reality (which per se is limitless), does it become meaningful. Accordingly, Weber considered Marx's theory about the succession of different modes of production to be a sociological hypothesis that provides essential insights into the nature and development of modern industrial societies, but on no account does Weber consider it as objectively valid scientific knowledge. In the former sense, namely as a ideal-typical construction, he regarded Marx's theory as extremely significant.[10] On the other hand, he was not prepared to accept it as ontological truth. He expressed this in "Objectivity in Social Science and Social Policy":

Liberated as we are from the antiquated belief that all cultural phenomena can be *deduced* as a product or function of the constellation of "material" interests, we believe nevertheless that the analysis of social and cultural phenomena with special reference to their economic conditioning and ramifications was a scientific principle of creative fruitfulness, and if applied carefully and free from dogmatic restrictions, will remain so for a long time to come. However, the so-called "materialistic conception of history" must be rejected most emphatically insofar as it is meant as a *Weltanschauung* or a formula for the causal explanation of historical reality.[11]

In this case Weber did not differentiate between Marx and Marxist theory in his own time.[12] Marx's conception of a necessary and irreversible process, leading from feudalism to capitalism and eventually to socialism, was not a purely ontological statement; it was also a theory for practical orientation, requiring human action to become reality. Capitalist society comes into being only through the actions of the bourgeoisie, and without a socialist revolution carried out by the proletariat there can be no socialist society. This activist element in Marx's theory was obscured by the later interpretations of Engels and, finally, Kautsky.[13] It was they who turned it into that rigid, mechanistic theory commonly called historical materialism.

When he wrote the above-quoted passages, Weber was apparently not fully aware of the substantial differences between Marx's theory and orthodox Marxist interpretations in his own time, even though it would appear that he discussed some of Marx's texts in his early academic classes in the 1890s. A careful comparison of their methodological procedures[14] shows that the two thinkers were actually not as antithetical as Weber himself claimed. Both Weber and Marx were concerned with extrapolating certain chains of causal association from the historical process. To be sure, unlike Marx, Weber was clear that one could grasp only segments of social reality, never its totality. Weber thought it impossible, indeed dishonest, to go beyond the construction of ideal-types: models that are used for describing particular historical sequences and for analyzing their social effects and human consequences. In other words, from Weber's methodological perspective, claims about the objectivity of the historical process were fictitious. It is no coincidence that he repeatedly took offense at precisely this element of Marx's teachings. Weber considered this view of history not only to be epistemologically false, but also axiomatically, or if one prefers, ethically, highly questionable. In his view it fatally weakened the responsibility of the autonomous individual, who is called upon constantly to decide between different ultimate values. The belief that history is determined by objective processes seduces individuals all too easily into adapting to the presumed objective course of things, rather than remaining faithful to their own ultimate convictions and value positions.

We also encounter this viewpoint in Weber's comments on the German Social Democrats.[15] He repeatedly expressed utmost contempt toward them precisely because they asserted persistently that world history was on their side and that, therefore, the victory of socialism over the bourgeois world was merely a question of time. In Weber's view, this posture was not only morally deplorable but also one of the essential causes of the political weakness of the Social Democratic Party in Wilhelmian Germany. In 1906 Weber sarcastically censured the German Social Democrats' blind confidence in the course of history:

Not the faintest likelihood supports the proposition that economic "socialization" *[Vergesellschaftung]* as such harbors in its bosom either the development of inwardly "freer" personalities or "more altruistic" ideals. Are we able to find the germ of anything of this sort among those who, in their opinion, are to be borne to inevitable victory by "material development"? "Correct" Social Democracy drills the masses to perform a sort of spiritual goose-step. Instead of directing them toward the otherworldly paradise (which in Puritanism *also* showed respectable achievements on behalf of this-worldly "freedom"), it points them to the this-worldly paradise and thereby turns the Social Democratic Party into a sort of vaccination which is to the advantage of those interested in the existing order of things.[16]

Not only the liberal in Weber, but also the follower of Nietzsche, protested against such an orthodox-Marxist and basically quietist position. Weber rejected strongly socialism dressed in pseudoscientific garb which seemed to guarantee scientific certainty of final victory. On the other hand, he had the greatest respect for socialists who, regardless of the chances of success, fought for their ideals. Revealing, in this regard, are Weber's close connections with Russian socialist emigrés in Heidelberg during the last years of the First World War. It is noteworthy that Weber always treated anarchism with unusual sympathy, primarily because he had high regard for positions based purely on ethics of conviction and an unwillingness to compromise with existing conditions.

For Weber, Marxism was acceptable in only two forms: (1) as a political theory which, instead of invoking objective scientific truths, proclaims revolutionary struggle against the purportedly unjust social order on the basis of ethical convictions and without regard for the possible consequences for the individual, or (2) as a systematization of brilliant ideal-typical hypotheses, which in themselves deserve closest attention from all sociologists and which are capable of substantially advancing knowledge of modern societies.

A more detailed analysis of Weber's view of Marxism shows that Weber took exception, above all else, to the Marxist theory of "superstructure." Weber never accepted the thesis that all social phenomena could be explained sufficiently by relating them to economic causes: "the common materialist view of history, that the 'economic' is in some sense an 'ultimate' in the chain of causation, is in my estimation totally worthless as a scientific statement."[17] Weber ignored the fact that Marx's and Engels's position on this matter was much more sophisticated.

Weber held that social phenomena could not, even in the final analysis, be explained by economic causes. However, neither did he express an idealist counterposition. Weber's famous essays on *The Protestant Ethic and the Spirit of Capitalism* are commonly viewed as an attempt to prove that idealist, and especially religious, factors play an independent role in the historical process. In 1918 Weber presented the results of this study in a series of lectures at the University of Vienna under the title, "A Positive Critique of the Materialist View of History." However, he did this with thoroughly ambivalent feelings.[18] He never claimed that his Protestant ethic thesis completely answered the question of how and why industrial capitalism arose. He pointed out repeatedly that he uncovered only one group of factors among others that had contributed to the rise of capitalism.[19] Incidentally, Weber drew considerably closer to Marx when he indicated that mature capitalism no longer needed the Protestant ethic. In almost Marxian language, he described modern capitalism as a social power that forces men to subject themselves to the societal conditions it has created, regardless of whether or not they are willing. They have no choice; they must be professionals *(Berufsmenschen)* because modern industrial capitalism permits nothing else.[20] In almost apocalyptic terms he argued that capitalism is forging the conditions for a new "cage of the serfdom of the future," which humanity will have to occupy as soon as the current phase of dynamic economic growth has reached its natural limits.[21] In describing the capitalist system's almost mechanical domination of man, which in the long run threatens to become a modern form of slavery, Weber came close to Marx's conviction that capitalism is an inhuman social order that contains the propensity for self-destruction.

On the other hand, Weber refused to identify this immanent trend of the capitalist system (which he endeavored to define precisely using sociological methods) with an objective developmental law. The universal-historical perspective of an approaching age of bureaucracy recurs repeatedly in Weber's scholarly writings; however, it is never hypostatized into an ontological statement of a philosophy of history. Here, the decisive difference between Weber's and Marx's conceptions of history becomes obvious. While Marx, in Hegelian fashion, framed his analysis in an almost apodictically conceived theory of history (although partly with political intentions), for Weber every holistic view of the historical process had only a hypothetical quality, serving orientation but not understood per se as true and immutable. Accordingly, Weber was only being consistent when he gave particular attention to those forces and tendencies which were counteracting this process and sought to discover the conditions under which these can display their optimal effectiveness.

Weber's reaction to individual elements of Marxist theory also conforms with this fundamental attitude. He accepted the thesis that the material conditions of existence pervasively determine human action only as a nomological model for the definition of concrete social conduct, but not as conceptualized truth; and it was precisely the significant deviations from this model that he sought to establish. With respect to the role of material, and particularly economic interests, Weber was fundamentally pluralistic. Weber found that even under industrial capitalism, development is not determined exclusively by "material interests." Alongside their dynamics, stand the dynamics of "ideal interests";[22] every analysis must take both sets of factors into account. In his essays on the Protestant ethic and later studies of the world religions, Weber was, above all, intent upon demonstrating that ideal interests can initiate social change of considerable magnitude; indeed, under certain circumstances they can have revolutionary effects although—or better, precisely *because*—they have nothing in common with economic motivations.

On this point Weber perhaps stood furthest from Marx. In contrast to Marx, he was firmly convinced that individuals who are consciously guided by ultimate values, of whatever sort—and the more these values stand in opposition to everyday reality, the more far-reaching their effects—can be an irreducible force that reshapes the given social reality to conform with their ultimate values. Naturally, the actual results of such individual actions are conditioned by the specific societal situation. But the original motivation of action cannot be explained perfunctorily by referring to the social conditions, which shape significantly the eventual results.

This concept of social change, which is directed primarily toward value-oriented actions of individuals or groups, corresponds to Weber's strictly individualistic thinking, and is, in principle, irreconcilable with Marxist theory. Nevertheless, there is common ground between Weber and Marx (at least with the *Philosophical Manuscripts of 1844*). In a brilliant essay, which still ranks among the best ever written on Weber, Löwith has shown that both thinkers were concerned with the same central problem: how a worthy human existence can be secured for the majority of the population under the conditions of industrial society. However, the realization that Marx was concerned equally with the liberation of "alienated man" was obscured, for Weber, by vulgar-Marxist interpretations.[23]

As a few scattered comments indicate, Weber doubted Marx's prognosis that, because of its inherent contradictions, the collapse of the capitalist system was inevitable. He believed that the pauperization theory, crisis theory, and concentration theory were all unsound, and, in this respect he agreed fully with contemporary critiques of Marxism. After a long and uninterrupted rise in real wages, the pauperization theory, even in modified form, was no longer tenable. Weber regarded the assumption that the transition to socialism would occur after a series of constantly intensifying economic crises with a mixture of disdain and irony, as can be gathered from his occasional polemical remarks about the "so-called anarchy of production," which nevertheless produces tremendous material achievements.[24] Weber's lecture on "Socialism," delivered to Austrian army officers in 1918,[25] used arguments of then contemporary political economists (also those of Eduard Bernstein) in pointing out the likelihood of increased capitalist self-regulation through the formation of cartels, syndicates, and the like, which would reduce the intensity of recurrent economic crises.[26] Specifically, Weber contradicted Marx's view that further capitalist development would cause an unavoidable polarization between the bourgeoisie and the overwhelming majority of the proletariat, absorbing all remaining social strata. Weber referred expressly to the rapid increase in " 'white-collar workers,' and, hence, of bureaucracy in the private sector," a development which, he believed, indicated increasing differentiation within the workers' ranks as well as within the middle classes.[27] Consequently, Weber regarded the German bourgeoisie's fear of revolution as pitiable and the Social Democrats' slogans of revolutionary agitation as a symptom of both political immaturity and the backwardness of the German political and social system, which denied workers political equality just as it denied them recognition as social partners of the entrepreneurs. Thus, Weber repeatedly blasted the patriarchalism of German entrepreneurs, who could not free themselves from their lord-of-the-manor perspective; he also considered them partially responsible for the radicalization of the workers.[28] Weber believed that a socialist revolution was extremely improbable in his time. In his view, the Russian "October Revolution" was a military revolt veiled in socialist drapery.[29]

Quite apart from the question of the prospects for socialism, Weber rigorously disputed that the abolition of private appropriation of the means of production and the transition to an economy that satisfies needs (*Bedarfsdeckungswirtschaft*), of whatever type, would substantially improve the lot of workers. Weber believed that the separation of workers from the means of production, which Marx emphasized so strongly, was by no means limited to a social order based on private property. Rather, he considered it to be an essential precondition of all modern, highly developed societies, capitalist or other. "It is," he opined, "a serious error to think that this separation of the worker from the tools of his trade is something peculiar to industry, especially to *private* industry. The basic state of affairs is unaltered when the person at the head of the machine is changed—when, for example, a state president or prime minister controls it instead of a private industrialist."[30] On the contrary, the separation of workers from the means of production exists in state-directed socialism just as much as in capitalism. In both an increasing divergence of formal ownership and managerial control becomes manifest, a split which Weber saw as a mark of advanced industrial systems and which, as we will see below, he took as the starting point for an ideal-typical theory of social stratification that differs significantly from Marxist theory.

From the foregoing, it can be concluded that Weber was convinced that neither private appropriation nor the uneven distribution of property can be regarded as the essential causes of the alienation and deprivation of the working classes. The elimination of private control over the means of production leaves the fundamental problem untouched, namely, the superiority of those in the dominant economic positions who exercise control over the masses of workers. It is the problem of control, not the formal disposition of property, which is crucial. Therefore, Weber saw the roots of alienation, not in property relations, but in omnipotent structures of bureaucratic domination, which modern industrial capitalism produced in ever-increasing numbers. Accordingly, he considered the demand for abolition of private control of production to be a fetish, which ignored the true state of affairs and glossed over the fact that individual workers had nothing to gain by such measures. "This would be true very particularly also of any *rationally* organized socialist economy, which would retain the expropriation of all workers and merely bring it to completion by expropriating the private owners."[31] However, this would be a further strengthening and bureaucratization of the economy and, indirectly, of the social system. Socialization would not liberate workers; it would make them more dependent upon those who control the means of production.

For workers it makes little difference whether the masters of the means of production are capitalist entrepreneurs or managers or government officials with entrepreneurial duties. In contrast to Marx's expectation that socialism would eliminate the profit motive, Weber posited soberly that individual workers would continue to be concerned only with their constellation of personal interests, whatever the structure of the society. Weber aimed at demonstrating that nationalization of production would lead only to a shift of interest positions, and it would certainly not eliminate "the domination of man over man." Workers would be confronted with a new, still more powerful bureaucracy and one far harder to control, whose members one might well call, with Djilas, "the new class." Consequently, any possibilities of improving their concrete working and living conditions within the system would be further restricted. According to Weber, it made no basic difference whether the transition to a socialist, planned economy that satisfies needs was achieved by a revolutionary or evolutionary path. Such a transition would curtail considerably the chances of attaining a maximum of freedom, in whatever sense.

In 1917, there was much discussion in Germany as to whether the forms of the wartime economy, with their high level of government control, should be maintained after the war and gradually turned into a socialist system. Weber protested passionately against such suggestions.

A progressive elimination of private capitalism is theoretically conceivable, although it is surely not so easy as imagined in the dreams of some literati who do not know what it is all about; its elimination will certainly not be a consequence of this war. But let us assume that some time in the future it will be done away with. What would be the practical result? The destruction of the iron cage of modern industrial labor? No! The abolition of private capitalism would simply mean that the *top management* of the nationalized or socialized enterprises would become bureaucratic as well.

This would endanger a free society's chances of survival in an age of bureaucratization; for it is bureaucracy that poses the real threat to a humane society.

Together with the inanimate machine it [i.e., bureaucracy] is busy fabricating the cage of bondage which men will perhaps be forced to inhabit some day, as powerless as the fellahs of ancient Egypt. This might happen *if* a technically good, i.e., a rational bureaucratic administration and provision of social services *were to be the ultimate and sole value* in the ordering of their affairs.[32]

From this universal perspective, Weber regarded the abolition of private ownership with great skepticism. In his view, nationalization of the means of production is incapable of contributing to a solution of the most pressing problem of our time. This is the question of how, in the face of "omnipotent tendencies towards bureaucratization . . . some remnants of 'individualistic' freedom of movement" can still be rescued?[33] Nationalization would make the situation still worse and only lead to an increase in the power of functionaries, not of workers. "It is the dictatorship of the official, not that of the worker, which, for the present at any rate, is on the advance."[34]

Yet Weber distinguished himself radically from Marx not only in his estimation of the chances for eliminating the structural deficiencies of industrial capitalism but also in his analysis of the nature of capitalist society. According to Weber, even mature capitalist societies are not as monolithically structured as the Marxist class model postulates. In principle he accepted the concepts "class" and "class struggle," unlike many of his bourgeois contemporaries, but he refused to assign them the dominant role that they play in Marx's theory.

Weber believed that class interest in the Marxist sense could be decisive in special situations, but that this is not necessarily so. Only in extraordinary historical situations, according to Weber, are there collective class actions that conform unambiguously to this behavioral pattern, and even in such cases the population achieves nothing without the leadership of persons (normally intellectuals) from other classes. Weber tersely rejected the so-called "false class consciousness" solution of Georg Lukács, who held that segments of a class can be mistaken concerning their actual class interests and that these interests are established objectively. Weber considered this to be a pseudoscientific strategy that obscured the key issues.

The fact that people in the same class situation regularly react in mass actions to such tangible situations as economic ones in the direction of those actions which are most adequate to their average interest is an important and after all simple fact for the understanding of historical events. However, this fact must not lead to that kind of pseudo-scientific operation with the concepts of "class" and "class interests" which is so common nowadays and which has found its most classic expression in the statement of a talented author, that the individual may be in error concerning his own interests, but that the "class" is "infallible" about its interests.[35]

Weber also rejected Lukács's thesis because he was convinced that the social action of particular groups is never determined solely by economic interests. People do not always act in accordance with their objective class situation; they are influenced by a multitude of other factors as well, including religious beliefs, traditional modes of behavior, and particular values. This means that instead of class, much more differentiated explanatory models of social action are necessary to deal with the complexity of social relations in industrial societies. Although Weber feared that, in the long run, capitalism would become a rigidly monolithic and bureaucratic system of gigantic proportions, he was convinced, contrary to Marx, that capitalist societies are, in principle, pluralistically structured. Class conflicts play an essential role, but actual social developments depend on many other social factors, such as strong, dynamic leadership.

Especially within complex industrial societies, distinctions between the individual's class situation and class interest are generally not clear. This is reflected in the ideal-typical schema of class stratification developed by Weber in *Economy and Society,* which differs most significantly from Marx's approach.[36] Instead of a single model of class stratification, Weber developed three different models, each based on a different criterion: the disposition of property; "the chance of utilizing goods and services in the marketplace"; and the social status of the respective social groups or strata. From these criteria, Weber distinguished between property classes, commercial classes, and social classes. He did so to make clear that class situation, defined as a set of shared interests of groups of individuals, is many-layered and totally unequivocal only in the exceptional case.

Weber also distinguished between property classes and commercial classes because, in his view, their social interests are quite different. A society based predominantly on class stratification according to property tends to stagnate, because the "positively privileged classes" are composed primarily of *rentiers,* who draw fixed revenues from private property. As a result, their central interest is maintaining the status quo; they are threatened by rapid economic growth and strong economic competition. The "negatively privileged classes" are, for the most part, either not free or directly dependent upon their masters. Because the *rentiers* are not interested in social change and the lower classes are unable to alter their lot, class stratification based on property is nondynamic. However, this model is not ideally suited for describing class relations in industrial societies. A more adequate approach emphasizes the chances of a specific class being able to exercise control of the means of production and the chances of its being able to obtain goods in the marketplace. Formal possession of property is not decisive in determining the economic and social position of the various social groups in a capitalist system; rather, the degree of their effective participation in the functions of economic leadership is the decisive factor. Admittedly, these functions are frequently closely associated with the possession of property, but this is not necessarily so, particularly where highly specialized knowledge and managerial skills are of increased importance. Here, also, Weber distinguished between positively and negatively privileged classes, while groups such as craftsmen and independent farmers stand between them. The positively privileged classes consist of entrepreneurs, managers, and members of the various professions "with sought-after expertise or privileged education" (e.g., lawyers, scientists, physicians, and artists), as well as, in rare cases, highly skilled workers who are not easily replaceable. The bulk of workers comprise the negatively privileged classes.

This bipolar model of class stratification, based on possession of property on the one hand and professional status on the other, is consistent with recent developments in industrial societies; science and technology are daily gaining in importance. Consequently the social status of those groups which supply the necessary specialized knowledge rises in importance, while the role of the formal proprietors of the means of production declines. What is the significance of this ideal-typical schema? First, under advanced capitalism, formal possession of property is less important than what Weber calls "the monopolization of entrepreneurial management for the sake of the business interests" of one's own class.[37] Second, the two models show that even within the ruling classes of industrial societies there exists a great diversity of economic and political interests. *Rentiers* usually favor a stable economic system and, accordingly, are more likely to be politically conservative. On the other hand, managers, filling important entrepreneurial positions, are supportive of dynamism and rapid growth, and therefore they are often more liberal in their political attitudes and more flexible in their social behavior.

Something similar can be said of workers. Weber was intensively concerned with the progressive differentiation of status groups within the working class and he pointed out that Marx, in his last years, also paid special attention to this issue.[38] Weber indicated that increasing differentiation would lead to corresponding differences in respect to economic interests and political views. Accordingly, he thought that the Marxist concept of class (i.e., that all societal conflict is ultimately attributable to conflicts between capitalists and their various bourgeois accomplices on the one side and workers on the other) was not sufficiently differentiated to do justice to the extraordinarily complicated network of competing material interests within capitalist societies. Weber did not deny that there is class struggle and class interest within capitalist societies, but he disputed the contention that these factors alone determine the way things develop. The status of particular groups or individuals within the production process, even more than the disposition of property, influences their interest positions within societal structure. The ideal-typical model of social class stratification that Weber developed, using social status as a standard, is designed to take account of this fact. Weber distinguished between four classes: (1) the working class; (2) the petit bourgeoisie; (3) the propertyless intelligentsia, highly qualified specialist, and white-collar workers; and finally, (4) "the classes privileged through property and education."[39] This classification is admittedly rather imprecise, but it indicates, nonetheless, that Weber made a clear distinction between class affiliation and social status and that he regarded them, to a certain degree, as independent variables.

At this point, a provisional balancing of accounts is in order. Weber's objections to the Marxist solution to the problems of industrial capitalist society have been confirmed, in many respects, by the development of socialist systems. Today, it is evident that eliminating private appropriation of the means of production does not solve the problems; it merely results in a displacement onto a different plane of the fundamental conflict of interests, determined by the technological constraints of industrial production. Nationalization has led to a replacement of the social strata in control of the means of production, but not, however, to the elimination or even the alleviation of the domination exercised by those groups over the working class. The problem of establishing effective social control from the perspective and in the interests of the bulk of the population proves much harder to solve in Marxist-Leninist societies than in the capitalist West. Accordingly, one must agree with Weber that, instead of the particular form of ownership, the omnipotence of bureaucratic structures (unavoidable as they are under modern industrial conditions) represents the real cause of alienation in the industrial work world and jeopardizes personal freedom. With a dispassionate eye Weber located the crucial problem, namely that in socialism merely a new strata of bureaucratic masters had gained control. His skepticism about the claim that socialist society gradually would engender a new type of man also has been justified. The insight expressed in his theory of the various types of class stratification— decisive importance rests not with property ownership but rather with the degree of control of the entrepreneurial function—has turned out to be valid. The key issue, namely how a humane existence can be assured for the working classes in industrial societies, is just as pressing as ever in existing socialist systems.

Weber's criticism of socialist theories does not mean that he was satisfied with capitalist social conditions. To be sure, he did not regard the situation of workers in Marx's despairing terms, and he considered Marx's proposals of how workers were to be helped as highly problematic. Nationalization could not end class struggle because it would only change the composition of the positively privileged classes, without significantly improving the lot of workers. Worse still, workers, henceforth, would be subjected to the omnipotent control of anonymous government bureaucracies. These would be far more powerful than a multitude of private entrepreneurs, who, among other things, always have to reckon with government intervention in the case of serious class conflicts. ''While at present the political and private industrial administrations (of cartels, banks, and giant concerns) stand side by side as separate bodies, and therefore industrial power can still be curbed by political power, the two administrations would then be one body with common interests and could no longer be checked.''[40]

Weber faced this problem on an even more fundamental level. He doubted whether the humane ideals of socialism could ever be realized. In a highly developed industrial society, full emancipation of workers was, in his opinion, unattainable. As early as 1908 he had written to Robert Michels that "every idea of eliminating the domination of man by man through any sort of socialistic social system or through ever so meticulously thought out forms of 'democracy'" was utopian.[41] This, of course, does not mean that he preached resignation. On the contrary, he had great sympathy with political movements that directed all their energies toward winning a maximum of social and political freedom for workers within a liberal, market-oriented capitalist economy. In his opinion the fact that workers rebelled against the capitalist system, instead of fighting for participation in it, was chiefly a result of the fact that they and their political organizations were not yet engaged adequately in political decisions. Weber derided the bourgeoisie's foolish fear of Social Democracy. If the Social Democrats were suitably involved in the political process, there would be little to fear from them. Accordingly, before 1914, Weber campaigned for political equality for the Social Democrats.

Again the question arises of how the sphere of individual personality could be asserted under capitalism and its great ally, modern bureaucracy, or, in other words, how the long-term, dehumanizing tendencies of modern industrialism might be counteracted? At first glance, Weber's answer seems paradoxical. Starting from the conviction that there was no simple solution to this problem and that nationalization would only worsen the situation, he inclined toward making the best of the capitalist system rather than abolishing it.[42] Weber defended liberal capitalism because it guaranteed a maximum of free competition on both the economic and social levels. His ideal was an expanding capitalist system with a high degree of social mobility and dynamism; he thought this would permit the greatest possible emancipation of the working classes. He considered two things vital: first, strengthening the dynamic factors within the capitalist economy, rather than encouraging bureaucratization through socialist measures; and second, creating a truly democratic political system, in which all social groups would be given the opportunity to pursue vigorously their social and economic interests within the limits of legal order. Weber conceded readily to Michels that this solution left much to be desired, but he added that its attainment would be "no small achievement."[43]

Weber's position contains problems, if not downright contradictions. On the one hand, Weber counted upon the dynamic effects of free competition in the economic as well as in the general societal realm, while, on the other, he viewed apprehensively the constant growth of cartels, trusts, and other monopolistic structures as typical forerunners of a bureaucratized economy. Weber never systematically discussed this contradiction. By 1906, at the latest, Weber questioned whether his model—in which conflicts of interest between the working classes and entrepreneurs were freely fought out in trade union struggles—was not outdated in the face of the development of giant corporations and powerful employer organizations. He emphatically advocated suitable legislative measures to restore the equality of opportunity between the working classes and their unions and the entrepreneurs in their continual struggle over wages and working conditions. Of course, the free, spontaneous action of the working classes would be encumbered with the fewest fetters possible. Therefore, Weber would hear nothing of governmentally established, consolidated unions or of arbitration bodies on which government officials would be represented. Likewise, Weber strongly supported progressive social legislation; this was not to serve ethical or moral ends, but rather during a period of growing entrepreneurial power it was to improve the position of the working classes in their battle with entrepreneurs.[44]

These observations could be generalized: the state should be, in some measure, a corrective to bureaucratization and petrification within the social structure. This was one of the reasons why Weber emphasized so strongly dynamic, future-oriented leadership and an effective system for the selection of qualified political leaders. It is open to question whether, under advanced capitalism, Weber would have favored a liberal or interventionist economic policy, or to put it sharply: would he have given preference to Keynes or Friedman? We can find support for both views. In principle, Weber favored the liberal model of freely contested conflicts within a society merely ordered by the rule of law. Yet, where the preconditions for this were imperiled, he did not hesitate to assign the state the task of intervening with appropriate corrective measures. Moreover, in Weber's view, as the political organization of society the state can be a source of dynamic economic growth and consequently of increased social mobility, though only by indirect means. Resolute and far-sighted politicians in top government positions are able, owing to their charismatic capacities, to set new societal goals and thereby counter routinization and petrification. This is also important because the underprivileged strata, especially the working classes, are particularly disadvantaged by economic stagnation and social petrification and their opportunities for emancipation are the first to suffer.

Such a solution presupposes that the government possesses a degree of independence from the economically powerful strata, or in Marx's terms, that the state is more than just a tool of the ruling classes. Here, difficulties, not resolved sufficiently in Weber's political sociology, appear and make his conceptual alternative to Marxism appear vulnerable. Certainly, Weber was quite clear that one could not simply grant the state the function of a *pouvoir neutre* in the conflicts of social interests within industrial society. His battle against Schmoller's policies in the *Verein für Sozialpolitik* was directed primarily toward destroying the illusion that the state could ever stand above the social classes. Occasionally Weber made it explicit.[45] In his view, it was important to organize the governmental system such that all social strata and groups, aided by plebiscitary leaders who have the people's confidence, could achieve a due share in political decisions. Weber did not doubt that, through their leaders, the working classes were capable of exerting a definitive influence upon the control of the governmental apparatus, thereby improving their social situation by political means.

Aside from this, there is the question of whether the state possesses a position of independent leadership vis-à-vis economic forces. In this regard Weber never clearly expressed himself. He always used the same sociological terms he applied to other social and economic institutions to describe the governmental power structure as a bureaucracy. Yet, the state was superior to these other institutions because of special legal privileges, in particular the right to employ physical violence; and it was, moreover, organized basically as an "autocephalous" institution. The state had to exercise independent authority, particularly with respect to the economic sphere; instead of being constantly affected by economic interests, it was, on the contrary, supposed to influence economic activities and dictate their political parameters.

Starting from these premises, Weber looked primarily to the political realm, rather than to profound changes of the capitalist economy, for a solution to the structural problems first addressed by Marx. In this connection Weber's advocacy of plebiscitary leadership democracy, with a charismatic element, deserves special notice (something to which Herbert Marcuse already drew attention, although, in my estimation, accompanied by an unacceptable interpretation).[46] A formally democratic political system, led by far-sighted, energetic, and skilled politicians with demagogic qualities, favored a high degree of social mobility. Consequently, this system had indirect emancipatory effects upon the lower classes without ever breaking the rule that the actual exercise of power rests in the hands of small groups. Beyond this, it allowed the underprivileged, at least formally, the possibility of overcoming the disadvantages of their social condition by political means. Weber considered as utopian the socialist option (i.e., smashing the power of the state), formulated by Lenin and then practiced. In the long term, history has shown Weber, rather than Lenin, to be right.[47]

Weber understood that there are possible socialist systems that would minimize worker domination by those controlling the means of production, for example, through extreme decentralization of economic organization and worker participation in management. Yet he believed that this could occur only under conditions that would eliminate both the regulatory mechanism of economic competition and the money economy. Thus, the cost of realizing certain socialist ideals would be a considerable reduction of formal rationality. Although Weber considered a variety of possible types of socialist societies, he assumed—and, thus far, existing socialist systems have proved him right—that a socialist economy could survive only as a centralized, state-operated system.

State socialist economic organization, with its powerful bureaucratic machinery to control production, distribution, and management, had, in Weber's view, obvious disadvantages when compared to the capitalist market economy *(Verkehrswirtschaft)*. In *Economy and Society,* Weber treated this problem in an ideal-typical schema. In a sense it was his last word on the relation between capitalism and socialism.[48] Weber contrasted the market economy with the planned economy. Although he explained clearly that it could not be determined on scientific grounds which of the two systems ought to be given preference, it is obvious that Weber believed market economies are more effective. Socialist economic systems would have to cope with a considerable reduction in the formal accountability *(Rechenhaftigkeit)* of the production and distribution system, especially if they broke with the capitalist practice of market-oriented pricing. Although Weber expressed himself very carefully, his argument nevertheless returned again and again to the thesis that capitalism was infinitely superior to all known economic systems because it alone was capable of rationalizing all economic operations on a purely formal basis. If one chooses the standard of highest achievement as the criterion for weighing the market economy against the planned economy, the former is far superior.

In contrast to some recent neo-Marxist interpretations, Weber was in no way inclined to glorify capitalism, particularly not a capitalist system with a maximum of formal rationality in all its social dimensions. Closer analysis reveals that the pure type of market economy, as Weber developed it in *Economy and Society,* is anything but attractive and is not at all identical with that form of capitalism which Weber favored. This model postulates that a maximum of formal rationality is attainable only if the following conditions are met:

1. "Constant struggle between autonomous groups in the marketplace"
2. the rational calculation of prices under conditions of unrestricted competition in the marketplace

3. "formally free labor" (i.e., work performed on the basis of freely contracted wage agreements, as distinct from fixed salaries or the like)
4. "expropriation of workers from the means of production"
5. private ownership of the means of production.[49]

The majority of these conditions were no longer sufficiently met under the advanced capitalism of Weber's time (assuming, for the moment, that they had been present in the early capitalism, which apparently served as Weber's model). Thus, was he describing a ghost that already belonged to the past? Such a question fails to grasp the core of the issue. Weber intended to describe the specifics of capitalism in its pure form (a procedure which had methodological similarities to Marx). Thus, Weber's process of concept formation must not be dismissed as a throwback to Manchester Liberalism. As already mentioned, he conceded, indeed, emphatically advocated, that under certain conditions departures from the pure form of capitalist market economy would be necessary—departures effected through appropriate state interventions and in some cases through a change in the legal and political parameters of economic activity. In a way, Weber anticipated the neoliberalism of the 1950s. In fact, he influenced its leading exponents (e.g., Friedrich Hayek, Hannah Arendt, and Alfred Müller-Armack) to a considerable extent.

By stressing formal rationality as its basic characteristic, Weber never intended to immunize modern industrial capitalism against criticism, as Herbert Marcuse and Wolfgang Lefèvre attempted to demonstrate.[50] Weber did not intend to elevate capitalism ontologically and thereby justify it ideologically, as Marcuse claimed. Marcuse's argument that Weber's emphasis on the formal rationality of all capitalist operations obscured capitalism's substantive irrationality is also erroneous. Weber discussed this very point repeatedly in *Economy and Society*, although not always without ambiguity.[51] Weber distinguished explicitly between formal and substantive rationality, but, again, not as consistently as the issue demanded. He stated several times that a maximum of formal rationality was inseparably linked with substantive irrationalities, for example, "the submission of workers to the domination of entrepreneurs."[52] Likewise, he never obscured the true nature of "formally free labor contracts," which are fundamental to capitalism; he soberly described them as a special form of domination. Weber proceeded from the premise that formal rationality and substantive rationality might diverge and conflict with each other. In fact, he believed this to be the rule.

Weber cleared the path for a fundamental critique of capitalism, a critique which rated substantive value positions, regardless of their sort, more highly than the formal rationality of the system. He also warned that the implementation of substantive principles must bring an unavoidable reduction in the efficiency and productivity of the economic system, but unfortunately he did not spend much time considering such alternatives. Proceeding from definite substantive value positions, he merely indicated that a large number of critical alternatives to the capitalist system was possible but in each case some setbacks in the areas of civilization and technology must be accepted as part of the bargain—an argument he used occasionally against Robert Michels.[53] The manifestly dogmatic point in Weber's position was his nearly boundless confidence in both the formally rationalizing effect of the economic struggle between competing groups in the market and, in a broader sense, the competition of political groups within society.

The typological dichotomy of the market economy on the one hand and different forms of socialistic planned economies on the other was by no means an apology for industrial capitalism. Weber did not aim to refute the socialists and Marxists with this extremely formal typology. Rather, his goal was to provide a value-free clarification of the respective social costs and consequences that the two opposing systems unavoidably generate. Thus, he stated: "The *purpose* of the discussion has been to determine the optimal preconditions for the *formal* rationality of economic activity and its relation to the various types of *substantive* 'demands' of whatever sort."[54] Weber wished to make perfectly clear that deviations from the pure type of market-oriented competition in capitalist economy entail a necessary reduction in formal rationality of the entire system or, in other words, a diminution of its economic efficiency.

Weber was certain that none of the conceivable theoretic models of ideal economic systems could be translated into social reality without compromising at least some of the aims and values which it was intended to serve. According to his position, it was, in principle, impossible to determine the best economic system. Moreover, "substantive and formal (in the sense of exact *calculation*) rationality," as he put it, were "unavoidably largely separate. This fundamental, and in the last analysis, inherent element of irrationality in economic systems is one of the important sources of all 'social' problems, and above all, of the problems of socialism."[55] As early as his Freiburg inaugural address, Weber had made clear that happiness and peace could not be had on this earth,[56] and he stuck to this conviction for the rest of his life with a "heroic pessimism," reminiscent of Nietzsche. Weber believed that a definitive answer to the question of the nature of a just economic order could never be found. For the forseeable future constant compromises between the principle of formal rationality and substantive value principles seemed to be the only humane solution.

It now should be evident why Weber never idealized capitalism, although he decided unequivocally in its favor. On the one hand, he was an enthusiastic partisan of capitalism as an economic system sustained by bourgeois values and as a source of rational social conduct largely experienced as binding; furthermore, he supported it as a system with a maximum of economic dynamism and social mobility. On the other hand, he was deeply concerned about the ultimate, socio-political consequences of capitalism, which, in the long run, would inevitably undermine worthy human life founded on the principle of the free, autonomous personality. The cool and matter-of-fact analysis of capitalism in *Economy and Society* corresponds to this perspective. Indeed, Weber did not hide the defects of capitalism, yet he was unable to imagine any workable alternative. Despite the high regard he had for the motives of sincere socialists, he did not believe the Marxist prescription could solve the real problems of modern western society. Despite all of capitalism's shortcomings, he preferred it to every conceivable form of socialist economy. He was convinced that socialists, insofar as they wished to be serious about realizing their moral principles, would either have to accept considerable regression in both technology and civilization or else be compelled to create gigantic bureaucracies in the face of which the people, including the workers, would be unable to accomplish anything. Compared to any form of socialism, capitalism appeared to offer far better conditions for the survival of free societies in the age of bureaucracy.

Following this basic conviction, Weber spoke out consistently for the preservation of the capitalist system even in the last years of the First World War and especially during the revolution of 1918–1919 in Germany. As early as 1916 he vigorously defended entrepreneurs against a mounting criticism of capitalism. The war could never have been waged so successfully without their services, and even in the postwar years it was necessary to retain the motto: not curtailment of entrepreneurial activity but "more capital, more capitalistic activity and dynamism," so that the economic losses incurred by the war might be made good again, and Germany's position in the world markets recaptured even in the face of superior competition from the United States.[57]

During the revolution, Weber, at first, made significant tactical approaches toward socialism in order to make what he considered the absolutely necessary coalition of the Social Democracy and the middle classes attractive to Social Democrats. "The paths of all honest, unreservedly peaceful and radical bourgeois democrats and Social Democrats" could "run together for decades 'shoulder to shoulder,'" he declared at a public rally in Frankfort on December 1, 1918.[58] He admitted occasionally that some socialization was necessary under the prevailing circumstances. But, in principle, he always stuck to his convictions that only a free, dynamic entrepreneurial class could restore Germany's economy. During the revolution (occasionally even in public), Weber asked himself repeatedly why he was not a socialist? He answered that, although he stood close "in his convictions to numerous economically schooled Social Democrats to the point of indistinguishability," he could not join the socialist movement because he was not ready to participate in the "grave-digging of socialism."[59] But these were political, tactical utterances.

Weber supported his conviction about the impossibility of thorough nationalization by political and economic arguments. For example, he suggested that Germany could not afford nationalization, at a moment of extreme need for credit and economic dependence on foreign capitalist nations, and that embarking upon such policies would, moreover, risk occupation and foreign rule.[60] Weber's belief in the fundamental superiority of dynamic capitalism became evident once again when the German Democratic Party invited him to represent them on the second Commission on Socialization, formed in 1920. Weber rejected this request with unusual harshness:

At all meetings, *everywhere*, both private and public, I have declared "socialization," in the sense now understood, to be "nonsense." We are in need of entrepreneurs (Herr Stinnes or his like). I have said about the Factory Councils Law: *"Ecrasez l'infame."* From the standpoint of the possible future of socialism, it is disastrous. Politicians should and *must* make compromises. But I am by profession a scholar. . . . The scholar dare not make compromises and cover up "nonsense."[61]

As a consequence of this step, Weber left the German Democratic Party and withdrew entirely from active politics.

Yet, there remained an element of ambiguity in Weber's attitude. He would not tolerate socialization in any form, but this verdict did not necessarily include Social Democratic politics. There was something more than tactical reasoning behind his recurring, although always ultimately rejected, thoughts of joining the Social Democrats—namely, a sympathy, in principle, with their efforts to win a position of equality for the proletariat within the existing society.[62] On the purely theoretical level as well, Weber appears to have felt that the confrontation with socialism was not over and that the final word on the topic had not yet been spoken. He had planned a series of lectures on "Socialism" for the summer semester of 1920, in Munich, and had already started on them when he died of pneumonia in June 1920.[63] Had Weber been granted a longer life, he surely would not have further postponed that systematic treatment of

Marxism, which we looked for in vain within his work; he would have set it forth, whether in the ambitious *Political Sociology* on which he was then working or as a separate inquiry. However, even in its present form, his sociological work can be regarded as an alternative to Marx's theory, one which is on a par with the latter in both breadth of vision and the rigor of its argument.

Clearly, any evaluation of Weber's critique of the Marxist idea should consider that he only lived through the first years of the Bolshevik regime and, therefore, lacked concrete experience with socialist systems. Regardless of this, his essential points are still worthy of consideration. His thesis—that the distribution of property is not as important as the groups who control the entrepreneurial positions—deserves special attention, as today's torpid Communist systems demonstrate. The abolition of private appropriation of the means of production may, under certain circumstances, be the way of resolving the pressing problems of our time, but it could also make things worse. A modern theory of socialism must, above all, be able to handle the problem of how economic decision making can be effectively controlled by the people at large instead of falling into the hands of indecisive bureaucrats or new authoritarian elites. In this respect, Weber's analyses deserve even the attention of those who do not share his convictions.

Weber presented no simple recipes for restructuring capitalist societies in order to end working class alienation and exploitation, but, at least, he emphasized the crucial problems. Thus, we are thoroughly justified in calling him a liberal sociologist who matched his great intellectual antipode, Marx, in probing deeply the problems of industrial capitalism.

Notes

This essay was first published as "Max Weber als Kritiker des Marxismus," *Zeitschrift für Soziologie* 3 (1974): 256–78, and was included under the title "Kapitalismus und Sozialismus: Die Auseinandersetzung mit Karl Marx," in the author's collection *Max Weber: Gesellschaft, Politik und Geschichte* (Frankfort: Suhrkamp, 1974). An earlier translation was "Max Weber as a Critic of Marxism," *Canadian Journal of Sociology* 2 (1977): 373–98. Gerd Schroeter and Robert Antonio contributed to the work on this translation.

1. Albert Salomon, "Max Weber," *Die Gesellschaft* 3 (1926): 144, wrote: "Thus, in the final analysis, it is not just methodological questions, but 'ideological' ones, which separated Weber from socialism and caused him to take the dialectics and ultimate goal of socialist society out of the Marxist philosophy of history. One can, to highlight the paradox of this position, call him a bourgeois Marx." Similarly, Ernst Topitsch, "Max Webers Geschichtsauffassung," *Wissenschaft und Weltbild* 3 (1950): 262.

2. Max Weber, *Gesammelte Politische Schriften* (Tübingen: Mohr, 1971), 20.

3. Letter to Michels, 6 November 1907. Cf. Wolfgang J. Mommsen, *Max Weber und die deutsche Politik, 1890–1920* (Tübingen: Mohr, 1974), 116.

4. In this regard see the analysis by Karl Löwith, *Max Weber and Karl Marx*, ed. Tom Bottomore and William Outhwaite (London: Allen and Unwin, 1982), 19ff.

5. Max Weber, "Socialism," in *Max Weber: The Interpretation of Social Reality*, ed. J. E. T. Eldridge (London: Michael Joseph, 1971), 205.

6. Eduard Baumgarten, *Max Weber: Werk und Person* (Tübingen: Mohr, 1964), 554–55n.1.

7. For a detailed exposition of this point of view see Wolfgang J. Mommsen, *The Age of Bureaucracy: Perspectives on the Political Sociology of Max Weber* (New York: Harper and Row, 1974), 103–7, and Mommsen, "Universalgeschichtliches und politisches Denken bei Max Weber," *Historische Zeitschrift* 201 (1965): 597ff., reprinted in Mommsen, *Max Weber: Gesellschaft, Politik und Geschichte* (Frankfort: Suhrkamp, 1974), 129ff.

8. Note the meager results of Guenther Roth's efforts to put together the textual documentation for Weber's attitude toward Marx in "Das historische Verhältnis der weberschen Soziologie zum Marxismus," *Kölner-Zeitschrift für Soziologie und Sozialpsychologie* 20 (1968): 429–47; also printed in Reinhard Bendix and Guenther Roth, *Scholarship and Partisanship: Essays on Max Weber* (Berkeley: University of California Press, 1971), 227–46. In addition, see Anthony Giddens, *Capitalism and Modern Social Theory: An Analysis of the Writings of Marx, Durkheim and Max Weber* (Cambridge: Cambridge University Press, 1971), 191ff., and Giddens, "Marx, Weber and the Development of Capitalism," *Sociology* 4 (1970): 289–310.

9. See Mommsen, "Universalgeschichtliches und politisches Denken," 563ff.

10. For an ideal-typical interpretation of the economic view of history as seen by Max Weber, cf. Judith Janoska-Bendl, *Methodologische Aspekte des Idealtypus: Max Weber und die Soziologie der Geschichte* (Berlin: Duncker and Humblot, 1965), 89–114.

11. Max Weber, *The Methodology of the Social Sciences,* trans. Edward A. Shils and Henry A. Finch (Glencoe, Ill.: Free Press, 1949), 68. (Translation modified slightly.)

12. We are relying on Jürgen Kocka's interpretation, "Karl Marx und Max Weber: Ein methodologischer Vergleich," *Zeitschrift für die gesamte Staatswissenschaft* 122 (1966): 328–57; also in Hans-Ulrich Wehler, ed., *Geschichte und Oekonomie* (Cologne: Kiepenheur and Witsch, 1973), in Kocka, *Sozialgeschichte* (Göttingen: Vandenhoeck and Ruprecht, 1977), and in English translation in this volume. See also Richard Ashcraft, "Marx and Weber on Liberalism as Bourgeois Ideology," *Comparative Studies in Society and History* 14 (1972): 130–68.

13. Cf. Helmut Fleischer, *Marxismus und Geschichte* (Frankfort: Suhrkamp, 1969), 52–55.

14. See the essay by Kocka in this volume; see also Erich Matthias, "Kautsky und der Kautskyanismus: Die Funktion der Ideologie in der deutschen Sozialdemokratie vor dem ersten Weltkrieg," *Marxismusstudien* 2 (1957): 151, and recently, in cautious defense of Kautsky, Hans-Joseph Steinberg, *Sozialismus und deutsche Sozialdemokratie: Zur Ideologie der Partei vor dem I. Weltkrieg* (Bonn-Bad Godesberg: Verlag Neue Gesellschaft, 1972), 60f.

15. See, as well, in greater depth, Mommsen, *Max Weber und die deutsche Politik,* 116–18.

16. Weber, *Gesammelte Politische Schriften,* 65.

17. Max Weber, *Gesammelte Aufsätze zur Soziologie und Sozialpolitik* (Tübingen: Mohr, 1924), 456.

18. Marianne Weber, *Max Weber: A Biography,* trans. Harry Zohn (New York: Wiley, 1975), 604.

19. Thus, in Weber's second essay on the Protestant Ethic (cf. *The Protestant Ethic and the Spirit of Capitalism,* trans. Talcott Parsons [New York: Scribner's, 1958], 183), he insisted it had not been his intention "to substitute for a one-sided materialistic an equally one-sided spiritualistic causal interpretation of culture and history. Each is equally possible." See also Max Weber, "Kritische Bemerkungen zu den vorstehenden 'Kritischen Beiträgen' " (article under review written by Karl Fischer), in Johannes Winckelmann, ed., *Die protestantische Ethik, II* (Gütersloh: Gütersloher Verlaghaus Mohn, 1972), 28, and Weber, "Bemerkungen zu der vorstehenden 'Replik' " (also by Karl Fischer), ibid., 46f. Here Weber protests explicitly against the assumption that he has "undertaken an idealistic construction of history" and states that he considers "the question of the influence of economic processes upon religious movements" has by no means been resolved by his "current observations regarding the way in which influence has moved in the *opposite* direction." For a systematic discussion of this problem, which we have largely neglected here, see Norman Birnbaum, "Conflicting Interpretations of the Rise of Capitalism: Marx and Weber," *British Journal of Sociology* 4 (1953): 125–41.

20. Cf. Weber, *The Protestant Ethic,* 181: "The Puritan wanted to work in a calling; we are forced to do so. For when asceticism was carried out of monastic cells into everyday life, and began to dominate worldly morality, it did its part in building the tremendous cosmos of the modern economic order. This order is now bound to the technical and economic conditions of machine production which today determine the lives of all the individuals who are born into the mechanism, not only those directly concerned with economic acquisition, with irresistible force. Perhaps it will so determine them until the last ton of fossilized coal is burnt. In Baxter's view the care for external goods should only lie on the shoulders of the 'saint like a light cloak, which can be thrown aside at any moment.' But fate decreed that the cloak should become an iron cage. Since asceticism undertook to remodel the world and to work out its ideals in the world, material goods have gained an increasing and finally inexorable power over the lives of men as at no previous period in history."

21. Cf. Weber, *Gesammelte Politische Schriften,* 63, and Mommsen, *Max Weber und die deutsche Politik,* 89–90.

22. Cf. H. H. Gerth and C. Wright Mills, eds., *From Max Weber: Essays in Sociology* (New York: Oxford University Press, 1946), 280.

23. Löwith, *Max Weber and Karl Marx,* esp. 50–51.

24. Cf. Weber, *Gesammelte Politische Schriften,* 64: "the much reviled 'anarchy of production,' " similarly, 333; see also, Weber, "Socialism," 202.

25. The lecture on "Socialism" (see note 5) should only be relied upon for Weber's understanding of Marx with caution, since it is not free of tactical political considerations. In it, Weber sought to counteract the uncertain atmosphere of Austria-Hungary. Cf. Mommsen, *Max Weber und die deutsche Politik,* 301–2.

26. Weber, "Socialism," 202–3.

27. Ibid., 207.

28. Cf. Mommsen, *Max Weber und die deutsche Politik,* 126–27.

29. Ibid., 299–302.

30. Weber, "Socialism," 199.

31. Max Weber, *Economy and Society,* ed. Guenther Roth and Claus Wittich (Berkeley: University of California Press, 1978), 139.

32. Ibid., 1401–2. (Translation modified slightly.)

33. Ibid., 1403.

34. Weber, "Socialism," 209.

35. Weber, *Economy and Society,* 930. (Translation modified slightly.)

36. For what follows, see *Economy and Society,* 302–3.

37. Ibid., 304.

38. Cf. ibid., 305. There Max Weber refers directly to an unfinished passage in the third volume of *Capital,* and speculates that Marx apparently became aware of this problem in the final years of his life and wanted to extend the analysis.

39. Ibid., 305.

40. Weber, "Socialism," 204.

41. Letter of 4 August 1908. See note 53 below and Mommsen, *Max Weber und die deutsche Politik,* 122.

42. Cf. Gerhard Hufnagel, *Kritik als Beruf: Der kritische Gehalt im Werk Max Webers* (Frankfort; Berlin; Vienna: Propyläen, 1971), 148–54. When Hufnagel attributes the fact that Weber refused to develop an alternative prescription for ending "alienation" "to the caution of the scientist" and to "the critic's bias not to go beyond the negative activity of critical destruction" (152), we are unable to follow him. It is not "caution," nor is it mere critical negativity, but rather realistic insight into the conditions of industrial societies which made Weber come to the realization that there was no quick solution to the problems that Marx had raised. It led him to develop a range of strategies designed to make the best of a situation which was in and of itself irreversible.

43. "Only political democratization is perhaps achievable in the foreseeable future, and it is not such a small thing. I cannot prevent you from believing that there may indeed be more to it, but neither can I force myself to think so." Letter to Robert Michels of 6 November 1907, quoted in Mommsen, *Max Weber und die deutsche Politik,* 114.

44. Cf. Weber's contribution to the discussion at the 1905 convention of the *Verein für Sozialpolitik* (Social Policy Association) held in Mannheim, reprinted in Weber, *Soziologie und Sozialpolitik,* 396–97, see also Mommsen, *Max Weber und die deutsche Politik,* 125ff.

45. Weber referred to the state as "the seat of political power which dominates national society." See "Die Lehrfreiheit der Universitäten," in *Münchner Hochschulnachrichten* 19

(1909), trans. Edward Shils in "The Power of the State and the Dignity of the Academic Calling in Imperial Germany: The Writings of Max Weber on University Problems," *Minerva* 11 (1973): 18–23 (quotation on p. 20); also see Weber, *Economy and Society,* 975, 983–90.

46. "Industrialisierung und Kapitalismus in Werk Max Webers," *Kultur und Gesellschaft* (Frankfort: Suhrkamp, 1965), 2: 125ff. Cf. Mommsen, *Max Weber: Gesellschaft, Politik und Geschichte,* 41ff.

47. In light of this, it is astonishing that Wolfgang Lefévre has tried once again to seek the solution to the problems posed (in quite different ways) by Marx and Weber by completely doing away with state power. This is on a level of utopianism exceeding that already reached by Marx. See Wolfgang Lefèvre, *Zum historischen Charakter und zur historischen Funktion der Methode bürgerlicher Soziologie: Untersuchungen am Werk Webers* (Frankfort: Suhrkamp, 1971), 86–97.

48. Weber, *Economy and Society,* 109–10.

49. Ibid., 151.

50. Here we approach Wolfgang Schluchter's brilliant analysis of Herbert Marcuse's critique of Max Weber, in *Aspekte bürokratischer Herrschaft: Studien zur Interpretation der fortschreitenden Industriegesellschaft* (Munich: List, 1972), 257–68.

51. Cf. Schluchter's point (ibid., 267) that "at the height of the inferno which he has set ablaze, Marcuse does not so much" unmask "Weber as that he truly understands him for the first time."

52. Weber, *Economy and Society,* 84, esp. 138: "The fact that the maximum of formal rationality in *capital accounting* is possible only where the workers are subjected to domination by entrepreneurs, is a further specific element of *substantive* irrationality in the modern economic order."

53. Letter of 4 August 1908: "There are two possibilities. Either: (1) 'My kingdom is not of this world' (Tolstoy), or syndicalism taken to its logical conclusion, which amounts to nothing but the proposition that 'the ultimate goal is nothing, the movement is everything'; this is translated into the revolutionary-ethical and personal spheres. However, you do not actually think it through to its logical conclusion, either. Someday I will probably write an article on this. Or: (2) *Acceptance* of civilization, with adaptation to the sociological conditions of every technology, be it economic, political or whatever (embodied above all in societies organized collectively). In the latter case, all talk of 'revolution' is a farce, and every idea of eliminating the domination of man by man through any sort of social system (however socialistic) or through ever so meticulously devised forms of 'democracy' is utopian. Your own criticism does not go nearly far enough. Anyone who wishes to live as a modern man—even if only in the sense of having his daily newspaper, trains, street cars, etc.—*renounces* all those ideals that you have vaguely in mind, the moment he stops being a revolutionary for the sake of revolution, now without any 'goal,' indeed without the very *idea* of a goal. You are a thoroughly honest fellow and will carry out the critique by yourself which long ago brought me to this way of thinking and *thereby* identifies me as a bourgeois politician as long as the little that one may hope for does not fade into the infinite distance." Weber Papers, Central Archives of the German Democratic Republic II, Merseburg. Partially quoted in Mommsen, *Max Weber und die deutsche Politik,* 112n.62.

54. Weber, *Economy and Society,* 118. (Translation modified slightly.)

55. Ibid., 111. (Translation modified slightly.)

56. Weber, *Gesammelte Politische Schriften,* 12.

57. Cf. the reports on Max Weber's speech before the Deutscher National-Ausschuss on 1 August 1916, printed in Mommsen, *Max Weber und die deutsche Politik,* Appendix II.

58. Weber, *Gesammelte Politische Schriften,* 487; cf. Mommsen, *Max Weber und die deutsche Politik,* 320–21.

59. Weber, *Gesammelte Politische Schriften,* 484. See also Weber's idea for a political speech, at the beginning of 1919, which confirms the report in the *Frankfurter Zeitung:* "Why not be a socialist? In order not to shield charlatanism, not [to join] in *grave-digging."* Arbeitstelle und Archiv des Max Weber-Ausgabe bei der Kommission für Sozial–und Wirtschaftsgeschichte der Bayerischen Akademie der Wissenschaften, Munich, Baumgarten manuscript bundle. Printed in Mommsen, *Max Weber und die deutsche Politik,* Appendix VII.

60. Weber, *Gesammelte Politische Schriften,* 458ff.; cf. Mommsen, *Max Weber und die deutsche Politik,* 320–21, 325–26.

61. Letter to Karl Petersen, 14 April 1920. Petersen papers 53, in the possession of Dr. Edgar Petersen, Hamburg. First published, but with numerous misreadings distorting its meaning, by Bruce F. Frye, "A Letter from Max Weber," *Journal of Modern History* 39 (1967): 122–24. For a corrected text, see Mommsen, *Max Weber und die deutsche Politik,* 333n.105.

62. As early as 1909 the idea of eventually joining the Social Democratic Party occurred to Weber as a theoretical possibility, because he thought that effective support of the interests of the proletariat would be possible for him only if he identifed with the Social Democrats. At that time he wrote to Toennies: "But I could not honestly subscribe to the credo of Social Democracy, and that prevented me from joining—even if I did not 'serve other gods' as well—although it is after all every bit as much lip service as the Apostles' Creed." Cf. Mommsen, *Max Weber und die deutsche Politik,* 137n.152. See also Weber, *Politische Schriften,* 485, and Weber's analogous statement in *Wiesbadener Zeitung,* evening edition of 6 December 1918 (cf. Mommsen, ibid., 294), and finally the letter of 14 April 1920 to Petersen: "I cannot become a 'majority socialist' *(Mehrheitssozialist),* because this party *must* make the same compromises concerning socialism (against the convictions of its scientifically trained members)," ibid., 333n.105. According to this, he might otherwise well have joined.

63. Letter to Mina Tobler, 10 December 1919 (date not quite certain), A. E. II, 116, in the possession of Professor Eduard Baumgarten: ". . . during the summer term I *hope* to find more pleasure in lecturing (government, socialism)." See also his letter to Lederer, 12 May 1920, Weber Papers, Central Archives of the German Democratic Republic II, Merseburg.

VAVA

| Franco Ferrarotti | **Weber, Marx, and the Spirit of Capitalism: Toward a Unitary Science of Man** |

WEBER AND VULGAR ANTI-MARXISM

Max Weber's studies in the sociology of religion are deservedly well-known, even to the nonspecialist.[1] From its first publication in the *Archiv für Sozialwissenschaft und Sozialpolitik* (1904–5), *The Protestant Ethic and the Spirit of Capitalism* quickly became a sort of best seller, and even in Italy it was widely known after its translation in 1928. The fame of *The Protestant Ethic and the Spirit of Capitalism* originated from a vulgar, oversimplified, and somewhat arbitrary interpretation of Weber's argument. There is no doubt that the exceptional reception of Weber's essay in the first decade of this century was largely due to its alleged upsetting of the Marxist theses concerning both the genesis and functioning of capitalism and, in a broader context, the materialist interpretation of history.

However, Weber's "spirit of capitalism" is not a one-sided idealist postulate. Instead, it is a heuristic tool that poses a developmental-historical hypothesis at the macrosociological level. Weber did not intend a polemic against Marxism; in fact, much of his theoretical and scholarly effort aimed to test Marx's ideas. However, Weber rejected Marx's claims to grasp history as a totality and, instead, treated his position as an ideal-type. The portrayal of Weber's thought as fashionable anti-Marxism, though responsible for his widespread public reputation, distorted the understanding of his efforts.

Weber's intention was to grasp what it means to be modern, to trace the origins of Western rationalism, and to understand the bureaucratization of organizational life. Instead of a simplistic rejection of Marx and abandonment of his theoretical and practical-political project, Weber desired to address some of the Marxian problems. Though he tried desperately to retain a conditioned appreciation of the impact of ideas, Weber recognized the centrality of material factors.

Weber was aware of vulgar Marxism, which derived from a mechanistic, nondialectical interpretation of Marx and Engels, and condemned it as a philosophically impoverished and dogmatic catechism. Weber rejected the contention of this "naive historical materialism": the ideas that make up the *ethos* or spirit of capitalism "originate as a reflection or superstructure of economic situations."[2] Critically understood, Marx's and Weber's positions are not in general opposition. In my view, Weber's investigation contributes to a sociology of capitalist development, conceived broadly as the study of its economic, political, juridical, cultural, and social elements. These aspects in mutual interaction are connected dialectically. Weber did not assume monocausality; his conception of cause is conditioned by dialectical relationships and their historical contexts.

THE MODERN, RATIONAL ENTERPRISE

Weber was very explicit about the "impulse to acquisition" and "pursuit . . . of the greatest possible amount of money." They are not particular to capitalism. These aspirations are present and have always been present amongst all sorts of persons and social conditions. The unbridled desire for profit should not be identified exclusively with capitalism, and much less with its "spirit," though capitalism can stimulate the rational pursuit of these irrational impulses.[3]

According to Weber, the capitalist order presupposes the modern rational enterprise, exact calculation of capital, and rational profit seeking. All this is based on a formally "free" organization of labor, the clear separation of domestic organization from the enterprise, and, finally, on rational accountability.

Despite scientific and technical innovations, the rise of industrial capitalism would not have been possible without its basic (in Weber's view) characteristic: the rational organization of free labor. This condition, which remained underdeveloped elsewhere, was most fully refined in the West because of the "rational structures of law and administration." Weber explained that "modern rational capitalism has need, not only of the technical means of production, but of a calculable legal system and of administration in terms of formal rules."[4] Why had such an administration and law developed only in the West? More precisely, what conditions generated these features? Mechanistic Marxists argued that the features were reflections of dominant economic interests. This is an oversimplified and clearly inadequate response. Weber's reply struck a different note:

Among other circumstances, capitalist interests have in turn undoubtedly also helped, but by no means alone nor even principally to prepare the way for the predominance in law and administration of a class of jurists specially trained in rational law. But these interests did not themselves create that law. Quite different forces were at work in this development. And why did not the capitalist interests do the same in China and India? Why did not the scientific, the artistic, the political, or the economic development there enter upon the path of rationalization which is peculiar to the Occident?[5]

Weber sought to demonstrate a meaningful correlation between the precepts of a lived, ethical-religious system and specific economic behaviors. In particular, his purpose was to seek "in the form of a survey of the relations of the most important religions to economic life and to the social stratification of their environment, to follow out both causal relationships, so far as it is necessary in order to find points of comparison with the Occidental development."[6] Thus, Weber did not present an a priori idealist, economic ethics as a one-sided causal framework of economic behavior, but rather he stressed an interactional relation, which is both cause and effect, and which binds in actual history, ethics and economics, structure and personality, religion and practical interests.

WEBER'S GLOBAL SOCIOLOGY

The greatness and lasting value of Weber's sociology lie basically in the style of his research—not simply its broad ranging erudition, but its global portrayal of the social world. The order found by Weber in the tangle of real historical experience was not the outcome of simple techniques such as the questionnaire, participant observation, or life histories, although Weber could use these skillfully. At the same time, however, his use of Benjamin Franklin's autobiography as an illustration of the new spirit of an entire epoch reflected an innovative methodological perspective in contrast to traditional historiography (which was still tied to history as artistic insight and the narration of the deeds of great men). Conventional historians were unable or reluctant to use descriptive and explanatory sociological categories, which uncover interconnected social, cultural, and economic factors and become the basis for interpreting great events in the context of global developmental-historical processes. Weber stated:

No economic ethic has ever been determined solely by religion. In the face of man's attitudes towards the world—as determined by religious or other (in our sense) "inner factors"—an economic ethic has, of course, a high measure of autonomy. Given factors of economic geography and history determine this measure of autonomy in the highest degree. The religious determination of life-conduct, however, is also one . . . only one, of the determinants of the economic ethic. Of course, the religiously determined way of life is itself profoundly influenced by economic and political factors operating within given geographical, political, social, and national boundaries.[7]

This global and multicausal approach was Weber's active methodological criterion and was demonstrated consistently in his research.

In his analysis of ancient Judaism, Weber stressed the covenant, which he linked to the ancient social system of Israel. This system was based on a contractually defined relationship between landed warrior families, guest-tribes, herdsmen, artisans, merchants, and priests. Weber observed that

the point at issue is not that the life conditions of the Bedouins and semi-nomads had "produced" an order whose establishment could be considered by something like the "ideological exponent" of its economic conditions. This form of historical materialist construction is here, as elsewhere, inadequate. The point is, rather, that once such an order was established the life conditions of these strata gave it by far the greater opportunity to survive in the selective struggle for existence against other less stable political organizations. The question, however, why such an order emerged at all, was determined by quite concrete religious-historical and often highly personal circumstances and vicissitudes.[8]

Thus, Weber sketched the famous reciprocal reaction—the *umwälzende Praxis* of which Engels spoke—between the ideological and the extra-economic elements and between the complex of personal qualities and biographical matters and their impact on the socio-economic base.

This "base" is not a *deus ex machina;* it is preeminent only in the sense that it has broad dialectical (interactive) connections with a wide variety of so-called superstructural elements. In fact, Weber argued:

Once the religious fraternization had proven its efficiency as a political and economic instrument of power and was recognized as such it contributed . . . tremendously to the diffusion of the pattern. Mohammed's as well as Jonadab ben Rechab's religious promises are not to be "explained" as products of population phenomena or economic conditions, though their content was co-determined thereby. They were, rather, the expression of personal experiences and intentions. However, the intellectual and social means which they utilized . . . [to] further the great success of creations of this very type are indeed to be understood in terms of such life conditions.[9]

If Weber's methodological acumen had stopped at this point, it would already have been a noteworthy contribution. It would have been, in itself, a successful effort to go beyond both vulgar materialism and abstract notions that preach dialectical analysis without undertaking the historical investigations to fill out abstract forms with specific historical contents.

Weber's emphasis on global historical analysis is a decisive advance that avoids the pitfalls of such approaches.

THE INTERCONNECTION BETWEEN PHENOMENA

Sociological analysis is characterized by the discovery of connections between phenomena and the clarification of substance and meaning that transcends commonsense understandings. The interconnections within sociological portrayals are more conditional, rather than "hard," cause-and-effect logic. Sociology reconstructs the significance of the social world by revealing the systematic connections between elements, which to the untrained eye appear to be discrete, fragmentary, and arranged by chance.

Weber's emphasis on the interconnections between phenomena is exemplified by his explanation of "castes and traditionalism" in India. Why did rational capitalism in India emerge with much difficulty only through English intervention? Weber noted at one of the few points he quoted Marx directly:

Karl Marx has characterized the peculiar position of the artisan in the Indian village—his dependence upon fixed payment in kind instead of upon production for the market—as the reason for the specific "stability of the Asiatic peoples." In this, Marx was correct. . . . In any case, insofar as social stratification is concerned, not only the position of the village artisan but also the caste order as a whole must be viewed as the bearer of stability. One must not think of this effect too directly. One might believe, for instance, that the ritual caste antagonisms had made impossible the development of "large scale enterprises" with a division of labor in the same workshop, and might consider this to be decisive. But such is not the case . . . ; caste has proved just as elastic in the face of the necessities of the concentration of labor in workshops as it did in the face of a need for concentration of labor and service in the noble household. . . . Hence no ritual factor would have been in the way of jointly using different castes in the same large workroom, just as little as the ban upon interest during the Middle Ages, as such, hindered the development of industrial capital. . . . The core of the obstacle did not lie in such particular difficulties . . . ; the obstruction was rather imbedded in the 'spirit' of the whole system. . . . Even if all this has come about, it must still be considered extremely unlikely that the modern organization of industrial capitalism would ever have *originated* on the basis of the caste system. A ritual law in which every change of occupation, every change in work technique, could result in ritual degradation is certainly not capable of giving birth to economic and technical revolutions from within itself, or even to facilitating the first germination of capitalism. . . . The artisan's traditionalism, great in itself, was necessarily heightened to the extreme by the caste order. . . . The traders themselves in their ritual seclusion remained in the shackles of the typical Oriental merchant class, which by itself has never created a modern capitalist organization of labor.[10]

There is no doubt that the interconnections Weber posed to explain specific historical phenomena are still too broad; they invoke categories like stability, traditionalism, and rationality. They might appear to cover historical and social situations which in reality do not correspond or which are indeed not even similar. Weber was conscious of this danger and drew attention to it: "A large number of possible relationships, vaguely perceived, occur to us. . . . It will now be our task to formulate what occurs to us confusedly as clearly as possible, considering the inexhaustible diversity to be found in all historical material. But in order to do this it is necessary to leave behind the vague and general concepts . . . and attempt to penetrate into the peculiar characteristics of and the differences between those great worlds of religions. . . ."[11] Weber was also aware of the danger of eclectic confusions that could occur when data relating to both historical conjunctures and long waves of developmental-historical change are compressed into a single theoretical framework.

THE PROBLEM OF METHOD

Weber was deeply concerned with methodological problems, though he did not have a formalist obsession with techniques. He understood that the method and object of inquiry are inseparable and that method cannot be clarified in a void. The idea that a method, defined exclusively in technical terms, could be applied automatically to any object of inquiry constitutes arbitrary methodologism, a fatal illusion for sociology.[12]

Weber often returned to the interactive character of his research: "It is hence our first concern to work out and to explain genetically the special peculiarity of Occidental rationalism, and within this field that of the modern Occidental form. Every such attempt at explanation must, recognizing the fundamental importance of the economic factor, above all take account of the economic conditions. But at the same time the opposite correlation must not be left out of consideration."[13] Weber was afraid of falling victim to the customary misinterpretation which confuses the awareness of a problem and the precise definition of the object of research with normative evaluation, transforming a typological directory into a scale of value priorities. According to Weber, "the constructed scheme, of course, only serves the purpose of offering an ideal typical means or orientation. It does not teach a philosophy of its own."[14]

Weber's ideal-types direct inquiry toward understandable segments of an infinite empirical world. The types establish a series of plausible and probable empirical interconnections, though these do not constitute absolutely certain empirical knowledge.

The theoretically constructed types of conflicting "life orders" are merely intended to show that at certain points such . . . internal conflicts are possible and "adequate." They are not intended to show that there is no standpoint from which the conflict could not be held to be resolved in a higher synthesis. As will be readily seen, the individual spheres of value are prepared with a rational consistency which is rarely found in reality. But they *can* appear thus in reality and in historically important ways, and they have. Such constructions make it possible to determine the typological locus of a historical phenomenon. They enable us to see if, in particular traits or in their total character, the phenomena approximate one of our constructions: to determine the degree of approximation of the historical phenomenon to the theoretically constructed type.[15]

METHOD AS A REFLECTION ON WORK

Weber stressed immersion in historical, cultural, and social situations and methods that must be elaborated through practice. Methodological questions are simply *reflections on work during work itself,* the thinking aloud of a tireless intellectual artisan. Concentration on method, independent of contents, implies a separation between concepts and techniques of research; this results in inevitable impoverishment of both. Weber recognized the dialectical and historical nature of sociological concepts, which must be constructed and weighed in relation to specific historical contexts; therefore, the object of sociology is society and its social problems. These human conditions are defined neither by the market nor by the customers who fund research but rather by the logic of methodological reflection, which provides the ultimate guarantee of the autonomy of sociological judgment.

The autonomy of sociology is not absolute. On the contrary, it is *directly related to the historical self-placement of the researcher.*[16] This delicate operation of self-placement—or the conscious choice of an explicit point of view—renounces naturalistic objectivism and frankly recognizes the futility of attempts by researchers to place themselves above material interests and the principled taking of positions. Such pure neutrality, if it were possible, would condemn sociology to irrelevance. Thus, Weber's recognition of the relativity of points of view is not an absolute relativism, reflecting universal skepticism and moral indifference. Every point of view, even the most plausibly established, must either be open to critical methodological reflection or risk petrification into dogma. In Weber's perspective points of view, linked to both given and experienced "historical consciousness," should never by hypostasized as eternal, metahistorical forms.

Weber did not resolve the exceptionally difficult methodological problems implied above, especially those concerning the relationship between knowing and evaluating and the equally controversial relationship between intellectual clarity and practical-political decisions (i.e., in the orthodox Marxist literature identified as the relationship between theory and practice). Though Weber understood the significance of these matters, the issue of methodology was, for him as for Marx and all of the great classical sociologists, always secondary to the primary substantive issues.

Classical sociologists did not have narcissistic self-concern about their own discipline. Instead, they attempted to take account of the historical situation in which they were living, its basic characteristics, and the probable historical developments. For them, sociology was *the science of historical social development and its direction and meaning.* Sociological theory and society did not confront each other as external, counterposed realities because theory lay within society. Theory constantly questions society and is continuously called upon to explain it. Therefore, sociology follows from the historical development of society and simultaneously acts as its inseparable shadow.

For these reasons Weber's argument should not be reduced to a critical examination of the relations between religion and society. This view is particularly objectionable when espoused by vulgar anti-Marxists who portray Weber's approach as completely antagonistic to that of Marx. Religion and society should not be conceived crudely as separate spheres because they are, in fact, dialectically related dimensions of the social-historical complex.

THE CONVERGENCE OF WEBER AND MARX: TOWARD A UNITARY SCIENCE OF MAN IN SOCIETY

Weber believed that there is a tension between the religious and the political-economic spheres; however, they do not, in his view, constitute mutually exclusive entities. Instead, the religious and the extra-religious (i.e., worldly and profane) are *at the same time integrated social situations.* The global outlook of Weber's sociological investigations and the search for interconnections, not readily apparent in common sense conceptions, were designed to penetrate this integrated reality. Here, Marx and Weber demonstrated a clear tendency to coincide.

While analyzing Confucianism and Taoism, Weber was struck by the religions' basic anti-individualism and observed: "In China, as in Egypt and Mesopotamia, the technique of knightly combat apparently never led to an individualist social order as strong as that of Homeric Hellas or the Occidental Middle Ages."[17] His explanation of this situation was not sought in ethics, in psychology, or in the socio-political system; rather, the interconnection is geographical and technological: since the population inevitably depended on the regulation of watercourses, the people's total subordination to the Prince's personal bureaucratic government "acted as a counterweight." Here, in a nutshell, is Karl Wittfogel's "hydraulic theory of oriental despotism." Moreover, Weber's observations recall Marx's comments regarding the rationalizing and antitraditional effects of a British-built railway on India's static and technically archaic social system.[18]

In addition, the structure of Weber's reasoning is not unlike that of Marx in *Capital,* where Marx reconstructs masterfully the framework and conditions of the erosion of the working class family through a series of interconnections which start from an innocent technical innovation, the incorporation of the tool in the machine. This seemingly neutral technical innovation specialized the machine while it deskilled the worker. The artisan not only lost control of the means of production, but he was also robbed of control over the disposition of his nervous and muscular energy and sense of direct responsibility regarding work. The worker no longer had the power to decide the inclination of the tool in the cutting of raw material, the machine's cutting speed, or time of production. On the other hand, the incorporation of the tool into the machine made possible the hiring of unskilled and docile female labor; thus, women were removed from their homes to displace their men at work. With a characteristic absence of proletarian sentimentalism, Marx noted that these same workers sold their wives and children on the capitalist labor market and became the new slavetraders.[19]

Marx's ability to develop social theory that captured meaningful interconnections was the basis of his perceptive awareness of nascent, long-term historical trends. Marx's foresight about capitalist concentration, proletarian development, and formation of a class-based industrial society was striking, given that these developments were in their early stages during his lifetime. Despite the proliferation of intermediate strata and status groups, the general thrust of his theory, concerning the concentration of power and the tendency toward a society divided between those who possess and control the means of production and those who are possessed, still represents a profound insight into the nature of modern capitalism.

Weber's sociology also had predictive power. For example, on the basis of a resemblance of the organization of landed property in China and Russia, Weber expressed an almost prophetic insight: "The solvent peasants . . . were typically at the mercy of the arbitrary *kuang kun* or the *kulaki* (fists), as one would say in Russian peasant terminology. . . . [T]he peasant as exposed to the non-propertied villagers organized by the *kuang kun,* thus the *bjednata,* the 'village poor': in the terminology of Bolshevism which, in this respect, might be attractive in China."[20] As with Marx's theory, the general thrust of Weber's sociology, particularly his analysis of rationalization and bureaucratization, was prescient about certain major, modern social developments. Also like Marx, this predictive power derived from the global nature of Weber's social theory and its sensitivity to interconnections between different societal components.

In Weber and Marx there is the foundation for a unitary science of man in society—a global orientation to research which surpasses the scholastic and merely instrumental conception of interdisciplinary approaches. The works of Weber and Marx contrast sharply with recent technocratic division of academic work into numerous independent specializations and the fracture of sociology into separate subareas. Though unitary and global, these approaches were not indulgent toward vague empirical generalizations and imprecise conceptualizations. Despite their encyclopedic scope, the works of Weber and Marx were indeed empirical and based on detailed historical research. They demanded an incisive conceptualization of history, civilizations, and cultures, and their goals were nothing short of understanding the macrotrends of history, converging and shaping the very modernity that the two great thinkers attempted to predict.

I have shown that the vulgar contrasts between Marx's and Weber's work are dated. Given both the fuller understanding of the two theorists that we now possess and our critical distance from the weaker aspects of their analyses, the convergence in their thought is now apparent. The works of Marx and Weber constitute the basis for a rich and unitary conception of man in society. It is our task to elaborate this conception further, applying it both in the continuing effort to understand history and in the action based on this historical knowledge.

Notes

1. Cf. in this connection, Franco Ferrarotti, *Una teologia per atei* (Bari: Laterza, 1983), di. IV; cf. also Ferrarotti, *Max Weber and the Destiny of Reason* (Armonk, N.Y.: M.E. Sharp, 1982).

2. Max Weber, *The Protestant Ethic and the Spirit of Capitalism* (New York: Scribner's, 1958), 55, see also 183, 277.

3. Ibid., 17.

4. Ibid., 25.

5. Ibid.

6. Ibid., 27.

7. Max Weber, *From Max Weber,* trans. and ed. H. H. Gerth and C. Wright Mills (New York: Oxford University Press, 1958), 268.

8. Max Weber, *Ancient Judaism* (Glencoe, Ill.: Free Press, 1952), 79–80.

9. Ibid., 80.

10. Weber, *From Max Weber,* 411–13.

11. Weber, *The Protestant Ethic,* 45.

12. Ferrarotti, *Max Weber and the Destiny of Reason,* 87–121.

13. Weber, *The Protestant Ethic,* 26.

14. Weber, *From Max Weber,* 323.

15. Ibid., 323–24.

16. See in this connection, Franco Ferrarotti, *Storia and storie di vita* (Bari: Laterza, 1981), partially translated in "Biography and the Social Sciences," *Social Research* 50 (1983): 57–80.

17. Max Weber, *The Religion of China* (New York: Free Press, 1968), 24–25.

18. Karl Marx, *The Portable Karl Marx,* ed. Eugene Kamenka (New York: Penguin, 1983), 337–41.

19. Karl Marx, *Capital* (New York: International Publishers, 1967), 1: 371–402.

20. Max Weber, *Religion of China,* 94.

PART V / Politics

V/XV/

Ira J. Cohen   **The Underemphasis on Democracy in
Marx and Weber**

In this essay I aim to challenge the adequacy of the
theoretical orientations of Marx and Weber as a means to analyze the more
positive characteristics of Western democracy. I have no intention to
diminish the value of their insight regarding the obstacles to democracy
inherent in the nature and consequences of capitalism and the bureaucratic
state. The systemic suppression of democratic opportunities and ideals
continues to be visible throughout the West. Yet these antidemocratic
forces need not blind us to the fact that Western societies are unique in the
extent to which democratic institutions have been established and employed. True, the consequences of this democratization have served
primarily as a defense against capitalist exploitation and other forms of
oppression. Moreover, the struggle to establish democratic institutions has
not been equally successful in all nations. These qualifications notwithstanding, the representative mechanisms and legally guaranteed rights of
political participation that are part of the way of life in most Western
societies represent notable achievements by contrast with the authoritarianism which prevails in both state-socialist and many Third World countries.

Marx's and Weber's failure to underscore the significance of these
achievements is exemplified in their respective observations on the development of state policy for social reform. Consider first Marx's approach to the
genesis of the British Factory Acts. The fact that an alliance of working-
class and other groups was primarily responsible for the passage of
legislation for the improvement of industrial working conditions fore-
shadows the opportunities for democratic initiatives by oppressed groups
which parliamentary institutions subsequently have introduced. Marx

discloses the massive exploitation untouched by the Acts, as well as the consequences of the Acts that augmented the development of the capitalist economy. He also acknowledges the democratic support which stood behind the Acts,[1] but he overlooks the significance of the parliamentary processes that facilitated their passage.

Although differing from Marx in many respects, Weber, too, overlooks the democratic origins of social reform. This is exemplified in his abstract account of the foundations of state welfare policies in which democratic institutions play no role. Rather, the foundations are located in the patrimonial status ethic of state bureaucratic officials and their related antipathy to the pursuit of profit. According to Weber, the same motives determine the limits and peculiarities of such policies.[2]

In fairness it must be acknowledged that neither Marx nor Weber could have foreseen the ways in which, over the last half century, labor movements and civil rights organizations have fought for and employed democratic institutions. If modern social scientists were less deeply indebted to the works of both theorists, matters might be laid to rest. Given their continuing influence this cannot be done: for unless we take notice of why Marx and Weber failed to emphasize the significance of Western democratic rights and institutions, we will perpetuate their oversights.

This paper concentrates on the nature and implications for democratic theory of central postulates in Marx's and Weber's theoretical frameworks. Marx presupposed an exaggerated conception of the capacity for democratization, while Weber postulated an imbalanced account of the inevitability of inequality and the imposition of domination.[3] Although almost diametrically opposed, these assumptions predispose a similar deflation of the positive aspects of modern democracy. I suggest one reason for this outcome is the failure of Marx and Weber to adopt a concept of the exercise of power suitable for the analysis of democracy's possibilities as well as its impediments.

The claim that Marx underestimates the emergence of democracy in capitalist societies does not negate his views of the inverted development of democratic principles in the structures of the capitalist mode of production, nor does it deny his faith in the democratic *telos* of proletarian revolution. However, this faith no longer can be sustained against the backdrop of a century in which such democratic revolutions have yet to occur. The Marxian *oeuvre* is most often read as a source of insight into the alienation and exploitation endemic in the structure and relations of capitalist societies. Though I draw upon the concept of democracy which informs Marx's historical materialist outlook, his philosophy of history is not of central concern; rather, attention will focus on how this concept of democracy figures in his analysis of capitalist society.

Along a different line, to argue that weaknesses exist in Weber's orientation to democracy is not to overlook his interest in the liberal implications of modernization processes. The freedom of the individual is a deep concern throughout his work, but this concern for individual freedom is not equivalent to a concern for democracy. An analytical difference between these concepts must be recognized.

Though democracy must presuppose individual freedom, the concept more directly refers to the nature of socio-political relationships. Two basic categories must be identified. *Representative democracy* refers to a state that provides structural means to ensure the accountability of policy makers to the politically expressed interests of those whom they serve. *Substantive democracy* refers to democratic communities or public spheres within which reciprocal relationships generate broad or specific interests in the direction and consequences of public affairs. Although a comprehensive theory of democracy requires attention to both categories and their interrelationship, for present purposes they will be treated as analytically distinct.

I

THE INVERSION OF SUBSTANTIVE DEMOCRACY IN MARX'S ACCOUNT OF CAPITALIST SOCIETY

A basic theme in Marx's early writing is the critique of Hegel's claim that the state pursues a universal interest in the common good which transcends the conflicts over private interests in civil society. Marx has no quarrel with the notion that society should be organized to pursue universal ends, but the Hegelian theory of the state mistakes this ideal for reality. According to Hegel, the transcendence of private struggles requires both that the state be severed from civil society and that it abstract political allegiance from all other relationships in the civil sphere. For Marx the modern state has no capacity to perform such abstractions; rather, the state is itself the outcome of the conduct of affairs in civil society. Since the latter consists of egoistic conflicts, it is impossible to claim that the state pursues the universal interest in the common good.[4]

During the course of his arguments Marx by no means overlooks the transformation of state structures. He is well aware that Western constitutions had begun to recognize the rights of man (i.e., formal freedoms). However, though he appreciates the struggle to establish these rights, he deflates radically their significance. These constitutional rights, he asserts, leave untouched and indeed facilitate the selfish pursuit of private interests. The individual remains supreme while the political community formally preserves his/her personal prerogatives.[5]

Marx's early conception of substantive, or "true," democracy underlies this critical line of thought. "True" democracy refers to a situation where the formal constitution no longer stands in abstraction from civil society. Rather, the constitution is determined by the people and in return permeates their social life.[6] Hence in "true" democracy:

Man does not exist because of the law but rather law exists for the good of man. Democracy is *human existence* while in other political forms man has only *legal* existence. . . . In [true] democracy the formal principle is simultaneously the material principle. For that reason it is the first true unity of the universal and the particular.[7]

The equation of "true" democracy and human existence provides the ultimate justification for this argument. In a variety of references to species characteristics and to man's communal nature, Marx proposes that the human existence of man is something other than egoistic individuation. Man has the unique capacity to control the production of the material and intellectual circumstances of social life and to be absorbed within the communal context which is the ongoing creation of the species.[8] Human existence occurs when the needs and relationships of the individual draw upon and reaffirm man's social or communal being,[9] and true democracy is a political conceptualization of the species' capacity to transcend the distinction between societal and individual interests.

Marx's early writings draw attention to the fact that this capacity has not yet been realized. Marx viewed, against the backdrop of true democracy, the selfish conflicts in civil society as rule by the "inhuman conditions and elements [of] the whole organization of our society." Man "is not yet a real species being."[10] While democracy is the concommitant of human existence, modern civil society is its antithesis, the dehumanized, "political animal world."[11]

Although these arguments are developed in philosophical terms, they reveal an important element of Marx's overall analytic strategy. Both "true" democracy and the species characteristics establish capacities for a mode of social existence which far exceeds present limits. These concepts are intrinsic to Marx's philosophy of history, but they also are baseline criteria against which the fundamental characteristics of modern society are examined and assessed. As a result, analysis and critique are joined in a common endeavor: the disclosure of the suppression in capitalistic society of the human capacity to be absorbed in the production and reproduction of a substantive democratic community. Marx's dismissive account of constitutionally guaranteed freedoms is consistent with this approach. The legal protection of individual rights appears of little intrinsic importance in contrast to the communal relationships in true democracy. There is much in Marx's work which is augmented and transformed in his analyses of capitalist societies, but this general strategy appears throughout his work; his accounts of alienation and the consequences of exploitation provide opposite examples of how this occurs.

Marx's conception of alienation developed during his transition from the critique of Hegel to the critique of political economy. It is here that the significance of labor and class analysis becomes central to his thought, and at the same time he no longer refers to "true" democracy. However, this does not mean that he shed his concern for a democratic society in which the interests of one are united with the interests of all. In a précis of social relationships in communal production written in 1844, Marx transforms his democratic vision in a manner consistent with his new theoretical perspective. Such relationships involve: (1) the objectification of the producer's individuality in his/her product; (2) the producer's gratification from knowing that the product has satisfied the need of another; (3) the sense of complementarity in social relationships that proceed on this basis; and (4) the confirmation through this sense of the producer's "human, communal nature."[12] The last of these points reaffirms Marx's emphasis on the species potential for democratic relationships. The four points, *in toto,* imply the transcendence of egoistic individualism, central to the earlier concept of true democracy. But now Marx infuses this transcendence by developing emphasis upon the importance of labor.

This account undoubtedly constitutes an early conception of Marx's vision of communist society.[13] However, it does not contradict the concept of "true" democracy. Although communism may be a more comprehensive concept, several commentators have observed that there is no fundamental difference in the nature of the socio-political relations to which both terms refer.[14] Since the term communism has taken on antidemocratic connotations in modern state-socialist societies, henceforth I shall note this continuity by employing the term *communist democracy.*[15]

The preceeding summary of social relations in communist democracy has implications for the interpretation of Marx's analysis of alienation. Like "true" democracy in this earlier work, it can be shown that the account of communal relations of production serves as a criterion which is used to disclose the oppressive characteristics of capitalist social relations; alienation appears as the suppression of the human capacity to engage in these communal relations. Before illustrating how this occurs, the class-specific nature of capitalist alienation should be mentioned.

Since the potential for communist democratic social relations refers to humanity at large, to interpret alienation as the suppression of this potential requires that the concept apply to both the bourgeoisie and the proletariat. Marx establishes this when he observes:

The propertied class and the class of the proletariat present the same human self-alienation. But the former class finds in this self-alienation its confirmation and its good, its own power: it has a semblance of human existence. The class of the proletariat feels annihilated in its self-alienation; it sees in it its own powerlessness and the reality of an inhuman existence.[16]

Thus, though alienation is common to both classes, only the proletariat experiences the annihilation and powerlessness which capitalism entails. The inhuman existence of the alienated proletariat corresponds to Marx's description of the "political animal world" of civil society. Both usages imply that the human capacity for democratic relationships has been suppressed.

This point is demonstrated by reading the four forms in which Marx describes the alienation of labor[17] against the four-fold précis of communal social relations summarized above: alienation from the product suppresses gratification from knowledge that the product satisfies a human need (point two above); alienation from the labor process suppresses the objectification of individuality in the product (point one above); alienation from fellow workers suppresses the sense of complementarity in social relations (point three above); and alienation from species-being suppresses the confirmation, through labor, of the worker's communal nature (point four above). In general, the two sets of concepts appear diametrically opposed. The alienation of the proletariat is the inversion of their capacity to conduct social relations in a communist democracy.

Capitalist exploitation of the proletariat becomes central to Marx's thought only after he is immersed fully in the critique of political economy and has developed the theory of surplus value. At that time changes occur in his vision of communist democratic social relations. On the one hand, references to species-capacities are submerged entirely within his philosophy of history and the *telos* of proletarian revolution; on the other, his conception of post-capitalist society introduces a realm of freedom beyond the production processes per se. These changes notwithstanding, above all else Marx remains committed to the view that a democratization of social relations is possible to achieve.[18] Thus, this view continues to provide a context against which the consequences of proletarian exploitation are disclosed and assessed. The discussion of the intensification of production provides a crucial case in point.

Capitalist intensification of production (which, importantly, does not advance in a linear direction) increases the extraction of surplus values.

Yet, in Marx's view, the satisfaction of human needs, measured in terms of use value, does not require the exhaustive expansion of productive output. Were capitalist exploitation to cease, "socialized man, the associated producers [would] govern the human metabolism with nature in a rational way, bringing it about under their collective control instead of being dominated by it as a blind power; accomplishing it with the least expenditure of energy and in conditions most worthy for their human nature." As a result, all needs would be met, and, at the same time, a realm of freedom beyond production would be created in which the development of human powers would be an end in itself.[19]

Since capitalism is not under the worker's control, these desirable possibilities undergo a complete inversion.[20] As the exploitation is intensified:

all means for the development of production becomes means of domination and exploitation of the producers, they distort the worker into a fragment of a man, they degrade him to the level of an appendage of a machine, they destroy the actual content of his labor by turning it into torment; they alienate from him the intellectual potentialities of the labor process . . . ; they deform the conditions under which he works, subject him during the labor process to a despotism the more hateful for its meanness. . . .[21]

As in the case of alienation, the consequences of the intensification of capitalist exploitation appear inversely related to Marx's vision of communist democracy. Marx summarizes that within capitalism: "individuals are subordinated to social production which exists . . . as a sort of fate, but social production is not subordinated to the individuals who manipulate it as their communal capacity."[22]

From Marx's critique of constitutional freedoms to his accounts of proletarian alienation and the consequences of exploitation, the capacity for a comprehensive substantive democracy serves as a criterion against which he establishes the oppressive nature of the capitalist system. Incisive as it is, this strategy is inadequate to disclose the more positive, albeit limited, trends toward democratization in capitalist societies; the problem is that the capacity for democracy anticipates harmonious social relationships where the interests of society and the interests of individuals converge (i.e., the good of one is the good of all). But presupposing this standard to assess the degree of democratization compares to the adoption of the potential for exemplary virtue as a basis to establish the moral character of human behavior. In both cases it is far easier to disclose deviations than approximations.

This strategy, in some measure, accounts for the asymmetry between the theoretical depth of Marx's analyses of alienation and exploitation and his superficial treatment of the democratic character of the proletarian movement, which fails to incorporate a corresponding theory. From a teleological standpoint Marx assumed, far more than he demonstrated, that the revolutionary *praxis* of the proletariat would realize the principles of communist democracy that were immanent but inverted in capitalist societies. However, once this philosophy of history is set aside, the remaining image is of a proletariat almost completely overwhelmed by capitalist oppression. Hence, Marx speaks of the alienated worker as feeling annihilated, while increasing exploitation leaves that worker distorted, degraded, and subordinated to capitalism as "a sort of fate."

To describe the proletariat in these terms may have been correct in Marx's own era, but not in the twentieth century. Though nothing resembling the revolutionary formation of a substantive democracy has occurred, labor movements have succeeded in establishing barriers against significant forms of capitalist oppression; the positive accomplishments of these democratic movements require explanation. Marx's overriding concern for the ways in which proletarian alienation and exploitation suppress the potential for democratic social relationships does not contribute to this goal. Indeed Marx often deflates the significance of labor movement programs which do not conform to his radically democratic communist standards,[23] an outlook also characteristic of Marx's approach to representative democracy.

MARX'S CRITIQUE OF REPRESENTATIVE DEMOCRACY

Marx's most extensive observations on representative democracy are in his Hegelian critiques. For Hegel, legislative representation mediates between the individual interests in civil society and the universal interest pursued by the state. Marx objects to this point because political representation leaves the social relationships in civil society untouched; hence, legislative delegates pursue their private interests,[24] and the mediation between the universal and the individual interest never occurs.[25]

As indicated, the central element of Marx's early conception of "true" democracy is the resolution of this distinction between universal and individual interests. "True" democracy merges the civil and political social realms. Given this unity, Marx holds that the meaning of representation is thoroughly transformed.

In this situation legislative power altogether loses the meaning of representative power. Here, the legislature is a representation in the same sense in which every function is representation. For example, the shoemaker is my representative in so far as he fulfills a social need, just as every definite social activity, because it is a species-activity represents only the species.[26]

Legislative representation is simply a political aspect of the complementarity in social relationships intrinsic to his view of true democracy. This conception of representation underpins Marx's critical analysis of modern forms of political representation. Beyond parliamentary politics per se this critique extends to the universal suffrage movement. Marx recognizes that implicit in this development is the principle that the state should represent the universal interest. Indeed this marks an important advance over preceding forms of state.[27] However, where civil society forms an arena of material conflict, rather than a substantive democratic community, this principle remains unrealizable. Thus, the removal of property qualifications for voting rights in itself does not institute popular sovereignty; rather, "the state . . . allows private property, education, occupation, to *act* after *their* own fashion . . . and to manifest their particular nature. Far from abolishing these *effective* differences [the state] only exists so far as they are presupposed."[28]

The critique of representative democracy in Marx's early writings reduces the *form* of political representation to the *content* of interests in civil society.[29] Once Marx embarks upon his analysis of capitalist society, this critique is no longer central to his theoretical arguments. However, a passage in *Capital* reveals the continuity in his thought on the topic. In capitalist societies the antagonistic relationship between the owners of the means of production and the producers "is the . . . hidden basis of the entire social edifice, and hence also the political form of the relationship of sovereignty and dependence, in short the specific form of state."[30]

Representative political processes are dealt with more extensively in Marx's later political and historical writings. At moments Marx endorses parliamentary institutions and universal suffrage as devices conducive to the development of proletarian revolution.[31] There is also the brief but well-known passage in *The Civil War in France,* where Marx mentions the need for a minimal, democratically controlled state in the socialist transition from capitalism.[32] More generally, however, he adopts a denunciatory tone.[33] For example, he dismisses the goal of the German "democratic constitutional" petit-bourgeois to establish a federated democratic republic. Though such movements are to be exploited for revolutionary ends, nowhere is it indicated that a more democratized state is significant in its own right.[34] A similar position is adopted in the *Critique of the Gotha Program.* The German Workers' Party's demands to establish universal suffrage and direct legislation contain nothing beyond "the old democratic litany." Such demands are inadequate because they leave the basis of the bourgeois state untouched when it is crucial to convert the state "from an organ superimposed upon society into one completely subordinated to it."[35] Just as in his Hegelian critiques, the resolution of the antimony between state and civil society remains the criterion against which Marx assesses all movements toward democratization.

One need not deny that the structure of the state in capitalist societies restricts the control it may exercise over the exploitation of labor in order to criticize Marx's dismissive approach to representative political processes. Although the outcome of these processes often serves capitalist interests, it is also true that twentieth-century parliamentary representation based upon universal suffrage has become a resource of great consequence in the struggle against working-class oppression. Marx's failure to anticipate the configuration of political struggles, introduced by representational politics, provides the clearest indication of the weaknesses in his approach to democratic issues.

THE DEMOCRATIC IRONY OF MARX'S THOUGHT

A commitment to substantive democracy pervades the entirety of Marx's thought. On this basis he perceived the manifold ways in which capitalism suppresses and obstructs a society, democratic in fact as well as in name. Ironically, this same commitment inhibits his analysis of the democratizing trends in Western societies.

Marx underemphasizes the significance of Western democracy because he presupposes a society can be created in which communal harmony reigns supreme. This complete fulfillment of substantive democratic ideals presumes that society can transcend all institutional and personal imbalances of power. Although this image is compelling in principle, few would argue that it is possible to achieve in modern societies. The need to coordinate the massive institutions in the West (industrially and administratively diversified and culturally heterogeneous) generates problems in the exercise of power which the presupposition of the capacity for communist democracy does not address. Analyses which assume this capacity may identify sources of capitalistic oppression, but because they lack a realistic theory of postcapitalist democratic exercise of power they cannot establish the positive foundations for a democratic society. The inevitability of the exercise of power certainly requires that even the most ideal socialist society retain the traditional guaranteed rights of political participation and mechanism of representative democracy which are part of our heritage. But Marx fails to emphasize the significance of this legacy.

Hal Draper observes that Marx drove the political logic of democratic demands to its end, thereby coming into conflict with bourgeois democracy.[36] Beyond all else, this exaggerates the prospects for substantive democracy. If we continue to regard Marx's analysis of alienation and exploitation as important resources for the development of modern social theory and if the formation of a socialist society remains an impelling goal, the inadequacies of Marx's work present a formidable challenge. We must develop accounts of the possibility for more extensive democratization and employ them as a backdrop for realistic analyses of the foundations of, as well as impediments to, democracy.

II

WEBER AND WESTERN DEMOCRACY

While Marx overstates the logic of democratic demands, Weber exaggerates the forces which impede them. This is not to say that Weber dismisses the virtues of the democratic agenda; in fact, his political writings reveal a lifelong struggle to reconcile commitments to liberalism and democracy with German nationalism and the German role in international power politics. The significance of this particular constellation of values and objectives is difficult to disengage from the peculiar context of post-Bismarckian social and political relationships addressed in Weber's political essays. But this problem can be overlooked insofar as Weber, unlike Marx, did not fuse his analytical and critical perspectives. The value-relevant theme that informs his analytical writings derives from his interest in the extent to which various modes of impersonal and amoral formal rationality have penetrated all spheres of life in Western civilization. The value postulates behind this theme reflect Weber's concern for the individual's autonomy and commitments.[37] Though this theme is relevant to democratic socio-political relationships, it does not provide the analytical assumptions which predispose his view of the dismal prospects for democracy.

Although Weber may have been methodologically averse to universal postulates, several assumptions of this kind appear in his work. They are universal in the sense that they admit no exceptions. At the same time, they are defined to allow polymorphic variations, preserving the historical flexibility which is a hallmark of Weber's analytic perspective. Two of these postulates are particularly relevant to Weber's orientation to democracy.

The first postulate refers to the inevitability of selection processes which establish forms of inequality, based upon social or biological criteria, in all social orders. In Weber's terms:

Selection is inevitable because apparently no way can be worked out of eliminating it completely. Even the most strictly pacific order can eliminate means of conflict and the objects and impulses to conflict only partially. . . . [E]ven on the utopian assumption that all competition were completely eliminated, conditions would still lead to a latent process of selection which would favor the types best adapted to the conditions, whether their relevant qualities were mainly determined by heredity or environment.[38]

Because of ineradicable social conflict in every society, selective factors afford certain types of persons the opportunity to rise to positions of superiority.[39]

The second postulate concerns the ubiquitous influence of structures of domination.

Without exception every sphere of social action is profoundly influenced by structures of dominancy. In a great number of cases the emergence of rational association from amorphous social action has been due to domination and the way in which it has been exercised. Even where this is not the case, the structure of dominancy is decisive in determining the form of social action and its orientation toward a "goal."[40]

Domination refers to authoritarian powers which establish a relationship of command and obedience between the rulers and the ruled.[41] Weber nowhere indicates that structures of domination are homologous with structures of inequality, but it is obvious that selection processes will operate to fill the ruling positions in social structures.

It is important to stress the unqualified nature of Weber's remarks on the inevitability of both the selective generation of forms of inequality and the ubiquitous influence of structures of domination. Indeed, they are unparalleled in Weber's work by any similarly universal postulates concerning communal or consensual social relations. In fact, Weber notes that coercion is common and selection is inevitable in communal relationships.[42] Consensual order, on the other hand, is specifically limited to the special case of voluntary personal agreement among all members of a social organization; all other forms of social order are said to be imposed in some measure on acquiescent actors. For example, constitutions are conceived to establish specific limits within which the administrative staff and the actions of groups members at large will be at the disposal of the leader.[43]

It would be difficult to overstate the differences between these analytical postulates and Marx's presupposition of the potential creation of a full, substantive democracy, and, given these differences, it is not surprising that Weber disagrees with Marx in both tone and substance about Western democracy. Yet, despite these disagreements, the fact remains that Weber's presuppositions, like those of Marx, stand behind the underestimation of democracy in his ideal-types addressed to Western political life.[44]

DOMINATION AND INEQUALITY IN WEBER'S VIEW OF REPRESENTATIVE DEMOCRACY

Weber devotes more attention than Marx to the structures and processes of representative democracy. Over the past twenty years, Weber's views on this topic have been interpreted in a number of excellent commentaries,[45] but these analyses have not focused on how Weber's position develops from his universal postulates concerning inequality and domination. The emergence of this line of thought can be traced to Weber's exposition of the direct democracy concept.[46] Direct democracy refers to a situation where the powers of command in small groups are controlled by the will of its members; however, inequality and domination pose problems (introduced at the start of this discussion), and even the smallest group must delegate at least some "imperative powers" to designated officials. Democratic control over officials is maintained only if there is no need for technical expertise. Once this seemingly minor degree of competence-based inequality is introduced, the democratic exercise of power is threatened; and once the size of the organization exceeds a few thousand members, administrative domination is inevitable.[47]

The need for expertise is not the only path from inequality to domination in direct democracy. Economic differentiation produces similar results because the economically advantaged (especially those also privileged in status-honor) alone possess the time and income to undertake the administrative offices of the group; this results in rule by notables.[48]

The antidemocratic influence of technical expertise and socio-economic advantage increases as the group expands in size and develops more hierarchical structures of inequality. On the one hand, as inequality develops, control of administrative positions becomes an object of conflict between the advantaged (notables and others) and those less advantaged in wealth and prestige; as a result, political parties emerge to pursue domination within the group. On the other hand, the need for an expansion of the administrative structure necessarily accompanies an increase in group size; the rise of a competence-based stratum of officials is now inevitable. Weber asserts that once mass administration is involved, the meaning of democracy must be radically transformed.[49]

The ideal-typical account of the control of public policy in the massive administrative structures of the modern state portrays overwhelming antidemocratic trends; this is the realm of representative democracy. Although Weber presents five types of representation, only two are relevant to the modern state. The less significant of the two is representation by agents of interest groups. This form clearly corresponds to the Durkheim-ian conception of corporatist representation in parliamentary bodies, and Weber is far less optimistic than Durkheim. The inequalities and antagonism of class (and analogous divisions in socialist societies) make it likely that internal conflicts, rather than consensus on issues of parliamentary deliberation, will predominate in corporatist political organizations.[50] This leaves the election of parliamentary delegates as the principal modern form of political representation. These delegates are free in the sense that they are not bound to follow the dictates of the electorate. Marx casts this freedom in an antidemocratic light insofar as it facilitates the influence of class-bound private interests. Weber, too, underscores the obstructions to the democratic potential of political representation, but his discussion places more emphasis on the bureaucratic dynamics of political parties.

Weber's conception of the way that the "law of small numbers" (which in some measure replies to Michels's "Iron Law of Oligarchy")[51] operates in political parties does not require detailed recapitulation. The central points are that the pursuit of domination in the state results inevitably in the bureaucratization of party structures and that the administration of these pursuits necessarily impels the formation of a coordinated party elite who quite often live "off politics."[52] What is less often discussed is that the law of small numbers establishes party leadership through a selective process based upon political expertise: the more bureaucratization of the party advances and the greater the interests in the rewards which accrue to its leaders, the more surely political experts will assume the positions of party controls.[53] Thus, it is not surprising that domination and inequality are emphasized in Weber's account of party organization as a whole and its relationship to the citizenry. In all forms of political parties

there is a central group of individuals who assume active direction of party affairs, including the formulation of programs and the selection of candidates. There is secondly, a group of "members" whose role is notably more passive, and finally the great mass of citizens whose role is only that of solicitation by the various parties. They merely choose between the various candidates and programs offered by the different parties.[54]

Political parties constitute specific instances of selective inequality which collectively dominate the relationship between the state and the governed. Party existence reverses the representative democratic process; instead of directing public policy, the citizenry and party members are reduced to passively responding to the policies and candidates presented by the party elites. It is noteworthy that Weber places little emphasis on the need of the elites either to appeal to the voters or to curry the favor of parliamentary delegates. Rather at one point, he suggests that the voters are "merely objects" whose votes are sought at election time,[55] and, at another, he observes that elected representatives tend to become the "servants" of the party elites.[56]

Weber's view of the conduct of political campaigns suggests additional reasons for the reversal of representative democratic procedures. The cost of such campaigns, combined with the need for stable government, precludes the possibility of frequent elections and referenda. When elections *are* held, the appeal to voters relies heavily on superficial advertising and emotional rhetoric rather than on the substantive interests represented by party policy and candidates (Weber makes an exception for economic interests).[57] Because of the expense such campaigns incur, the source of party funds becomes an equal, if not greater, force than all other influences on party affairs; frequently a "crypto-plutocratic" distribution of power results.[58]

It is important to consider the role of the legislative body in the formation of state policy where a new constellation of inequality and domination further impedes the prospects for representative democracy. The leaders of the state administrative agencies form bureaucratic elites who employ the indispensability of their agencies, their technical expertise, and their control of official secrets as means to advance their own "pure power interests" over and against parliament itself. Regardless of their particular form, parliamentary bodies are said to be ill-equipped to confront administrative leaders who possess these resources.[59]

The only political official who can effectively forestall the domination of state policy by the bureaucratic elite and simultaneously allow an avenue of democratic access to policy formation is the plebiscitarian, or "Caesarist," head of state. Although the charismatic appeal of this type of leader may catalyze public opinion and thus ultimately transcend the restrictions of party politics, it seems difficult to consider this appeal a basis for the representation of citizen interests. Despite a complex of legal restraints, the plebiscitarian leader appears to lead the people more than that leader is led by them.[60] This point is illustrated in the autonomy of the leader's decision which is presupposed in Weber's exposition of the political ethics of responsibility and ultimate ends.[61]

The preceding discussion underscores the extent to which Weber's ideal-typical analysis of representative democratic process is consistent with his postulates of the universality of inequality and the influence of structures of domination. This account all but forecloses the possible means by which the electorate may influence policy formation. Indeed, with the exception of the "Caesarist" leader, the power of party elites, their financial supporters, and the elites controlling the bureaucratic agencies of state is so pervasive that there is no separate category devoted exclusively to the successful influence of the citizenry on the conduct of state affairs in *Economy and Society*. To understand the limits of Weber's point of view this omission should be contrasted with the prominence of representative political processes in the works of theorists such as Tocqueville or T. H. Marshall.

THE WEBERIAN IMPEDIMENTS TO SUBSTANTIVE DEMOCRACY

Since inequality and domination compromise the development of communal action and consensual order in large-scale societies, it follows that the prospects for substantive democracy do not figure prominently in Weber's conceptual analyses. Even his occasional remarks on the personal freedoms made possible by the differentiation of spheres of life must be construed in this light. Such freedoms refer to the individual's decision to commit to participation in particular spheres; however, once the actor does so, the actor's freedom becomes enormously limited.[62] Weber's accounts of the legitimation of authority and the demands for social justice in his sociology of law suggest a focus on the formation and pursuit of popular interests in the conduct of state affairs, but in each instance there are limiting qualifications. Moving against such trends toward democratization of socio-political relations are the modes of inequality and domination introduced by the capitalist economy and the bureaucratic state.

According to Weber, capitalism is the "most fateful force in our modern social life,"[63] if only because the class situations which it generates "have become unambiguously and openly visible to everyone as the factor determining every man's fate."[64] Class situation consists in differential life chances distributed through competition in various labor and commodity markets. Such markets, therefore, constitute the most influential means for the production of selective inequality in modern Western societies.[65]

Although Weber's definition of class differs from that of Marx, his most salient class distinction remains between capitalist employers and the proletariat. Within the firm or enterprise this class inequality is transformed into a relationship of domination; domination occurs despite the existence of the formally free labor contract. In general, the worker's freedom to accept or reject such contracts is severely limited by the pressing nature of the worker's economic needs. Therefore, the employer normally can impose contractual terms on a "take it or leave it" basis.[66] Once employed, workers are often subjected to quite severe discipline. Weber's account of the most advanced forms of industrial discipline such as "scientific management" (which he believed to be advancing in an inexorable manner) resembles Marx's analysis of alienation.[67] Weber also echoes Marx's outlook when he observes that the proletariat is subjected to impersonal, "masterless slavery" within the formal-rational capitalist enterprise.[68]

Although Weber frequently acknowledges the existence of socialist political parties in a disparaging manner, he presents few means by which workers can forestall the authoritarian powers of command imposed upon them by their capitalist employers. Indeed, it is quite surprising that the massive compendium of categories and definitions in *Economy and Society* includes no section dedicated to the nature or consequences of unions, strikes, or other rebellious industrial actions. Rather, the most prominent means for the redress of workers' grievances to appear in this work (other than political parties dominated by their elites) is the judiciary's responsiveness to the proletarian demand that the legal code recognize "social justice" as a foundational principle.[69] Such demands soften the formal rational amorality of legal codes and juridical decisions, but it is by no means certain that their implementation will serve working class interests.[70] Even where the degree of legal formality is relatively low (e.g., in the case of British Common Law), Weber observes that the interests of the legal profession and the cost of legal services often dispose the administration of justice against those with inadequate means.[71] This does not amount to a dismissal of all possibilities that the workers' demands for social justice will be met; however, it does limit the frequency of the occasions when such will be the case.

The bureaucratic state is the second sphere where inequality and domination interfere with the formation of effective democratic interests. Inequality appears on two levels. First, within state administrative agencies bureaucratic elites achieve power on the basis of their technical and political competence in a manner analogous to the formation of elites in political parties.[72] This domination involves the submission of subordinate officials to their superiors, based upon the formal requirements of the lower office. Second, the distinction between the bureaucratic state and the society which it governs is of crucial importance since it depends on a relationship of domination that is, in part, the ironic result of demands for democratization.

Weber recognizes that belief in the rights of man now penetrates to some degree all quarters of Western political life. Stimulated by a commitment to these rights, advocates of democratization seek to proscribe all elements of socio-economic privilege or bias in the conduct of state affairs. These demands translate into an interest in the abstract routinization of the exercise of authority, which, in turn, supports the bureaucratization of the state.[73] The result is to "level" the significance of all socio-economic differences among those who must seek or who are subjected to the services of the state. Therefore, Weber asserts, "one must always remember that the term 'democratization' can be misleading. The *demos* itself, in the sense of a shapeless mass never governs larger associations, but rather is governed."[74]

There are several qualifications. Weber observes that the democratic aversion to the arbitrary exercise of authority at times may generate the demand for the election of bureaucratic officials. Such elections can modify the rigidity of the bureaucratic hierarchy of subordination, but they could have democratic implications only if the electoral process were conceived to transmit the interests of the governed. As it is, the candidates generally owe their allegiance to the party elites. Moreover, even when this is not the case, the technical inexperience of elected officials often results in subsequent demands for administrative reform. These demands redound upon the party in power at the next election and strengthen the likelihood that administrative officials will be appointed in the future.[75]

Second, a concern for the welfare of the governed is present among bureaucratic officials. However, this orientation does not arise in response to the self-expressed interests of the state clientele; rather, it results from the presence of a status ethic within the state bureaucracy rooted in premodern patrimonial forms of administration. From this standpoint the satisfaction of the needs of those subject to state authority corresponds to the interest of the officials in the protection of their positions and preservation of public peace.[76] (I alluded to these interests in my introduction.)

Finally, the concept of legitimacy must be addressed. At first glance there is an inconsistency between this concept and Weber's analysis of the domination of the governed by the bureaucratic state. For if the *demos* is sincerely motivated to accept the legal norms which legitimate state edicts, then presumably they have given their democratic assent to be governed. But several recent analysts have established that Weber's conception of legitimacy does not imply that all those who accept the legitimacy of such norms are impelled by a belief in their validity,[77] although it is likely that at least some of those subjected to authority will be so motivated. In his most extensive discussion of the issue, Weber offers a wide range of reasons why actors may submit without belief to legitimate norms. Loyalty may be hypocritically simulated by individuals or groups on opportunistic grounds (i.e., carried out for reasons of material self-interest), and, alternatively, individuals may submit to authority out of sheer weakness or helplessness.[78] Hence, legitimacy does not necessarily imply the consent to be governed.

Weber's brief remarks on democratic legitimacy[79] must be construed in this light. Democratic legitimacy rests on the formal freedom to elect officials and the belief in the plebiscitary right to enact, recognize, or appeal laws. In the strongest sense democratic legitimacy only implies the confidence of the ruled: a far cry in itself from the direction of public policy by the *demos*. Recalling his implicit skepticism toward the sincerity of belief in legitimating norms, Weber further weakens this concept in his commentary on the democratic plebiscite: "Regardless of how its real value as an expression of the popular will may be regarded, the plebiscite has been the specific means of *deriving* the legitimacy of authority from the confidence of the ruled, *even though the voluntary nature of such confidence is only formal or fictitious*"[80] (my emphases). Democratic legitimacy thus appears of more significance as a derivation of authority than as a sincere expression of the assent to be governed.

WEBER'S UNBALANCED ORIENTATION TO THE PROSPECTS FOR DEMOCRACY

The preceding discussion draws attention to the ways in which Weber's underlying emphasis on inequality and domination are implicated in his ideal-typical analysis of the impediments to democracy. His accounts of the subversion of political representation by party and administrative elites and his analysis of the relationships between capitalists and workers, as well as between political and administrative officials and the citizenry, raise severe doubts about the possibility of democracy. Yet, Weber's discussions of both working-class demands for substantive justice and attempts by democratic partisans to limit the autonomy of bureaucratic state officials establish a subdued recognition that democratic demands sometimes emerge from the body politic. At one point, Weber extends himself further, albeit in a heavily qualified passage, and asserts that "democratization" may, in certain situations, imply "an increasingly active share of the subject of the subjects in government."[81]

Here, we arrive at the limits of his outlook. While party politics, capitalism, and the bureaucratic state continue to impede the realization of anything resembling a fully democratized society, in certain situations broad segments of the population in Western societies have met with success in directing public policy on behalf of their interests. Aside from the labor movements, prominent examples include the international movements for women's rights, the protection of the environment from toxic pollution, the state guarantee of welfare services, mobilization against the Vietnam war, and the ongoing struggle for racial and ethnic equality (the latter are more specific to the United States). It is noteworthy that, among other means, these movements have made skillful use of representative political mechanisms. Moreover, few of these groups (the United States civil rights movement being the most prominent exception) have depended upon either bureaucratic organizations or charismatic leadership during the periods of their greatest gains.

Given that Weber's ideal-types permit contrasts as well as correspondence, one searches in vain for concepts which refer to the formation, the means employed, or the successful consequences of democratic movements. Likewise, he makes no reference to the potential strength of the public spheres which such movements represent. These omissions constitute the most telling deficiencies in the Weberian approach to modern democracy. None of the above denies the significance of the antidemocratic forces conceptualized by Weber. However, what is suggested is an imbalance in his orientation. The problem can be traced to his universal postulates of inequality and domination. One cannot quarrel with the assertion that selective inequality and structures of domination are ubiquitous. On this score Weber offers a useful corrective to Marx's presuppositions regarding the possibility of a comprehensive, substantive democracy. Problems arise from the fact that his analysis *begins* from the position of unequal advantage and control of the means of domination and only thereafter proceeds to establish the relationship of the advantaged and dominant to the disadvantaged and obedient. Thus, the universality of inequality is conceived in terms of the selection of certain types of persons for superior positions,[82] rather than positions of disadvantage. Similarly, structures of domination are initially defined in terms of the exercise of authoritarian powers of command, rather than the complex balance of control between elites and society.[83] The problem is not that Weber ignores subordinate groupings, but rather that he defines them by looking down from positions of advantage and control.

The predisposition to place initial emphasis upon upper-level positions stands behind the prominence which Weber's ideal-types ascribe to the impediments to democracy and his neglect of the possibility for the democratic exercise of power. He devotes far more attention to antidemocratic consequences of modes of domination and the existence of elites in both capitalism and the state than he does to the limits on their autonomy by democratic forces which emerge from below. Alvin Gouldner recognized a crucial facet of this problem in an early critique of Weber's concept of bureaucracy: he observes that Weber's stress on the authoritarian implications of organizational constraints stacks the deck against democracy. Weber overlooks the fact that moving against the ''iron law of oligarchy'' is the ''iron law of democracy'': ''if oligarchical waves repeatedly wash away the bridges of democracy, this eternal recurrence can only happen because men [and women] doggedly rebuild them after each inundation.''[84] Had Weber incorporated a countervailing emphasis on the reaction of the dominated and the disadvantaged into his universal postulates, it would have been necessary to consider this and other trends which point to the significant achievements of Western democracy. As it is, in his work the impediments to democratization loom far greater than the prospects for democracy.

III

DEMOCRACY BEYOND MARX AND WEBER

Marx and Weber provide powerful insights into the obstacles which confront the full realization of democracy, but the significance of the West's democratic achievements and the realistic prospects for their expansion are obscured. It is undeniable that the systemic constraints of both capitalism and the bureaucratic state generate imposing barriers to democratization. Nevertheless, the reduction in oppression, facilitated by Western democratic rights and institutions, is significant in itself, and Western democracy provides an essential foundation for further advances. To ignore these facts is to lapse into either cynicism and dogma or pessimism and resignation— diverse attitudes which are sadly evident in many works beholden to Marx and Weber.

The paradox of the perspectives of Marx and Weber is that proceeding from presuppositions almost diametrically opposed, they concur in the overwhelming nature of the obstacles which confront democracy. However, this paradox is resolved once it is realized that each of their presuppositions contains an unnecessary exaggeration. Marx, on the one hand, exaggerates the extent to which substantive democratization is possible to achieve; on the other hand, Weber overstates the forces of advantage and domination which democracy confronts. The opposition between these positions can be elaborated in the theories of power which each view reflects. For Marx, the possibility exists that a society can be created in which the exercise of power poses no problems; for Weber, the exercise of authoritarian powers of command by those who possess superior resources is inevitable.

A program to overcome the difficulties in Marx's and Weber's orientations to democracy must continue to recognize the wisdom of their insights regarding the capitalist and bureaucratic impediments to democracy. But unlike Marx, new theories must be based upon the inevitability of the institutionalized exercise of power in all large societies, including all imaginable forms of socialism. Unlike Weber, we need not assume that this means the *demos* is incapable of exercising a powerful force in the direction of public policy. An adequate theory of democracy's prospects as well as its impediments must be capable of explaining the complex relationships in the exercise of institutional power between the dominant and the citizenry. A theory of this kind could grasp the capitalist and state oppression which continues to exist, but it would also be sensitive to the resources and the success of democratic resistance to these forms of oppression. Moreover, this theory would permit the generation of realistic, counterfactual possibilities for the development of more democratic modes of socio-political organization, permitting a greater latitude for public control than presently exists. Such counterfactuals would be useful for analytical and evaluative purposes in the same way that Marx employed his communist-democratic baseline; they might also serve as a valuable contribution to the creation of practical political agenda.[85]

However, there are basic problems which extend beyond issues connected with the exercise of power. Despite the success of democratic mass movements, it remains true that the majority of citizens in Western societies are far more concerned with their personal needs than they are with the creation of a democratic society.[86] The central problem of substantive democracy (i.e., the maintenance of vigorous public spheres in which democratic interest is formed and advanced) is perhaps less well addressed than any other aspect of democratic theory. Marx's account of the democratic *telos* of the proletariat offers little help in this regard, and Weber's work is all but bereft of positive suggestions. Moreover, Habermas's recent work, valuable as it is, presupposes an "ideal-speech situation" which is far too abstract to offer the kind of insight which is required. There is room here for a reconsideration and reconstruction of pertinent insights by Tocqueville and Durkheim, but this is a topic for another occasion.

Notes

This work was funded by a grant from the Rutgers University Fellowship Program. An earlier draft was presented at the Max Weber Colloquium, in Wayne, New Jersey, in October 1983. Robert Antonio, Jeffrey Goldfarb, and Stephen Kalberg provided extensive comments on an earlier draft. The views that are expressed, however, are strictly my own, as are all deficiencies that remain in this work.

1. Karl Marx, *Capital: A Critique of Political Economy* (1867; reprint, New York: Vintage, 1977), 1: 389–411. Marx also notes the self-interested participation of certain capitalist groups.

2. Max Weber, *Economy and Society: An Outline of Interpretative Sociology* (1921; reprint, Totowa, N.J.: Bedminster, 1968), 1107–9, also 226.

3. While the implications of these postulates extend beyond Marx's and Weber's orientations to democracy, I make no claim that the meaning or significance of their theories or concepts is grounded solely in these presuppositional standpoints.

4. Cf. Shlomo Avineri, *The Social and Political Thought of Karl Marx* (Cambridge: Cambridge University Press, 1968), 19 passim.

5. Karl Marx, "On the Jewish Question," in *Karl Marx: Early Writings,* ed. T. B. Bottomore (1843; reprint, New York: McGraw Hill, 1963), 26.

6. Karl Marx, *Critique of Hegel's Philosophy of Right* (1843; reprint, Cambridge: Cambridge University Press, 1970), 29–31.

7. Ibid., 30.

8. Karl Marx, "Economic and Philosophical Manuscripts," in *Karl Marx: Early Writings,* ed. Bottomore, 126–30, 157–58, 202. It should be mentioned that this point refers only to man's potential or capacities. Marx does not postulate an *essentialist* ontology such as those of natural law theorists.

9. Ibid., 157–61.

10. Marx, "On the Jewish Question," 20.

11. Karl Marx, "Letter to Arnold Ruge, May 1843," in *The Letters of Karl Marx,* ed. Saul K. Padover (Englewood Cliffs, N.J.: Prentice-Hall, 1979), 26–27.

12. Karl Marx, "Excerpts from James Mill's 'Elements of Political Economy,'" in *Karl Marx: Early Writings,* ed. Quintin Hoare (1844; reprint, New York: Vintage, 1975), 277–78.

13. Cf. Marx, "Economic and Philosophical Manuscripts," 155.

14. Shlomo Avineri, *The Social and Political Thought of Karl Marx,* 34; Anthony Giddens, *Capitalism and Modern Social Theory: An Analysis of the Writings of Marx, Durkheim, and Weber* (Cambridge: Cambridge University Press, 1971), 16.

15. This phrase inverts Hal Draper's description of Karl Marx as a "revolutionary-democratic communist." Hal Draper, *Karl Marx's Theory of Revolution,* volume 1: *State and Bureaucracy* (New York: Monthly Review Press, 1977), 31.

16. Karl Marx and Friedrich Engels, "The Holy Family," passage in *Karl Marx: Selected Writings,* ed. David McLellan (1845; reprint, New York: Oxford University Press, 1977), 134.

17. Marx, "Economic and Philosophical Manuscripts," 124–29. For a similar account see Steven Lukes, "Alienation and Anomie," in *Essays in Social Theory* (1967; reprint, London: Macmillan, 1977).

18. Ali Rattansi, *Marx and the Division of Labor* (London: Macmillan, 1982), 177.

19. Karl Marx, *Capital: A Critique of Political Economy* (1894; reprint, New York: Vintage, 1981), 3: 959.

20. Cf. Marx, *Capital* 1: 798.

21. Ibid., 799.

22. Karl Marx, *The Grundrisse,* ed. David McLellan (New York: Harper, 1971), 68 (written in 1857–1858).

23. E.g., Karl Marx, *The Poverty of Philosophy* (1847; reprint, New York: International Publishers, 1963), 69–79; Karl Marx and Friedrich Engels, "The Communist Manifesto," in *Karl Marx: Selected Writings,* ed. McLellan, 238–45; cf. Avineri, *The Social and Political Thought of Karl Marx,* 149.

24. Marx, *Critique of Hegel's Philosophy of Right,* 64.

25. Ibid., 123, 126.

26. Ibid., 119.

27. Ibid., 121.

28. Marx, "On the Jewish Question," 12.

29. Cf. Marx, *Critique of Hegel's Philosophy of Right,* 116.

30. Marx, *Capital* 3: 927.

31. E.g. Karl Marx, "British Political Parties," in (1852) *Karl Marx: Selected Writings,* ed. McLellan, 331–32; Karl Marx, *The Eighteenth Brumaire of Louis Bonaparte* (1852; reprint, New York: International Publishers, 1963), 65 ff.

32. Karl Marx, *The Civil War in France* (1871; reprint, New York: International Publishers, 1940), 65ff. The weaknesses in this passage are summarized by Ali Rattansi, *Marx and the Division of Labor,* 194.

33. Cf. Ralph Miliband, *Marxism and Politics* (Oxford: Oxford University Press, 1977), 76.

34. Karl Marx and Friedrich Engels, "Address to the Communist League," in (1849) *Karl Marx: Selected Writings,* ed. McLellan, 281–83.

35. Karl Marx, "Critique of the Gotha Program," in *The Portable Marx,* ed. Eugene Kamenka (1875; reprint, New York: Penguin, 1983), 549–50.

36. Draper, *Karl Marx's Theory of Revolution* 1: 58.

37. Cf. Karl Löwith, *Max Weber and Karl Marx* (1932; reprint, London: Allen and Unwin, 1982), ch. 2.

38. Max Weber, *Economy and Society,* 39.

39. Max Weber, "The Meaning of Ethical Neutrality in Sociology and Economics," in *The Methodology of the Social Sciences,* ed. E. A. Shils and H. A. Finch (1917; reprint, New York: Free Press, 1949), 27.

40. Weber, *Economy and Society,* 941.

41. Ibid., 948, cf. 941.

42. Ibid., 42.

43. Ibid., 50–51.

44. It is illegitimate to interpret Weber's ideal-types in empirical terms. However, though ideal-types admit empirical contrast as well as correspondence, they are nonetheless "one-sided viewpoints which illuminate the aspect[s] of reality with which [they] can be related." Max Weber, "Objectivity in Social Science and Social Policy," in *The Methodology of the Social Sciences* (1904), 105. Therefore, it will be Weber's ideal-typical viewpoint or perspective which will be at issue in the following account.

45. See Wolfgang J. Mommsen, *The Age of Bureaucracy: Perspectives on the Political Sociology of Max Weber* (New York: Harper, 1974); Anthony Giddens, *Politics and Sociology in the Works of Max Weber* (London: Macmillan, 1972); David Beetham, *Max Weber and the Theory of Modern Politics* (London: Allen and Unwin, 1974); Ernest Kilker, "Max Weber and the Possibilities for Democracy," in *Max Weber's Political Sociology,* eds. R. Glassman and V. Murvar (Westport, Conn.: Greenwood Press, 1984), 55-65.

46. Weber, *Economy and Society,* 289-90, 948-52.

47. Ibid., 291.

48. Ibid., 949.

49. Ibid., 951. It is noteworthy that Weber presents no comprehensive ideal-type of modern democracy in *Economy and Society.*

50. Weber, *Economy and Society,* 297-99.

51. On this point see Lawrence A. Scaff, "Max Weber and Robert Michels," *American Journal of Sociology* 86 (1981): 1282.

52. Ibid., 957; Max Weber, "Politics as a Vocation," in *From Max Weber,* ed. H. Gerth and C. W. Mills (1918; reprint, New York: Oxford University Press, 1946), 86 passim.

53. Weber, *Economy and Society,* 1131.

54. Ibid., 287-88.

55. Ibid., 285.

56. Ibid., 297.

57. Ibid., 288, 1128-30.

58. Ibid., 989.

59. Ibid., 992-93, 997.

60. Ibid., 267-69, 1132. Cf. Beetham, *Max Weber and the Theory of Modern Politics,* 266.

61. Cf. Weber, "Politics as a Vocation," 120-28.

62. Cf. Donald Levine, "Rationality and Freedom: Weber and Beyond," *Sociological Inquiry* 51 (1981): 18.

63. Max Weber, "Author's Introduction," *The Protestant Ethic and the Spirit of Capitalism* (1920; reprint, New York: Scribners, 1958), 17. This is a historical generalization rather than an ideal-type.

65. Weber, *Economy and Society,* 953.

65. Cf. Weber, *The Protestant Ethic,* 55-56.

66. Weber, *Economy and Society,* 729-30, cf. 110.

67. Cf. ibid., 1156, and Marx, "Economic and Philosophical Manuscripts," 124-29.

68. Weber, *Economy and Society,* 600. On the formal rationality of the capitalist enterprise see Ira Cohen, "Max Weber on Modern Western Capitalism," in Weber, *General Economic History* (New Brunswick, N.J.: Transactions, 1981), pt. 1.

69. Weber, *Economy and Society,* 886.

70. Ibid., 893.

71. Ibid., 891-92.

72. Ibid., 960-61.

73. Ibid., 983.

74. Ibid., 984-85; see also 226.

75. Ibid., 960–62, cf. 985.

76. Ibid., 226, 1107–9.

77. Jere Cohen, Lawrence Hazelrigg, and Whitney Pope, "De-Parsonizing Weber: A Critique of Parsons' Interpretation of Weber's Sociology," *American Sociological Review* 40 (1975): 239; Mommsen, *The Age of Bureaucracy,* 84 ff.

78. Weber, *Economy and Society,* 214–15.

79. Ibid., 266–69.

80. Ibid., 267.

81. Ibid., 985.

82. Cf. ibid., 38–40; "Ethical Neutrality," 27.

83. Cf. *Economy and Society,* 53–56, 212–15, 947–48.

84. Alvin Gouldner, "Metaphysical Pathos and the Theory of Bureaucracy," *American Political Science Review* 49 (1955): 506.

85. The most promising attempt to construct a theory of the exercise of power which opens up these possibilities is Anthony Giddens's structuration theory. See *A Contemporary Critique of Historical Materialism.*

86. See Nicholas Abercrombie, Stephan Hill, and Bryan S. Turner, *The Dominant Ideology Thesis* (London: Allen and Unwin, 1980), ch. 6; Michael Mann, "The Social Cohesion of Liberal Democracy," *American Sociological Review* 35 (1970): 423–39; Robert Bellah, *The Broken Covenant: American Civil Religion in Time of Trial* (New York: Seabury, 1975) x–xiii passim.

VXV\

*Stephen L.
Esquith*

Politics and Values in Marx and Weber

Since this is an essay on the political significance of
the historicity of values, it answers two related questions: what is the
historicity of values? why is it politically significant? After some preliminary remarks, my answer rests on a comparison of Marx and Weber.
Despite well-known political differences, both Marx and Weber recognized
in their later writings the historicity of the value of work and its potential
for restructuring power in capitalist society.

INTRODUCTION

Value of work means the value which work has for those doing it. Thus, the
value of challenging work is often connected to the development of talents
and skills, while routine, mind-numbing work has a different value. It may
pay the bills or distract us from our troubles. For Marx, the value of work
in capitalist society is more than its exchange value in a technical sense, as
important as that is; it is also the value which work, reduced to the
production of exchange value, has for workers. Similarly, for Weber the
value of routinized work is more than its efficiency; it is the value which
hierarchical, specialized work—manual, administrative, or intellectual—
has for the worker. I aim to examine how, according to Marx and Weber,
the sociological value of work affects both the shape of collective identity
and the balance of political power.

HISTORICITY AND POLITICS

Too often historicity is nothing more than an obscure name for the
nonlinearity and relevance of history. In this section I present a meta-

physically modest conception of historicity whose main virtue is that it highlights the political significance of the general concept while avoiding the larger Heideggerian traps that surround grander conceptions.[1] First, one must clarify the relationship between history and historicity, and the best way to do this is to examine the historicity of objects and persons. Then, the more complex notion of the historicity of values and its political significance can be clarified. When I enter a room, I often see more than a strange tableaux: the people and things have a story which defines the setting and marks off the immediate future. Thus, the historicity of the scene is the way the dramatic history, symbolized by the objects and persons in the scene, shapes an understanding of the present and the social trajectory of action.

Imagine you are entering the home of Mme. Aubain as it is masterfully described in the opening passage of Flaubert's short story "A Simple Heart." Try to put yourself in this place.

This house had a slate roof and stood between an alleyway and a lane leading down to the river. Inside there were differences in level which were the cause of many a stumble. A narrow entrance-hall separated the kitchen from the parlour, where Mme Aubain sat all day long in a wicker chair by the window. Eight mahogany chairs were lined up against the white-paned wainscoting, and under the barometer stood an old piano loaded with a pyramid of boxes and cartons. On either side of the chimney-piece, which was carved out of yellow marble in the Louis Quinze style, there was a tapestry-covered arm-chair, and in the middle was a clock designed to look like a temple of Vesta. The whole room smelt a little musty, as the floor was on a lower level than the garden.[2]

Mme. Aubain's home is a testament to her chastity and the belief that individuality can be tightly arranged like carefully chosen possessions, but even before we face the clock and tapestry our field of vision is fixed. The "differences in level" which protect Mme. Aubain from an impetuous caller at the same time create the space for these reified objects and channel our steps in certain directions rather than others by surprising us, catching us off balance, and disorienting us in this musty atmosphere.

The historicity of this scene refers to the way that unfolding social relations between actual persons are refracted through the history embodied in an object or person either peculiarly situated or strategically located. The historicity of an actual scene such as this cuts across our path in two directions. On the one hand, certain choices are foreclosed; social relations are mediated only through prized possessions. On the other hand, Flaubert presents Mme. Aubain in such a way that it is possible to reach her, appeal to her admittedly bourgeois sensibilities, and convey respects. As important as her "eight mahogany chairs" are to her, they are more than mere reflections of her staid character; they face the reader in a way she never could, keeping him at arms length while inviting him to visit briefly. In short, the historicity of the scene creates an opportunity to enter Mme. Aubain's small world, but on her terms.

The historicity of values is, however, a more complex notion. While Mme. Aubain's home is a collection of cultural artifacts which partake of value-laden symbolic meaning as well as physical shape, they are located in time and space in a way that intangible values (e.g., the value of meaningful work) are not; therefore, the historicity of concrete objects shapes social relations in a more determinate way. Values do not surround the way objects and persons do: a scene can haunt or thrill, but a value can enslave or liberate a people. The impact of the historicity of values is less determinate than the impact of the historicity of objects and persons, but it may reverberate through the collective identity as myth and tradition. Because values exist within a larger cultural field of energy, their potential to shape social relations extends much further.

It is this potential power which gives the historicity of values political significance. While the historicity of a concrete scene creates an opportunity for determinate, irreversible action, the historicity of values provides a political opportunity for the community as a whole. Whether this cultural energy field is tapped depends upon particular historical circumstances and the corresponding theoretical stance toward the past.

Consider the familiar value of independence: when it is persuasively linked to practices like active political membership and political equality, its historicity broadens moral ties; when it is associated with possession and industry, it narrows them. Garry Wills's recent interpretation of the United States Declaration of Independence is an attempt to capture the unifying power of the value of independence. Wills argues that the traditional Lockean reading of the Declaration overlooks its Hutchesonian origins. Independence is not necessarily reducible to the individuating claims of wronged property owners. It can be a statement of common purpose emanating from a common moral sense, and property can be the basis for moral reciprocity, not heartless interest group politics.[3]

Leaving aside the strength of Wills's evidence, his project is noteworthy because it calls attention to the unexplored potential for decentralizing political power by the value of independence. If Wills is right, there is a countertradition: widen the boundaries of political discourse in the United States, and fellow feeling deepens. The historicity of a value like independence is not limited to personal relations in the way that the historicity of a concrete scene is. Granted, the text of the Declaration is no less concrete than the vestal clock in Mme. Aubain's parlor; however, the clock is confined to that room in a way that the Declaration is not confined to Independence Hall. Independence is something shared by a people; it defines part of our collective identity. As laudable as Mme. Aubain's chastity may be, it remains hers alone.

Work, not independence, is the key value for Marx and Weber; it is work which the capitalist division of labor degrades according to Marx and which rationalization empties of meaning according to Weber. For both theorists the value of work was initially simply a transcendental moral standard against which they measured capitalist society and found it wanting. In *The Economic and Philosophic Manuscripts* Marx used the value of work to bring out the dehumanizing effects of wage-labor.[4] In *The Protestant Ethic and the Spirit of Capitalism* Weber implicitly relied on it to criticize the compulsive nature of work in a secular capitalist society.[5] However, both Marx and Weber deepened their critiques of capitalism in the wake of unanticipated political events by elaborating the historicity of the value of work in a more dialectical way.

By expanding the notion of alienation to include the fetishism of commodities, Marx hoped to exploit the historicity of the value of work under capitalism. He could no longer moralistically denounce wage-labor. After 1851 he argued that under the right interpretation wage-labor could be the basis for a new collective consciousness centered around the political struggle over the working day. Weber's mature writings after World War I also focused on the value of work in this dialectical sense, though obviously with different ends in mind. Instead of dismissing academic specialization as a form of alienated intellectual labor, Weber attempted to carry forward what was valuable in intellectual work under capitalism in a way that would move his audience toward a more meaningful conception of vocation appropriate to a scaled down national political domain. By interpreting the phenomenal forms which work takes under capitalism, Marx and Weber hoped to redefine the political domain so that genuine political action, as they understood it, would be possible.

MARX

Two things should be stressed in Marx's treatment of the value of work: the shift from morality to historicity and the political events which occasioned this rethinking. When Marx and Engels called for a proletarian revolution in *The Communist Manifesto* in 1848, their specific proposals fell short of a communist conception of justice. The emphasis was on the abolition of private landed capital, state control of communications and transportation, and the establishment of a state bank, but not the abolition of industrial capital. They called for the "equal liability of all to labor," but not the abolition of wage-labor.[6] They believed that temporary "democratic" alliances with the bourgeoisie, particularly in Germany, were necessary in the early stages of radical social transformation.[7]

While the *Manifesto* was a transitional program, it was also a hopeful and optimistic one. In France and especially Germany, where economic development lagged behind that of England and the urban proletariat did not constitute a majority, Marx and Engels argued that workers and peasants would make common cause based on similar economic interests. Even in *The Class Struggles in France* of 1850, Marx retained this hope, though by that time he urged the proletariat to push the bourgeoisie beyond its earlier positions endorsed by the *Manifesto*. He no longer felt that the transition to communism would be possible if the initial revolutionary program gave too much attention to strictly bourgeois economic interests, but he retained faith in a worker-peasant alliance.[8]

The Eighteenth Brumaire of Louis Bonaparte (1852) abandoned this qualified optimism and signaled a new theoretical stance toward history on Marx's part. Marx argued that the French peasants had mistaken Louis Napolean Bonaparte for his uncle, thrown their support to him, and sealed the fate of the urban proletariat.[9] The failure of the worker-peasant alliance was not simply a matter of peasant myopia; it was indicative of a deeper theoretical problem that required rethinking the very notion of a proletarian revolution. Carried out in an unreflective way the proletarian revolution would be stillborn, but it was precisely this unreflective attitude which the *Manifesto* had encouraged.

From the standpoint of the *Manifesto,* history and its political implications were virtually transparent: "The history of all hitherto existing society is the history of class struggles."[10] Earlier class struggles had not been neatly organized, but now that proletariat and bourgeoisie met each other in open combat it was possible to see that this is simply the culmination of a "long course of development, of a series of revolutions in the modes of production and exchange."[11] According to the *Eighteenth Brumaire,* because the "tradition of all dead generations [weighs] like a nightmare on the brain of the living,"[12] revolutionary action could no longer model itself on swift, decisive declarations of right.[13] History is hardly transparent. Without the proper orientation toward past moral and political values, such as the Napoleonic Code, attempts at a radical break with the past would only be tragic reenactments of famous scenes from it.[14] The logic of a proletarian revolution was long, drawn out, and burdened by setbacks as well as advances. Conventional political history must be excavated and viewed from a new perspective to strengthen the proletariat for this odyssey.

More specifically, Marx realized that revolutionary political discourse was not merely a technique and the past not simply a storehouse. As long as the proletariat translated new actions, decisions, and problems back into old idioms, it would lack the wherewithal to sustain a revolutionary struggle.

Thus Luther donned the mask of the Apostle Paul, the Revolution of 1789 to 1814 draped itself alternately as the Roman Republic and the Roman Empire, and the Revolution of 1848 knew nothing better to do than to parody in turn, 1789 and the revolutionary tradition of 1789 to 1795. In like manner the beginner who has learnt a new language always translates it back into his mother tongue, but he has assimilated the spirit of the new language and can produce freely in it only when he moves in it without remembering the old and forgets in it his ancestral tongue.[15]

Thus, Marx later argued, a new political language would have to be pieced together from the fragments of the working day which is neither the divisive ordinary language of individual exchange nor the archaic language of the bourgeois revolution. The new language would draw on the history of the struggle over hours and wages, a collective struggle "congealed" in the seemingly abstract language of classical political economy.[16]

The sober analysis of the *Eighteenth Brumaire* did not lead Marx to abandon the worker-peasant alliance. However, he believed that the proletariat would have to undergo a fundamental change if it were to be capable of pursuing radically new ideals of social cooperation. The proletariat would need its own historical theory, not just an agenda. Marx opposed the overanxious "great men of exile" who turned to ad hoc conspiratorial action, not simply because he thought it would be some time before new economic crises would make revolution possible. "While we say to the workers, you have fifteen or twenty or fifty years of civil and national wars to go through, not just to alter conditions but *to alter yourselves* and qualify for political power—you on the contrary say: we must obtain power at once or we might as well lay ourselves down to sleep" (emphasis added).[17] How the proletariat is "to alter" itself is addressed by Marx in *Capital* and its early drafts. He approached this problem obliquely through a critique of classical political economy for good reason. In fact, this oblique approach to the political education of the proletariat—one that would lead Marx to think that *Capital* could be serialized and widely distributed[18]—emerges most clearly and convincingly when comparing the historicist treatment of work in *Capital* to Marx's earlier moralistic formulations.

In *The Economic and Philosophic Manuscripts* of 1844 Marx questioned the fundamental assumptions of classical political economy from a moral rather than a sociological perspective. The facts of classical political economy, according to Marx, were not "actual economic facts" but derivative of unexamined assumptions about the nature of labor.[19] Classical political economy took alienated labor as a given and then constructed the laws of production and exchange on this basis. Alienated labor is not the result of the system of private property, but rather its cause. Private property is the "consequence" of alienation because once sensuous labor is reduced to a "sense of having," the world can only be accounted for by the laws of classical political economy.[20] In 1844 Marx added that the relations between laboring persons no longer need be competitive bargaining relations and their relationship to nature no longer need be an appropriative one when the potential vitality of the labor process is recognized. If the "actual economic facts" to be accounted for are the more aesthetic and sensuous potentials inherent in human "species-being," then classical political economy is built upon morally flawed premises.[21]

In the *Grundrisse* (1857–58) Marx still believed that alienated labor is dehumanizing, but he suspected that there was something more paradoxical about productive activity than simply its weak, unacknowledged moral presuppositions. Abstract labor appears on its face to be thoroughly ahistorical. It unites what is common to all wage-labor, regardless of who does it and where. On closer examination it contains the key to the history of all previous producing classes.[22] This Darwinian analogy represents a first effort to come to terms with the dilemma which history had posed for Marx in the *Eighteenth Brumaire;* however, it is never fully developed in the *Grundrisse.*

Instead, *Capital* located the activity of abstract labor of the individual worker within a larger abstract environment represented by the language of political economy. Not only had labor grown abstract, but laborers' own abstractions held dominion over them; this Marx called the fetishism of commodities.[23] Because the fetishism of commodities exists, classical political economy cannot simply be rejected on moral grounds. In a world that has grown abstract—where power and productive forces seem to move in an ethereal realm of their own, where workers do not see the conflict-ridden history of the products they produce—the first revolutionary step must reveal to them how they have indeed created those products through their own collective effort. This means disabusing them of the ordinary belief that they are merely individual sellers of their own labor-power. Marx had to develop an interpretation of the categories of classical political economy that revealed the political history of the self-genesis of labor-power. This achievement, he believed, could demonstrate to the proletariat how it had in part shaped its own collective fate and was capable of even more class-conscious action. Here was the suppressed political history to replace the conventional political history of the *Eighteenth Brumaire.*

The paradoxical nature of labor is now clearer: labor is the source of power in capitalist society, but workers do not share in this power as long as they remain ignorant of its genesis. As "abstract labor," its history is masked by the seemingly abstract language of classical political economy which presumes to explain it. To gain a knowledge of its origins so they can eventually control it, workers must understand labor through the more general notion of fetishism. The fetishism of labor-power is the most important fetishism of all, and hidden behind it is the history of the collective struggle over hours and wages, not the competitive bargaining relationship between individual worker and entrepreneur.[24]

Fetishism is not, therefore, simply a restatement of the notion of alienation found in the 1844 *Manuscripts.*[25] The section on commodity fetishism is perhaps, as Lukács suggested,[26] the most important part of *Capital.* It goes beyond the notion of alienation because it analyzes a collective enterprise. Alienation, marked by the lack of social cooperation, can be overcome by uniting conceptual understanding and execution, as in craft labor, within a cooperative environment; thus, the *Manuscripts* are often criticized as romantic. In contrast, to overcome commodity fetishism, the fetishism of *individual* labor-power must first be recognized and abandoned. Fetishism is a critical notion that calls attention to more than just the need for free, self-actualizing labor under conditions of social cooperation; it fastens onto the fact that capital is a social product whose mysterious strength derives from the illusion that it is produced by *independent* owners of capital and labor-power. Therefore, fetishism is a form of false consciousness that masks the collective history of the exchange and reproduction of labor-power.

The historical values which handicapped the working class, according to the *Eighteenth Brumaire,* can now finally be mastered. The values and interests which had blinded the peasants to the fragmenting effects of supporting the Second Empire can now be seen in a more political light. The pursuit of individual economic self-interest only exacerbates the political powerlessness of the working class whose interests in strictly economic terms are too heterogeneous for building a collective political movement. Just like the individual sellers of labor-power, peasants and workers only weaken their bargaining positions and worsen their lots when they compete against each other. *Capital* is an attempt to loosen the hold which a commoditized self-image has on the members of the working class through an interpretation of the historicity of the value of labor.

In response to Marx's call for a theoretically armed proletariat, Weber argued that collective political action of any sort would only replace one oppressive bureaucracy with another. Weber believed there was no theory of industrial and manufacturing work which the proletariat could grasp and which would then alter it significantly. Instead, the answer to alienation lay in a theory of academic work which reshaped the character of social scientists themselves. Eventually, this would limit the growth of bureaucratic institutions and demonstrate the possibility of individual meaningful work within a fixed national political domain.

In the *Freiburg Inaugural Address* (1895), in addition to stressing the nationalist merits of recolonizing the East Elbian provinces, Weber defended recolonization in the name of political education and considered it his duty *as a social scientist* to advance national values.[27] After his illness at the turn of the century Weber retreated from this initial position and formulated the concepts of value-freedom and value-relevant interpretation which put a greater distance between science and politics. This was the period of his first foray into methodology (1903–1906), the publication of *The Protestant Ethic* (1904–1905), and the writing of the early sections of *Economy and Society* (pre-1913).

However, after 1913, Weber was dissatisfied with this second position for several reasons. The middle class was not developing as a responsible political class, and Germany, Weber believed, would have to make a more concerted effort to develop political leaders committed to nationhood. Bismarck's legacy and the bureaucratization of existing political institutions made the need for strong individual leaders more acute, yet more problematic; the parliament could not be counted on as a school for political leaders.[28] Consequently, Weber favored World War I because he saw it as an opportunity to renew the nation. (Hughes suggests that not until the War did Weber snap out of his depression.)[29] Weber said that there was no reason to get involved in this kind of conflict if only the form of German government was at stake, but he hoped, under a capable leader, the War would restore German political culture.[30]

Although Weber's concern with political education and national political culture predated the War, the post-1913 period represented a new approach to this problem. Because Parliament was an inadequate forum for educating political leaders, the scholarly community would have to play a larger role in political education by shaping national sentiments, not just imparting cognitive skills. At the same time, it was impossible to return to the unscientific strategy of the *Freiburg Inaugural* because the university as the center of humanistic studies had lost its privileged place in German political life; now only science could speak authoritatively above the din of particularistic political voices since the old "mandarin" scholarly community had atrophied.[31] In this context, in the absence of a politically committed bourgeoisie, the only available strategy was to adapt social science to the task of educating strong leaders more directly. Against this background Weber's appreciation of the historicity of social science as a vocation emerges.

The reorientation of social science around the historicity of the value of work occurs at two related levels in Weber's later writings. His own social scientific research took a new direction, illustrated most clearly in the shift in his treatment of "charisma" in *Economy and Society* and the contrast between *Ancient Judaism* and his earlier studies of religion. To legitimate this new project, Weber extended the boundaries of social scientific inquiry to encompass the self-transformative notion of value interpretation.

As Mommsen has shown, the pre-1913 sections of *Economy and Society* treat "charisma" as an institutional form of legitimate authority located chronologically before traditional and rational-legal authority.[32] After 1913, Weber was more concerned with the charismatic leader and the particular role he might play in a rationalized world than with the routinization of charismatic authority; he was more interested in individual gifted leaders as potential sources of political renewal than he was in the structural causes of routinization.

The most interesting manifestation of this shift, the one which reveals Weber's new orientation toward intellectual work, is his treatment of the pre-exilic prophet in *Ancient Judaism,* composed near the very end of his life. Marianne Weber reported that when Weber read those sections of the manuscript to her dealing with Jeremiah, she saw "his own fate expressed in many passages."[33] The pre-exilic prophet, for Weber, was preeminently a political figure, but he was not a mass leader; he was political in an "objective" or nonpartisan sense.[34] His aim, according to Weber, was to preserve the nation at a time when it was deprived of state power. Furthermore, the prophet was an unwilling leader. He responded to his calling reluctantly and had no interest in living "off politics"; yet he lived for politics despite the pain it caused him. Thus, the prophet was able to forge a new sense of political order in the midst of chaos. He could persuasively explain how the community's "collective fate" resulted from a violation of the covenant with God.[35] In contrast to his earlier sociological work on religion, in *Ancient Judaism* there was no effort to continue the comparative project begun with *The Protestant Ethic.* Weber was no longer concerned primarily with causal arguments of this sort; instead, he wanted to isolate the political significance of the prophet's calling: how it affected the prophet's character and, through him, the shape of the nation as a whole. Weber concluded that it was the prophet's speech, his confrontation with kings and priests through the spoken word, which forged the sentiments upon which the nation rests.[36]

Weber considered the pre-exilic prophets "exemplary," not "ethical," prophets.[37] They taught by example to a small circle of disciples, not by rallying large numbers to a new cause. The "false prophecy" Weber warned against in *Politics as a Vocation* (1918)[38] referred to a contemporary ethical, not exemplary, prophet. Inspired by the work of the exemplary prophet, the social scientist could then show how human practices and institutions could both be guided by the prophetic virtues of commitment, "objectivity," and matter-of-factness and how they might structure political discourse on a national scale. What is the basis for Weber's belief that social scientists can transform themselves along exemplary prophetic lines? To answer this difficult question, we have to compare his prewar methodological writings with the later ones.

In *The Protestant Ethic* and the methodological essays appearing at that time, Weber, although committed to *verstehen* and causal explanation, believed social science was possible only through a broad comparative approach. He admitted that specialists were supreme within their own domain, perhaps entitled to some kind of final judgment on parts of the generalist's work.[39] However, the comparative generalist was forced to trespass "on other special fields" despite the risk of being proved wrong[40] because something greater was at stake which specialists could not see. In the dark concluding paragraphs of *The Protestant Ethic* it was "the specialist without spirit" and the "sensualist without heart" who failed to grasp the ominous spirit of the age; ultimately, specialists could not be trusted.[41]

This same rejection of the specialist can be seen in the faint praise with which Weber opened his 1905 critique of Edward Meyer. Weber noted that the methodological naiveté of specialists like Meyer may be useful for specialists in neighboring disciplines. However, their methodological reflections also resembled "a diagnosis not by the physician but by the patient himself."[42] In a more caustic note in "Knies and the Problem of Irrationality" Weber referred to the work of a lesser known specialist who "makes one wish that the current fashion according to which every first work must be embellished with epistemological investigations would die out as quickly as possible."[43] The "dilettantish logical blunders" of specialists who feel compelled to justify their methods[44] so aggravated Weber that he considered them a "methodological pestilence." There was only one alternative: "Only by laying bare and solving substantive problems can sciences be established and their methods developed."[45] Thus, only the generalist was capable of assessing the relative merits of competing methods because only the generalist used these methods in actual research. This was the ultimate test of any method for Weber, and the generalist, by definition, was the only one in a position to evaluate the competing knowledge claims of, for example, Rickert's historical economics and abstract "Manchesterism."

However, by the close of the war, Weber tempered this rejection of expert knowledge. In "Ethical Neutrality" and *Science as a Vocation* Weber was reconciled to the fact that science must be done by specialists.[46] He aimed in these pieces to demonstrate how the power of expert knowledge could be enlisted in the search for a politically meaningful conception of progress (i.e., progress toward a stable national culture) without grossly violating the canons of science. By this time Weber had shifted to a position that favored what we might call specialization-with-a-difference.

In "Ethical Neutrality" Weber repeated that one could logically distinguish between value judgments and judgments of fact. This, however, did not solve the more difficult question whether a teacher or scholar who separates the two should present value judgments as well as facts to students; Weber stated that this depended upon one's conception of the university. If the purpose of the university is "molding human beings"[47] rather than the more focused purpose of developing the "intellectual integrity" of the specialist, then scientists have a duty to present separately their values as well as their findings. Weber favored the more focused purpose for two reasons: first, not all value positions were permitted to be aired in the German university of 1917; second, and more important, given the lack of consensus regarding what kind of life one should make for oneself, there was a great danger that the personal values of individual professors would be passed off as universally valid when delivered from the lectern.

In political situations such as this, lacking national agreement over how one should make the highest "ethical/personal" decisions, Weber believed truly strong persons can only be formed through devotion to a task which gains its meaning when they exercise the restraint proper to it.[48] This kind of restraint can be taught only by example, not by preachment. The exemplary teacher and scholar does have a "powerful personality," but it is one that "does not manifest itself by trying to give everything a 'personal touch' at every possible opportunity."[49] In restraining themselves from presenting their own value judgments, scientific experts inculcate the virtues of self-discipline, intellectual honesty, and a general ethical attitude in their students; to succumb to the temptation to personally tint their lectures with value judgments is to court disaster. As Weber stated in *Science as Vocation,* scientists were not "personalities,"[50] and if they chose to be, they would threaten the fragile balance of power. Their values must remain private, not public; like art in the modern world, they must be "intimate" or else they invite a grotesque response.[51] This does not mean their values must remain unspoken; on the contrary, it means they must be introduced only to a small circle in a circumspect, exemplary way.

Weber defended specialization despite the fact that he believed bureaucratic expertise was the foundation of a form of power which threatened the world with "mechanized petrification embellished with a sort of convulsive self-importance."[52] The crude alternative to the specialist which the "younger generation" yearned for was unacceptable in his eyes.[53] But what precise differences did Weber want to introduce into the practice of social science which would extend this disciplinary rigor in a characterological direction?

It is clear that in his 1917 essay Weber wanted to discuss the meaning, not the logic, of ethical neutrality. Logically, he was satisfied with unargued a priori claims.[54] The body of the essay was devoted to the meaning of value-free science which rested on a particular method, the "value interpretative approach." Value interpretation went beyond technical assessments of progress to consider the values underlying human action and their significance as national sentiments. In the process, Weber claimed, it had a profound effect on the social scientist.

After covering some familiar ground on the question of causality,[55] Weber fastened on the central problem of facticity. A socio-cultural fact is something true of a socio-cultural object or event, but such an object or event can entail a very complex conception of progress which, Weber asserted, often involves "an entanglement with value."[56] Vocation is the key socio-cultural object for Weber. For a proposition to be true of a socio-cultural object like vocation, it must grasp correctly its historical meaning (i.e., the potential contribution which that object might make to human progress, be it negative or positive). For Weber, this meant the potential contribution which the notion of vocation can make to the development of a fixed national culture. In short, national cultural progress, not the philosophical problem of causation, was at the heart of the meaning of ethical neutrality. There was nothing inevitable about this conception of progress; above all, it depended on the exemplary behavior of social scientists and leaders to trigger it.

Weber argued that there were three possible conceptions of progress, but only two of interest to the scientist. First, progress can be thought of in purely evaluative terms. For example, we might compare and order a series of aesthetic or moral values on the basis of some nonempirical standard of taste or goodness; in either case, science must remain agnostic according to Weber. Second, progress can be understood in strictly empirical terms, and here the scientist is best suited to judge whether or not there has been "technical progress." For example, technical progress in economics can be measured in terms of the effectiveness of institutions and policies designed to achieve certain agreed upon ends like free trade. Finally, Weber believed that scientists can also study progress through a "value interpretative approach," which differs from the empirical approach they take toward technical progress. It is this "value interpretative approach" which addresses the historicity of socio-cultural objects outside the causal nexus in which mere technical progress is embedded. When social scientists take this value interpretative approach they legitimately step into the political domain, according to Weber.[57]

The "value interpretative approach" is not a secondary feature of the social scientist's vocation. On the contrary, Weber believed that causal explanations which strive for higher and higher levels of generality were less important than interpretations of "individual concrete situations" which bring out their "value relevance."[58] "[K]nowledge of cultural events is inconceivable except on a basis of the *significance* which the concrete constellations of reality have in certain individual concrete situations."[59] Significance can be measured in two ways: first, what light does the value implicit in a particular socio-cultural object shed on other values associated with it;[60] second, what effect does value interpretation itself have on the social scientist?[61] According to Weber, value interpretation "extends his 'inner life' and his mental and spiritual horizon." It makes him more "sensitive to values."[62] Weber believed that the character of the social scientist and the student are indeed shaped by their work and approach to socio-cultural significance. If scientists limit themselves to the problems of technical progress and causal explanation, they will remain insensitive to the values which guided their own exemplary precursors. In *Ancient Judaism* Weber practiced what he preached.

In sum, specialization-with-a-difference is science which includes a concern with technical progress within a detailed division of labor, but it also examines the roots of culturally significant values and expands them. This form of specialization indeed implicates the whole person, and this is the desired sensitization underlying Weber's final plea in *Science as a Vocation* that scientists do more than clarify the consequences attached to alternative means. They must warn students from collective values which will only enlarge the scale of bureaucratic power and invite false prophets to take the helm. Only the gradual reintroduction of the meaning of responsibility to one's calling and matter-of-factness among a small set of disciplined followers, not a headlong rush into communal salvation, promises genuine (for Weber, national) progress. Specialization-with-a-difference enables social scientists to teach future leaders how to cope with "the demands of day," which again according to Weber, explicitly following Isaiah, can lead man out of exile to become a separate nation.[63]

CONCLUSION

In a sense, this analysis of the political significance of the historicity of values is a commentary on one of the most famous passages in the Marxian *corpus*. In the *Eighteenth Brumaire* Marx wrote:

Men make their own history, but they do not make it just as they please; they do not make it under circumstances chosen by themselves, but under circumstances directly found, given and transmitted from the past.[64]

As anxious as Marxists have been to cite approvingly this passage as proof that Marx was neither a crude determinist nor a naive antideterminist, they have rarely subjected it to careful scrutiny. The argument I have made concerning Marx is that one of the "circumstances" of history is the set of values inherited from the past. These values are not only "directly found" or "given," but sometimes they are also transmitted through complex theoretical interpretations.

In Weber's essay "The Social Psychology of the World Religions," the same kind of suggestive remark occurs. "Not ideas, but material and ideal interests, directly govern men's conduct. Yet very frequently the 'world images' that have been created by 'ideas' have, like switchmen, determined the tracks along which action has been pushed by the dynamic of interest."[65] Contrary to the popular view of Weber, his critique of materialism was a highly qualified one.[66] However, this passage, like the one from the *Eighteenth Brumaire*, must be viewed as a general thesis in need of careful development. How, for example, do these "switchmen" work? Do they all work the same way or are some more discriminating than others? The metaphor can only be sharpened if we examine the differences between ideas which play this historical role. I have argued that the value of vocation is an idea which Weber believed advances national interests when appropriated by social scientists themselves.

It would be a mistake, however, to conclude that because both Marx and Weber appreciated the way theory can politically exploit the historicity of the value of work, all their political differences have heretofore been exaggerated. Despite this common appreciation, they disagreed vehemently about the scale on which meaningful political action must begin. According to Weber, mass political action, no matter how historically informed and resonant, only exacerbates the problem of bureaucracy by necessarily expanding the scale of power in society and hollowing out the socio-cultural traditions that make the nation whole. Thus, the work Weber called attention to had to bear a restrained personal signature because only those committed to science as a vocation could, he thought, exemplify the virtues which a unified national culture requires. In contrast, Marx focused on the collective struggle over wages and hours precisely because he believed this was the only way to restore meaningful work. This difference, more than the disagreement over nationalism, is at the heart of Weber's and Marx's political differences. It explains why they addressed the historicity of the value of work in the particular ways they did.

Notes

I would like to thank Peter Lyman, whose views on Weber's conception of political leadership I am greatly indebted to, and Robert J. Antonio, Richard Peterson, A. P. Simonds, David Weiman, and M. Richard Zinman for helpful comments on an earlier draft.

1. Martin Heidegger, *Being and Time,* trans. John Macquarrie and Edward Robinson (New York: Harper & Row, 1962), sec. 72-76, 424-49. See David Couzens Hoy, "History, Historicity and Historiography in *Being and Time,*" in *Heidegger and Modern Philosophy,* ed. Michael Murray (New Haven, Conn.: Yale University Press, 1978), 329-53.

2. Gustave Flaubert, "A Simple Heart," reprinted in *Three Tales,* trans. Robert Baldick (Middlesex: Penguin Books, 1975), 17.

3. Garry Wills, *Inventing America* (New York: Random House, 1979), 167-255.

4. Karl Marx, *Economic and Philosophic Manuscripts,* reprinted in *The Marx-Engels Reader,* ed. Robert C. Tucker, 2nd ed. (New York: Norton, 1978), 70-81. All subsequent references to the work of Marx and Engels are to this edition unless otherwise stated.

5. Max Weber, *The Protestant Ethic and the Spirit of Capitalism,* trans. Talcott Parsons (New York: Charles Scribner's, 1958).

6. Karl Marx and Friedrich Engels, *Manifesto of the Communist Party,* 490.

7. Alan Gilbert, *Marx's Politics: Communists and Citizens* (New Brunswick, N.J.: Rutgers University Press, 1981), 125-35.

8. Ibid., 201-6.

9. Ibid., 206-11.

10. Marx and Engels, *Manifesto,* 473.

11. Ibid., 475.

12. Marx, *The Eighteenth Brumaire of Louis Bonaparte,* 595.

13. Ibid., 597.

14. Ibid., 595.

15. Ibid.

16. Marx, *Capital* 1: 305.

17. Quoted in Gilbert, *Marx's Politics,* 250.

18. Marx, *Capital* 1: 298.

19. Marx, *Economic and Philosophic Manuscripts,* 71.

20. Ibid., 87.

21. Ibid., 121-25.

22. Marx, *Grundrisse,* 241.

23. Marx, *Capital* 1: 319-29.

24. Ibid., 364. "Hence is it that in the history of capitalist production, the determination of what is a working day, presents itself as the result of a struggle, a struggle between collective capital, i.e., the class of capitalists, and collective labor, i.e., the working class."

25. For a representative discussion of alienation and fetishism which obscures the difference between these two concepts, see Shlomo Avineri, *The Social and Political Thought of Karl Marx* (New York: Cambridge University Press, 1968), 96-123.

26. Georg Lukács, *History and Class Consciousness,* trans. Rodney Livingstone (Cambridge, Mass.: MIT Press, 1968), 170.

27. See Lawrence A. Scaff, "Max Weber's Politics and Political Education," *American Political Science Review* 67 (1973): 124-41.

28. Max Weber, "Parliament and Government in a Reconstructed Germany," reprinted in *Economy and Society,* ed. Guenther Roth and Claus Wittich (Berkeley: University of California Press, 1978), 2: 1381-69.

29. H. Stuart Hughes, *Consciousness and Society* (New York: Vintage Books, 1961), 325-26.

30. Marianne Weber, *Max Weber: A Biography,* trans. Harry Zohn (New York: Wiley & Sons, 1975), 585.

31. Fritz K. Ringer, *The Decline of the German Mandarin: The German Academic Community, 1890-1933* (Cambridge, Mass.: Harvard University Press, 1969).

32. Wolfgang Mommsen, *The Age of Bureaucracy; Perspectives on the Political Sociology of Max Weber* (Oxford: Blackwell, 1974), 15-21.

33. Marianne Weber, *Max Weber,* 594.

34. Max Weber, *Ancient Judaism,* trans. Hans H. Gerth and Don Martindale (New York: Free Press, 1952), 275.

35. Ibid., 315. I owe this argument to Peter Lyman.

36. Ibid., 269, 290.

37. Max Weber, *The Sociology of Religion,* trans. Ephraim Fischoff (Boston: Beacon Press, 1964), 46-59.

38. Max Weber, *Politics as a Vocation,* reprinted in *From Max Weber,* ed. Hans H. Gerth and C. Wright Mills (New York: Oxford University Press, 1958), 122.

39. Max Weber, *The Protestant Ethic,* 28.

40. Ibid., 29.

41. Ibid., 182.

42. Max Weber, "Critical Studies in the Logic of the Cultural Sciences," reprinted in *The Methodology of the Social Sciences,* trans. Edward A. Shils and Henry A. Finch (New York: Free Press, 1949), 113.

43. Max Weber, "Knies and the Problem of Irrationality," reprinted in *Roscher and Knies,* trans. Guy Oakes (New York: Free Press, 1975), 275.

44. Quoted by Oakes in his introductory essay to *Roscher and Knies,* 12-13.

45. Weber, "Critical Studies," 116.

46. Max Weber, *Science as a Vocation,* reprinted in *From Max Weber,* 134.

47. Max Weber, "The Meaning of 'Ethical Neutrality' in Sociology and Economics," reprinted in *The Methodology of the Social Sciences,* 3.

48. Ibid., 6.

49. Ibid., 5.

50. Weber, *Science as a Vocation,* 138.

51. Ibid., 155.

52. Weber, *The Protestant Ethic,* 182.

53. Weber, *Science as a Vocation,* 152.

Politics and Values in Marx and Weber 317

54. See Richard W. Miller, "Reason and Commitment in the Social Sciences," *Philosophy and Public Affairs* 8 (Spring 1979): 241–66.

55. Weber, "The Meaning of 'Ethical Neutrality,' " 11.

56. Ibid., 28.

57. Ibid., 33.

58. Ibid., 42.

59. Max Weber, " 'Objectivity' in Social Science and Social Policy," reprinted in *The Methodology of the Social Sciences,* 80.

60. Weber, "Critical Studies," 142.

61. Ibid., 143.

62. Ibid.

63. Weber, *Science as a Vocation,* 156.

64. Marx, *The Eighteenth Brumaire,* 595.

65. Max Weber, "The Social Psychology of the World Religions," reprinted in *From Max Weber,* 280.

66. See the essay by Robert J. Antonio in this volume.

The Editors

Robert J. Antonio (University of Kansas, sociology) works in sociological theory, economy and society, and historical sociology. He is the author of "The Contradiction of Production and Domination in Bureaucracy," *American Sociological Review* (1979); "Weber vs. Parsons: Domination or Technocratic Model of Social Organization," in *Max Weber's Political Sociology* (1983); "The Origin, Development, and Contemporary Status of Critical Theory," *Sociological Quarterly* (1983); and "Immanent Critique as the Core of Critical Theory," *British Journal of Sociology* (1981).

Ronald M. Glassman (William Paterson College of the State University of New Jersey, sociology) has published numerous books and articles, among them: *The Political History of Latin America* (1969); *Conflict and Control: The Challenge to Legitimacy of Modern Governments,* edited with Arthur Vidich (1979); *Max Weber's Political Sociology: A Pessimistic Vision of a Rationalized World,* edited with Vatro Murvar (1983); *Democracy and Despotism in Primitive Societies* (1984); and *Bureaucracy against Democracy and Socialism* (1984); *The New Middle Class and Democracy* (1985). His best-known articles are: "Legitimacy and Manufactured Charisma," *Social Research* (1975), and "The Limiting Structural and Culture Conditions for Latin American Modernization," *Social Research* (1970). Professor Glassman has been president of the Section on Comparative Historical Sociology of the American Sociological Association and is currently the convener of the Max Weber Colloquium.

⌁⌁⌁

The Contributors

Thomas Clay Arnold (University of Arizona, political science) is a doctoral student, working with Lawrence A. Scaff. Arnold's interests are in American political theory, philosophy of the social sciences, and critical theory. His dissertation is on language and political theory.

Ira J. Cohen (Rutgers University, Newark and New Brunswick, sociology) has published works in social theory and historical sociology. Among his works are: "Max Weber on Modern Western Capitalism," appearing as the introduction to Weber's *General Economic History* (1982); "Toward a Theory of State Intervention: The Nationalization of the British Telegraphs," *Social Science History* (1980); "Participant Observation and Professional Sociology: Transposing and Transforming Descriptions of Everyday Life," *Current Perspectives in Social Theory* (1984). He is presently completing a study of the analytical dimensions of structuration theory (London: Macmillan, forthcoming).

Stephen L. Esquith (James Madison College, Michigan State University, political science) works in political theory. He has presented papers on the problem of political education and on the justification for participatory democracy. His current research is on political education in liberal political philosophy.

Franco Ferrarotti (University of Rome, sociology) has written extensively on methodological and substantive issues. Among his published works are: *Toward the Social Production of the Sacred* (1977); *An Alternative Sociology* (1978); *Max Weber and the Destiny of Reason* (1982); *A Theology for Atheists* (1983; forthcoming in English translation); "The Paradox of the Sacred," *International Journal of Sociology* (1984); *The Myth of Inevitable Progress* (1984).

Stephen Kalberg (Harvard University, Center for European Studies) has, as his main interests, sociological theory, comparative sociology, and political sociology. Among other publications, he has written several articles on Max Weber, including "The Search for Thematic Orientations in a Fragmented Oeuvre: The Discussion of Max Weber in Recent German Sociological Literature," *Sociology* (1979); "Max Weber's Types of Rationality," *American Journal of Sociology* (1980); "Max Weber's Universal-Historical Architectonic of Economically-Oriented Action: A Preliminary Reconstruction," *Current Perspectives in Social Theory* (1983); and "Max Weber, *The Social Science Encyclopaedia*" (1984). He is presently completing a manuscript in which he reconstructs Weber's comparative historical sociology (Routledge & Kegan Paul, forthcoming).

Douglas Kellner (University of Texas, philosophy) is author of *Karl Korsch: Revolutionary Theory* (1977) and *Herbert Marcuse and the Crisis of Marxism* (1984). He has published numerous articles on Marxism and critical theory, and in recent years he has published extensively on the mass media and popular culture from a neocritical-theory standpoint.

Jürgen Kocka (University of Bielefeld, modern history) has published extensively on German and United States history, particularly in the field of eighteenth- to twentieth-century social and economic history and on theoretical and methodological problems of history. Among his works are *White Collar Workers in America, 1890–1940* (1980) and *Facing Total War: German Society, 1914–1918* (1984). He is coeditor of the journal *Geschichte und Gesellschaft: Zeitschrift für historische Sozialwissenschaft*. He is presently engaged in research on the formation of the German working class in the nineteenth century.

Wolfgang J. Mommsen (University of Düsseldorf, modern history, and director of the German Historical Institute, London) has published extensively on Max Weber, modern German and British history, and the history of imperialism. He is coeditor of the *Complete Works of Max Weber,* currently being prepared in cooperation with the Bayerische Akademie der Wissenschaften of Munich. Volume 15, *Politik im Krieg: Schriften und Reden, 1914–1918,* edited in cooperation with Gangolf Hübinger, was published in 1984. His *Max Weber and German Politics, 1860–1920* (first published in 1959) will appear in English translation in 1985 (University of Chicago Press). Another well-known work by Professor Mommsen, available in English, is *The Age of Bureaucracy: Perspectives on the Political Sociology of Max Weber* (1974).

Guenther Roth (University of Washington, sociology) is the author of *The Social Democrats in Imperial Germany* (1963); *Scholarship and Partisanship,* with Reinhard Bendix (1971); and *Max Weber's Vision of History,* with Wolfgang Schluchter (1979). He edited, with Claus Wittich, *Max Weber's Economy and Society* (1968) and translated Schluchter's *The Rise of Western Rationalism* (1981). A companion piece to the present essay appeared in *Theory and Society* (July 1984) under the title "Max Weber's Ethics and the Peace Movement Today."

Lawrence A. Scaff (University of Arizona, political science) has published work in political theory and on the thought of Max Weber. Among his works are: "Max Weber's Politics and Political Education," *American Political Science Review* (1973); "Max Weber and Robert Michels," *American Journal of Sociology* (May 1981); and "Weber before Weberian Sociology," *British Journal of Sociology* (1984). He is presently engaged in a major study of Max Weber. During 1984/85 he is a Fulbright scholar at the University of Freiburg.

Gerd Schroeter (Lakehead University, sociology) is interested in the expansion of sociology in Germany after World War I and in the impact that the writings of Max Weber, Georg Simmel, and other "classical" theorists had upon European scholarship during the years immediately after their deaths. His publications include "Max Weber as Outsider," *Journal of the History of the Behavioral Sciences* (1979), and "The Marx-Weber Nexus," *Canadian Journal of Sociology* (1985). Together with Alan Sica he edits the journal *History of Sociology: An International Review.*

Alan Sica (University of Kansas, sociology) recently published: *Hermeneutics: Questions and Prospects,* edited with Gary Shapiro (1984); "Parsons, Jr.," *American Journal of Sociology* (1983); and "Sociogenesis vs. Psychogenesis: The Unique Sociology of Norbert Elias," *Mid-American Review of Sociology* (1984). He has been a frequent contributor to *Telos* and edits, with Gerd Schroeter, *History of Sociology: An International Review.* His central interest concerns irrationality as a problem for social theory. During 1984/85 he is teaching sociology at the University of Chicago and is associate editor of the *American Journal of Sociology.*

Stephen P. Turner (University of South Florida, sociology, and Center for Interdisciplinary Studies in Culture and Society) has authored *Sociological Explanation as Translation* (1980) and *Max Weber and the Dispute over Reason and Value,* coauthored with Regis Factor (1984).

Turner is currently completing a revision and expansion of his scattered articles on Durkheim's and Weber's methodological writings, which locates these writings in the history of scientific methodology and, specifically, in relation to the nineteenth-century debates over the relation between statistical and causal explanation.

Johannes Weiss (University of Kassel, Social Science Department) specializes in sociological theory and philosophy of the social sciences. His other areas of interest are cultural sociology and social philosophy. He is presently involved in research projects on representation and deputyship and on social causality. Among his major publications are: *Weltverlust und Subjektivität: Zur Kritik der Institutionenlehre Arnold Gehlens* (1971); *Max Webers Grundlegung der Soziologie* (1975); *Das Werk Max Webers in der marxistischen Rezeption und Kritik* (1981; forthcoming in English translation).

Index

287-88; and petrifaction, xviii, 10, 34, 249; politicians as countervailing force to, 24, 249; precise calculation in, 31, 58, 91; technical superiority of, 23; and Weber's erroneous predictions about, in the U.S., 216, 223-25; and welfare and garrison state, 216, 221, 224-25, 229
Burnham, James, 96

Caesarism. *See* Democracy: plebiscitary
California, 218-20, 225
Capitalism: agreement about, between Marx and Weber, 10, 182-85; ambivalence of Weber toward, xiii, 235; concentration of property in, xv, 270; and concentration theory of Marx, Weber's doubts about, 241; contradictions and problems in Weber's analyses of, 248-49, 252-53; and the destruction of traditionalism, 234; dynamic form of, valued by Weber, 234, 239, 248, 254-55; entrepreneurs' role in, 254; erroneous predictions about, by Marx, 215-16; and formal rationality, 251-52, 290; individual personality in, 248, 254 (*see also* Autonomy of the individual in Weber's thought); and inequality, Marx's view, xiii-xiv, 10, 20; and inequality, Weber's view, xiii-xiv, 23-25, 222, 248-50, 255-56, 275, 284-94; and liberalism, 234-35, 248, 252 (*see also* Liberalism); origins of, 8, 182-85; pure type vs. modern form of, in Weber's thought, 11, 251-52; relation of state to economy in, Weber's view, 250; spirit of, 160n.13, 262-63; stagnation of, 10, 239; trade type of, 184; Weber's views about the positive effects of economic and political competition in, and of countervailing powers in, 25, 253; and the world economy, predictions by Marx and Engels, 217-21
Carter, Jimmy, 228-29
Cassirer, Ernst, 70, 80
Caste order, 12, 266
Causality: von Kries's conception of, 168-71; Marx's conception of, 145-47 (*see also* History: core features of, and Marx's method); probabilistic, 168; Weber's conception of, xx, 21, 141, 147, 167-85 passim, 264-66. *See also* Monocausality; Multicausality

Cause: adequate, 169, 172-74, 180 (*see also* Objective possibility); necessary, 170; sufficient, 170
Cavell, Stanley, 68
Celine, 70
Cervantes, Miguel de, 74-75
Charisma: institutional, 223, 309; as leadership attribute (heroism), 49, 56, 128, 225, 249, 309; outbreak of, and social upheaval, 31, 225; presidential, 222; shift in Weber's treatment of, 309. *See also* Democracy: and charisma
Chicago, 225
China, 60, 219, 264, 269-70
China, People's Republic of, 216, 220
Cicero, 72
Civil society, 276, 279, 281-83
Class: analysis, Marxian, 200-207, 278; analysis, Marx's abandonment of, 206; analysis, Weberian, 200-205, 244-46, 289-91; conflict, Marx's view of, xviii, 27, 122, 148, 190-211 passim, 217, 221, 229, 304; conflict, Weber's criticism of Marxian view of, 203, 241, 244; conflict, Weber's view of, 7, 203-5, 226, 244, 247-49; consciousness, 26, 34; false consciousness of, and Weber's critique of Lukács, 244; real or objective interests of, Weber's rejection of, 27, 201-4, 244. *See also* Interests: class
Clientelism, 216, 224-25, 227
Cohen, Jean, 106
Collins, Randall, 9
Communism, 26-27, 102; agrarian form of, 203-5, 208; as post-capitalist and emancipated society, 278-79 (*see also* Democracy: communist)
Communist Party: Second International of, 29; Spanish International of, 75
Concept-reality: dualism, 29, 123, 142; relation, 134-58 passim; unity, 148
Consciousness, false, 77, 79, 143, 146, 307. *See also* Alienation; Fetishism; Reification
Convergence theory, of capitalism and communism, 102
Core structure. *See* History: core features of, and Marx's method
Crisis theory: Marxian, Habermas's reconstruction of, 108; Marx's, Weber's doubts about, 241
Critical theory: xiv, xvi-xvii, xix, 32-37, 43n.89, 89-112 passim; Weberian elements in, 112

Critique, immanent, 38, 150-52, 164n.83. *See also* Rationality: emancipatory *and* immanent; Rationalization: immanent

Cultural significance, 21, 26-27, 32-33, 154-56. *See also* Reality, Weber's view of; Value: relevance, and Weber's view of reality

Culture industry, 96-97

Dante, 74

Decisionism, xii, xvii, xix, 32, 38, 43n.89, 66-67n.62, 99, 134-58 passim

Demetz, Peter, 78

Democracy: achievements of, xviii, 294; adequate theory of, 295; and charisma, 222-23, 225; communist, 278-80, 283, 295 (*see also* Communism: as post-capitalist and emancipated society); conflict of, with organizational rationality, 221, 230; conflicting interest groups in, 25, 28; and constitutional rights, 276, 280; contradiction of, with bureaucracy, 24, 223, 291; and decline of class-based politics in the U.S., 229; and demagoguery, 25, 250; direct, 25, 222-23, 225-26, 230, 286; iron law of, 294; and legitimacy, 290 (*see also* Legitimacy); liberal, 194, 284; mass, xii, 24, 216; obstacles to, xviii, 274-95 passim; parliamentary, 24-25, 222, 287-88; plebiscitary, xvii-xviii, 25, 222, 225, 227, 250, 288, 292; political machines in, 222, 225, 227; primary system in, 224-25; public spheres in, xviii, 276, 293, 295; representative, 25, 222, 274, 276, 281-83, 286-89; and resistance to oppression, 295; and right of recall, 223; and rights of political participation, 274, 283; substantive, xii, xviii, 276-77, 280, 282-85, 289, 293-95; true, 277-78, 281-82; and universal suffrage, 282-83; in Weber's developmental history, 222-25

Despotism, hydraulic theory of, 269

Determinism: areas of agreement about, between Marx and Weber, 31, 236; economic, of Weber's teachers, 7; in Marx's theory of history, 122, 137-38, 314; Weber's opposition to, xiv, 28-31, 123-24. *See also* History: Marx's theory of; Marxism: orthodox; Materialism: historical, approach to, of Marx *and* historical, and stages of history; Teleology: Marxian

Dibble, Vernon, 6, 12

Dickens, Charles, 74

Dilthey, Wilhelm, 80-82

Disenchantment, 10, 12, 22-2?, 182

Djilas, Milovan, 243

Domination: critical theory c⊂ 100-101, 126-28; defined by ⌐⌐⌐⌐⌐, ⌐⌐, 41n.28, 285; inevitability of, in Weber's approach, 22-25, 275, 285-91, 293; legitimate, 31, 54 (*see also* Legitimacy); of nature, 97-98, 103-4, 127; organizations, 54-59; organizations, feudal, 55; organizations, patriarchal, 54; organizations, patrimonial, 56-57, 228; organizations, rational-legal, 57-58; reaction to, 294; traditional, xvii; voluntary servitude and happy submission, Marcuse's theory of, 101

Dostoevsky, Feodor, 72

Draper, Hal, 283

DuBois-Reymond, Emil, 220

Durkheim, Emile, 287, 295

East Elbia: farm workers of, Weber's study of, 6, 12; recolonization of, Weber's defense of, 308

Egypt, 269

Eisenhower, Dwight, 227

Emancipation, xvii, xix, 26-28, 34-35, 37, 70, 102, 111, 249-50; as a standard of valid knowledge, 26, 29, 71; *telos* of, 26, 275, 279, 295. *See also* Communism: as post-capitalist and emancipated society; Critique, immanent; Rationality: emancipatory *and* immanent; Rationalization: immanent

Engels, Friedrich, 4, 29-30, 36, 74, 77-78, 218-19, 237, 265

England, 304

Enlightenment: and goals of freedom and rationality, xix, 37-38, 70, 80, 208-9 (*see also* Emancipation); is totalitarian, 97

Ethic: of absolute ends, 28, 34, 238; of brotherhood, 52-53; of fraternal allegiance, 55; of mutual assistance, 53-54; of personal accomplishment, 56; of responsibility, 24; status, 49-52, 291

Ethical commitment, Weber's respect for acts based on, 238, 254

Ethos, 263-64; feudal, 55; patriarchal, 54; patrimonial, 56-57; bureaucratic, 57-59

Evangelisch-Sozialer Kongress, 7

Evolution: Habermas's approach to, 111; Marxian theories of, 26, 29, 191-92,

194, 196, 209, 217; Parsons's approach to, and Weber, xxi n.1, 20. *See also* Materialism: historical, and stages of history; Progress; Rationalization: progressive; Teleology

Explanation: individual, areas of agreement in approaches of Marx and Weber, 124-26; genetic, 180-81, 267; individual, as aspect of Weber's method, 180, 240; probabilistic, 71

Exploitation, Marx's theory of, 279-81

Fact-value dualism, 21-22, 26, 29, 99-100, 121-22, 151, 311-12. *See also* Value: freedom

Fallows, James, 227

Fascism, 93-94, 96-97

Fatalism. *See* Pessimism, Weber's

Fetishism, xix, 92; of commodities, 303, 306-7. *See also* Alienation; Consciousness, false; Reification

Feuerbach, Ludwig, 138, 143

Flaubert, Gustave, 301

Fleischmann, Eugène, 6

Foucault, Michel, 69

France, 190-211 passim, 304

Frankfort, 254

Frankfurt: parliament, 198; School, xvii, 35, 99, 118 (*see also* Critical theory; Institute for Social Research)

Franklin, Benjamin, 264

Freud, Sigmund, 70, 94, 98, 100, 102

Friedman, Milton, 249

Fromm, Erich, 93-95, 99

Functionalism, xii-xiv, xxi, 20, 37, 110

Gadamer, Hans-Georg, 68

Garfinkel, Harold, 68

Generalists, Weber's view of, 310-11

Germany, 219, 238, 243, 254-55, 304, 308

Germany, Democratic Republic of, 118

Germany, Federal Republic of, 98-99, 226

Gerth, Hans H., xiii, 2-3

Giddens, Anthony, 6-7, 9-10

Goethe, Johann Wolfgang von, xix, 72-82 passim, 210

Gouldner, Alvin, 293

Grün, Karl, 77

Habermas, Jürgen, xvii, 32, 69-71, 80-81, 89-112 passim, 295

Hamburg, 218

Hayek, Friedrich, 252

Hegel, George W. F.: critique of, by Marx, 77, 152, 198, 276, 278, 281; idea of development in, 210-11; and influence on Marx and Marxism, xx, 11-12, 25-27, 122-23, 134, 146-47, 149-52, 190-91, 196, 207-11; relation of critical theory to, 98

Heidelberg, 90, 107, 238

Hermeneutical circle, problem of, 153, 165n.100

Herodotus, 72

Herzen, Alexander, 209

Heuristic devices, Weber's conception of theories as, 22, 31-32, 36, 59, 136, 147, 191, 262. *See also* Ideal type; One-sidedness: necessary methodological; Reality, Weber's view of: and perspectivity, selection, and relativity of knowledge

Hiatus irrationalis. See Concept-reality: dualism

Historical individual, and Weber's method, 141, 161n.39, 169-70, 217. *See also* Ideal type

Historical inevitability. *See* Historical necessity

Historical necessity, 27, 30, 105, 122, 138, 207, 217. *See also* Determinism: in Marx's theory of history; Teleology: Marxian

Historicity, xix, 300-315 passim

History: core features of, and Marx's method, 26-27, 120-21, 140, 146; developmental, Weber's approach to, xix, 26-27, 136-40, 190-211 passim, 217, 223; as foundation of classical sociology, 268-69; Marx's theory of, xix, 26-27, 136-40, 190-211 passim (*see also* Determinism: in Marx's theory of history; Materialism: historical, approach to, of Marx *and* historical, and stages of history); rejection by Weber of contentions about objective meaning of, 121, 149, 236-37; and surface phenomena, 146

Hodges, H. A., 71, 81

Hofmann, W., 121

Hollis, Martin, 68

Homer, 72, 74

Hong Kong, 220

Horkheimer, Max, 82, 89-112 passim

Hübner, Kurt, 68

Hughes, H. Stuart, 308

Human rights and civil liberties, 38, 128, 203, 276, 290, 294

Hypostatization. *See* Reification

Idealism: Marx's view of, 25-26; orthodox Marxist critique of, xvi, 118-21; vs. materialism, xv-xvi, 31-32, 60-61, 119; Weber criticized for, xvi, 118-21; Weber disagreed with, 31-32, 121
Ideal type: as basic feature of Weber's method, 21-22, 48, 59, 121, 123-24, 171-74, 180, 236, 267-68; of class stratification, 242, 245-46; and democracy, 285-86, 288, 292-93; as distinct from abstraction, 124, 171; genetic, 172-73, 180-82, 185; as ideology of empiricism, 100; as model of particular historical sequences, 191, 237; of planned economy vs. market economy, 251; and the Protestant ethic, 167, 172; Weber's approach to religious ideas in the context of a real type instead of an, 177; in Weber's formulations of traditional and rational, 176. *See also* Heuristic devices; Knowledge; Materialism: historical, as heuristic device; Objective possibility; One-sidedness: necessary methodological; Reality, Weber's view of
India, 12, 60, 78, 264, 266, 270
Individualism, ethical, and Weber's method, xix, 26, 32-34
Infrastructure. *See* Base
Institute for Social Research, 89, 93, 95-96, 98-100. *See also* Frankfurt: School
Instrumentalist interpretation of Weber, xii, 48, 61, 62n.4, 66-67n.62
Interests: class, 27, 65, 122, 143, 201, 244-45 (*see also* Class); conflict of, 23, 247, 249; ideal, in Weber's work, xvi, xix-xx, 46-61, 202, 240; individual, 277, 281; material, in Weber's work, 36, 246, 263; relation of material and ideal, in Marx's work, xvi, 31-32, 36; relation of material and ideal, in Weber's work, xvi, 31-32, 36, 46-61 passim, 240, 314; universal, 27, 276, 281. *See also* Idealism; Materialism
Iron cage, 73, 93, 128, 134, 195, 208, 239
Irrationalitätsproblem. See Irrationality
Irrationality: critical theory approach to, 93-94, 96-97, 103, 106, 109, 144; critical theory critique of, in Weber's approach, 32-33, 92-93, 98-99, 104-5, 128; Lukács's approach to, 92, 97; Marx's approach to, xix, 68-82 passim, 128, 134; and orthodox Marxist critique of, in Weber's approach, 118, 128 (*see also* Nihilism); Weber's approach to, xix,

68-82 passim, 134, 191 (*see also* Unintended consequences: in Weber's sociology). *See also* Decisionism
Isaiah, 314
Israel, 265
Italy, 262

Jacobinism, 198, 203
Jaffé, Edgar, 217
Janowitz, Morris, 229-30
Japan, 60, 220
Jaspers, Karl, 221
Jeremiah, 309
Johnson, Lyndon, 227
Judaism, ancient, Weber's analysis of, 265, 309-10
Jung, C. G., 69

Kant, Immanuel: his influence on Weber, xvi, xix-xx, 11-12, 21-22, 31, 33, 146, 169, 172; Weber criticized for being influenced by, 117, 119-21; Weber's deviation from, 22, 121
Kantian dualism. *See* Fact-value dualism
Kathedersozialisten, 30
Kaufmann, Walter, 80
Kautsky, Karl, 30, 217, 237
Keynes, John Maynard, 103, 249
Kierkegaard, Soren, 71
Kissinger, Henry, 227
Knies, Karl, 81
Knowledge, partial, Weber's conception of science, 141, 146, 150-51, 237. *See also* One-sidedness: necessary methodological; Reality, Weber's view of
Kocka, Jürgen, 3, 11
Kofler, Leo, 118
Kon, I. S., 122
Kozyr-Kowalski, Stanislaw, 6-7
Kries, Johannes von, 168-72
Kronman, Anthony, 181
Kuczynski, J., 122
Kugelmann, Franzisca, 75

Labor, abstract, 92, 306-7. *See also* Alienation: Marx's approach to, and labor
Lafayette, Marquis de, 198-99
Lamprecht, Karl, 217
Langer, Suzanne K., 124
Lavrov, Peter, 209

Laws: of motion, Marx's, 146, 194, 196, 207, 210; of nature, Marx's conception of, 119, 138-39; of nature, Weber's misunderstanding of Marx's conception of, 139-40, 144; nomothetic, Weber's approach to, 21-22, 156, 236, 240
Lefargue, Paul, 78
Lefèvre, Wolfgang, 252
Legitimacy: 23, 31, 56-57, 111, 222, 291-92, 309; crisis of, 108. *See also* Domination: legitimate
Leibniz, Gottfried Wilhelm, 70
Lenin, V. I., xvi, 117, 119-20, 198, 207, 209, 250
Lermontov, Mikhail, 75
Lessing, Gotthold, 82
Leveling, 24, 56, 291
Liberalism, Weber's adherence to bourgeois values, 234-35. *See also* Capitalism: and liberalism
Lichtheim, George, 3
Liebknecht, Wilhelm, 74-75
Lifshitz, M., 78
Livy, 72
Löwith, Karl, 2-3, 6, 10, 12, 80, 191, 208, 240
London, 218
Louch, A. R., 167
Louis XVI, 198-99
Luethy, Herbert, 177
Lukács, Georg, 71, 78, 89-112 passim, 118, 180, 244, 307
Lukes, Stephen, 68

MacIntyre, Alasdair, 167
Mann, Thomas, 70, 80-81
Mannheim, Karl, 80
Marcus, Steven, 81
Marcuse, Herbert, xii, xvii, 32, 89-112 passim, 118, 127-28, 250, 252
Marshall, Gordon, 167
Marshall, T. H., 289
Martov, Y. O., 198
Marx, Eleanor, 75, 217
Marxism: crude, vulgar, mechanistic form of (*see subhead* orthodox); and dogmatism, xvii, 29, 135-58 passim, 208, 263; orthodox, xiv, xvi, 4-6, 30, 32, 34-35, 117-28 passim, 191, 237-38, 263-64; and revisionism, 118-19; structuralist form of, and Weber's method, 11-12; Weberian, 110; Western, 29-30, 108. *See also* Critical theory; Hegel: and influence on Marx and Marxism; Materialism

Massachusetts, 226
Materialism: crude, xv, 29, 136 (*see also* Marxism: orthodox); crude, of Lenin, 119-20; crude, and pseudo-value freedom, 29-30; crude, and Weber's criticism of historical materialism, 4-6, 29-31, 135-36, 171, 174-75, 236, 238, 240 (*see also* Social Democratic Party: and Weber's criticism of historical materialism); historical, abandonment of, by Marx, xviii, 201, 211; historical, agreement with, in Weber's thought, 6-7, 137; historical, approach to, of Marx, 25-32, 34-35; historical, as heuristic device, 5, 31-32, 36, 137, 173, 175, 196, 235-36, 238, 262 (*see also* Heuristic devices; Ideal type); historical, and stages of history, 26-27, 29, 139, 190-91, 196, 208, 210-11, 217, 236-37 (*see also* Evolution: Marxian theories of; Progress: in Marx's theories; Teleology: Marxian); historical, Weber's criticism of, 4, 26-32, 136-40, 142, 149, 207-8, 236-46, 265, 314 (*see also* History: rejection by Weber of contentions about objective meaning of; Social Democratic Party: and Weber's criticism of historical materialism); as starting point for a Weber-Marx dialogue, 36, 38. *See also* History: Marx's theory of
Mayer, Carl, 11
Merquior, J. G., 73
Mészáros, István, 79
Mexico, 220
Meyer, Edward, 310
Michels, Robert, 235, 248, 253, 287
Mill, John Stuart, 170; and Method of Difference, 167, 178-79
Mills, C. Wright, xiii, 2-3
Mitzman, Arthur, 73
Modernization, xiv, 108, 111, 203
Mommsen, Wolfgang, 3, 5, 10-11
Monocausality: Marx's critique of, 137-40; Weber's critique of, 28-29, 136, 139-40, 175, 263
Morawski, Stefan, 75-76
Mueller, Gert H., 10
Müller-Armack, Alfred, 252
Multicausality: in Marx's approach, 145, 147-48, 265; in Weber's approach, 265-67; in Weber's approach and Engels's, 265
Mumford, Lewis, 96
Munich, 255

Narodniki, 196, 203
Nationalism, Weber's 25, 30, 93, 284, 308
Nationalization, socialization of production.
   See Socialism
National Socialism, 96-97
National-Sozialer Verein, 6
Natural resources, exhaustion of, ecological
   deterioration, and technological threats
   to humanity: Marx and Engels's lack of
   sensitivity to, xviii, 215, 220; Weber's
   approach to, 220-21
Nelson, Benjamin, 3, 178-79
Neumann, Franz, 97
Neustadt, Richard, 228
Neusychin, Alexander, 118
New Deal, 96, 224
New Zealand, 220
Nicholas II, 193, 198-99
Nietzsche, Friedrich, 5-6, 28, 71, 77, 80,
   98, 207, 235-36, 253; his influence on
   Weber, xix-xx, 6, 22-23, 27, 33, 40n.22,
   191, 238
Nihilism, Weber criticized for, 118-19,
   134-35. See also Irrationality: and
   orthodox Marxist critique of, in Weber's
   approach
Nixon, Richard, 228

Oakes, Guy, 11
Objective possibility, 22, 35, 123-24, 152,
   172-73, 180. See also Cause: adequate
Oligarchy, Iron Law of, 287, 293-94
One-dimensional society, Marcuse's con-
   cept of, 106, 108
One-sidedness: in Marx's and Weber's
   philosophy of science, 135; necessary
   methodological, 22, 171-72, 174; uncriti-
   cal, 29, 106, 140, 150, 173; uncritical,
   Weber's attempt to avoid, 173, 262, 264.
   See also Ideal type; Knowledge
Ontic dimension, xvii, 11, 140-41, 154,
   156, 161n.39
Ossian, 72
Ostwald, Wilhelm, 220
Ouspensky, P. D., 69

Panama, 219
Parsons, Talcott, 2, 20, 27n.2, 69, 107,
   110
Pauperization theory, Weber's doubts
   about Marx's, 241
Pears, David, 68

Peasants: Marx's analysis of, 184-85,
   203-5, 304-5, 307; Weber's analysis of,
   203-5
Personal rulership, failure of, to decline,
   xvii, 216
Pessimism, Weber's, xix, 99, 105, 108,
   128, 253, 294
Philosophy: of history, Weber's rejection of
   materialist approaches to, 236; of lan-
   guage, 109
Plekhanov, G. V., 207
Poland, 118
Political economy, Marx's critique of classi-
   cal, 305-6
Politics, Weber's view of, as struggle over
   interests, 24. See also Interests: conflict of
Pollock, Friedrich, 97
Popper, Karl, 100, 107
Positivism: xiii, 32-35, 37, 99-100, 105,
   118-19; dispute over, 107
Post-capitalist society, Marx did not at-
   tempt a theory of, 27
Post-industrial society, xiii-iv, 37, 102
Prawer, S. S., 71, 74-79
Praxis, Marx's conception of, 13, 134,
   142-44, 151, 153-54, 158, 281
Preunderstanding, as guide for the formulation of scientific categories, 153,
   156-57
Probability: dependent, 169-70; outcome,
   169; theory, 168; true, 168-69
Progress: in Marx's theories, 121-22, 191,
   209, 215; in Weber's theories, 121,
   312-14. See also Evolution; Rationalization: progressive; Teleology
Progressive era, 222, 225-26
Proletariat, dictatorship of, 193-94, 196,
   207. See also Socialism: Weber's critique
   of the repressive consequences of the
   ensuing nationalization and bureaucratization of
Prophets, Weberian: ethical, 310; exemplary, 310, 313; pre-exilic, 309-10
Pushkin, Alexander, 75

Radbruch, Gustav, 174
Rationality: capitalist, 24, 102-3, 105, 108,
   127-28; communicative, 109-11, 128;
   contradiction of formal and substantive,
   xii, 24, 94, 106, 127-28, 252-53,
   260n.52; emancipatory, xvii, 70, 105,
   107, 109-11; formal, 57, 94, 98, 102,
   106, 127-28; immanent, xvii, 26-27, 69,

Index 331

152 (*see also* Rationalization: immanent); individual, 95; instrumental, 94-111 passim; Marcuse's misinterpretation of Weber's concept of, 103-4, 107, 126-28, 252; means-end, 57, 59, 69, 98, 144; naturalistic, 208-9; objective, 98-99; practical, 51; pragmatic, 208-9; subjective, 99; substantive, 94, 98-99, 128; technological, 37, 89-112 passim, 127-28

Rationalization: capitalist, 13, 91, 105-6; cultural, 98, 111; formal, xix, 106, 109, 284; Habermas's agreement with Weber's approach to, 110, 112; Habermas's critique of treatment of, in tradition of social theory, 110; Habermas's critique of Weber's approach to, 108; Habermas's portrayal of emancipatory social, 111-12; immanent, 167, 177-78, 182 (*see also* Rationality: immanent); of modern state, 205-6, 211; partial, 178; progressive, xii, xiv, 20, 176-78 (*see also* Evolution: Habermas's approach to *and* Parsons's approach to); and religion, 8, 20, 176-79; technological, 128; theoretical, 51

Rayburn, Sam, 227

Reagan, Ronald, 228-29

Reality, Weber's view of: as amorphous detritus of appearances, 141, 144, 154; as heterogeneous continuum, 141, 146-47, 149, 154, 156-58, 162n.42; and perspectivity, selection, and relativity of knowledge, 21-22, 120, 140-45, 156, 170-74, 237, 268. *See also* Concept-reality; Cultural significance; Decisionism; Heuristic devices; Ideal type; Knowledge; One-sidedness; Value: relevance, and Weber's view of reality

Reason: critical, 94, 98; cunning of, 78, 81

Reflection theory of knowledge, 119-20, 143. *See also* Materialism: crude *and* crude, of Lenin

Reification: and ahistorical categories, 27, 32, 35, 109, 123, 126, 143, 145, 175, 239, 268; of capitalism, 77-78, 143; of collectivities, 21; Habermas's approach to, 111; ideal types counteract, 123; Lukács's approach to, 92, 101; Marx and Weber in agreement about, 124-26; opposition to, by substantively rational conceptions of human and civil rights, 128; of proletarian emancipation, 36; of science, 208. *See also* Alienation; Fetishism

Resignation. *See* Pessimism, Weber's

Revolution: bourgeois, 197, 203, 305; modern, 196-98, 201, 208-10; proletarian, xix, 26-27, 193-97, 201, 304-5; Russian October, 193, 241; socialist, 218-19, 237, 241; success of, in Weber's view, 198

Rickert, Heinrich, 22, 311

Rickman, H. P., 68

Robespierre, Maximilien, 206

Roman civilization, Weber's study of, 7

Roosevelt, Theodore, 225

Roscher, Wilhelm, 81

Roth, Guenther, xiii, 4, 7-9

Rousseau, Jean-Jacques, 80

Russia, xix, 75, 117, 190-211 passim, 270. *See also* Union of Soviet Socialist Republics

Salomon, Albert, 2

Salvation religions, 47, 60

Schick, Frederic, 68

Schiller, Friedrich, 72

Schleiermacher, Friedrich, 81

Schluchter, Wolfgang, xiv, 177

Schmoller, Gustav, 250

Schopenhauer, Arthur, 71, 80

Schumpeter, Joseph, 3

Science: autonomy of, xix, 34, 36; and politics, xvi, 34-35, 135, 207, 308

Scott, Walter, 72

Secularization. *See* Disenchantment

Shakespeare, William, 74-75, 80

Simon, Herbert, 69

Singapore, 220

Smith, Adam, 125, 183

Social Democratic Party: bourgeoisie's fear of, 241, 248; Lenin's association of petit bourgeois strains in, with Kantian influences, 119; and Weber's bourgeois background, 235; and Weber's criticism of historical materialism, 8, 30, 238 (*see also* Materialism: crude, and Weber's criticism of historical materialism); and Weber's views on class and class politics, 254-56, 261n.62 (*see also* Class)

Socialism: as a bureaucratization of top management, 10, 28, 206, 243, 247; caste rule in, and stagnation of, 206, 243 (*see also* Bureaucracy: and petrifaction); as a command economy, 216; and the decline of formal rationality, 28, 206, 251, 253-54; as expropriation of workers,

and the selection of scientific problems, 22; pluralism, xvii, xix, 32-34, 36; premises, 154; relevance, and the positivist concept of value freedom, 32-33, 107; relevance, and Weber's emphasis on the division of science and politics, 308; relevance, and Weber's view of reality, 21-22, 120, 126, 140-42, 313 (*see also* Cultural significance; Reality, Weber's view of); surplus, 183, 279; universally valid, Weber's view of, 311; use, 280; of work, Marx's, xix, 300, 303-7; of work, Weber's, xix, 308-14

Veblen, Thorstein, 96, 221

Verein für Sozialpolitik, 6

Verstehen. See Understanding

Virgil, 72

Vocation, xix, 58, 303, 309-14

Wallace, Henry, 96

Wallerstein, Immanuel, 218

Walton, Paul, 6

Weber, Alfred, 221

Weber, Marianne, 8-9, 32, 71-72, 309

Weiss, Johannes, 3

Wertbeziehung. See Cultural significance; Value: relevance

Wieland, Christoph Martin, 72

Wiener, Jonathan, 7

Wills, Garry, 302

Wittfogel, Karl, 118, 269

Work, rational organization of, 184-85, 263-64, 266

Worker's control, 92

World-systems approach, 217-18

Wrong, Dennis, 8

Zander, Jürgen, 6

Zemstvo, 198-99, 202

Znaniecki, Florian, 118